CONQUEST

CONQUEST

The English Kingdom of France
1417–1450

JULIET BARKER

Little, Brown

LITTLE, BROWN

First published in Great Britain in 2009 by Little, Brown

Copyright © Juliet Barker 2009

The moral right of the author has been asserted.

Maps and family trees drawn by John Gilkes

A CIP catalogue record for this book
is available from the British Library.

ISBN 978-1-4087-0083-9

Typeset in Sabon by M Rules
Printed and bound in Great Britain by
Clays Ltd, St Ives plc

Papers used by Little, Brown are natural, renewable and
recyclable products sourced from well-managed forests and certified in
accordance with the rules of the Forest Stewardship Council.

Little, Brown
An imprint of
Little, Brown Book Group
100 Victoria Embankment
London EC4Y 0DY

An Hachette UK Company
www.hachette.co.uk

www.littlebrown.co.uk

This book is dedicated to Judith Bateson who died on 23 May 2009. She was not just my beloved mother but my 'man on the Clapham omnibus' for every book I have written. I am bereft without her.

CONTENTS

CONTENTS

PREFACE

The Hundred Years War is defined in the popular imagination by its great battles. The roll-call of spectacular English victories over the French is a source of literary celebration and national pride and even those who know little or nothing about the period or context can usually recall the name of at least one of the most famous trilogy – Crécy, Poitiers, Agincourt. It is curious therefore that an even greater achievement has been virtually wiped from folk memory. Few people today know that for more than thirty years there was an English kingdom of France. Quite distinct from English Gascony, which had belonged to the kings of England by right of inheritance since the marriage of Eleanor of Aquitaine and Henry II in 1152, the English kingdom was acquired by conquest and was the creation of Henry V.

When he landed a great English army on the beaches of Normandy at the beginning of August 1417 Henry opened up an entirely new phase in the Hundred Years War. Never before had an English monarch invaded France with such ambitious plans: nothing less than the wholesale conquest and permanent annexation of Normandy. Yet, after he had achieved this in the space of just two years, the opportunity presented itself to secure a prize to which even his most illustrious ancestor, Edward III, could only aspire: the crown of France itself. On 21 May 1420 Charles VI of France formally betrothed Henry V of England to his daughter and recognised him as his heir and regent of France. In doing so he disinherited his own son and committed both countries to decades of warfare.

By a cruel twist of fate, Henry died just seven weeks before his father-in-law, so it was not the victor of Agincourt but his nine-month-old son, another and much lesser Henry, who became the first (and last) English king of France. Until he came of age and could rule in person, the task of defending his French realm fell to his father's right-hand men. First and foremost among these was his brother John, duke of Bedford, a committed Francophile who made his home in France and for thirteen years ruled as regent on his nephew's behalf. His determination to do justice to all, to rise above political faction and, most important of all, to protect the realm by a slow but steady expansion of its borders meant that, at its height, the English kingdom of France extended from the coast of Normandy almost down to the banks of the Loire: to the west it was bounded by Brittany, to the east by the Burgundian dominions, both of which, nominally at least, owed allegiance to the boy-king.

Bedford's great victory at Verneuil in 1424 seemed to have secured the future of the realm – until the unexpected arrival on the scene of an illiterate seventeen-year-old village girl from the marches of Lorraine who believed she was sent by God to raise the English siege of Orléans, crown the disinherited dauphin as true king of France and drive the English out of his realm.

The story of Jehanne d'Arc – better known to the English-speaking world today as Joan of Arc – is perhaps the most enduringly famous of the entire Hundred Years War. The fact that, against all the odds, she achieved two of her three aims in her brief career has raised her to iconic status, but it is the manner of her death, burned at the stake in Rouen by the English administration, which has brought her the crown of martyrdom and literally made her a saint in the Roman Catholic calendar. The terrible irony is that Jehanne's dazzling achievements obscure the fact that they were of little long-term consequence: a ten-year-old Henry VI was crowned king of France just six months after her death and his kingdom endured for another twenty years.

Of far more consequence to the prosperity and longevity of the English kingdom of France was the defection of the ally who had made its existence possible. Philippe, duke of Burgundy, made his peace with Charles VII in 1435, just days after the death of Bedford. In the wake of the Treaty of Arras much of the English kingdom, including its capital, Paris, was swept away by the reunited and resurgent French but the reconquest stalled in the face of dogged resistance from Normandy and brilliant tactical military leadership from the 'English Achilles', John Talbot. For almost a decade it would be a war of attrition between the two ancient enemies, gains by each side compensating for their losses elsewhere, but no decisive actions tipping the balance of power.

Nevertheless, the years of unremitting warfare had their cost, imposing an unsustainable financial burden on England and Normandy, draining both realms of valuable resources, including men of the calibre of the earls of Salisbury and Arundel, who were both killed in action, and devastating the countryside and economy of northern France. The demands for peace became more urgent and increasingly voluble, though it was not until Henry VI came of age that anyone in England had the undisputed authority to make the concessions necessary to achieve a settlement.

The Truce of Tours, purchased by Henry's marriage to Margaret of Anjou, the infamous 'she-wolf of France', proved to be a disaster for the English. In his determination to procure peace at any price, the foolish young king secretly agreed to give up a substantial part of his inheritance: the county of Maine would return to French hands without compensation for its English settlers who had spent their lives in its defence.

Worse was to follow, for while the English took advantage of the truce to demobilise and cut taxes, Charles VII used it to rearm and reorganise his armies so that, when he found the excuse he needed to declare that the English had broken its terms, he was ready and able to invade with such overwhelming force that he swept all before him. The English kingdom of France which, against the odds, had survived for three decades, was crushed in just twelve months.

It seems extraordinary to me that the history of this fascinating period has been so neglected. French historians have, perhaps for obvious reasons, generally declined to engage with the subject beyond celebrating Jehanne d'Arc and, to a much lesser extent, the Norman brigands whom a few have chosen to glorify as a medieval version of the French Resistance. At a more basic level, the websites of most French towns, even those which played a critical role in the events of this period, make no reference to them at all, creating a gaping hole in the centre of their civic existence.

Even English historians have proved remarkably unforthcoming over the years. Though there have been many excellent scholarly studies of the Hundred Years War, its last thirty years have not attracted a dedicated narrative history. One might have expected the great Victorian antiquarians to have been attracted by such a colourful subject but, perhaps because the history of the English kingdom of France ends in defeat and failure, it failed to appeal.

In more recent times, and particularly since the 1980s, there has been a surge of interest among scholars, led by Professors Christopher Allmand and Anne Curry, who have trawled the remarkably detailed financial, military and legal records of the English administration to produce a wealth of invaluable studies on particular aspects of the regime. Without their dedication to the minutiae of scholarship which inform and shape the broader-brush approach of narrative history, this book could not have been written, and I am indebted to them and their fellow historians who have pioneered research in this field. Though the extent to which I have drawn on their labours will be clear from my notes and bibliography, I have, perhaps, abused their academic standards by rebranding what they would call 'the Lancastrian occupation' as 'the English kingdom' of France. The former may be more politically correct but my excuse is that the latter more accurately reflects how contemporaries (other than die-hard supporters of Charles VII) saw and referred to the situation.

I have two main aspirations for my book. The first is that it will introduce this extraordinary period of history to a much wider audience: the many remarkable people at every level of society and on both sides of the conflict whose lives were shaped by the dramatic events of their times deserve to be remembered. The second is that it will provide the cogent and reliable chronological narrative which is so difficult to achieve in the face of conflicting contemporary sources but which is so badly needed by anyone with an interest in the Hundred Years War. As an enthusiast myself I hope that the reader will be entertained as well as informed.

NOTES TO THE TEXT

I: Money

All references to money are given in the original coinage followed by the approximate modern-day equivalent in brackets: for example, £7333 6s. 8d. (£3.85m). This is intended simply to give an indication of worth, rather than an exact valuation, as rates fluctuated according to the gold or silver content, which varied considerably, especially in France during the war years. Where a current equivalent is in the millions, the figure is accurate to two decimal places, or one place where a zero would follow (for example, £195.3m is £195.30m). The standard sterling units in England were the pound (£1), consisting of 20 shillings (s.) or 240 pence (d.), with the mark valued at 13s. 4d., the noble at 6s. 8d. and the crown at 5s. The standard units in France were the *livre tournois* (*l.t.*), which consisted of 20 *sous* (*s.t*) or 240 *deniers* (*d.t*), and the *livre parisis* (*l.p.*), which was worth 25 per cent more than the *livre tournois*. All my references to *livres* are to the *livre tournois* only. The reader should be aware, however, that no actual coin represented the pound sterling, the *livre tournois* or the *livre parisis*: these were simply convenient accounting terms for the weight of a collection of smaller coins.

The contemporary writer William of Worcester calculated one pound sterling as being worth 9*l.t.* and I have used this figure for ease of calculation, though the value of an English pound fluctuated from 6.6*l.t.* in the 1420s to 11.3*l.t.* in 1436–7, when inflation was at its height. The other French coins in common use at the time were the *franc*, which was the same as a *livre tournois*, the *salut d'or*, which was worth 1.375 of a *livre tournois*, and the *écu*, which was worth 25 *sous*.

The standard conversion rate for one pound sterling in the period 1410 to 1460 based on the retail price index as of January 2009 is £525.

II: Names

To avoid confusion between many individuals with similar names or whose status changed several times, I have continued to use the same name, even where this might be anachronistic or fail to indicate his elevated rank. 'Somerset', for instance, refers only to John Beaufort, earl of Somerset from 1418 and duke of Somerset from 1443. I have called his younger brother, Edmund Beaufort (1406–55), only by that name, despite his rise to become count of Mortain in 1427, earl of Dorset in 1442, marquess of Dorset in 1443, earl of Somerset in 1444 and duke of Somerset in 1448. John Talbot similarly remains a humble 'Talbot' rather than the earl of Shrewsbury and then earl of Wexford and Waterford he later became, and the Bastard of Orléans remains as his contemporaries termed him rather than referred to by his titles as lord of Valbonnais, count of Périgord, count of Dunois and count of Longueville. The only exception to this rule is Charles Valois, whom I have called 'the dauphin' until his coronation in 1429, when he becomes Charles VII.

Although I have anglicised all titles held by Frenchmen throughout this book, there is no English equivalent for 'sire de', which I have retained.

III: Distances

All distances between places have been calculated using the 'walking' option on Google maps: http://maps.google.co.uk.

IV: Chronology

A chronology of key events can be found on p. 447.

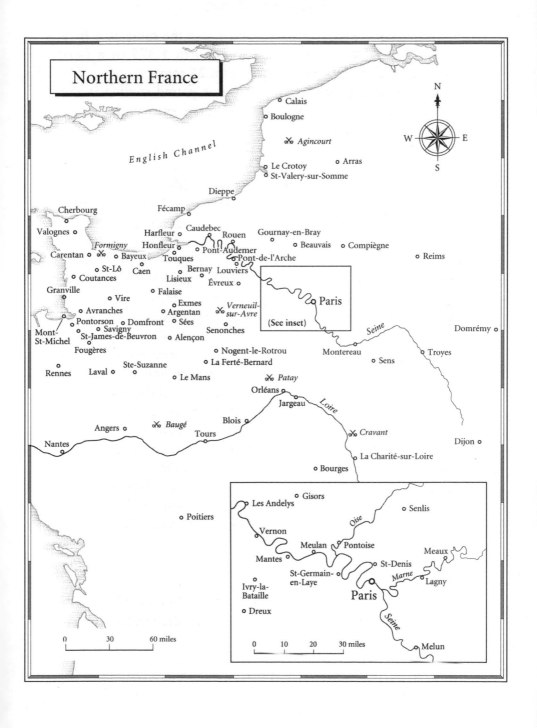

Northern France

English Channel

Calais
Boulogne
⚔ *Agincourt*
Le Crotoy   Arras
St-Valery-sur-Somme
Dieppe
Fécamp
Cherbourg
Valognes   Harfleur Caudebec Rouen Gournay-en-Bray
Formigny Honfleur   Pont-Audemer   Beauvais   Compiègne
Carentan Bayeux Touques   Pont-de-l'Arche   Reims
St-Lô Caen   Bernay Louviers
Coutances   Lisieux   Évreux
Granville   Falaise
Vire   Exmes   *Verneuil-
Avranches   Argentan   sur-Avre*
Pontorson Savigny Domfront Sées   Paris
Mont- St-James-de-Beuvron   Senonches   (See inset)   Seine
St-Michel   Alençon
Fougères   Nogent-le-Rotrou   Montereau   Sens   Troyes   Domrémy
Rennes Laval Ste-Suzanne   La Ferté-Bernard
Le Mans   ⚔ *Patay*
Orléans   Dijon
Jargeau   *Loire*
Angers ⚔ *Baugé*   Blois   ⚔ *Cravant*
Nantes   Tours   La Charité-sur-Loire
Bourges
Poitiers

N
W   E
S

Gisors
Les Andelys   Senlis
Vernon   *Oise*
Meulan   Pontoise   Meaux
Mantes   St-Denis
St-Germain-   *Marne*   Lagny
en-Laye   **Paris**
Ivry-la-   *Seine*
Bataille
Dreux   Melun

0   30   60 miles

0   10   20   30 miles

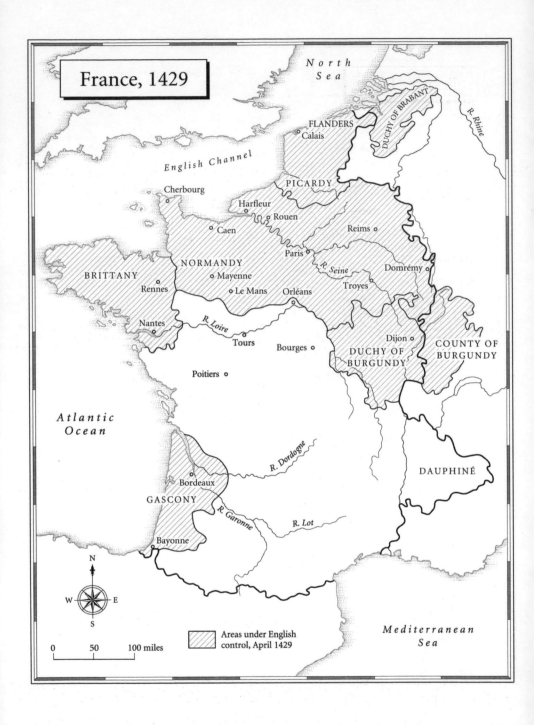

France, 1429

*North
Sea*

FLANDERS
Calais o

DUCHY OF BRABANT

R. Rhine

English Channel

PICARDY

Cherbourg o

Harfleur o
o Rouen

Reims o

o Caen

Paris o

Domrémy o

NORMANDY

R. Seine

BRITTANY

o Mayenne

Troyes o

Rennes o

o Le Mans

Orléans o

Nantes o

R. Loire

Tours o

Bourges o

Dijon o

DUCHY OF
BURGUNDY

COUNTY OF
BURGUNDY

Poitiers o

*Atlantic
Ocean*

R. Dordogne

DAUPHINÉ

Bordeaux o

GASCONY

R. Garonne

R. Lot

Bayonne o

N

W   E

S

0   50   100 miles

*Mediterranean
Sea*

Areas under English
control, April 1429

France, 1436

Calais

English Channel

Le Crotoy
Arras
St-Valery-sur-Somme

Dieppe

Fécamp

Cherbourg

Harfleur
Caudebec
Gerberoy
Gournay-en-Bray
Rouen
Beauvais
Compiègne
Honfleur
Gisors
Creil
Reims

Caen
Bernay
Louviers
Coutances
Evreux
Mantes
St-Denis
Granville
Meaux
Vire
Ivry
Paris
Avranches
Exmes
Mortain
Argentan
Pontorson
Domfront
Sées
Senonches
Savigny
Seine
Mont-
St-Michel
St-James-
Mayenne
Alençon
de-Beuvron
Nogent-le-Rotrou
Montereau
Troyes
La Ferté-Bernard
Sens
Laval
Ste-Suzanne
Montargis
Le Mans

Orléans
Jargeau
Loire
Blois
Angers
Tours

Loire

N

W   E

S

Areas under English
control, May 1436

0   30   60 miles

Table 1: The English royal line from Edward III

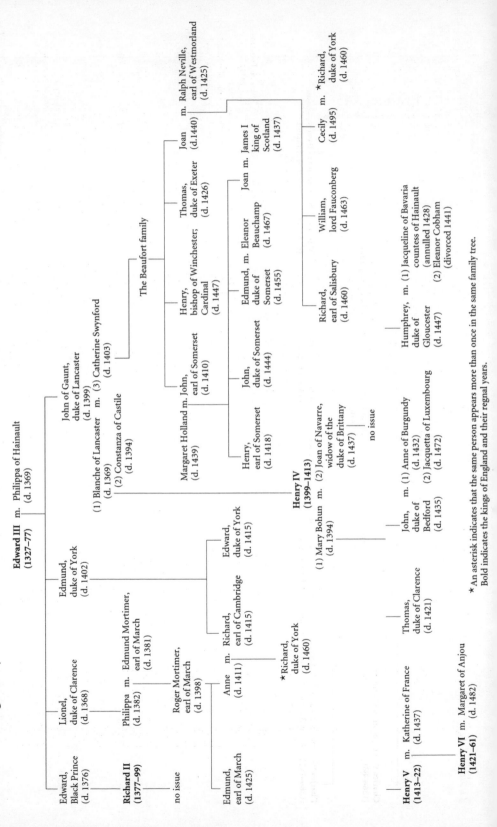

* An asterisk indicates that the same person appears more than once in the same family tree.
Bold indicates the kings of England and their regnal years.

Table 2: The French royal line: the House of Valois

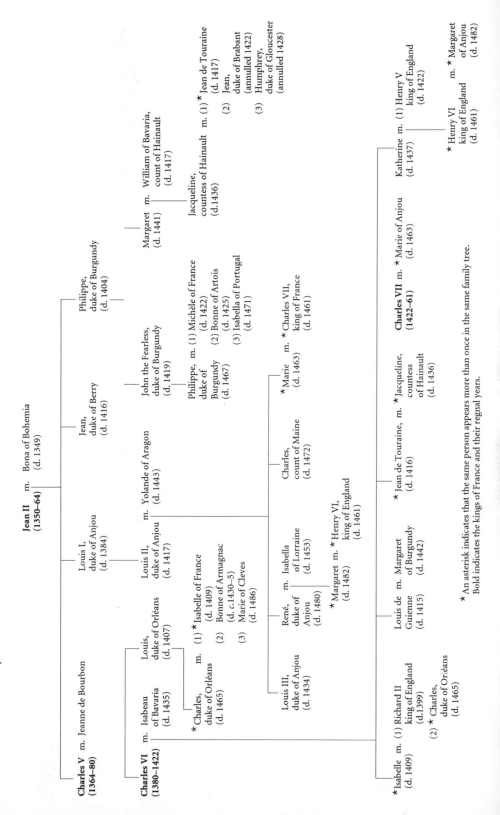

* An asterisk indicates that the same person appears more than once in the same family tree.
Bold indicates the kings of France and their regnal years.

PART ONE

ESTABLISHING THE KINGDOM

CHAPTER ONE

Invasion

On 10 February 1417 King Henry V ordered six wing feathers to be plucked from every goose in twenty English counties and sent to the Tower of London. A few months earlier he had, through parliament, prohibited the recently introduced practice of making clogs and wooden overshoes from ash instead of the traditional willow and alder.[1] These two acts might seem unrelated – even trivial – but together they marked a significant escalation in rearmament. The feathers and ash were required to make the flights and shafts of arrows, hundreds of thousands of which were now urgently needed. For, less than two years after he had first led an army into France, Henry was about to launch a second invasion. And this time he intended to stay.

The campaign of 1415 had been a triumph. It began with the capture of Harfleur, a powerful and strategically significant town at the mouth of the river Seine whose port had not only threatened the security of the English coast and Channel shipping but also controlled access to the interior of France. Harfleur was now a second Calais, with an English garrison twelve hundred strong, commanded in person by the king's own uncle, Thomas

Beaufort, duke of Exeter.[2] Though this was an important English success, it paled into insignificance beside the great victory which was the culmination of the campaign. On 25 October 1415 the king himself had led his small army into battle against an immensely superior French force at Agincourt and defeated it comprehensively. Thousands of Frenchmen were killed, including three royal dukes, eight counts and four of the most senior military officers of France; the dukes of Orléans and Bourbon, the counts of Richemont, Eu and Vendôme and the great chivalric hero Marshal Boucicaut were taken prisoner. By contrast, the English had lost only two noblemen, Edward, duke of York, and Michael, earl of Suffolk, a handful of men-at-arms and perhaps a hundred archers.[3]

The shock of Agincourt had reverberated throughout Europe. In Henry V's own eyes, and indeed those of many of his contemporaries, victory on such a scale could only have been possible if God had been on his side. It therefore followed that Henry's reason for undertaking the campaign – the refusal of the French to restore to him what he called his 'just rights and inheritances' in that realm – had divine approval and sanction. Quite what those 'just rights and inheritances' were, however, was a fluid concept which varied according to the king's ambition and the strength of his political hand. At the very least they included an expansion of the duchy of Gascony, which had belonged to the English crown since the marriage of Henry II to Eleanor of Aquitaine in 1152, though its borders had been eroded and pushed back over the years by its French neighbours. These were relatively recent losses but the duchy of Normandy, which Henry V claimed by 'inheritance' from William the Conqueror, had been in French hands for over two hundred years, having been annexed by Philippe Auguste in 1204.

Even bolder was Henry's demand that the crown of France itself should be handed over to him. It was, he said, also his by right of inheritance since his great-grandfather, Edward III, was the only surviving grandson and direct lineal descendant of Philippe IV of France. In 1328, however, the young Edward III had been unjustly deprived of this inheritance when the crown was seized by his French cousin who had established the new Valois dynasty of kings.[4]

The representative of that dynasty was now Charles VI, who had become king of France in 1380 as a child of eleven. Until 1388, when he came of age, he had been subject to the guardianship of his uncles but the strain of taking over the reins of government in person had proved too much for him. After only four years he lapsed into the first of what would become lengthening periods of intermittent madness in which he believed that he was made of glass and was afraid to sit down in case he shattered. At these times he was unable to recognise those closest to him, denied that he was married or had children, and was capable only of looking at picture books.[5]

The vacuum this created at the heart of France naturally drew in those ambitious for power themselves and in the ensuing struggle by the king's uncles for control of the king's person, and with it the regency, two fiercely opposed parties emerged: the Burgundians (led by the duke of Burgundy) and the Armagnacs (led by the duke of Orléans). An already bitter quarrel was further envenomed when John the Fearless, duke of Burgundy, had his rival, Louis d'Orléans, assassinated in 1407. From that moment the two parties were irreconcilable and France was torn apart by civil war.

This situation had provided Henry V with the perfect opportunity to exploit their differences for his own ends. Both parties hated each other more than their traditional enemies, the English, so they were prepared to offer him concessions in order to secure his aid. Henry had negotiated simultaneously with them both, offering his military services to the highest bidder in an effort to secure his 'just rights and inheritances' by diplomatic means. When this had failed to achieve all he wanted, he went to war on his own account.

The Agincourt campaign had demonstrated that Burgundians and Armagnacs could not unite against a common enemy, even in the face of invasion and the loss of Harfleur. John the Fearless, whom the Armagnacs rightly suspected of having made a secret non-intervention pact with Henry V, had given the invaders a wide berth and been a notable absentee from the battle. It was not until ten days after the defeat that he finally mobilised the forces he had been ordered to raise to resist the English – only to lead them in an attempt to take Armagnac-held Paris. The people of that city, who were ardent supporters of the duke, were even said to have received the news of Agincourt with joy because they regarded it as a defeat for the Armagnacs rather than for France.[6]

The Armagnacs, however, were by no means crushed. They had lost some of their most important military leaders, including Charles, duke of Orléans, who suffered the indignity of spending his twenty-first birthday being paraded through the streets of London with the other prisoners of Harfleur and Agincourt. Many more had been killed in the battle. The dauphin, Louis de Guienne, an ardent supporter of the Armagnac cause, ought to have been a rallying point in place of his insane father, but he too died, in December 1415. His brother, the next heir to the throne, seventeen-year-old Jean de Touraine, was living in Hainault, where he had been brought up in the court of the duke of Burgundy's sister and had married her daughter.

Yet the Armagnac cause was not completely lost. They still had Paris, the seat of government. The new dauphin might have been out of reach, but they had the king and could rule in his name. They had also found a replacement for Constable d'Albret, the chief military officer of France, who had fallen at Agincourt: Bernard, count of Armagnac, father-in-law of Charles d'Orléans and veteran of many campaigns against the English in Gascony. Able and ruthless as a soldier, but short on diplomatic skills, his leadership would ensure that France would remain as divided as it had been before the English invasion.

Henry was far too much of a realist ever to have imagined that the success of the Agincourt campaign would force the concessions he wanted from the French. Further military action would be needed, the only question being when that should take place. Even before he left France in November 1415, he had held a council at Calais to discuss whether 'as ought to follow a great victory, he should go on to besiege neighbouring towns and castles'.[7] It might have been advantageous to strike again while the French were still in disarray but Henry had in mind plans far more ambitious than merely the acquisition of a few strongholds. He had his sights set on nothing less than the conquest of the entire duchy of Normandy and the next eighteen months would be dedicated to the meticulous planning and preparation of that campaign.

His first priority was the security of Harfleur. Having suffered heavy bombardment during the English siege, its fortifications and large areas of the town were in a parlous state, offering little protection in the event of an attack. Though work was begun immediately to rectify this, the gates and ramparts were still being repaired in 1417 when orders were given to fill in the English mines under the walls.[8] More importantly, unlike Calais, Harfleur had no surrounding occupied territory to provide a buffer against French attack and food and firewood for the inhabitants. The garrison's soldiers risked their lives every time they ventured out for supplies, and on one disastrous occasion suffered heavy losses of both men and horses when they were ambushed by Bernard d'Armagnac at Valmont, twenty miles from Harfleur. Beaufort, who had led the expedition, only escaped by making for the coast and leading the survivors back at night along the sands.[9]

By the late spring of 1416 the situation of the garrison was becoming increasingly desperate as the Armagnacs tightened their siege by land and, with the aid of twenty galleys hired from Genoa, laid a blockade by sea to prevent English supply ships getting through. (One ship carrying corn which successfully ran the blockade did so only by the stratagem of flying the French flag.) Just when the French were convinced that Harfleur was on the point of surrender, relief arrived in the form of an English fleet under the command of the king's brother John, duke of Bedford. On 15 August, in his first action in what would be a long and illustrious military career in France, Bedford launched an assault on the blockade and, after five or six hours of fighting at close quarters, succeeded in scattering the enemy ships, capturing some and sinking others. He then sailed triumphantly into Harfleur to reprovision the town.[10]

Bedford had won an important victory but another, of a different kind, was secured by his brother on the very same day. On 15 August 1416 Henry V and Sigismund, the Holy Roman Emperor, signed the Treaty of Canterbury, committing themselves and their heirs to perpetual friendship and to support each other in the pursuit of their 'just rights' in France. The significance of the treaty was that for the previous six months Sigismund had dedicated himself to securing peace between England and France. His frustration at his failure and his conviction that French duplicity was entirely to blame were set out at length in the preamble for all to see. There could not have been a clearer or more public endorsement of Henry's own oft-stated view that the French were not to be trusted and, unlike himself, did not genuinely desire peace.[11]

The Treaty of Canterbury was formally ratified in the parliament that met at Westminster in October. The king's uncle Henry Beaufort, bishop of Winchester, gave a rousing opening speech as chancellor: Henry, he said, had generously tried to come to a good and peaceful agreement with his adversary, but the French were 'full of pride' and had 'absolutely refused' to reach a settlement.

> For which reason our said sovereign lord is again of necessity obliged to have recourse to the issue of the sword if he wishes to achieve an end, peace and termination of his just aim and quarrel, thereby fulfilling the words of the wise man, who says, 'Let us make wars so that we may have peace, for the end of war is peace.'[12]

Medieval English parliaments only met when summoned to do so by the king and Henry, a master of propaganda, ensured that this parliament was in session for the first anniversary of Agincourt, which was celebrated with a *Te Deum* in the royal chapel at Westminster. The House of Commons duly responded with a patriotic grant of a double subsidy – a tax of two-fifteenths on the value of movable goods rising to two-tenths for those living in towns – enabling the business to begin in earnest of stockpiling weapons and provisions, recruiting men-at-arms, archers, gunners, miners, carpenters and surgeons and hiring ships to carry them all across the Channel.[13]

By the end of July 1417 everything was in place. The duke of Bedford, reprising his role during the Agincourt campaign, had been appointed as the king's lieutenant in England. (Bedford's older brother Thomas, duke of Clarence, and his younger brother Humphrey, duke of Gloucester, would accompany the king to France.) Some fifteen hundred ships had been hired or forcibly pressed into service, including, despite their protestations, Venetian merchant vessels. The Genoese, however, whose mercenary principles were stronger than their alliance with France, had accepted £1667 (£875,175) to provide six transports. An army of around ten thousand fighting men, three-quarters of whom were archers, had been contracted to serve for a year and was mustered, reviewed and waiting to embark at Southampton.[14]

The only obstacle to their safe passage had been removed. John, earl of Huntingdon, a veteran of Agincourt though still only twenty-two, had been dispatched to destroy the nine Genoese galleys which had escaped Bedford's defeat of the blockade of Harfleur. On 29 June he had won a decisive naval battle off Cap-de-la-Hève, capturing four of the ships, their French commander (a bastard brother of the duke of Bourbon) and a useful haul of treasure. 'And so we know for certain,' one Venetian chronicler noted, in words which demonstrated just how widely Henry V's interpretation of events had come to be accepted in Europe, 'that the wrath of God has brought these defeats upon the French because of their arrogance and pride.'[15]

On 30 July 1417 the great invasion fleet set sail for France. Its objective was known to no one except the king himself and a small group of his closest advisers, and even the king had changed his mind. In February he had sent troops under the command of two trusted knights, John Popham and John Pelham, to Harfleur, ordering them to stay there until his arrival.[16] Perhaps he realised that this was too obvious a choice of destination. The French were certainly expecting him to land there and had appointed special commissioners to 'repair and fill with provisions and munitions, the towns of Honfleur and Montivilliers, and the other towns, castles and fortresses of Normandy to enable them to resist English attacks'.[17] The special emphasis on the two named towns reflected their strategic importance: Honfleur lay across the Seine from Harfleur and its capture would cut off the vital river supply line to Rouen; Montivilliers was just six miles from Harfleur and therefore, in the phrase that would be used repeatedly over the coming years, 'held the frontier against the English'.

Despite their best efforts, the French were wrong-footed, just as they had been in 1415. On 1 August, almost exactly two years to the day since his last invasion, Henry landed at the mouth of the Touques, the river in the Calvados region of Normandy that now divides the fashionable resorts of Deauville and Trouville. The site was chosen for two reasons. The long, flat stretches of sandy beach enabled even a fleet the size of Henry's to disembark its cargoes of men, horses, munitions and supplies within a single day, freeing some ships to return immediately to England to pick up those who had been left behind for lack of space.[18]

The second reason for choosing Touques was that it was less than ten miles from Honfleur – close enough to deceive the French into thinking that this was indeed Henry's objective. Instead, after several days gathering intelligence, during which all the castles in the neighbourhood surrendered with unseemly haste and without striking a blow, the king led his army in the opposite direction, south-west towards Caen.

Before he left Touques, Henry issued a final challenge to the French, calling upon Charles VI in the name of the God 'in whose hands are the rights of kings and princes' to give him 'in fact and in reality' the crown and kingdom of France, his rightful inheritance which had so long been unjustly withheld.[19] This was not mere bravado but the formal and legal requirement of the laws of war: before hostilities began in earnest, the enemy had to be offered one last chance to avoid the spilling of Christian blood. And since they had failed to respond to that request, the blame for the consequences would rest squarely on the shoulders of the French.

Henry had claimed the crown but, for the moment, his ambition was limited to a lesser prize. Even this was no easy task. The duchy of Normandy was prosperous, with a large number of towns or *bonnes villes* which were the local centres of trade and financial, judicial and military administration. The surrounding areas of open countryside, known as the *plat pais*, provided food, wine and fuel for their local town. They were also an important source of taxation and of manpower for the urban-based military levies.

To conquer Normandy – and keep it – Henry needed to capture not only the castles and fortresses which were the traditional first line of defence but also the towns which would give him control of their wider administrative districts. The French, however, had learned the lesson of Edward III's invasion in 1346, when the towns had been defenceless and at his mercy. Since then every urban centre of any importance had built great walls behind which the population of the neighbouring country-side as well as the townspeople could take refuge in times of danger. A sophisticated system of civilian defence – keeping watch on the walls at night and guarding the gates during the day – had also been introduced. In the larger towns this was supplemented by a local garrison of professional soldiers who manned a fortress within the walls which could hold out long after the town itself had surrendered.

The two most important towns in Normandy were Rouen and Caen. To attack Rouen, the regional centre of government, some forty miles up the Seine from Harfleur, would mean running the gauntlet of all the castles and fortified towns with which it was ring-fenced and the risk of being stranded deep in enemy territory. Caen, capital of lower Normandy, was less than twenty-five miles from the point of invasion but, more importantly, it lay just nine miles from the Channel with a navigable river leading into its heart. The English fleet could therefore keep up a regular supply of victuals and armaments, avoiding the need to plunder the surrounding countryside and further antagonise the population. In the event of dire necessity it could also quickly and easily evacuate the army back to England.

On 18 August 1417 Henry laid siege to Caen, 'a strong town and a fair, and a royal castle therein',[20] in what was to become a model for the rest of his campaign and indeed the years of occupation which were to follow. Caen had walls seven feet thick, defended by thirty-two towers and twelve fortified gates, and it was encircled by the river and water-filled ditches. The castle had a massive square stone keep built by William the Conqueror, who had also founded the two great abbeys of Saint-Étienne and La Trinité as burial places for himself and his wife. Like so many other French abbeys, they were heavily fortified and as capable of withstanding siege as any castle. Unfortunately, as was also the case elsewhere, both abbeys lay outside the town walls. The nuns and monks had fled and the small castle garrison, wary of dispersing its strength, had been forced to abandon its defence at Henry's approach.

The standard procedure for a medieval town threatened by siege was to clear away any building lying outside the town walls to prevent it giving shelter to the enemy. A pious reluctance to commit sacrilege and, more likely, the sheer impossibility of razing two vast stone structures within the short space of time available, meant that the necessary demolition of the two abbeys was not carried out. However, in a scenario that was to become familiar in the coming years, the mere threat of demolition provoked treason. At dead of night one of the monks crept into the English camp, found his way to Henry's brother, the duke of Clarence, and offered to show him a way in. 'It is especially suitable for you to save our abbey', an English chronicler reported him to have said, 'seeing that you are descended from the line of kings who founded, built and endowed it.' With the monk's aid, the duke and his men scaled an unprotected part of the abbey walls and gained possession of Saint-Étienne, giving the king a bird's-eye view of the town and enabling him to train his cannon from the roof and towers of the monastery. La

Trinité on the other side of Caen was also taken and artillery stationed there.[21]

Having duly summoned the town to surrender (an important formality before the attack could take place legitimately) but been refused, Henry ordered the bombardment to begin. Two weeks of continuous shelling by gunners working in shifts throughout the day and night damaged the walls sufficiently to enable a full-scale assault to be launched. This was a relatively rare occurrence in medieval warfare, though Caen was unfortunate to have suffered the same fate and its consequences before, when Edward III sacked the town in 1346. According to the laws of war, the town's refusal to capitulate meant that its inhabitants and their property were at the mercy of its attackers. And very little mercy was shown.

The king and Clarence attacked simultaneously from opposite ends of the town. Henry's men were kept at bay by a vigorous defence in which one knight, who fell from a scaling ladder, was burned alive 'by those inhuman French scum' but Clarence's company forced their way through a breach and made their way through the streets towards the king, killing all in their path, shouting 'à Clarence, à Clarence, Saint George!' and sparing neither man nor child. Though the king had ordered that women and clergy were to be spared, the streets were said to have run with blood. Once victory was assured, the town was turned over to the soldiers to pillage at will, only churches being spared at the king's insistence.[22]

The brutal sack of Caen was an exemplary punishment authorised by the Bible[23] and meted out in accordance with the laws of war by a king who believed he was simply carrying out God's will. It was designed to teach 'his' subjects in the duchy of Normandy the penalty of 'rebellion', as he termed any act of resistance, and the lesson was not lost on the Normans. Five days after the fall of Caen, the castle garrison came to terms: if Charles VI, the dauphin or the count of Armagnac did not come to their aid in the meantime, they agreed to surrender on 19 September, together with fourteen other towns and villages in the vicinity, including the important town and castle of Bayeux.[24]

No relief was forthcoming. For, just days before the English invasion, the duke of Burgundy had begun his own military operations against the Armagnacs in a campaign designed to secure him the mastery of Paris. Advancing on two fronts, from his lands in Burgundy and in Flanders and Picardy, he had captured many of the towns along the Oise and lower Seine valleys, cutting off the principal supply lines from Normandy and Picardy and gradually encircling Paris. As he drew closer to the city, the count of Armagnac was faced with the choice of resisting the English invasion in far-off Normandy or defending his own seat of power. Naturally he chose the latter and recalled his men-at-arms from the frontiers of the duchy for the defence of Paris. 'And so it was', wrote the Burgundian chronicler Monstrelet, 'that the king of England . . . had an even greater advantage in his campaign of subjugation, having no impediment and no danger at all.' The way now lay open for Henry to expand his conquest into the heart of Normandy.[25]

CHAPTER TWO

Conquest

The sack of Caen had shown that Henry was prepared to be ruthless in pursuit of his goals, but if his conquest were to acquire any sort of permanence he needed to win the acquiescence, if not the support, of the local population. He had therefore issued proclamations that anyone who was prepared to submit and swear allegiance to him would be taken into his royal protection and allowed to enjoy their property and the right to continue in business. Those who did not wish to take the oath would be free to depart, but all their possessions would be forfeited.[1]

The administrative records of English Normandy reveal that one thousand inhabitants of Caen had refused to take the oath. They were given safe-conducts, valid for three days, enabling them to reach the safety of Falaise, some twenty-two miles further south. More generous terms were given to Bayeux, because the town had surrendered without resistance. The inhabitants there were allowed to take with them all the movable possessions they could carry and 250 wagon-loads were granted safe-conducts lasting fifteen days.[2]

The confiscated houses and business premises they left behind them were taken into the king's hands to do with as he wished. Within days of the fall of Caen, Englishmen were invited to settle in the town, though they showed an unsurprising reluctance to uproot themselves until the conquest became more secure. An enterprising exception was John Convers, who married the daughter of Richard Caunet 'of our town of Caen' a mere ten days after the formal surrender and was granted all his father-in-law's property in and outside the town. It may have been the first, but it was certainly not the last, marriage of convenience between victor and vanquished in Normandy.[3]

Henry himself took up residence in his ancestor's castle and, in a pointed gesture, turned the building where the townsmen used to hold their official meetings into a munitions store. Before he left to continue his military campaign at the beginning of October, he appointed tried and trusted Englishmen to key positions: Gilbert, lord Talbot, became captain-general of the marches around Caen, Sir Gilbert Umfraville captain of the town itself, Sir John Assheton seneschal of Bayeux and Richard Wydeville captain of Lisieux.[4] With an acquiescent French population and a growing English presence, Henry could afford to leave Caen, his conquest of the town complete.

He now had to decide where to strike next. At this point the diplomatic agreements he had made before his campaign proved their worth. The dukes of Burgundy and Brittany had each held a separate face-to-face meeting with Henry. Their discussions remained secret but it was now evident from their actions that both had agreed to hold aloof from Henry's campaign.[5] With Burgundy actively pursuing his own ends and holding the Armagnacs hostage in Paris to the east and Brittany nervously looking the other way to the west, Henry was free to plunge through the heart of lower Normandy. Fifteen days after leaving Caen he arrived before Alençon, having taken every town and castle on his sixty-five-mile route, including the strongholds of Exmes, Sées and Argentan. Not one of them had offered even a token resistance.[6]

It had been breathtakingly easy, not least because the Normans lacked leadership. The duke of Alençon, for whom the duchy had been created within Normandy in 1414, had been killed at Agincourt and his son, Jean II, was only eight years old. He could claim kinship with Henry V, since his grandmother was Joan of Brittany, the king's own stepmother, but so could many other Armagnacs and there was no room for family senti- ment in the world of medieval politics. With no one round whom to rally, and the example of Caen all too recent, even Alençon surrendered immediately, despite being well prepared for a siege. Within a fortnight of Henry's arrival at the town the rest of the child-duke's lands were in his hands, creating an English-held corridor from Normandy's northern coast to its southern border.[7]

This rapid success brought Jean VI, duke of Brittany, to Alençon for a second personal meeting with Henry. He did not come to assert the rights of his dispossessed nephew, the duke of Alençon, but to protect his own interests. On 16 November 1417 he signed a year-long truce, promising that his subjects would abstain from all acts of war against the English in return for a commitment from Henry to refrain from attacking his lands. At the same time he obtained a similar agreement for Yolande of Aragon, the dowager duchess of Anjou, whose fourteen-year-old son was betrothed to his own daughter.[8]

Assured of freedom from attack to the west and south, Henry could now begin the business of expanding his conquest. The duchy fell geographically, historically and administratively into two parts divided by the Seine. To the east lay the relatively flat and featureless, though fertile, chalk plains of upper Normandy which extended round the north of Paris towards Picardy; to the west lay the more isolated and dramatic landscape of lower Normandy, with its granite bluffs and plateaux, enclosed valleys and ancient woodlands. Henry's first objective was to obtain control of lower Normandy. Having cut it in two by his initial advance and secured the central region by garrisoning the places he had captured, he planned to extend his conquest systemat- ically outwards by the simultaneous deployment of divisions of his army against the key fortresses to the east and west.

Military campaigns were usually suspended for the winter

because of the difficulty in obtaining supplies, particularly fodder for the horses upon which the army was dependent, but Henry understood the importance of maintaining the momentum of his conquest. On 1 December, with his brothers Clarence and Gloucester, he laid siege to Falaise, birthplace of William the Conqueror, a town he had avoided initially because of the strength of its defences. Now, however, since he intended to advance further and deeper into lower Normandy, he could not afford to leave such an important stronghold in enemy hands. Though the town at first refused to surrender, it took just three weeks for the English guns to reduce it to submission. The great white-walled castle, soaring above the town on a cliff of solid rock, held out for another month but when no relief was forthcoming it too surrendered, on 16 February 1418. As punishment for this obstinacy the captain and his garrison were not allowed to leave until they had repaired the artillery damage to the walls at the town's expense and to the king's satisfaction.[9]

A special clause in the terms of capitulation also marked a hardening of the king's attitude towards those who refused to take the oath of allegiance to him. All those not from Falaise who had fought against Henry elsewhere in Normandy were to be at his mercy. This was undoubtedly aimed principally at those who had left Caen a few months earlier with safe-conducts to Falaise. Having spared their lives once, Henry was determined that his generosity should not be abused by having them take up arms against him again.[10]

Throughout the coming months Henry's captains extended the boundaries of his conquest. In the south-west the capture of a line of border towns and castles, including Avranches, Pontorson and Saint-James-de-Beuvron, established English control up to the frontier of Brittany. In the meantime Gloucester and the earl of Huntingdon pushed into the Cotentin peninsula, gathering in Saint-Lô, Coutances, Carentan and Valognes before settling down to a five-month siege of the last remaining stronghold, Cherbourg, 'one of the strongest castles in the world . . . in a place impossible to besiege or fight'.[11]

Henry himself, with Clarence and their uncle, Thomas Beaufort, who had brought over from England much-needed reinforcements of five hundred men-at-arms and fifteen hundred archers, was slowly advancing towards the Seine and Rouen, taking Évreux on 20 May and Louviers on 23 June. When Pont-de-l'Arche also fell to him, on 20 July 1418, Henry had completed the conquest of virtually the whole of lower Normandy in the astonishingly short period of just less than a year.[12] Only two places had evaded him: Cherbourg, which would capitulate at the end of September, and Mont-Saint-Michel, which would remain defiant to the end.

This was a significant achievement but it was not enough to sate Henry's ambition. Nothing less than all of Normandy would do. The capture of Pont-de-l'Arche marked an important stage in the realisation of his plans, giving him control of his first bridge over the Seine and with it the capability of leading his armies across the river and into upper Normandy. Only one other major obstacle stood in his path. A dozen miles north of Pont-de-l'Arche lay the wealthy and powerful city of Rouen. Ancient capital of the duchy of Normandy, larger and more populous than any contemporary English city except London and, as Henry himself acknowledged, 'the most notable place in France save Paris', Rouen would have to be taken before the conquest of upper Normandy could begin.[13]

As Henry closed in on the capital of the duchy, a dramatic coup took place in the capital of the kingdom, transforming the political situation in France. Paris had remained in Armagnac hands, despite the fact that most of the ordinary citizens and poorer inhabitants were solidly pro-Burgundian in sentiment. Neither a bloody popular uprising within the city in 1413 nor several attempts by the duke of Burgundy himself to take it by military force had succeeded. In the early hours of 29 May 1418 the son of an organiser of the night-watch stole his father's keys to the Saint Germain gate and secretly admitted the sire de l'Isle-Adam and a party of armed Burgundians into Paris. Their battle-cries roused their Parisian partisans, who swiftly joined them with any arms they could find to hand and the city was engulfed in a tidal wave of violence. While the soldiers seized the major seats of government and arrested prominent Armagnacs, the mob went on the rampage, pillaging the houses of Armagnac sympathisers whom they dragged from their beds, and murdered without compunction in the street. Their bodies, plundered of everything except their underclothes, were heaped up in piles in the mud 'like sides of bacon'.

A few days later the volatile mob was unleashed again. Perhaps deliberately inflamed by calls for vengeance on the deposed Armagnac leaders, they stormed the city jails and massacred the prisoners indiscriminately, leaving their corpses naked and their faces mutilated beyond recognition. Among the most eminent victims who met their end in this brutal way were the count of Armagnac and three Norman bishops who had fled the English invasion. The Burgundian victory was complete and on 14 July the duke arrived in Paris to the acclamation of the crowds. He now had control of the king and the government. Only two things marred his triumph. The new dauphin, sixteen-year-old Charles, the fifth and last surviving son of Charles VI, had escaped his clutches and fled to the safety of his Armagnac friends.[14]

More importantly, having seized power, the Burgundian party now represented France and therefore had the obligation to resist her enemies. This was forcibly brought home the day after the duke made his formal entry into Paris, when he received two messengers from Pont-de-l'Arche. The first brought news from the garrison's captain that the town would surrender unless relieved before 20 July; the second, a herald from Henry V, sought to know if the duke would respect his truces with the English. The only possible reply to both – officially at least – was that England and Burgundy were now at war.[15]

Nevertheless, Pont-de-l'Arche was not relieved and nine days after it surrendered the English army appeared before Rouen. The next stage in Henry's master plan for the conquest of Normandy had begun. Well aware that if Rouen fell, upper Normandy would surely follow, the citizens had done all they could to protect themselves and their city. Every building outside the city walls which might afford assistance to the enemy had been ruthlessly demolished, including several churches and the famous royal shipyards. The stone had been carried into Rouen to reinforce and repair the five miles of wall which surrounded the city. Guns had been placed in each of the sixty towers on the walls and in those flanking the five gates. Some four thousand extra troops had been poured into the garrison and both city and castle had been placed under the overall command of Guy le Bouteiller, a renowned Burgundian captain. The citizens had even raided the cathedral treasury for items which could be pawned to ensure that the soldiers' wages were paid. They had also taken up arms themselves and around sixteen thousand were now ready and willing to repel the English. Every person living in Rouen, regardless of status, had been ordered to lay in supplies sufficient for a six-month siege; those who could not afford to do so were told to leave the city. Though some did go, many thousands of refugees who had fled the English advance did not. And the siege began before the harvest could be gathered in.[16]

Henry set up four great camps around the city, linking them with trenches which kept his men out of the sight and range of gunners on the walls: thorn bushes were piled along the tops of the trenches to prevent assault or ambush. Huge piles were hammered into the bed of the Seine and three rows of massive iron chains were suspended above, below and on the water-line, preventing any ships bringing aid to the besieged. A fleet of English ships, meanwhile, kept the king's army well stocked with victuals and ammunition, some of it brought over from England via Harfleur. The only bridge across the Seine nearer than Pont-de-l'Arche was heavily fortified and lay out of reach in the heart of Rouen, so Henry built another to facilitate communication between his forces on the left and right banks of the river. This temporary structure, made of hides stretched over a wooden frame, had originally been built in England by the king's master-carpenter, but it dismantled into sections so that it could be stored and transported for use in the field.

Henry had also brought with him 'a great multitude of siege engines and artillery' and these were trained upon the city walls and gates so that the bombardment could begin. His entire army was now gathered round Rouen as he concentrated all his military effort on the single objective of bringing the mighty city to its knees.[17]

Henry's plan, however, was not to take Rouen by assault but to starve it into submission. By the beginning of October, food was beginning to run out and the increasingly desperate citizens were driven to eat dogs, cats and rats, paying huge sums for the privilege of doing so. Even water was in short supply after the English dammed the river Renelle above the city. As the death toll rose, the decision was taken to expel those unable to fight: the poor, the old, women, children and the sick. If they had hoped for mercy from Henry V they were mistaken. He would not allow them to pass and, trapped in the ditches between the city walls and the English army, they slowly starved to death, in full view of both besieger and besieged. John Page, an English eyewitness, described their plight: 'some unable to open their eyes and no longer breathing, others cowering on their knees as thin as twigs . . . a woman . . . clutching her dead child to her breast to warm it, and a child . . . sucking the breast of its dead mother'. Henry remained inexorable. When asked to take pity on them, he simply replied that 'they were not put there at my command'.[18]

Summer turned to autumn and then winter but still the English army maintained its relentless and vice-like grip on the city: nothing and no one were allowed to leave or enter. Every attempt to make a sortie was driven back with heavy losses and a regular bombardment kept up the pressure on the unfortunate besieged. The citizens' increasingly desperate pleas for aid to both Armagnacs and Burgundians went unanswered. At the end of November the duke of Burgundy was eventually pressured into gathering an army and marched as far as Pontoise, where he lingered for five weeks, but he dared not risk another Agincourt and, fearing the Armagnacs might seize Paris in his absence, he retreated without making any attempt to engage the English in military action. Deprived of this last hope, Rouen capitulated. On 19 January 1419, almost six months after he had first laid siege to the city, Henry accepted its formal surrender. The next day he rode through the shattered streets where dead and dying still lay, and gave thanks for his victory in the cathedral of Notre Dame.[19]

The siege had cost Henry a great deal of time and several of his commanders, including Gilbert, lord Talbot, and Thomas Butler, prior of the Knights Hospitallers at Kilmainham in Ireland; Butler had only recently arrived, bringing fifteen hundred Irish foot soldiers whose distinctive dress and savage behaviour had caused consternation among French and English alike.[20] The terms of the rendition were little harsher, except in scale, than those of other Norman towns. Henry demanded eighty hostages as surety for the payment of a fine of 300,000 *écus* (£21.88m); all English prisoners were to be freed; Norman members of the garrison were to remain as prisoners, but those of other nationalities could leave so long as they swore not to take up arms against him for one year; the town's ancient privileges were ratified and its inhabitants confirmed in their possessions, providing they took the oath of loyalty.[21]

Guy le Bouteiller was among those who did so and was rewarded for changing his allegiance by being appointed lieutenant to the duke of Gloucester, the new captain of Rouen. The French regarded his defection as treachery, so it was ironic that one of the few executions which did take place was that of another traitor whose betrayal had actually benefited the English. Nicolas de Gennes had accepted a bribe and a safe-conduct as far as Rouen to surrender Cherbourg to the English the previous August: as a result, only Mont-Saint-Michel remained in French hands in the whole of western Normandy. Instead of being grateful to de Gennes, Henry had him arrested, tried and executed for treason. To modern eyes this seems like impartiality taken to excess, but contemporaries applauded this very unusual action as further evidence of Henry's punctiliousness in observing the laws of war. Once more he emerged with his reputation enhanced.[22]

The fall of Rouen was a turning point in the conquest of Normandy. Fourteen neighbouring towns and castles surrendered under the terms of Rouen's capitulation. Two months later the whole of the Caux region was in English hands, including the important strongholds of Caudebec, Lillebonne, Tancarville and Honfleur on the Seine and Dieppe and Fécamp on the Channel coast. Henry's captains pushed the eastern boundaries as far as Gournay, Vernon and Mantes, most places surrendering without even a token resistance. The frontier town of Ivry, which did resist, was swiftly taken by assault and though the castle garrison held out for another six weeks, no relief came and it too was obliged to surrender. It was becoming increasingly clear to the Normans that they had been abandoned by Burgundians and Armagnacs alike.[23]

Yet the strain of continuous warfare was also beginning to tell on the English. They had been fighting on French soil for almost two years – one of the longest periods of sustained military activity of the entire Hundred Years War – and though almost all of Normandy was now in their hands, the conquest had drained England's resources of both money and men. The cost of putting garrisons into every conquered stronghold while also maintaining armies on active service in the field was prohibitive, particularly since Henry insisted that his men should pay their way rather than live off the land. He was also finding it harder to recruit soldiers in England. The Privy Council reported in May 1419 that it had been unable to find any willing volunteers among the leading gentry, adding that all the 'most able' were already in Normandy with the king. And some of those who were in Normandy were now hankering to go home. 'There may no hope be had as yet of peace', wrote John Feelde from Évreux. 'I pray you to pray for us that we come soon out of this unlusty soldier's life into the life of England.'[24]

A diplomatic solution was the best hope of obtaining a permanent peace and resolving these difficulties but Henry's sweeping military success entitled him to remain resolute in his twin demands for territorial concessions and marriage with Charles VI's daughter Katherine. He had continued his policy of negotiating separately with each party throughout 1418 and 1419, successfully ratcheting up the tensions and suspicions between them, but failing to win the concessions he wanted. As always, the English blamed the French: they were 'yncongrue', Feelde complained after the dauphin failed to turn up for a summit meeting at Évreux, 'that is to say, in [the] old manner of speech of England, they be double-dealing and false'.[25]

The Burgundians at least honoured their promise to attend a meeting arranged on neutral ground between English-held Mantes and Burgundian-held Pontoise in the early summer of 1419. This was not the usual conference of ambassadors and diplomats but a meeting at the highest level, raising hopes on both sides that a settlement might be achieved. The presence of Henry V himself, his brothers Clarence and Gloucester, the duke of Burgundy, Queen Isabeau and Princess Katherine (whose hand in marriage had consistently been one of Henry's demands since before the Agincourt campaign) indicated that business was meant to be done: it would not be possible to rely on the usual stalling tactic of referring back for further instructions. There was only one notable absentee and significantly that was Charles VI, whose attendance had been promised. The Burgundians claimed he was too unwell to travel from Pontoise but his absence was a convenient insurance policy, providing them with an excuse to avoid committing to a final treaty.

Nevertheless, it seems possible that they might indeed have accepted Henry's terms. Queen Isabeau later wrote to Henry claiming that they were 'agreeable enough to us' but that, if they had been accepted, 'all the lords, knights, cities and good towns would have abandoned us and joined with our . . . son; whence even greater war would have arisen.'[26] At their final meeting Henry allowed his frustration to show: 'Good cousin', he said to the duke,

'we wish you to know that we will have the daughter of your king and all that we have demanded with her, or we will drive him, and you also, out of his kingdom.' To which words the duke replied: 'Sire, you say as you please. But before you drive my lord and me out of his kingdom, you will be very tired, and of that I have no doubt.'[27]

What the duke knew, but Henry did not, was that Burgundians and Armagnacs were about to sign the Treaty of Pouilly, ending the war between them and committing both parties to unite against the English for the recovery of Normandy. Henry's reaction on learning this news can only be guessed, but his response was swift and punitive. The day after his truces with Burgundy elapsed, he sent the earl of Huntingdon and the Gascon Captal de Buch to Pontoise, which the duke and royal court had just vacated. Under cover of night the Captal and his men scaled the walls and took the town by surprise; the fleeing citizens were intercepted and slaughtered by Huntingdon. Those who escaped fled to Paris, bringing a shocking and premature end to public celebrations of the peace.[28]

Pontoise was a mere seventeen miles from Paris and its fall meant that nothing now stood between the capital and 'the cruel, bloody English'. The Parisians were thrown into a blind panic, which escalated as the duke decamped to the safety of Troyes, taking the king and the court with him, and English raiding parties appeared before the city gates. In answer to their desperate pleas the duke and the dauphin agreed to hold a second meeting to put their treaty into effect. If ever there was a time to put aside their differences and work together to save France from the common enemy, this was it. Actions, not words, were needed and action there was, though not of the kind that the plight of the kingdom demanded. Since neither man trusted the other, the security arrangements took several weeks, so it was not until 10 September 1419 that they met on the neutral ground of the bridge over the river Yonne at Montereau. As the duke knelt before the dauphin, his hand upon his sheathed sword, Tanneguy du Chastel, the former provost of Paris, who had rescued the dauphin in the Burgundian coup of the previous summer, cried out, 'It is time!' and struck the duke in the face with an axe. The rest of the dauphin's attendants closed in, raining sword blows upon the dying duke and overpowering those who ran to his aid.[29]

Whether the assassination was a premeditated plot involving the dauphin, as the Burgundians claimed, or a reaction to an attempt by the duke to seize the dauphin, as Charles himself asserted, the murder changed the course of history. Any hope of cooperation between Armagnacs and Burgundians ended at that moment: both parties were now committed to each other's utter destruction, even if it meant alliance with their country's most deadly enemy. As the Carthusian prior of Dijon would later say, when showing François I the duke's skull, it was through the hole in that skull that the English entered France.[30]

Just ten days after the murder the dauphin's own mother, who was said to have been Burgundy's lover, wrote to Henry, urging him to avenge his murder and offering to resume peace negotiations. Before the end of September Henry had also received overtures from both the city of Paris and the new duke of Burgundy.[31]

Since the Burgundians needed him more than he needed them, Henry increased the price of peace. Only a few months earlier he had been willing to renounce his claim to the French crown in return for recognition that Normandy and an enlarged Gascony were his in full sovereignty, and marriage with Katherine of France. Now he saw his opportunity to win the crown itself. The negotiations which followed were lengthy and tortuous, since any agreement had to be acceptable to as many people as possible and legally binding, but Henry also kept up the military pressure, advancing his troops into the Île-de-France, taking Meulan, Poissy and Saint-Germain-en-Laye, and tightening his economic grip on Paris, where the price of food and fuel soared. The fear that he might take Paris itself was enough to persuade both Philippe of Burgundy and the Parisians that English alliance was better than English conquest.[32]

On Christmas Day 1419 – a day carefully chosen for its Christian significance as the anniversary of the birth of the King of Peace – a preliminary treaty was agreed between Henry V and the duke of Burgundy. The old demands for 'just rights and inheritances' were quietly dropped and in their place a completely different structure was created. This was to be a 'final peace' between England and France, based on Henry's marriage to Katherine of France and his formal adoption as his father-in-law's heir. During Charles VI's lifetime the government would continue to be carried out in his name but Henry would act as regent and be styled 'our very dear son Henry, king of England, heir of France'; the lands that Henry had conquered inside and outside the duchy of Normandy were to remain his absolutely. When Charles VI died the crown would pass to Henry, his heirs and successors, and Normandy, with the *pays-de-conquête* as conquered territory outside the duchy was known, would once again become part of the kingdom of France.

At the heart of this arrangement was the concept of the union of the two crowns which, after Charles's death, would be indivisible in the person of the king. In response to unease in both England and France, however, it was explicitly stated that neither kingdom was to be subject to the other: they were to be governed separately and each would preserve its own institutions, laws and customs.[33]

The treaty became the foundation stone upon which the edifice of the English kingdom of France was built. The sheer scale of what was at stake, and the likelihood that the settlement would be contested, meant that everything possible had to be done to make the treaty legally water-tight and morally binding. Once the final form had been agreed, the principals of both parties met at Troyes in Champagne, residence of the French royal court. (In the light of recent events, Henry demonstrated a remarkable degree of confidence in his new ally by travelling so far into Burgundian territory: Paris would have been a more obvious choice.)

On 21 May 1420 the Treaty of Troyes was formally signed and sealed on the altar of the cathedral, this holiest of places being chosen to emphasise the sanctity of the settlement. Immediately after the ceremony Henry and Katherine were betrothed at the same altar, and all those present, including Queen Isabeau, Philippe of Burgundy, Henry and his current heir, Clarence, swore to observe the treaty. The next day fifteen hundred eminent Frenchmen took the oath, led by Philippe de Morvilliers, first president of the *parlement* of Paris, which, as the ultimate court of appeal in France, would be responsible for upholding the settlement. Its legal status was further underpinned by the requirement that both the English parliament and its French counterpart, the national estates-general, should formally ratify the treaty.[34]

All Charles VI's subjects were expected to swear the oath to what its supporters called 'the final peace'. Many were prepared to do so, believing an English king of France to be a lesser evil than a realm disintegrating through civil war and foreign conquest. Henry had, after all, a reputation for enforcing justice and order which even his enemies respected. In the longer term, if Katherine produced a son, then at least the crown would pass to an heir who was half Valois. Nevertheless, even some Burgundians had reservations about this 'unnatural' alliance and the duke had to pay a personal visit to Dijon, capital of his duchy of Burgundy, to enforce its obedience.[35]

The elephant in the room was the dauphin. A proclamation in his father's name earlier in the year had accused him of the murder of John the Fearless and declared him unfit to be the heir to the crown. The treaty effectively disinherited him, though this was nowhere stated explicitly. Indeed he was mentioned only twice. One clause prohibited either side from negotiating independently with 'Charles, who calls himself dauphin' on account of the 'horrible crimes and offences' he had committed. Another bound 'our son' (Henry) to do all in his power to regain all the places and people within the realm belonging to 'the party commonly called dauphin or Armagnac'.[36]

This was the fatal flaw in the settlement. For the Treaty of Troyes was not really a 'final peace' but a commitment to continue the war. The dauphin had already set up a rival court and administration in Poitiers and virtually all France below the Loire and between Gascony and Burgundy remained resolutely loyal to him, as did much of the upper Seine valley and the area east of Paris. If Henry was to achieve his aims, it would only be at the point of the sword.

On Trinity Sunday, 2 June 1420, the archbishop of Sens married Henry of England to Katherine of France in the parish church of Troyes. The king was almost thirty-four, his bride just eighteen. Katherine can have had few illusions about her husband's character but she might have expected at least some of the customary celebrations which attended a royal wedding. Instead, the very next day, when knights from both parties proposed a tournament, Henry ordered that 'tomorrow morning we all of us be ready to go and besiege Sens, where my lord the King's enemies are. There we may all tilt and joust and prove our daring and courage, for there is no finer act of courage in the world than to punish evildoers so that poor people can live.'[37]

CHAPTER THREE

Heir of France

Henry's main objective in his first campaign as regent of France was to clear away the Armagnac strongholds to the south of Paris. A mere nine days after his marriage Sens surrendered to him and Henry was able to say to its archbishop, 'You have given me my bride; I now give you yours.' His next gift was for Philippe of Burgundy. On 24 June 1420 their joint forces carried Montereau-sur-Yonne by assault and the body of John the Fearless, which had been buried in the parish church, was disinterred and taken to Burgundy for reburial in the Charterhouse of Dijon.[1]

On 13 July the Anglo-Burgundian forces laid siege to Melun, a strongly fortified town on the Seine twenty-seven miles upstream of Paris. There they were joined by Henry's brother, the duke of Bedford, who had brought two thousand reinforcements from England, and their brother-in-law, Louis, the 'Red Duke' of Bavaria, at the head of seven hundred Germans whose wages Henry had agreed to pay. The English, unlike the French, did not usually employ foreign mercenaries but Henry was short of men for a campaign outside Normandy and needed to strike a decisive blow against the dauphin.

The captain of Melun, Arnaud Guillaume, sire de Barbazan, was 'expert, ingenious and renowned in arms'. Unfazed by either the size of the besieging army or the heavy bombardment from the great guns of England and Burgundy, he succeeded in holding them at bay for eighteen weeks. He shored up the damaged defences and personally led regular sorties to inflict damage and casualties: the English responded in the customary fashion by fortifying their camps, surrounding them with ditches and wooden walls so that they formed a series of temporary castles encircling the town. They also threw another temporary bridge across the Seine to maintain communications between the besieging forces.[2]

When Henry ordered a huge mine to be dug under the walls, Barbazan began a counter-mine to intercept it. This was a difficult and dangerous feat of engineering. The miners had the advantage of knowing where they were heading and, since the mine had to be large enough to bring down a section of wall, they could employ packhorses to bring in pit props and carry away the earth and rubble. Once they were underground their location and direction could only be guessed by listening for the sound of their digging. Counter-miners would often sink several trial shafts before hitting on the correct place and even then the tunnels might have to twist aside or plunge downwards in the frantic attempt to locate the mine before it brought down the defences. Working against the clock and by the light of candles and torches in these cramped, airless conditions, the counter-miners could only dig tunnels wide and high enough to admit one man. Once they had broken into the mine they had two options: to collapse it by burning the props or to attack the miners by sending in a file of men-at-arms.[3]

In the latter instance, the point where mine and counter-mine met would often become an impromptu set of lists, where men-at-arms from each side could test their valour and skill in feats of arms. Like other chivalric combats, such as jousts and tournaments, these were not intended to be fights to the death but simply an opportunity to excel in difficult and dangerous conditions. Because the participants risked their lives, however, fighting in mines acquired a special place in knightly lore. It was held to create a bond of brotherhood-in-arms between the opponents: they had mingled their blood in combat and therefore owed each other a personal duty of service, aid, counsel and protection, despite the fact that their nations were at war.

One of the most famous contests of this kind took place at the siege of Melun, where the miners had created a tunnel so large that it was possible to hold a joust on horseback underground. Among those who fought against each other in single combat were the two commanders, Henry and Barbazan, an unusual encounter of which no details survive, though it would later save the Frenchman's life. After the fall of Melun, Barbazan was put on trial by Henry as one of the dauphin's chief councillors, found guilty and condemned to death. Normally there was no appeal from the king's judgement but in this case Barbazan claimed the privilege of judgement by heralds. The law of arms, he said, forbade a man to put to death a brother-in-arms who was at his mercy: he had fought hand to hand with Henry in the mine at Melun, 'which battle was held by the heralds of arms in like strength as if he had fought with the king body to body within the lists.' Henry was always punctilious in his administration of justice but he was also scrupulous in enforcing his sovereign rights. Faced with this clash between the two spheres of his authority, as a knight and as a king, it is extraordinary that, in this instance, he chose to abide by the rules of the international order of chivalry. He accepted Barbazan's argument and commuted his death sentence to life imprisonment.[4]

Despite its importance in deciding Barbazan's fate, the fighting within the mines was little more than a distraction from the serious business of effecting the reduction of Melun. As the siege dragged on Henry's patience began to wear thin. He had already had his wife brought to him, installing her in a house which he had built for that purpose near his own tents. There – in the nearest he ever came to a romantic gesture – he had her serenaded by musicians for an hour every dawn and dusk. English musicians were renowned for their 'sprightly concordance and angelic sweetness' and Henry, a passionate lover of music, even bought harps for himself and Katherine about this time.[5]

More significantly, Henry had two other kings brought to join him at the siege: poor, mad Charles VI and James, the twenty-five-year-old king of Scotland, who had been a prisoner in England since 1406. What he wanted them to do was to issue a summons to surrender to the defenders of Melun. According to the laws of war, any subject of a king who refused to obey such an order issued in person by their sovereign was a rebel and a traitor who could therefore be executed. The Armagnacs might not recognise Henry's right to demand their submission but they could not ignore that of Charles VI.

The fact that Henry thought it necessary to involve James I was an indication of the growing threat posed by Scottish mercenaries in France. The 'auld alliance' between Scotland and France began with the Treaty of Paris in 1295 (though both countries claimed it went back to the days of Charlemagne) and a contemporary French poet described it as 'not traced on a charter of vellum but on the flesh and skin of men . . . not written in ink but in the flowing, intermingled blood of the allies.'[6]

The dauphin, who with good reason did not trust his compatriots, had retained a company of Scottish archers, under John Stewart of Darnley, to act as his personal bodyguard in 1418. The same year he had sent recruiting agents into Scotland to raise an army in his father's name to resist the English conquest of Normandy. This could not be done with the official support of the government – the duke of Albany, regent of Scotland in James's enforced absence, would have been in breach of the terms of his truces with England – but the recruits included his own son John, earl of Buchan, together with Archibald, earl of Wigtown, son and heir of another great magnate and prime mover in Scottish affairs, Archibald, earl of Douglas. Their involvement, and the fact that between six and seven thousand troops contracted to serve with them, were indications not only that the 'auld alliance' still held good but also that the prospect of enriching oneself by fighting in France was more alluring than being forced to remain unemployed in Scotland.[7]

A fleet of forty Castilian ships brought this army over to La

Rochelle in October 1419. It then deployed along the southern frontiers of Normandy to hold back the English advance into Maine. On 3 March 1420 a combined Scottish and French force sent from Le Mans to relieve Fresnay was ambushed and wiped out by the earl of Huntingdon and Sir John Cornewaille; the booty included Sir William Douglas's standard, which was sent for public display in Rouen, and, more importantly, the Scottish war chest. This defeat was counterbalanced by an Armagnac raid from Dreux which captured the castle of Croisy, freeing the famous captain, Ambroise de Loré, who had been an English prisoner for almost a year, and an attack by the garrison of Le Mans which killed sixty-three and captured fifty-eight.[8]

On 18 November 1420, after a siege lasting four months, Melun was eventually starved into surrendering. Twenty Scottish mercenaries found in the town's garrison were among those excluded from the terms of the capitulation. In the hope of stemming the flow of Scotsmen coming to the dauphin's aid, Henry had decided to make an example of them and he therefore hanged all twenty for disobeying their king's order to submit. Melun's Armagnac defenders were also treated more harshly than usual as punishment for their defiance of their king and regent. All those who had taken up arms, including civilians, were to be held captive until they paid a ransom and gave security that they would never serve the king's enemies again. Several hundred prisoners were deported to Parisian jails, including the sire de Barbazan and others who were to stand trial on suspicion of involvement in the murder of John the Fearless.[9]

On 1 December 1420 Henry made his first formal entry into Paris, riding beside Charles VI with the dukes of Burgundy, Clarence and Bedford in attendance. He came as regent, rather than conqueror, so the crowds greeted him with cries of 'Noël!' and a living representation of Christ's passion. 'No princes were ever welcomed more joyfully than these', a citizen noted in the journal he kept throughout these troubled times; 'in every street they met processions of priests in copes and surplices carrying reliquaries and singing *Te Deum laudamus* and *Benedictus qui venit*.'[10]

Henry had not come to Paris for acclamation but to do business. Two formal legal processes were required to strengthen his hand against the dauphin: the ratification of the Treaty of Troyes by the estates-general of the realm and the trial of those guilty of the murder of John the Fearless. Since none of the dauphin's supporters was present, the treaty was duly ratified without protest. Twelve days later a special court was convened to hear Philippe of Burgundy's demand for justice: both kings were present, together with the chancellor of France, Philippe de Morvilliers and other representatives of the *parlement*, and members of the estates-general. The dauphin was summoned to respond to the charges in person; when he failed to appear the royal council and *parlement* banished him from the realm and declared him incapable of succeeding to the crown.[11] The legal process of disinheriting him had been completed.

Henry did not linger in Paris for he had more important business in Rouen, where for the first time he had summoned a meeting of the local estates-general of the duchy and *pays-de-conquête*. They too agreed to ratify the Treaty of Troyes but they also took a significant step in implementing its terms. In January 1421 the assembly at Rouen granted Henry a hearth tax on the laity worth 400,000*l.t.* (£23.33m), with the first payment due on 1 March. The clergy also offered a tax of two-tenths, which was of equivalent value, though their generosity did not prevent Henry collecting the arrears of another tenth which, ironically, they had previously granted to Charles VI for the purpose of resisting the English invasion.[12]

There was one final piece to put in place. Henry also needed the English parliament to ratify the Treaty of Troyes. He had not visited England since first embarking on his conquest three and a half years earlier and both parliament and country were becoming increasingly concerned by his absence. Legal processes had been suspended since August 1417 to protect those away on campaign; heavy taxation to pay for the war had led to a shortage of bullion and an epidemic of counterfeiting; and the most recent parliament, held in December 1420, had demonstrated a marked reluctance to endorse the 'final peace'.[13] It was time for the king to return.

On 1 February 1421 Henry and his new French queen landed at Dover to an enthusiastic welcome, the barons of the Cinque Ports rushing into the sea to carry them shoulder-high to shore. Seven days later Henry was back at work in London, leaving his wife to follow at a more leisurely pace. On Sunday 23 February Katherine was crowned by Henry Chichele, archbishop of Canterbury, in the church of Westminster Abbey, the ceremony being followed by a celebratory banquet in Westminster Hall.[14]

Three days later Henry issued the writs summoning parliament to meet on 2 May, then he and Katherine set out on a tour of the country, taking in the major towns of Bristol, Leicester and Nottingham, the cathedral cities of York, Lincoln and Norwich, the royal castles at Kenilworth and Pontefract and the popular shrines at Bridlington, Beverley and Walsingham. This was no belated honeymoon, though the declared object was to introduce the new queen to her subjects. It was partly a pilgrimage to the great shrines of England by a king renowned for his piety, partly a propaganda mission designed to stimulate flagging enthusiasm for his French ambitions and, as a consequence, partly a fund-raising tour to sustain those ambitions. He had already achieved great things, he told his people, but he needed money and men to defeat the dauphin, who still held the greater part of France.[15]

This message had little appeal to a country already tired of the constant strain of war and it undermined the hard selling of the Treaty of Troyes as a 'final peace'. Henry's difficulties were compounded when, having just paid his devotions at the shrine of Saint John of Beverley – whose tomb had miraculously exuded holy oil during the battle of Agincourt – he received disastrous news. On 22 March 1421 his brother and heir, Clarence, to whom he had given supreme military command in France during his absence, had unexpectedly intercepted a newly arrived contingent of four thousand Scots at Baugé in Anjou. Clarence was desperate to prove himself his brother's equal but succeeded only in demonstrating that he was not. Against the advice of his captains, he had not waited for the slower columns of English and Welsh archers to arrive but had launched an immediate attack. Riding at the head of his men-at-arms he had caught the first troops he encountered by surprise and swept them away, only to see the main body of the army, rallied by the earl of Buchan, appear on the horizon. Under a hail of Scottish arrows and hampered by the marshy ground by the river, he had suffered the first major defeat of an English army in France for more than a generation.

The casualties were enormous. Clarence himself was killed; so were two veteran captains of Henry's wars, Sir Gilbert Umfraville and Sir John Grey. Among others taken prisoner were the able John, earl of Huntingdon, and two of Clarence's own cousins, the seventeen-year-old John, earl of Somerset, and his fifteen-year-old brother, Thomas Beaufort. Huntingdon was fortunate to secure his release in 1425, in exchange for Raoul de Gaucourt and Jean d'Estouteville, who had been prisoners since the Agincourt campaign of 1415, and a ruinous ransom. Thomas Beaufort was also ransomed, for 7000 marks (£2.45m) in 1430, but his elder brother, whose entire life would be shaped by the fortunes of the English in France, had to wait seventeen years to win his freedom.[16]

The only crumb of comfort in this disaster was that Thomas, earl of Salisbury, a seasoned and clear-headed warrior, had gathered the troops left behind by Clarence and, avoiding the victorious Scots who barred their way, led an orderly retreat back to the safety of Normandy. There he had taken charge, prohibiting anyone from leaving the duchy without a licence issued under the great seal and ordering all Englishmen and soldiers to report at once to the military authorities.[17]

Writing from Baugé just hours after the battle, to inform the dauphin of their victory and to send him Clarence's captured standard, the earls of Buchan and Wigtown urged him to invade Normandy immediately 'for, with God's help, all is yours'. The pope too recognised the significance of the defeat, remarking that 'truly the Scots are the antidote to the English'. All across Anglo-Burgundian France the fear and expectation were that the dauphin would follow this victory with an invasion of Normandy or an attack on Paris.[18]

In this crisis Henry revealed his mettle. 'In adversity, just as in success, he possessed remarkable composure', a contemporary French chronicler wrote admiringly. 'If his troops suffered a reverse, he would repeatedly say to them "You know, the fortunes of war are changeable; but if you want good fortune, you should preserve your courage unchanged."'[19]

Henry had already promised that he would return to France with reinforcements before midsummer but he now stepped up his efforts to raise men and money. His finances were in dire straits. A report submitted to him by the treasurer at this time revealed that the ordinary revenues of the kingdom brought in £56,743 10s. 10¼d. (£29.79m) but his annual defence expenditure, excluding the cost of the war in France, was £52,235 16s. 10½d. (£27.42m), leaving a surplus of just £4507 13s. 11¾d. (£2.37m) to pay for all the king's personal expenses, which, bizarrely, included responsibility for artillery, embassies and the lions kept in the Tower of London.[20]

In the circumstances a grant of taxation by the parliament which met at Westminster in May 1421 would have been extremely useful but it was more important to secure the ratification of the Treaty of Troyes. That very act, however, would mean that Henry's English subjects were no longer responsible for financing a war he was now conducting in his role as regent and heir to France. With his usual mastery of the situation Henry obtained the ratification in return for deferring a request for taxation to the next parliament. The immediate shortfall he had to make up by obtaining loans worth £36,000 (£18.9m), almost half the sum coming from his uncle, Henry Beaufort, bishop of Winchester.[21]

Less than three weeks after parliament ended Henry was back in France at the head of a new army of between four and five thousand men on short-term contracts of six months. Salisbury had the situation in Normandy under control. On 21 June he wrote cheerfully to Henry from Argentan, informing him that the duchy 'stood in good plight and never so well as now'. To counteract Clarence's disastrous foray into Anjou, Salisbury had led another as far as Angers, returning with 'the fairest and greatest prey of beasts, as all they said that saw them, that ever they saw . . . And truly, we were before several places, that what time it liketh you to besiege them, or to command any other man to besiege them, they be not able, with God's grace, to hold against you any length of time.'[22]

Knowing that Normandy was in safe hands, Henry made a swift trip to Paris, which was in turmoil. Thomas Beaufort, duke of Exeter, whom he had appointed captain of the city in January 1421, had proved to be a disaster. Unfairly accused of having shut himself in the Bastille after Baugé until Henry's arrival, he had in fact been forced to retreat there in June when he caused riots by arresting the popular Burgundian Jean, sire de l'Isle-Adam, on suspicion of plotting to betray Paris to the dauphin. L'Isle-Adam was not cleared of all charges and restored to office until November 1423 but Henry immediately removed Beaufort from office and, recognising that the Parisians were unlikely to warm to an Englishman in the sensitive post of captain, tactfully replaced him with a Burgundian.[23]

Henry could now turn his attention to the dauphin. Charles had appointed Buchan constable of France in acknowledgement of his role at Baugé but he ignored his Scottish captains' advice to invade Normandy. Instead – and perhaps thereby giving credence to the rumours of l'Isle-Adam's treason – he had launched a campaign from Le Mans towards Chartres, which lay less than sixty miles south-west of Paris. Important strongholds, including Nogent-le-Roi and Gallardon, had fallen and Chartres itself was under siege. Perhaps even more serious was the fact that he had with him two thousand Breton troops: Clarence's defeat at Baugé had frightened the vacillating duke of Brittany into abandoning his English alliance and joining forces with the dauphin.[24]

Henry was clearly a more feared opponent than his brother. As he assembled his troops on the Seine to relieve Chartres, the dauphin abandoned his siege and withdrew across the Loire to Vendôme, leaving Henry free to recover the places he had lost and to capture the isolated but powerful and troublesome fortress of Dreux. Then, hoping to engage the dauphin in battle, he pressed on towards the Loire, even making a provocative raid on the suburbs of Orléans, but in vain. As both armies were discovering, an exceptionally long and harsh winter, followed by a poor summer, made it extremely difficult to find enough supplies to keep an army in the field. The citizen-diarist of Paris observed that even the wolves had grown so hungry that they swam across rivers and scavenged at night in the towns, eating the limbs of dismembered traitors hung over the gates and digging up newly buried corpses in the countryside. What might be dismissed as pardonable exaggeration finds confirmation in an Act of 14 December 1421 appointing wolf-hunters in Normandy because of the increase in their numbers and their attacks on animals and humans.[25]

Famine and dysentery, the scourge of medieval armies, put an early end to the campaign but Henry was determined to make the best use of his soldiers before their service contracts ran out. The Parisians had long pleaded with him to take the town of Meaux, thirty miles to their east, whose Armagnac garrison had regularly raided up to the gates of the city, attacking travellers, disrupting trade and destroying supplies. The town stood in a loop of the Marne and was also protected by walls and ditches; at its heart was the Market, a fortified island stronghold, with a garrison of a thousand men under the command of the notoriously brutal Bastard of Vaurus. It was said of him that he had executed a young man whose heavily pregnant wife could not pay the ransom demanded, then tied her to the tree where he usually hanged his victims; as she gave birth her cries attracted wolves which killed her and her baby.[26]

On 6 October 1421 Henry laid siege to Meaux, surrounding the town with his camps, deploying his artillery and throwing temporary bridges across the river. Despite the usual heavy bombardment, the town held out for five months, falling only when Guy de Nesle, lord of Offémont, attempted to bring a hand-picked band of men-at-arms to its aid; they succeeded in stealing through the English camp but as they scaled the walls a plank gave way and Offémont fell into the ditch. He was wearing full armour, so the noise alerted the English sentries, and after a brief scuffle in which he was badly wounded in the face Offémont had the humiliation of being taken prisoner by a cook from Henry's kitchen.

The Bastard was so dismayed by this failure that he decided to fire the town and retreat into the Market. Informed of this by one of the townsmen, Henry seized his opportunity: he ordered an immediate assault and took the town without any real opposition. Sparing the townsfolk, who had taken shelter in the churches, he began the reduction of the Market, but it was another two months before the garrison surrendered. They knew they could expect no mercy and none was shown. Four of their leaders, including the Bastard, were tried and executed for their crimes. A trumpeter who had publicly insulted Henry during the siege was also put to death, together, it was said, with the gunners because they were responsible for killing several important Englishmen.

Several hundred prisoners were sent for lengthy incarceration in castles throughout Normandy, England and Wales. Unusually these included clergymen: the bishop of Meaux, who was committed into the custody of the archbishop of Canterbury, and Philippe de Gamaches, abbot of Saint-Faro, which had been Henry's headquarters during the siege. Gamaches was an extraordinary character: not merely an abbot but a warrior abbot who, with two other monks, had taken an active fighting role in the defence of Meaux. Taken to Paris for trial, he was threatened with being tied in a sack and thrown into the Seine to drown. This was not an unusual punishment inflicted by the vengeful English: it was the customary French method of executing churchmen found guilty of treason. Three Dominican friars accused of having plotted to deliver Montauban to the English were similarly drowned at Toulouse in 1433–4. Gamaches only escaped this fate because his brother Guillaume was the Armagnac captain of Compiègne, who agreed to surrender the town to the English if Philippe's life was spared.[27]

The fall of Meaux on 10 May 1422 brought more security to Paris and yielded a rich haul of booty but it had been achieved at great cost. The English had lost many men to sickness, and Richard, earl of Worcester, John, lord Clifford, and the seventeen-year-old heir of Sir John Cornewaille were all killed by cannon-fire. Cornewaille himself, a Knight of the Garter and one of Henry's most trusted and able captains, was wounded by the same shot that killed his boy and, overcome with grief at the death of his only son, was said to have sworn never to fight Christians again. It is certainly true that he left the siege early and, having served continuously in France for six years, he did not take up arms there again until the crisis of 1436.[28]

The full cost of taking Meaux was not immediately apparent. On 12 May Bedford sailed from England with a thousand new recruits for the next campaigning season. His sister-in-law, Katherine, accompanied him and made a triumphal progress from Harfleur to Rouen and then to Paris. Her status was now considerably enhanced, for she was not only the crowned queen of England but also mother of the heir to England and France. On 6 December 1421 she had given birth to a son, another Henry, at Windsor Castle.[29] Contemporaries believed that the blood of both Charlemagne and King Arthur were united in him, a propitious lineage that demanded his birthplace should also be that of the founder of the Round Table. It was unfortunate, perhaps, that no one at the time remembered the ultimate fate of Arthur: mortally wounded, fighting against his own kin, in a realm riven by civil war.

Katherine had left her baby in the care of a wet-nurse in England while she travelled to France. As breast-feeding was a form of contraception, most medieval aristocratic women did not suckle their own babies, in order to return to fertility as soon as possible. (For the opposite reason, peasant women tried to breast-feed their babies until the age of three.) Infant mortality rates were high: at least a third of the babies born to the kings of England between 1150 and 1500 died in their first year.[30] It was therefore important that Katherine should become pregnant again as soon as possible. She had not seen her husband for eleven months and her return to France at this point was a pragmatic necessity to ensure the royal succession.

There was not to be a second pregnancy. Henry met Katherine at Bois-de-Vincennes and they went together to Paris, where the citizens obsequiously performed a mystery of the passion of Saint George to celebrate their arrival. June and July were unusually hot and dry, causing a welcome abundance of fruit and corn, but also a virulent outbreak of smallpox. It was probably to avoid the heat and contagion that Henry and Katherine, with her parents, transferred the royal court thirty miles north of Paris to Senlis. Unfortunately for Henry, it was already too late.

The king had always enjoyed robust health, despite his punishing regime and the rigours of campaigning. In February, during the siege of Meaux, he had become unwell and an English physician was dispatched to treat him. By July he was so ill that he summoned another from England. When he then attempted to lead a relief force to the aid of Cosne, he had to be carried in a horse litter because he was unable to ride. Sheer willpower forced him on as far as Corbeil, but there he accepted that he could go no further, and was conveyed back to Bois-de-Vincennes.[31]

Henry made his preparations for death with his usual efficiency and coolness. He had never seen his eight-month-old son, but his prime concern was to protect him and the inheritance that would come to him. On 26 August he added codicils to his will: his youngest brother, Humphrey, duke of Gloucester, was to have 'chief guardianship and wardship of our dearest son'; the king's uncle, Thomas Beaufort, duke of Exeter, was to have the boy's 'government and management' and select his personal servants; and two of Henry's closest friends, Henry Fitzhugh and Walter Hungerford, were specifically commanded that 'one or other of them should always be with him'. The will had committed Katherine to the protection of John, duke of Bedford, and Henry Chichele, archbishop of Canterbury, but a new codicil ordained that she should also reside with her son.[32]

Exactly what arrangements Henry made for the future governance of France and England during the minority of his son were to be a matter of dispute, since they were made verbally. The problem was that the Treaty of Troyes had not foreseen that

Henry would die before Charles VI or that an infant would inherit the two crowns. The likelihood is that he created three regents for the duration of Charles VI's life: Bedford for Normandy, Philippe of Burgundy for the kingdom of France and Gloucester for England. Once Charles was dead, Normandy and the *pays-de-conquête* would return to the French crown and Henry probably envisaged that Bedford would become regent for all his nephew's French possessions.[33]

Henry V died at Bois-de-Vincennes in the early hours of 31 August 1422. He was just sixteen days short of his thirty-sixth birthday and had been king of England for nine and a half years. The exact cause of his death is not known: contemporaries suggested smallpox, leprosy or dysentery, the last being the most probable, since it had afflicted so many of his troops at the siege of Meaux. He died as piously as he had lived, with prayers upon his lips and his confessor and priests of the royal chapel at his bedside.[34]

His will had specified that he should be buried in Westminster Abbey and, characteristically, that his funeral rites should be appropriate to his royal status but avoid excess. His entrails were removed, his body embalmed and enclosed within a lead coffin, upon which an image was placed of him bearing royal robes, crown, orb and sceptre. The bier then began a two-month progress back across northern France to England. Requiem masses were held at every stopping point, including Saint-Denis, Rouen, Calais and Canterbury, and crowds came to pay their respects. Even his enemies offered him their grudging admiration: 'he was the prince of justice', declared one, 'he gave support to none out of favour, nor did he suffer wrong to go unpunished out of regard for kinship.'[35]

The great irony of Henry's life was that he came so very close to achieving his ultimate goal. Charles VI died on 21 October 1422, just seven weeks after his son-in-law. It was not Henry V, but Henry VI, who would unite the two crowns of England and France.

CHAPTER FOUR

The English Kingdom of France

'All manner of perfection is contained in the number six,' the archbishop of Canterbury declared in his speech opening the first English parliament of the new reign, 'and also, inasmuch as God finished all his work in six days, it is thus understood that the completion of all the good deeds begun by the father will be finished by this son who is, by God's grace, King Henry the sixth since the conquest.' Chichele was, necessarily, taking an optimistic view of the future, but for most subjects of the new king the biblical text 'Woe to you, O land, when your king is a child' seemed a more apt assessment of the situation.[1]

The prospects were certainly not good: assuming he lived to come of age, Henry VI's minority would be the longest in England's history. To compound the problem, there were two kingdoms to rule, each with its own institutions, laws, customs and personnel. Quite how this was to be done became a matter of fevered debate in both countries. In England, Gloucester tried to assert his right to be regent on the grounds that his brother had appointed him to the 'chief guardianship and wardship' of Henry VI. Parliament would have none of it: the codicil referred only to the young king's person, not to the realm, and in any case the late king had no power to alter precedent and law without the assent of parliament. Constitutionally the right to govern England should fall to Gloucester's elder brother, who was next in line to the succession, but Bedford was still in France and likely to remain there. A compromise was therefore reached. On 5 December 1422 Bedford was appointed protector, defender and chief councillor of England, but he would only exercise these powers when he was in the country: in his absence they would be held by Gloucester. This arrangement ensured the separation of crowns envisaged by the Treaty of Troyes and prevented Bedford from ruling England from France. It also limited the powers of the office by avoiding the term 'regent', a technically more powerful and contentious role, and by appointing a sixteen-strong council of bishops, peers and knights 'to assist with the governance' of the realm.

Though Bedford was happy to accept this settlement, believing it best fulfilled the late king's wishes and the country's needs, Gloucester's simmering discontent at being denied what he believed was his inalienable right to exercise full regal authority in England on behalf of his nephew would place considerable strain on the relations between the brothers. More seriously, it would lead to a bitter personal feud with the most senior member of the council, their uncle, Henry Beaufort, bishop of Winchester, which would bring the country to the brink of civil war. Beaufort's own overreaching ambition had been firmly held in check by the late king. Now, however, despite having been assigned no formal role in Henry's will, he was determined to emerge from the political wilderness as the elder statesman of the new reign. He had orchestrated the opposition to Gloucester's assumption of the regency, for which his nephew never forgave him, and his views on how best to preserve Henry V's legacy were diametrically opposed to those of the belligerent Gloucester. Beaufort, like Bedford, was a passionate believer in the importance of the Anglo-Burgundian alliance. Gloucester was suspicious of Burgundy's loyalty and motives, abhorred any idea of concession and put his faith in military might alone. His selfish pursuit of his own territorial ambitions, his rash, quarrelsome temperament, his vendetta against Beaufort and his jealous conviction that he could do a better job in France than Bedford would encourage faction on the English council, undermine Bedford's authority both at home and abroad and even foster conflicts of interest between the two kingdoms. For these reasons, though denied the regency of England, he would be a pivotal figure in the fortunes of both that country and the English realm overseas for years to come.[2]

In France the situation was different and more straightforward: the office of regent already existed because of the king's mental incapacity. Though a regent was expected to be advised by a council (as indeed was the king himself) ultimately the right to exercise supreme power and authority rested with him alone. The dauphin had unilaterally claimed the regency in December 1418, setting up an alternative court, *parlement* and financial administration in the three cities of Toulouse, Poitiers and Bourges, otherwise disparagingly known as the kingdom of Bourges. Neither of his parents had acknowledged the legitimacy of his title, bestowing it instead upon Henry V by the Treaty of Troyes.[3]

For the short period between the deaths of Henry and Charles, Philippe of Burgundy had probably exercised the role of regent. Burgundian chroniclers, anxious to explain why their duke did not continue in office, would later claim that Henry had intended that Philippe should be given first refusal of the regency after Charles's death; only if he declined should it pass to Bedford.[4] Burgundy might have had good reason to decline such an offer. It was one thing to be regent of France on behalf of a mad but unquestionably legitimate king and quite another on behalf of an infant Englishman imposed on the realm by treaty with a foreign conqueror. To have accepted the office would have laid the duke open to charges of treason in a way that his alliance with the English did not.

However, it is inherently unlikely that Henry envisaged Burgundy retaining the regency. The Treaty of Troyes had laid down that Normandy would return to the French crown after

Charles's death and Henry would not have handed his hard-won conquests to his ally in preference to his own brother.[5] It was Bedford therefore before whom the sword of state was carried after the burial of Charles VI in a symbolic demonstration, as the watching Parisians recognised, that he was regent of France. Some days later, on 19 November 1422, he formally assumed the title of regent in a full session of the *parlement*, swearing to maintain peace and justice and declaring his intention to reunite the duchy of Normandy with the crown; all present then renewed their oath to the Treaty of Troyes, placing their hands between those of the chancellor of France.[6]

Burgundy was a notable absentee from the funerals of both Henry and Charles but there is no indication that he was unhappy with Bedford's assumption of the regency. He had already renewed his own oath to the treaty on 7 November and on 12 December his sister Anne was formally betrothed to Bedford. This was a significant step for both parties and potentially for the future of France: Bedford was heir apparent to his baby nephew and Anne was co-heiress to her brother, who did not father a legitimate child until 1430.[7]

The marriage of Bedford and Anne of Burgundy became a cornerstone of the Anglo-Burgundian alliance. Bedford was thirty-four, his bride nineteen, when they married at Troyes (as Henry V and Katherine of France had done three years earlier) on 14 June 1423. Such disparity in age was not unusual in medieval dynastic alliances, but there seems to have been a genuine bond of affection between them, as there was between brother and sister. Anne also enjoyed great personal popularity, particularly in Rouen and Paris, from which her husband and the English alliance benefited.

Bedford was in many ways ideally suited to the role of regent of France. He perhaps lacked his brother's charisma, but he was intensely loyal to Henry's aims, devoted to the interests of his nephew, an able soldier and administrator: it was his decisive action in going to Paris to claim the regency on behalf of his nephew that persuaded the waverers in *parlement*, who had been looking at the dauphin's legal claim to the crown, to commit to Henry VI. Bedford was also a passionate Francophile who gave generously to churches and abbeys, patronised French artists, writers and craftsmen, owned extensive lands throughout northern France and palaces in both Paris and Rouen, and, rarest of all in an Englishman, would insist on burial in France. Like Henry, but unlike their brother Gloucester, he was regarded as being above faction and commanded universal respect.[8]

The kingdom over which Bedford would rule as regent was united in theory but in practice divided into areas of English conquest or Burgundian influence. (It did not, of course, include the Armagnac kingdom of Bourges, which, in 1422, extended through the central region of France from the southern coast to north of the Loire, including Anjou and part of Maine.)

Normandy had a strong tradition of independence from the French crown which was enshrined in a thirteenth-century summary of customary law and a fourteenth-century charter of liberties and franchises. Normans even had their own 'nation', or racial group, at the University of Paris and, like Bretons and Gascons, were generally distinguished from Frenchmen by their contemporaries.[9] Henry V had deliberately played up to this separatist feeling: he had constantly reiterated throughout the conquest that Normandy was his by right of inheritance and, having summoned the Norman nobility to appear before him at Rouen in the spring of 1419, he received them wearing the robes of the duke of Normandy rather than those of the king of England.[10]

Henry had also made no attempt to impose English-style institutions on the duchy, preferring to take over the existing administration and make it independent of the French monarchy. As each new town or castle fell into his hands – and sometimes even before that, in order to give an incentive for its capture – he appointed an English captain and installed a garrison. At the same time he also appointed new officials to run the civil administration. The most important of these were the *baillis*, whose role corresponded roughly to that of an English sheriff. There were seven *baillis* in the duchy, each responsible within his own area for administering justice, executing royal decrees and raising and leading the local militia. Of necessity these also had to be appointed as and when each *bailliage* was conquered, but in every case the new *bailli* was an Englishman.[11]

Their subordinates, however, were almost uniformly Normans, who took advantage of the olive branch offered to change allegiance and continue in office. The most important were the financial officials: the *vicomtes*, who were responsible within a subdivision of each *bailliage* for collecting and paying out the regular revenues from royal lands and vassals; the receivers, to whom the parish officials paid the sums collected whenever an estates-general had granted a hearth-tax; and the *grênetiers*, who built salt warehouses and accounted for the revenue of the salt-tax, a valuable source of money at a time when salting was the most effective way of preserving meat and, more especially, fish, which all good Christians were required to eat on Fridays and during Lent. The collection of other taxes, such as those on sales, was generally farmed out to the highest bidder, who paid a discounted lump sum and was then able to keep all the money his diligence brought in.[12]

One of Henry's first acts at the very beginning of his conquest was to set up a *chambre-des-comptes* in Caen, which had been the ducal financial centre before the French conquest of 1204. Like the English exchequer, the *chambre-des-comptes* would be responsible for authorising payments and auditing accounts, but all transactions were made in French currency (*livres tournois*) and documented in French. Again the most important officer, the treasurer-general of Normandy, would always be English but his clerks included Englishmen, Normans and later Frenchmen.[13]

These arrangements were part of a deliberate policy to reconcile the native population to a conquest which Henry intended to be permanent. It was never his intention to expel the indigenous people and replace them with English settlers: England did not have the population to support emigration on such a scale and in any case Henry wanted acceptance by the Normans as a visible demonstration of the legitimacy of his claims. From the very beginning, as we have seen, he offered his protection to those who were prepared to swear allegiance to him, confirming their right to keep the lands, homes and offices they had held on 1 August 1417, the date of the English invasion and the start of the new era.[14]

At first he had been willing to allow those who refused to take the oath to leave but the scale of the exodus soon became a matter for concern: 1000 from Caen, 1700 from Argentan, 1500 from Sées and Exmes, 2500 from Alençon. Such a loss of population was unsustainable, especially as many of those who fled were artisans or merchants, whose skills were important to the Norman economy.[15] To draw them back again, Henry needed to address the reasons why they had left. For most of them it was not loyalty to the French crown but fear – fear of being oppressed or persecuted by a foreign military regime and fear of violence and instability if the war was prolonged.

The story of one refugee, the chronicler Thomas Basin, was not untypical. Basin's father was a wealthy grocer and spice merchant in Caudebec, twenty-one miles north-west of Rouen. In 1415 or 1416, when Basin was three years old, his family moved to Rouen to escape 'the insults, outrages and violence' of the French troops installed at Caudebec to protect the town from the English garrison at Harfleur. There were so many refugees in Rouen that food was in short supply and plague broke out, so the Basins moved to Vernon for several months, returning only when the plague ended. In 1417, fearing that Henry would land at Harfleur and head straight for Rouen, they packed up their valuables and fled for the safety of Falaise. When Henry landed at Touques instead, they made for the Breton border, taking up residence in St-James-de-Beuvron, until the English advance drove them into Brittany. For almost a year they lived at Rennes, but English troops were raiding and pillaging along the border, so they retreated to the greater security of Nantes. It was more than a year later, in 1419, when Rouen had fallen and all Normandy seemed to be 'in some sort pacified', that the Basins finally returned to Caudebec, preferring to take the oath of submission rather than spend the rest of their lives in exile.[16]

A critical factor in the Basins' decision to go home was

Henry's offer of a general amnesty to all returning Norman refugees. These had been offered at irregular intervals since the fall of Falaise in February 1418 and were backed up with the threat that those who failed to return would be considered 'rebels and brigands' and their lands and movable property confiscated. After the surrender of Rouen the punitive element became more pronounced. On 12 March 1419 the *baillis* were ordered to record the names of all those who had not taken the oath, together with the value and extent of their lands; three months later these were seized into the king's hands ready for distribution to his loyal subjects. A final proclamation was issued on 29 September 1419 urging all absentees to return 'to the king's obedience' by 1 November and offering a general safe-conduct protecting those who chose to do so.[17]

The majority of landowners were thus persuaded to accept the English conquest. In the Carentan *bailliage*, for instance, three-quarters of fiefs remained in the same hands, indicating that their proprietors took the oath. Significantly, however, these were all petty landholders and it was a matter of serious concern, as Henry informed his privy council in England, 'that in substance there is no man of estate come in to the king's obedience and . . . right few gentlemen, the which is a thing that causeth the people to be full unstable and is no wonder.'[18]

After the capture of Rouen, Henry determined to take a harder line with the recalcitrant nobility. If they could not be persuaded to submit, then they too should be dispossessed. Among those who therefore had their lands formally confiscated were the young duke of Alençon (with his marshal, the Agincourt veteran Ambroise de Loré), Jacques d'Harcourt, count of Tancarville, and his cousin Jean d'Harcourt, count of Aumâle, Louis d'Estouteville and Jean de la Haye, sire de Coulances. It will come as no surprise to learn that all of them would commit the rest of their lives to the war against the English.

The lands and properties confiscated from 'rebels', whatever their status, passed into Henry's personal possession, providing him with the means of rewarding his supporters and establishing a permanent English presence in Normandy. Henry's distribution of the confiscated lands was slow and carefully planned: this was no rush to enjoy the spoils of victory but a measured attempt to secure the long-term future of the duchy. Of 358 recorded grants made between September 1417 and June 1422, almost exactly two-thirds were made in 1419, the year of consolidation after the surrender of Rouen.[19]

The policy of distribution was carried out with Henry's usual attention to detail. Every grant was recorded. The name of the original owner was checked against the register of those who had taken the oath to ensure that the property was legitimately forfeit and the value, expressed in terms of its annual income, was calculated. Efforts were made to ensure that the recipient had a connection with the area and that there was a correlation between the size of the gift and his status. In 1419, for example, Richard Wydeville, who was appointed *bailli* of Gisors, was given the lordship of neighbouring Dangu, while Nicholas Bradkyrk, a merchant-draper, acquired houses in the ports of Harfleur and Caen, and Roger Waltham, a clerk in the *chambre-des-comptes* at Caen, also received a house in that town.[20]

This careful targeting of grants helped to create a class of Englishmen with entrenched interests in maintaining the conquest in their particular area but without overburdening them with duties they could not afford to fulfil. Property ownership went hand in hand with office in either the civilian or military administration, but it also carried obligations. Sir Gilbert Umfraville was restored to his family's ancestral lands at Amfreville-sur-Iton, which had been confiscated from Jean d'Estouteville and Pierre Amfreville, but he had to provide garrisons for all their castles and a further twelve men-at-arms and twenty-four archers for the army. At the other end of the scale, Roger Waltham's house in Caen came with the annual obligation to pay a rent of 40 *sous* (£117) and his share of the costs of the town watch for one night.[21]

To ensure that such conditions were fulfilled, Henry V made virtually every grant of land or property in fee tail, a legal device which meant that only heirs of the body could inherit, thereby preventing ownership passing out of the family. If there were no children, ownership reverted automatically to the crown. When the childless Umfraville was killed at Baugé, for instance, his French lands were taken into the king's hands again and then regranted to Sir Robert Brewes, even though he had a living English heir, his uncle, Sir Robert Umfraville. Englishmen were permitted to buy or acquire other French lands, but they were forbidden to sell their fiefs from the king, except to other Englishmen and with the king's approval. Disputes arising out of royal grants were to be decided by the council in Rouen rather than appealed to the *parlement* in Paris, ensuring that Henry's hand remained firmly at the helm.[22]

At the heart of the land settlement was the concept that the conquered lands should provide the manpower for their own defence. Failure to perform the required military services could therefore result in confiscation, as James Linde and Walter Hasclat discovered when they failed to answer the summons to 'several campaigns, sieges and armies against our enemies': their lands were taken from them and given to the more reliable Richard Wydeville.[23]

Lands owned by the church did not owe military service, though they were expected to provide horses, wagons and victuals for armies operating in the duchy. Nevertheless, these too were taken into the king's hands as the conquest progressed and not restored until the relevant bishop, abbot or other church authority made the profession of obedience. The royal accounts reveal that the property of every bishop and sixty-six abbeys and monasteries (two-thirds of the total number) of Normandy passed through Henry's hands in this way.[24]

From the very beginning Henry was fortunate that his reputation as a defender of the church preceded him. The strict discipline he imposed on his troops, and his express commands safeguarding the persons and property of the clergy, were unusual for the period and won him many friends. Indeed it was said that some Normans adopted the tonsure so that they might be mistaken for clergymen and enjoy the king's protection. It was noticeable too that within eight weeks of Henry's landing at Touques 483 parishes had surrendered to him, suggesting that it was local parish priests who led the submission rather than the officials of the secular administration.[25]

The higher echelons of the church, just like the secular nobility, were significantly more resistant. Only the bishop of Sées,[26] whose seat fell into English hands in October 1417, made an early submission: Henry pointedly made him take the oath of fealty in person at the Saint George's Day celebrations held in Caen in 1418. The archbishop of Rouen, Louis d'Harcourt, and the five other bishops of the province all fled as the English approached. Jean de Saint-Avit, bishop of Avranches, would return and take the oath in 1420, though his loyalty remained suspect and he was later imprisoned on suspicion of plotting to deliver Rouen to the French.[27]

The rest would never return. Fortunately for Henry, in 1418 the bishops of Lisieux, Évreux and Coutances were killed in the Parisian massacres that followed the Burgundian coup, leaving him with three empty sees which he could legitimately administer until their successors were appointed. This both gave him a healthy income and allowed him to influence the appointment of clergy within the sees. Fortunately again, through the Burgundian alliance he had access to a steady stream of graduates from the University of Paris who were hungry for the benefices which years of Armagnac dominance had denied them.

The relationship was mutually beneficial. Clerics had always been the backbone of secular government – the term 'clerk' derives from the clerical status of those serving in the offices of state – and graduates were always clergymen, though not all had been fully ordained as priests. Self-interest made such men eager to accept and promote the English conquest, while Henry needed literate, numerate, intellectually capable men to serve in his administration.[28]

Henry was also able to exert his influence on the appointment of new bishops. The new pope, Martin V, was in a difficult position. His election on 11 November 1417 at the Council of Constance had ended thirty years of schism in the western church, but his position was by no means secure. He was reluctant to commit himself to either side in the Anglo-French conflict since he could not afford to offend either ally. Henry needed papal support to legitimise his conquest but was determined that no Frenchmen should be appointed to vacant bishoprics in Normandy. The extraordinary compromise they reached was that the three bishops killed in Paris were all replaced by Italians: Cardinal Branda da Castiglione was appointed to Lisieux, Paolo da Capranica to Évreux and Pandolfo di Malatesta to Coutances. This was not a situation Henry would have permitted in England but it flattered the pope, an Italian himself, while also allowing Henry to continue to exert authority over the sees because their bishops would inevitably be non-resident.[29]

Henry's luck continued with the remaining recalcitrant bishops. The bishopric of Bayeux became vacant in July 1419 when Jean Langret, who was at the Council of Constance when Henry invaded and did not return home, died in self-imposed exile. His replacement, Nicholas Habart, was not an Italian, but he took the oath to Henry immediately and was rewarded with being allowed to enjoy the temporalities of his see even before his formal installation.[30]

The most senior Norman clergyman, archbishop Louis d'Harcourt, had absented himself even before the siege of Rouen. Despite Henry's attempts to lure him back, he remained obdurate, defiantly taking up residence in the dauphin's court at Poitiers. One of Henry's first acts on taking possession of Rouen was to order, on 9 February 1419, the forfeiture into his hands of all lands belonging to any lay or ecclesiastical lord who refused to swear obedience to him. This gave him control over the absentee archbishop's lands. Two years later he ordered that any remaining absentee clergymen would now face the church's own sanction of deprivation of office if they did not return and take the oath. The archbishop declined to do so and on 14 July 1421 he was removed from his post; a week later the vicars-general acting in his place deprived twenty-six clergy of the diocese who had taken up residence 'in enemy parts', including the archdeacon, cantor, sub-cantor and ten canons of the cathedral.[31]

Henry was able to do this because he had established cordial relations with the cathedral chapters which exercised spiritual authority in the absence of the archbishop and bishops. The relationship between the canons of the chapter and their bishop was often a power struggle, so Henry won the chapters over by confirming their charters and respecting their rights and privileges. On 19 August 1419, for instance, some English soldiers violated the right of sanctuary when they arrested and returned to prison a priest who had escaped and taken refuge in the choir of Rouen cathedral. The canons immediately stopped singing the offices of the day and sent a delegation to the lieutenant of the duke of Exeter demanding his release, which was granted so promptly that they were able to resume singing where they had broken off. Such swift and decisive action in their favour helps to explain why, when Louis d'Harcourt died at Poitiers on 19 November 1422, the Rouen chapter obliged by electing the pro-English Jean de la Rochetaillée in his place.[32]

Significantly, the only chapter which gave Henry trouble was the one whose bishop had so promptly accepted the English conquest. The twelfth-century cathedral of Sées, fifteen miles north of Alençon, also served as the town's fortress. At the very end of 1420 the canons came up with an ingenious plan to betray the town to the dauphin. They made a secret approach to the local Armagnac captain, Louis de Tromagon, and suggested that it would be possible to gain access to the fortress through the adjoining cathedral treasury. Tromagon summoned several of his tenants from La-Chapelle-près-Sées, the canons let them into the treasury and they set to work covertly digging a hole through the party wall. The workmen were sworn to secrecy but the plot was almost discovered on the very night that the French made their entry into the fortress. A barber-surgeon employed by the canons was on night-watch when he ran into a man armed with an axe. He challenged the intruder but, hearing the commotion, one of the canons leaned out of an upper-floor window, ordered him upstairs immediately and then held him there against his will (or so the barber claimed) throughout the night. The coup was successful, though Sées remained in French hands for only eight weeks before being retaken.[33]

What is striking about Henry's policy towards the church in Normandy is its restraint. It would have been easy to fill every post with English clergymen but relatively few were appointed and only in areas where there was an English enclave: Rouen cathedral chapter admitted several English canons and a royal clerk of Gascon origins, Jean de Bordiu, was appointed to the parish church of Harfleur. For the most part, however, Henry was prepared to give churchmen every opportunity to return. Some would take many years of persuading. Thomas de Saint-Lô, abbot of Blanchelande in the Cotentin, fled to Brittany with all his abbey's treasures, including reliquaries, chalices and charters, as soon as the English army landed at Touques. Thirteen years later, in 1430, he received letters of amnesty, took the oath of loyalty and was restored to his abbey.[34]

A more spectacular conversion was that of Robert Jolivet, abbot of Mont-Saint-Michel since 1411. The abbey church, perched 240 feet above sea-level on top of a solid granite outcrop just over half a mile wide, had been a stronghold and place of refuge for centuries. Accessible only twice a day when the tides went out to reveal the narrow strip of causeway over treacherous quicksands, the island possessed natural defences that had been reinforced by the sheer granite walls of the abbey soaring parallel to the cliff face and by a fourteenth-century barbican. When the English invaded, Jolivet had begun a major programme of repairs to the defences, building ramparts round the town at the foot of the mount, laying in supplies for a siege and commissioning the building of a water cistern chiselled out of the solid rock. In 1418 and again as late as November 1419 the dauphin had responded to his petitions for financial assistance, authorising him to collect taxes locally to pay for these works and the wages of the garrison installed to prevent Mont-Saint-Michel falling into enemy hands.[35]

In the spring of 1420 Jolivet finally succumbed to Henry's attempts to persuade him to change allegiance. The catalyst seems to have been the arrival of Jean d'Harcourt, count of

Aumâle, whom the dauphin had appointed as captain of Mont-Saint-Michel. One of Aumâle's first actions was to raid the abbey treasury, where many local churches and wealthy individuals had placed their goods for safe-keeping. His intention was to take the treasure to the dauphin but, as John Assheton, captain of Coutances, reported to the king on 15 June 1420, when he left the island 'in dividing the goods amongst them, there fell great debate, and was great fight', since many of the garrison wanted to keep the treasure to melt down into money which could pay for the island's defence. 'Their cistern in which their water is wont to be kept is broken', Assheton added, 'so that for lack of water and of wood they cannot stay'. All this information had undoubtedly come from Jolivet himself, since Assheton referred the abbot's request for a safe-conduct to the king in the same letter.[36]

These events, combined with the signing of the Treaty of Troyes, had evidently persuaded Jolivet that he was on the losing side. As one of the most senior Norman clergymen his defection was a major coup for the English, so he was quickly admitted into the inner circles of power, becoming a member of the councils of both Normandy and France, which advised the king on policy and supervised the administration of the duchy and kingdom respectively. There could be no more powerful illustration of the divisions that had torn France apart than the fact that the abbot of Mont-Saint-Michel became one of the pillars of the English administration but his abbey, defiant to the last, remained the only territory in Normandy to elude capture and occupation.

CHAPTER FIVE

Resistance

The death of Henry V put new heart into the dauphin and his supporters. Ambroise de Loré and Jean, sire de Coulances, launched a raid into lower Normandy, attacking and pillaging the town of Bernay, which was abandoned by its garrison on their approach, and inflicting a heavy defeat on those sent to pursue them.[1] On 30 October 1422, just six days after the death of his father, the dauphin had himself proclaimed king Charles VII at Mehun-sur-Yèvre, and began negotiations with the Scots and Castilians for a new army, eight thousand strong, to be brought from Scotland to expel the English from France in the new year.[2]

In Paris a plot to betray the city to the dauphin was discovered. A priest walking in his garden outside the city walls early one morning observed the wife of the royal armourer in secret conversation with some men-at-arms. He reported his suspicions to the guards at the gate, she was arrested, found to be carrying letters from the dauphin to his supporters in Paris and, together with her fellow conspirators, was put to death by drowning. Not long afterwards Meulan was betrayed to the Armagnacs, who placed a strong garrison in the fortress at the bridge which disrupted supply lines to Paris and raided far and wide.[3]

Throughout all these trials Bedford kept his nerve. He ordered all soldiers to return to their captains immediately and Norman subjects to assemble in arms at Domfront. Pilgrimages to Mont-Saint-Michel – often a cover for illicit dealings with the enemy garrison there – were prohibited. Suspected Armagnacs in Paris were rounded up and imprisoned and everyone in the city, 'citizens, householders, carters, shepherds, cowmen, abbey pig-keepers, chambermaids, and the very monks', was required to take the oath of allegiance to Bedford as regent. Meulan was besieged and, after holding out for two months, capitulated on 1 March 1423.[4]

Bedford now decided to take the war to the enemy. The Norman estates-general and clergy, responding to an impassioned plea from Robert Jolivet, had each granted taxes worth 50,000*l.t.* (£2.92m) for the defence of the duchy and the recovery of Mont-Saint-Michel, Ivry and other places. In May, John Mowbray, the earl marshal, brought over the first contingent of an English army, totalling 380 men-at-arms and 1140 archers, which had been recruited for six months' service in the field. With these additional resources at his disposal Bedford was able to wage war on several fronts.[5]

The earl of Salisbury, appointed governor of Champagne and Brie, began the systematic reduction of the remaining Armagnac strongholds between Paris and Chartres. In Picardy the earl of Suffolk, admiral of Normandy, and Sir Ralph Bouteiller, *bailli* of Caux, jointly began a blockade by sea and land of Le Crotoy. This great fortress, guarding the north bank of the entrance to the bay of the Somme, was a haven for Breton pirates and its garrison, commanded by Jacques d'Harcourt, made regular sorties into Normandy and the Burgundian-controlled Low Countries to rob, pillage and take prisoners for ransom. An attack had long been expected, so Le Crotoy was well stocked with artillery and supplies, but its capture was a priority. Bedford had ordered three large new guns to be forged at Rouen and withdrawn fifteen hundred men from garrisons throughout Normandy to serve at the siege.

Harcourt held out for nearly four months, agreeing in October to surrender Le Crotoy on 3 March 1424, but only on condition that Bedford would come there on each of the first three days of March prepared to meet him in personal combat. Whoever ended in possession of the field, either through victory or by the other's failure to attend, would also win Le Crotoy. Challenges of this kind were not uncommon in chivalric circles, and the more valuable the prize the greater the honour bestowed on the participants, but it was very unusual for the fate of a major fortress to depend on one. Perhaps this was just a chivalric flourish, for Harcourt left Le Crotoy long before the encounter was due to take place and did not return, so no further combat was necessary.[6]

The third front opened up by Bedford in 1423 was in southwest Normandy, where Mont-Saint-Michel stood alone in its defiance. In February the English began to fortify Tombelaine, a priory set on a rocky islet 459 feet high out in the bay halfway between Mont-Saint-Michel and the Norman coast. The previous summer the prior had sent more than 3000 pounds of lead to Mont-Saint-Michel for safe-keeping 'because of the uncertainty caused by the wars'; ironically the monks there had purloined it for their own defences. With a permanent garrison of thirty men-at-arms and ninety mounted archers, Tombelaine would now become one of the most important English fortresses holding the frontier against Mont-Saint-Michel and keeping the raiding activities of its garrison in check.[7]

On 30 July 1423 Bedford charged Sir John de la Pole, captain of neighbouring Avranches, with the task of recovering Mont-Saint-Michel 'by all ways and means possible . . . by force of arms, by amicable means or otherwise'. Pole was given power to call up the feudal levies and draw on the garrisons of Caen and Cotentin but, before he began his siege in earnest, his attention was fatally distracted by the prospect of easier pickings elsewhere. The dauphin's army, under the command of the earl of Buchan, constable of France, had laid siege to the Burgundian town of Cravant, 115 miles south-east of Paris. A combined Anglo-Burgundian force, some four thousand strong, had been sent to relieve it and on 31 July won a decisive victory. The

Scots, who were in the forefront of the fighting, suffered heavy casualties and among the many prisoners was Buchan himself, who was blinded in one eye, and John Stewart, constable of the Scottish army in France. (The dauphin was callously dismissive of the defeat: 'almost none of the nobles of our kingdom [were] there,' he wrote, 'but only Scots, Spaniards and other foreign soldiers, accustomed to live off the country, so that the harm is not so great.')[8]

Perhaps hoping to take advantage of the situation, while the enemy was regrouping far away on the other side of France, Sir John de la Pole decided to lead the forces he had gathered for the siege of Mont-Saint-Michel on a strike into Anjou. Like Clarence before him, he got as far as Angers and, like Clarence, he was caught in an ambush on returning with his plunder. On 26 September 1423 Ambroise de Loré, Jean, sire de Coulances, and Louis de Tromagon intercepted him near Laval with a small band of mounted men-at-arms and lured him to La Brossinière, where Jean d'Harcourt, count of Aumâle, was waiting with the main body of the army on foot.

Caught between the two French forces, with no artillery and impeded by the thousands of cattle they were driving back to Normandy, the English were slaughtered. Only a handful escaped, among them Pole himself, who was taken prisoner. His folly exposed the weakness of the English military administration, for many of the Norman garrisons which had contributed to his army were now themselves under-strength and vulnerable. Aumâle pressed home his victory, laying siege to Avranches and, boldly striking through the heart of Normandy, spent several days plundering the suburbs of Saint-Lô. He withdrew from Avranches only on learning of the approach of an English relieving force.[9]

As early as 4 June Bedford had complained to Jolivet that the campaigns had bled his treasury dry and he had nothing left to pay the wages of the Norman garrisons. The estates-general met at Vernon in July and granted another levy of 60,000*l.t.* (£3.5m) but it needed a further meeting – the third of the year – to raise sufficient funds to meet his needs. This last meeting, in December at Caen, was significant for several reasons. It granted 200,000*l.t.*

(£11.67m), plus a tax of a tenth on the clergy, but, in an implicit reproof to Pole's diversion of money and men away from their intended purpose, the proceeds were specifically designated for the payment of Norman garrison wages, the sieges of Mont-Saint-Michel, Ivry, Dreux, Gaillon, Nogent-le-Rotrou, Senonches and Beaumont-le-Vicomte, and the extirpation of brigandage.[10]

The subject of brigandage is a fascinating one but it is fraught with difficulties. Did its inclusion on the agenda for the first time since the English invasion mean that the problem had recently grown worse? Or had it only become a priority because the war of conquest was over and there was a greater degree of security across the duchy? Were the brigands simply criminals, taking advantage of the instability of the times to rob, steal and kidnap for their own ends? Or were they, as some French historians[11] believe, a medieval French Resistance, committing acts of sabotage to undermine and eventually expel the English regime?

This confusion was apparent even to contemporaries. The Caen meeting of the estates-general addressed the question of how to deal with captured brigands, ruling that they must all be examined by the judiciary to determine whether they were malefactors who should be punished within the judicial system or prisoners of war who should be returned to their captors for ransom.[12]

It was not always easy to make such nice distinctions. The Norman records rarely note the execution of a mere 'brigand', preferring to use sweeping catch-all phrases, most commonly 'traitor, brigand, enemy and adversary of the king' but sometimes adding 'thief', 'highwayman' or 'murderer'. 'Enemy and adversary of the king' was the administration's description of all those who bore arms against Henry V or Henry VI, including Armagnac supporters and prisoners of war, but also outlaws in the literal sense of those who had, like brigands, put themselves outside the king's law by committing capital offences. The term 'traitor', however, was only used in the specific legal context of someone who had sworn the English oath of allegiance and then broken it.

Convicted brigands who had not taken the oath were normally executed by hanging like common thieves. A much harsher fate awaited those who had taken the oath: as traitors they were drawn on hurdles to the place of execution, beheaded and quartered, their dismembered bodies then being put on public display.[13] An even more unpleasant fate awaited women who aided and abetted brigands: since it was considered indecent to expose their nakedness by dismembering them, the customary punishment was to bury them alive at the foot of the gibbet. At least three instances are recorded during the English occupation: Thomasse Raoul at Caen in 1424, Jehanne la Hardie at Falaise in 1435 and Thassine de Foullon at Coutances in 1447. The Falaise executioner was paid 28s. 4d.t. (£82.64) for la Hardie's execution: 5s.t. for bringing her to the gibbet, 10s.t. for digging the ditch, 10s.t. for burying her and 3s. 4d.t. for two pairs of gloves.[14]

After the fall of Rouen, Henry V had made restoring order to Normandy a priority. To encourage the arrest of brigands, on 10 May 1419 he introduced a bounty system. Anyone bringing to justice a brigand who was subsequently tried, convicted and executed was awarded 6l.t. (£350) the equivalent of thirteen days' pay for an English man-at-arms or twenty-seven for an archer. (No bounty was payable if the brigand was pardoned or imprisoned, even if convicted.) The captor was also allowed to keep all the goods of the convicted man, except for his clothes, which traditionally went to the executioner. Bounty-hunting could therefore be a very profitable business: in 1424 the captain of Carentan and one of his soldiers captured a single brigand carrying 113l. 12s. 6d.t. (£6628) in cash and seven silver cups which they shared between them.

This was an unusual case, but soldiers out on patrol could usefully add to their ordinary wages by bringing in brigands: the marshal and some his men from the Saint-Lô garrison shared 72l.t. (£4200) for capturing twelve brigands, eleven of whom were beheaded as traitors and the twelfth, a Breton who had never taken the oath of allegiance, hanged.[15]

Many of those arrested for brigandage were, or had been, members of enemy garrisons. Henriet Pellevillain, for instance, left the Armagnac garrison at Nogent-le-Rotrou in February 1423 and, with four other men, took up residence in the forest of Brotonne, which lies in a loop of the Seine halfway between Pont-Audemer and Caudebec. The forest had long been a notorious haunt of brigands: as early as January 1408 mounted troops had been sent there to root out gangs operating in the area. Pellevillain's men preyed on merchants travelling by road and river to Rouen, kidnapping them and holding them to ransom. Their downfall came when, in their most daring exploit, they went to Caudebec with a trumpeter, seized a number of people in broad daylight and escaped back to the forest with their hostages.[16]

Was this real-life Robin Hood a partisan or a robber? There is no evidence to suggest that his activities benefited anyone other than himself and his group and they were operating far from their base at Nogent-le-Rotrou. The involvement of the trumpeter, however, suggests an operation with legitimate military overtones, as do the facts that Pellevillain had never taken the English oath of obedience and, from the age of twenty, had been actively in the dauphin's service. These were extenuating circumstances which explain why he was allowed to sue for pardon and not simply hanged as a highwayman.

After Nogent-le-Rotrou was captured by the earl of Salisbury in October 1424, another notorious gang from the same garrison also operated out of the forest of Brotonne. Their leader, Guillaume de Hallé, had served in the garrison for three years. During that time he had been taken prisoner on a raid near the English stronghold of La-Ferté-Frênel, some forty miles away. His father, who still lived near Pont-Audemer, had paid his ransom and pledged that his son would not rejoin the enemy if released. Hallé took the oath of allegiance and was set free but then became captain of a large band of brigands, whose profile and activities are recorded in the pardons some of them received in the spring of 1426.[17]

The gang consisted almost entirely of young men in their late teens and twenties, many of whom came from around Pont-Audemer and were involved in the leather-working industry.

Huet de Quesnoy, a shoemaker, was known locally as the captain's recruiting agent, intermediary and enforcer: he threatened to kill and burn down the houses of anyone who failed to respond to Hallé's demands for weapons, food, drink and shelter.[18] Guillaume Bouchier claimed that such threats had compelled him not only to take the gang supplies but also to join them in their kidnapping expeditions.[19] Eighteen-year-old Jeannin Beaudouyn's excuse was that he was in love with Yolette, widow of Jean de Hallé, Guillaume's brigand brother: she had taken him to meet the captain and he had forced him to marry her and join his company. Seventeen-year-old Colin du Quemin had become a member only for his own protection, he said, because Beaudouyn had discovered that Yolette was also sleeping with him and wanted to kill him.[20] A more convincing reason for joining was given by Laurens Hue, an impoverished apprentice shoemaker with an epileptic wife, who confessed he was persuaded by the prospect of earning more than half as much again as a brigand.[21]

Hallé's band were responsible for the usual brigand catalogue of kidnappings, extortions, murders and arson, even raiding as far afield as Harfleur in their quest for victims. No one was safe from their violence. One woman, who refused to reveal where her absent husband was, suffered what seems to be the earliest recorded example of waterboarding: Hallé personally 'tortured her on a bench, forcing her to drink a vast amount of water, causing her serious injury and pain'.[22]

On another occasion seven of the group were sent on a secret night mission to Préaulx Abbey. They were led by Hallé's Friar Tuck, one brother Jehan de Guilleville, a renegade monk from the abbey who was already a veteran kidnapper and robber. With the aid of a ladder stolen from a nearby cottage he scaled the abbey walls and then broke down the door to enable his men to enter. Guilleville informed the seven terrified monks they found inside that they would be held hostage until they obtained the release of one of their brethren, his friend, who was being held prisoner at Pont-Audemer. This time, however, the brigands had overreached themselves. They carried off their hostages into hiding in nearby woods but the alarm was raised and within a few hours they were rounded up and all but two, who escaped, were thrown into prison.[23]

It would be easy to dismiss Hallé's band as nothing more than a particularly vicious criminal gang. The only thing that gives one pause for thought is the formal initiation that each applicant was made to undergo before he was admitted. As Laurens Hue explained it, he was obliged to swear that he would serve Hallé loyally and well 'and that he would do everything in his power to damage and injure the English and all [their] subjects'. Having promised to do this, he was then given a complete new suit of clothing, including a hat and shoes (possibly a uniform?), together with a sword, bow and quiverful of arrows. The initiates were allowed to keep half of everything they won.[24]

Though there remains room for doubt, the telling argument would seem to be that Hallé's activities, like those of most brigands then operating, did nothing to undermine English rule: despite the initiates' oath, there were no attacks on English natives, on English officials or on the infrastructure which made their administration possible. His victims were all Norman civilians, of the same humble class as himself (Hallé was the son of a poor labourer), and many of them were his neighbours, whom he attacked in their own homes. When he was captured again Hallé could not ransom himself a second time because he was now in breach of his oath: he was therefore executed as a traitor, not because he was a guerrilla warrior.[25]

There are occasional references to Englishmen being murdered by brigands in the records of the Norman chancery but for the most part it was ordinary villagers who, especially in the first two years after the invasion, attacked and killed English soldiers who ventured out alone or in twos or threes. Naturally, since they were seeking to justify the offence to obtain a pardon, the killers claimed that they were acting in self-defence or were provoked by violence against themselves or their neighbours.[26] These excuses might not always have been true but there were many examples of English soldiers who did abuse their position to rob, steal and rape, despite the best efforts of the English authorities to prevent and punish such behaviour because it antagonised the local population.[27]

What is perhaps most striking about the evidence of the chancery records is that most of the crimes were not concerned with national identity or political difference. Racially abusive terminology abounds: the English are usually referred to as the 'Goddons', or God-damns, an allusion to their habitual cursing. The stock character invariably swears 'by Saint George' and drinks ale: a riot broke out at Le Crotoy in 1432 when Breton mariners insulted some men from Dieppe by calling them 'treacherous English dogs, Goddons full of ale'. Nevertheless, race was seldom the sole cause of crime. An English merchant living in Rouen was stabbed to death in a quarrel over payment for goods he had received; an over-zealous tax-collector was killed (and his receipts thrown into the sea) by an angry man who thought he had already paid enough; the Norman lieutenant of the *bailli* of Tancarville was killed in a public-house fracas when drinking with a man he had previously arrested for assault.[28] These were not the actions of politically motivated freedom fighters but the unintended consequences of petty squabbles in daily life which are still the staple diet of courts today.

The true resistance was to be found elsewhere, among those prepared to risk their lives to regain territory for the dauphin, either as a civilian fifth column plotting to seize English-held towns and castles or in military service at a frontier garrison such as Mont-Saint-Michel or under a die-hard loyalist commander such as the Harcourts, Ambroise de Loré or Poton de Xaintrailles.

One could be forgiven for thinking that there was sometimes little to distinguish the activities of these Armagnac captains from simple brigandage. The raids of Jean d'Harcourt, count of Aumâle, on Saint-Lô in 1423 and Ambroise de Loré on Caen fair in 1431, for instance, caused terror and consternation because they struck unexpectedly and deep into the heart of Normandy, but in essence they were opportunist attacks whose principal objective was plunder and prisoners.[29] (The same was also true, of course, of English raids into enemy territory.) To a peasant working in the fields perhaps the only observable difference between the smaller marauding groups of armed soldiers and brigand bands was that the former would ride with the banners of their captains displayed and wear the French badge rather than the red cross which Normans were required to bear. It was an important difference, however, as these identified the combatants as the legitimate enemy who were subject to, and protected by, the laws of war.[30]

The French system of levying *appâtis* in times of war was also little more than legalised banditry. *Appâtis* were a form of protection money, paid every quarter in money and in kind, by the parishes of the surrounding countryside to their local garrison. The payments subsidised or even replaced the wages of the soldiers, who in return would refrain from seizing goods and persons without compensation. A parish paying *appâtis* might expect military protection from raids by other garrisons but, since the payments were theoretically voluntary, it laid itself open to the charge of being subject to that garrison and therefore a legitimate object of plunder by the enemy. For ordinary villagers trying to scrape a living by plying their trade or cultivating the fields and vineyards in frontier regions, it was simply a question of choosing the lesser of two evils: to be despoiled by the resident soldiers who would take an agreed sum or by marauding ones who might seize or destroy everything they had.[31]

The plight of the inhabitants of L'Aigle was a case in point. They had been loyal English subjects since their submission on 13 October 1417, but the town had no walls and was regularly terrorised by the three Armagnac garrisons of Nogent-le-Rotrou, Ivry and Senonches, all less than forty miles away. Faced with the prospect of having to abandon their homes and farms, they decided to offer *appâtis* to the captain of the nearest, Senonches, but for just three months' freedom from attack he would accept nothing less than 80 *écus* (£5833) and thirty-six war lances. The money was bad enough but to provide the enemy with arms was a capital offence. The parish priest who negotiated the deal was denounced to the English authorities and obliged to sue for a costly pardon. And his parishioners did not, for the moment, get the security they needed.[32]

For those who were unable to buy their way out of trouble, the only option was to help the enemy or even join them. The story of one Norman gentleman from this same frontier area demonstrates how hazardous this could be. Gilet de Lointren had served as a man-at-arms in Armagnac garrisons from the very beginning of the English invasion. In 1422 he was captured by the Damville garrison and held prisoner for seven months until he raised a ransom of 81 *écus* (£5906). On his release he went to Senonches, serving six months there before joining five comrades who 'went to seek adventures in the land of Normandy, as men-at-arms are accustomed to do'.

When he was captured by the English at Verneuil Lointren's ransom was again set at 81 *écus* but the men at Damville had already taken everything he had. After six months' captivity, when it became clear he could not raise the money and would otherwise die in prison, he agreed to change allegiance and serve one of the four men who had shared the rights to his ransom. Eight days later Lointren was captured by the Armagnacs at Nogent-le-Rotrou and, since his masters at Verneuil would not contribute to his ransom, he reverted to his former allegiance and returned to Senonches. Captured again, this time by the English at Beaumesnil, he was given a safe-conduct allowing him to raise a ransom of 40 *écus* (£2917) at Senonches, only to be taken prisoner for a fifth time as he made his way back with the money. His captors were from Verneuil, recognised him and brought him before the *bailli*, who condemned him to death. Before the sentence could be carried out there was an extraordinary turn of events. A fifteen-year-old girl from Verneuil, 'a virgin and of good reputation', sought an audience with the captain of the garrison, Thomas, lord Scales, and, with her family's approval, offered to marry Lointren. Scales granted her request, returning Lointren to prison only until his pardon could be obtained. The idea that marriage was a suitable alternative to execution seems to have been peculiarly French: in 1430 a 'very handsome' twenty-four-year-old brigand was actually on the scaffold in Paris when another young girl 'boldly came forward and asked for him'; she got him too, and married him, thus saving his life.[33]

Lointren's story was remarkable for the number of times he was taken prisoner and the fairy-tale ending, but otherwise it was by no means unusual. For those living within striking distance of Armagnac strongholds or on the frontiers, where the fortunes of war meant that castles frequently changed hands, some sort of accommodation with the enemy was a necessity. For most of them, fear, poverty and the simple desire for a quiet life were far more potent than political conviction in deciding an allegiance that was as pragmatic as it was ephemeral.

Bedford was aware that his best chance of preserving his brother's legacy and making the English occupation permanent was to provide security and justice for all. In December 1423 the estates-general, which was then in session at Caen, complained that civilians in Normandy could not 'safely live, trade, work or keep that which is their own' because of the 'excesses, abuses, crimes and wrong-doings' daily perpetrated by the military. Bedford responded immediately by issuing a series of reforming ordinances which, by addressing specific issues, provide a damning indictment of the behaviour of English soldiers.

The ordinances drew together into a single document nearly all the measures which had been issued over the years to control the worst excesses of the soldiery. The most important innovation was that captains were prohibited from interfering directly or indirectly in matters of justice: their sphere of jurisdiction was limited to the purely military, distributing gains of war and dealing with discipline within the garrison. They, and all other soldiers, were strictly enjoined to obey the civilian officers of justice, especially the *baillis*, 'the principal chiefs of justice' under Bedford himself.

In response to many complaints that captains, 'French as well as English', were levying *appâtis*, Bedford reiterated what had been standard English practice since the beginning of the invasion: nothing whatever was to be taken without due payment and tolls levied on travellers entering towns or castles or crossing bridges, or on boats, carts and horses carrying merchandise, were declared illegal. Anyone who seized civilians for ransom on the pretext that they were 'Armagnacs or brigands' was to be punished according to the criminal law. And because some soldiers were pillaging and robbing outside their garrisons, all were ordered to report to their captains within fifteen days and prohibited from living anywhere except within the garrison. All knights and esquires were to be suitably armed and mounted, in readiness for campaigns against brigands, traitors and the enemy.

One clause stands out because it was not strictly concerned with military matters, though it reflects a genuine concern. We understand, Bedford declared, that some of our subjects, 'English as well as Normans and others', when speaking of 'our enemies, rebels, traitors and adversaries who are known as Armagnacs' or of 'he who calls himself the dauphin', refer to them as 'French' and 'the king'. This was now forbidden and anyone who continued to do so, in speech or writing, was to be severely punished, a first offence meriting a fine of 10*l.t.* (£583) for noblemen or 100 *sous* (£292) for non-nobles, rising to ten times those amounts or, if the offender was unable to pay, 'the tongue pierced or the forehead branded' for a second offence, and criminal prosecution and confiscation of all goods for a third.

The ordinances were to be published 'at the sound of the trumpet' in the usual way of proclamations, and all captains, *baillis* and their lieutenants were to swear to uphold them. Finally, in a gesture of his determination to deal with the problems caused by indiscipline among his own men, Bedford publicly set his seal to the ordinances in the presence of the estates-general.[34]

These measures were not to be a dead letter but to be enforced by some judicious new appointments. Thomas, lord Scales, was made lieutenant of the regent and captain-general of the Seine towns and Alençon: with twenty men-at-arms and sixty archers he would patrol the Seine between Rouen and Paris to prevent incursions by Armagnacs and brigands. John Fastolf was appointed governor of the triangle south of the Seine between Pont-de-l'Arche, Caen and Alençon, with authority to receive all manner of complaints, punish crimes, execute royal orders, resist the enemy and suppress brigandage. And in April 1424 'prudent and powerful knights' were sent to certain *bailliages* 'to ride in arms . . . in order to expel and extirpate the enemies, brigands, and pillagers therein, and to maintain the king's subjects in peace and tranquillity'.[35] Having reimposed internal discipline and order, Bedford was now in a position to concentrate on his strategy for the defence of his nephew's realm.

CHAPTER SIX

A Second Agincourt

As the new campaigning season opened in the late spring of 1424, both sides made preparations for a major offensive. The dauphin had a war chest of a million *livres* (£58.33m) granted him by the estates-general of the kingdom of Bourges, and the backing of a new Scottish army, 'two thousand knights and esquires, six thousand good archers and two thousand Scots with axes', commanded by the elderly earl of Douglas and his eldest son. The dauphin's declared intention was to fight his way to Reims so that he could be crowned in the cathedral, the place where for centuries kings of France had received their coronation.[1]

Bedford's plans were equally ambitious: to wipe out the remaining Armagnac garrisons on the frontiers of Normandy and then secure the border by extending the conquest south into the counties of Anjou, Maine and Dreux. On 3 March 1424 Le Crotoy was handed over in accordance with the terms of capitulation agreed the previous year.[2] Twelve days later Compiègne agreed to surrender. The town had been captured some months earlier in a daring raid by the Armagnac captain Étienne de Vignolles, better known as La Hire, who had taken advantage of thick fog and an inadequate night-watch to take it by surprise from the Burgundians. The siege to recapture it had dragged on until Bedford, uncharacteristically losing patience, took Guillaume Remon, captain of neighbouring Passy-en-Valois, under whom many of the garrison of Compiègne had fought, and paraded him before the town with a halter round his neck, threatening to hang him if they did not surrender, but release him if they did.

Though this produced the desired effect, it cost Sir John Fastolf a considerable amount of money because Remon was his prisoner and he thereby lost not only Remon's ransom but also those of a group of merchants from Hainault and Brabant whom Remon had captured bringing food to sell in Paris. Fastolf was not a man to allow his loss to go unchallenged. He sued the merchants, unsuccessfully, in the *parlement* of Paris and complained to Bedford for nine long years until the regent finally succumbed and gave him lands in compensation.[3]

The garrison of Compiègne was allowed to withdraw with its arms intact – an unfortunate error of judgement as its soldiers avenged themselves by seizing the castle of Gaillon, eighty miles away in Normandy. Two months and eight hundred men were required to recover it and this time no mercy was shown: the Armagnacs were put to the sword and the castle itself demolished to prevent its being retaken.[4]

While Scales besieged Gaillon, the earl of Suffolk was dispatched to retake Ivry, a tenth-century fortress on a hilltop overlooking the Eure valley. In August 1423 Géraud de la Pallière had scaled the walls and taken it by surprise, installing an Armagnac garrison of four hundred men-at-arms who had raided far and wide, pillaging, robbing and terrorising the countryside without check. The captain of Ivry, Pierre Glé, a Norman and one of the richest lords of the region, absconded rather than face prosecution for his failure to safeguard the castle, and all his goods, lands and possessions were confiscated to the crown. He was eventually persuaded to throw himself on Bedford's mercy and was duly pardoned in March 1424 on the grounds that he was guilty only of negligence and had had no knowledge of, or part in, the treason which led to the castle's seizure.[5]

Besieged for just three weeks, Pallière agreed to surrender on 15 August 1424 if no assistance was forthcoming from the dauphin in the meantime. This was, as we have seen, the standard form of capitulation: the suspension of hostilities was usually the prelude to an orderly handover. This time it would be different. The dauphin had gathered a formidable army at Tours: French troops from Anjou and Maine commanded nominally by the fifteen-year-old duke of Alençon but in reality by the highly experienced Jean d'Harcourt, count of Aumâle, captain of Mont-Saint-Michel, lieutenant and captain-general of Normandy; at least ten thousand Scots led by the earls of Buchan and Douglas; and the dauphin's latest acquisition, two thousand heavy cavalry hired from Milan, a city famed throughout Europe for the skill of its armourers. If anything could withstand English arrows it was Milanese steel. Together, according to Bedford's own estimate, the dauphin's army numbered some fourteen thousand men.[6]

Bedford had also recently received reinforcements, the earl of Warwick, lord Willoughby and Sir William Oldhall having brought sixteen hundred men on six-month contracts from England in April and May. He had issued a general call to arms in Normandy, summoning all those holding lands from the crown and accustomed to bear arms 'of whatever nationality they might be' to meet him at Vernon on 3 July. About two thousand men were also taken from Norman garrisons, an exercise which revealed that some enterprising soldiers from the army recently arrived from England, who had already received their wages until November, had left their captains and enrolled on garrison duty 'to defraud and deceive us and take double wages'. A clampdown was immediately put in place but Bedford was left with fewer men than he had anticipated for his approaching showdown with the dauphin's forces. Even after he was joined by a Burgundian contingent, led by the sire de l'Isle-Adam, the chronicler Jehan Waurin, who served in this army, reckoned that Bedford had only eighteen hundred men-at-arms and eight thousand archers at his disposal.[7]

Bedford led his troops in person to Ivry, arriving on 14 August, the day before the fortress would have to surrender if not relieved. He deployed his men ready for battle but the Armagnac forces did not come. They were thirty miles away to the south-west at Verneuil, which, on 15 August 1424, they captured by an ingenious ploy. Knowing that everyone was waiting for the outcome of the battle for Ivry, they took some of the Scots who could speak English, tied them up, splashed them with blood and set them backwards on their horses, as if they were prisoners. As they were paraded before the town they cried out in English, bewailing their fate and the utter destruction of 'their' army before Ivry. The terrified townspeople were then presented with the sire de Torcy in a similar condition, who confirmed that all was lost. What they did not know was that he had just deserted the English cause and sworn allegiance to the dauphin. Convinced that there was no point in holding out, the citizens opened their gates and the dauphin's men took control of the town.[8]

Bedford set out for Verneuil immediately after accepting the surrender of Ivry. He arrived on 17 August 1424 to find the massed forces of the dauphin's army waiting for him in the flat fields to the north of the town. The site had been chosen to give the greatest advantage to the Milanese cavalry, whose heavily armoured men and horses were to ride down the English archers before they could launch their deadly storm of arrows. Both armies deployed in the traditional manner for battle. Regardless of rank, everyone dismounted to fight on foot, apart from the Milanese on the French wings. The English archers were arrayed opposite the Milanese and, repeating the anti-cavalry tactics used so successfully at Agincourt, each one was protected by a stake driven into the earth in front of him, its sharpened end pointing towards the enemy. All the English horses were tied together so that they could not run away and placed with the wagons at the rear of the army, forming a barrier to protect it from attack.

The battle began at about four in the afternoon with a devastating charge by the Milanese, who swept the archers before them, drove straight through the army and then, instead of regrouping to strike again from behind, proceeded to pillage the baggage in the wagons. The English, demonstrating the discipline for which they were justly renowned, rallied and began a counter-attack against the advancing men-at-arms. Contemporary chroniclers make no mention of the English using their longbows but, given the sheer number of archers present and their ability to shoot a minimum of ten aimed arrows a minute,[9] it seems impossible that their capacity to inflict such destruction was not used.

As at Agincourt, however, it was the archers' willingness to engage at close quarters once their arrows had run out that proved the turning point in the battle. Bedford had given the order that there was to be no quarter and, inspired by his personal example, and that of the earls of Salisbury and Suffolk, who were with him, the English fought doggedly on, pushing the French line back into the Scots behind them and slaughtering all in their path. The dauphin, who had not accompanied his troops to the battlefield, now reaped the consequences of his signal failure of leadership.

It was a victory to match Agincourt. Despite his inferior numbers and the disadvantage of not choosing the field, Bedford completely routed the dauphin's forces. Seven thousand, two hundred and sixty-two French and Scottish soldiers lay dead, among them some of the dauphin's most effective military commanders, the count of Aumâle and the earls of Douglas and Buchan. The young duke of Alençon, newly married to the daughter of Agincourt's most famous prisoner, Charles d'Orléans, was himself a captive, together with Pierre, the bastard of Alençon, and Marshal Lafayette. The English, according to Bedford, had lost two men-at-arms and a 'very few' archers.[10]

The victory at Verneuil secured Bedford's reputation and the English conquest. The Scottish army, upon which the dauphin depended so heavily, was all but annihilated and would not be replaced. The king of Scotland, an English prisoner since 1406, had been released in April 1424, married off to a Beaufort and signed a seven-year truce with England which would prevent further mass recruitment of his subjects into the dauphin's service.[11]

The dauphin could not shrug off this defeat as he had that at

Cravant. Abandoning his plans for a coronation at Reims and also, to all appearances, for the recovery of his kingdom, he settled into a life of luxury and indolence in his kingdom of Bourges, leaving those still committed to his cause leaderless and without hope. Bedford, however, returned to Paris to a hero's welcome: the crowds wore red and shouted 'Noël!' as he passed and when he went to give thanks at Notre Dame 'he was received as if he had been God . . . in short, more honour was never done at a Roman triumph than was done that day to him and his wife.'[12]

Bedford's captains pushed home their advantage by seizing the military initiative from the disheartened Armagnacs. By October Salisbury and Suffolk had retaken Senonches, Nogent-le-Rotrou and other frontier fortresses in the south-east and La Hire agreed to evacuate his remaining strongholds in the spring. Guise, the last northern Armagnac outpost, had fallen to Sir Thomas Rempston and Jehan de Luxembourg after a five-month siege. In the south-west the earl of Salisbury joined lords Fastolf and Scales in extending English control over Maine and into Anjou, a year-long campaign designed to both secure the border of Normandy and reward those who had missed out on the profits of the first wave of conquest.[13]

The only failure in the immediate aftermath of Verneuil was, once again, at Mont-Saint-Michel. Earlier in the year Thomas Burgh, captain of Avranches, had tried to instigate a plot within the garrison. On 24 June, Jean, bishop of Julin, who had been imposed by the English as a deputy on the bishop of Avranches, whose loyalty was suspect, paid a visit to the abbey on the pretext of diocesan business. It was clearly a spying mission, for just two weeks later Henry Meudrac, a Norman esquire who had served in the garrison for at least three years, signed an agreement to deliver Mont-Saint-Michel to Burgh. For this he was to receive 1750*l.t.* (£102,083), a sum so large that the payment had to be specially authorised by both Bedford and the council in Rouen. Two days later, on 10 July, Meudrac received his payment and handed over his nephew, Raoulin, as a hostage for the performance of his part of the bargain. Meudrac either had a change of heart or failed in his attempt, for Mont-Saint-Michel was not betrayed to the English and his nephew was still in English service as a man-at-arms at Avranches eleven years later.[14]

While Burgh waited for his scheming to bear fruit, Bedford resorted to more conventional means. On 26 August, Nicholas Burdet, the *bailli* of the Cotentin, whom Bedford had knighted on the field of Verneuil, was commissioned to begin another siege of Mont-Saint-Michel. Robert Jolivet, the abbot of Mont-Saint-Michel, was appointed to advise and assist him and Bertrand Entwhistle, lieutenant of the earl of Suffolk in his capacity as admiral of Normandy, took charge of the sea blockade.

Burdet began by building a new wooden fortress, complete with drawbridge, two and a half miles away from the island on the southern coast at Ardevon. Intended to last only for the duration of the siege, Ardevon would remain in service for ten years, housing a garrison of up to 40 men-at-arms and 120 archers in what must have been extremely basic and uncomfortable conditions.[15]

Despite all these efforts, the siege proved as fruitless as its predecessors, dragging on for ten months before it was abandoned in June 1425. Although the defenders had lost their captain, Aumâle, at Verneuil, they secured two major coups, capturing Burdet himself and inflicting a naval defeat which allowed the garrison to resupply and precipitated the decision to withdraw.[16]

One of the consequences of the victory at Verneuil was that many people who had hitherto refrained from accepting the English occupation and the Treaty of Troyes now decided that resistance was futile. The weeks and months following the battle saw a flood of applications for pardon. Nicolas le Jendre, for instance, had been in English obedience since May 1419 but had gone to live at Ivry when it was captured by the Armagnacs, ostensibly because his priory was outside the walls and the supply of alms from pilgrims upon which he depended had dried up. Once inside Ivry, he had been elected abbot of Saint-Germain-de-la-Truite and was duly summoned to Évreux for consecration by his diocesan bishop. When he was told he must also take the oath of loyalty, le Jendre refused, fearing, he said, retribution from the Ivry garrison. Nevertheless, he had returned to Ivry, remaining there until he learned that the English were coming to lay siege to the place. He then fled the English kingdom altogether, returning only after the battle to sue for pardon and belatedly take his oath.[17]

Many other inhabitants of Ivry received the benefit of the doubt and were pardoned for colluding with the Armagnacs by supplying goods or even fighting in their service.[18] The inhabitants of Verneuil also won a general pardon for opening their gates to the enemy which Bedford actually signed 'in the army before Verneuil' the day after the battle.[19]

The pardon records also reveal what the chroniclers do not. When the Milanese smashed their way through the English ranks, a number of 'varlets, pages and others of feeble courage' ran away, spreading the news that the battle was lost. These rumours, confirming those that must already have been swirling about as a result of the Armagnac ploy to capture Verneuil, prompted an attempt to cause an uprising in Normandy. The rebels were quick to submit once they had discovered their mistake but not before they had robbed and murdered some of those who had fled the battlefield.[20]

Altogether more serious than these opportunistic acts of violence was the discovery – three years later – that there had been a plot to betray Rouen to the dauphin on the eve of Verneuil. A Franciscan friar, Étienne Charlot, was told by the dauphin that he had resolved to be crowned at Reims and invade Normandy because he had been personally approached by certain loyal citizens of Rouen 'wearing disguises'. Their leader was Richard Mites, a wealthy merchant who had signed the capitulation of Rouen in 1419 and profited from the conquest by becoming a supplier to the English regime and farmer of the town's revenues.

Mites had sought and obtained the expert opinion of Jehan Salvart, master-mason for the king's works in the Rouen *bailliage*, and Alexandre de Berneval, master-mason for the town's works, on how best to neutralise the castle, if Rouen itself 'was taken by storm and it was necessary to make a new oath and change allegiance'. Salvart and Berneval were working in the castle at the time. They conferred, and Salvart pointed out where the walls could be mined and cannon placed to break down the bridges and the gate so that the English garrison could be prevented from getting out of the castle.

Why the plot was not put into action is not known but it seems likely that it was aborted when Bedford unexpectedly snatched victory from the Armagnacs at Verneuil. Mites fled to the kingdom of Bourges and his property was confiscated as being that of a traitor, but Salvart and Berneval were among those arrested and imprisoned. Salvart was tried and condemned to be beheaded as a traitor, but received a last-minute reprieve when he was literally at the place of execution. He and Berneval were both pardoned after a spell of imprisonment and, remarkably, within a year were back in their original posts.[21]

Mites had been able to obtain the master-masons' cooperation because he persuaded them that the dauphin and the duke of Burgundy had made peace and were preparing to attack Rouen together. In the fevered atmosphere before Verneuil this was believable, not least because there had been a major quarrel between Philippe of Burgundy and Humphrey, duke of Gloucester. In the spring of 1423 Gloucester had married Philippe's cousin, Jacqueline of Bavaria, the countess of Hainault, Holland and Zeeland. Jacqueline had been married before, first to the dauphin Jean de Touraine, who had died in 1417, then to her cousin, John of Brabant. The second marriage was unhappy and she had fled to England, where her personal charms and valuable inheritance so captivated Gloucester that he determined to marry her. When the legitimate pope refused to grant her a divorce, they procured one from the schismatic pope at Avignon.

Gloucester's actions put a severe strain on the Anglo-Burgundian alliance because Burgundy, who had his own designs on Jacqueline's territories, sided with his cousin, John of Brabant. All that Bedford had achieved in France was now imperilled by his brother's impetuous actions, stupidity and greed. In October 1424 Gloucester and his bride landed at Calais at the head of an

English army and laid claim to Jacqueline's lands. They set up a government at Mons but the town quickly surrendered when besieged the following March by Burgundian and Brabantine troops. Gloucester's little adventure ended ignominiously with him abandoning his wife and returning to England with nothing to show for his efforts except a challenge from the duke of Burgundy to settle their quarrel in personal combat.[22]

The challenge was a deadly serious affair, a trial by battle, which could, and should, result in the death of either combatant. Burgundy went into strict training and spent an inordinate sum of money equipping himself, but the pope intervened to prohibit it and Bedford, holding a court of chivalry in Paris, declared honour was thus duly satisfied without the combat having to take place.[23]

Gloucester's unwelcome intervention in the Low Countries seems to have pushed Burgundy into making tentative concessions towards the dauphin. In September 1424 they signed the first treaty of abstinence from war between them. Though it covered only the mid-west of France, principally the duchy and county of Burgundy, the Bourbonnais, Mâconnais and Forez, it was of enormous importance for two reasons: the truces were regularly renewed, providing an ongoing dialogue between the two parties, and for the first time Burgundy referred to the dauphin in an official document as 'king of France'.[24]

At the same time Burgundy was also building up personal ties among the Armagnacs. In April 1423 Bedford had secured a major diplomatic coup with the Treaty of Amiens, a triple alliance between England, Burgundy and Brittany which personally committed the three dukes to 'true fraternity' and the preservation of each other's honour 'both in private and in public'. The alliance had been sealed with a double marriage: that of Bedford with Anne of Burgundy and Arthur de Richemont, Brittany's brother, with Anne's sister, Margaret.[25]

Arthur de Richemont was, like his brother, a man whose loyalties were determined by his own perceived advantage. At first a committed Armagnac, he had been captured at Agincourt and remained an English prisoner for seven years. After he took the oath of loyalty to Henry V he was released on licence, served with the earl of Suffolk against his former allies in France and was granted the lordship of Ivry as his reward.[26] When the earl of Buchan was killed at Verneuil, however, the dauphin offered Richemont the office of constable of France. Richemont consulted his brother-in-law and Burgundy, provoked by Gloucester's invasion of Hainault, advised him to accept. Richemont's second spectacular change of allegiance gave Burgundy a useful contact in the dauphin's court, a link that was strengthened by another double marriage: that of Burgundy himself with his uncle's widow, Bonne of Artois, countess of Nevers, and his sister Agnès with Bonne's half-brother, Charles de Bourbon, count of Clermont, a committed Armagnac whose father had been a prisoner in England since Agincourt.[27] Territorial ambition played a part in these marriages but they were undoubtedly a rebuff to the English alliance. More seriously, Richemont's defection was followed by that of his brother, the duke of Brittany, who in October 1425 signed with the dauphin the Treaty of Saumur, which gave him control of the finances of the kingdom of Bourges and supreme direction of the war 'for the expulsion of the English'.[28]

Bedford had been unequivocal in his support for Burgundy throughout the crisis caused by his brother, but Gloucester's penchant for causing mayhem was not limited to the continent. On his return to England he quarrelled spectacularly with his uncle, Henry Beaufort, bishop of Winchester, who had been appointed chancellor the previous year and had used Gloucester's absence to consolidate his own power in the council and exert his personal influence over the boy-king. Gloucester alleged that Beaufort was planning a coup to seize Henry and at the end of October 1425 there was an armed stand-off between their followers in the streets of London. As events threatened to spiral out of control, Beaufort appealed to Bedford to return home:

> as you desire the welfare of the king our sovereign lord and of his realms of England and of France, and your own weal and ours also, haste you hither; for by my troth if you tarry, we shall put this land at risk of a battle. Such a brother you have here.

God make him a good man. For your wisdom knows well that the prosperity of France stands in the welfare of England.[29]

Bedford could not ignore such an entreaty. On 26 November he appointed the earls of Salisbury, Suffolk and Warwick as his lieutenants in charge of military affairs in his absence. The same day he issued a set of ordinances to reform abuses of the night-watch which were causing great popular resentment. Captains were prohibited from levying excessive charges, extracting payments from those living outside the designated area or forcing local people to labour in the repair or construction of fortifications. To prevent them imposing arbitrary fines on those who defaulted on their performance of night-watch or physically beating those who fell asleep, a scale of fines was laid out. Finally, in an interesting sidelight on current military practice, captains were ordered to ensure that the watchword for the night was in French, so that those on duty could understand and easily remember it.[30]

Having completed these acts of housekeeping, Bedford left Paris for Calais. On the way, in an incident which must have sowed the seeds of doubt about the wisdom of his leaving France at this time, he survived an attempt on his life by a notorious brigand chief, Sauvage de Frémainville, who was later captured in the castle of l'Isle-Adam, taken to Paris and brutally executed, being beaten at the scaffold, refused permission to make a confession and, because the executioner bungled his hanging at the first attempt, falling, breaking his back and leg, and being forced to remount the scaffold for a second time.[31] On 20 December 1425 Bedford and his wife landed at Sandwich. He could not have imagined that it would be fifteen months before he would return to France.[32]

Apart from the four-year-old king, Bedford was the only person senior in standing to both Gloucester and Beaufort, and for that reason only he had sufficient authority to enforce a resolution to their quarrel. Gloucester proved truculent and difficult, refusing to meet his uncle or attend a council meeting to discuss the problem and demanding Beaufort's removal from office as chancellor. Bedford had to resort to ordering him to attend a meeting of parliament, held at Leicester, well away from Gloucester's sphere of influence in London, and setting up a committee of the House of Lords to arbitrate between them. The deal Bedford eventually brokered to achieve a public reconciliation was that Beaufort would resign the chancellorship, ostensibly so that he could go on pilgrimage to Rome, but in reality so that he could accept the cardinal's hat which Henry V had forced him to refuse in 1418. Beaufort thus lost the most important post in the English government but gained the most powerful position in the English church, with authority superior even to that of the archbishop of Canterbury.[33]

Gloucester appeared to have won but, before Bedford returned to France, a new set of ordinances was drawn up which asserted the right of the whole council to be involved in decision-making and emphasised the need to avoid disputes between magnates. Bedford personally and publicly committed himself to the principle that authority during the king's minority 'rests not in one single person but in all my said lords together'. Gloucester at first protested that 'after [Bedford's] going over into France I will govern as seems good to me' but then reluctantly gave way.[34]

On 25 March 1427 Bedford personally invested his uncle with the cardinal's hat at Saint Mary's church in Calais, just a week after his return to France.[35] In his absence much of the military effort had been directed against Brittany, upon which the English had formally declared war in January 1426 in response to the Treaty of Saumur. Sir Thomas Rempston, the earl of Suffolk's lieutenant, had mounted a serious offensive into Brittany which had struck as far as Rennes, before withdrawing to establish himself as a threatening presence at the border fortress of Saint-James-de-Beuvron. An attempt by Arthur de Richemont to besiege him there ended in failure after less than two weeks but in January 1427 the Bretons captured the neighbouring stronghold of Pontorson. The earl of Warwick, with six hundred men-at-arms and eighteen hundred archers, recaptured it on 8 May after a ten-week siege: Saint-James-de-Beuvron was then demolished and the garrison and its artillery transferred to Pontorson.

The threat of a full-scale assault on Rennes was now sufficient to bring the duke of Brittany to heel. He agreed a truce which, on 8 September 1427, became a full-scale alliance: the duke abandoned the dauphin again, accepted the Treaty of Troyes and declared himself to be Henry VI's liege man.[36]

This important diplomatic gain was overshadowed by the breaking news that just three days earlier, on 5 September, the English had suffered two major military defeats. The Bastard of Orléans and La Hire carried out a surprise attack on the English army, commanded by the earls of Suffolk and Warwick, which for more than two months had been besieging Montargis, an important Armagnac stronghold some seventy miles south of Paris. Several hundred soldiers and civilians were killed and the earls were forced to retire so quickly that they left behind their artillery and baggage.[37]

On the same day Ambroise de Loré ambushed and defeated a substantial force of Englishmen at Ambrières, a village less than two miles from Sainte-Suzanne, the fortress-base of Sir John Fastolf, governor of Anjou and Maine. Fastolf's nephew was taken prisoner, but most of his men were either slaughtered or put to flight. This victory put such heart into the Armagnacs that when, shortly afterwards, the castle of La Gravelle agreed to capitulate to Fastolf unless relieved in the meantime, the garrison went back on its sworn terms and refused to surrender. Bedford was so incensed by this that he personally ordered the execution of the unfortunate hostages for the surrender and not long afterwards removed Fastolf from office.[38]

Several other important strongholds in Maine fell to the resurgent Armagnacs in the wake of Ambrières, including Nogent-le-Rotrou, Nogent-le-Roi and La-Ferté-Bernard. Unusually a detailed description of how La-Ferté-Bernard was lost has survived in a non-chronicle source. The captain of this small but important fortress, twenty-eight miles north-east of Le Mans, was Robert Stafford, an esquire whose loyal service in Normandy had been rewarded with grants of land by Henry V in 1419. In February 1428 these were all confiscated from him as punishment for his negligence in allowing La-Ferté-Bernard to fall into enemy hands. It was alleged by the new governor of Anjou and Maine, lord Talbot, that Stafford had been warned that traitors were plotting to betray the place and been given a list of their names. Instead of arresting them and taking pre-emptive defensive measures, he had merely retreated into the castle 'which is impregnable' and then surrendered, despite there being neither an assault nor a bombardment. According to the law of arms, since he had put up no resistance his lands were rightfully forfeit.

Stafford's response to these charges was that he had appointed trusted townsmen and garrison members to guard the gates and sent out scouts to warn of the enemy's approach. Only then had he retired into the castle but, during the night, some of the local officials had opened the town gates to the enemy, who had set fire to the castle bridge and gate. He had been unable to defend the castle, he said, because the only gunner was absent, the sole cannon was in need of repair and there was just one crossbow left in the munitions store – and that had no string. In the face of such woefully inadequate equipment, the garrison had mutinied and forced him to negotiate a surrender. Stafford argued that he had done all that could reasonably be expected of him, in the circumstances: La-Ferté-Bernard had fallen 'by chance and bad luck, not by his fault'.

Stafford was so determined to clear his name that he appealed his forfeiture to the *parlement* of Paris, the highest court in the land. His honour had been impugned and he felt that he had been unjustly deprived of the estates he had built up in a hitherto unblemished career of almost a decade of loyal and continuous military service to the crown in France. To add insult to injury, as he plaintively informed the court, on his way to Paris to bring his suit he had been captured by the enemy, despite having a safe-conduct, and had been forced to pay a ransom of 800 *saluts* (£64,167). Surprisingly, since the embarrassing lack of weaponry in the castle would seem to have been prima facie evidence of his negligence as captain, Stafford was cleared of misconduct and his forfeiture was reversed. Nevertheless, it took him six years to achieve this result, and he may have won only on the technicality that the summary forfeiture of his lands without a hearing or a right of appeal was unjust.[39]

The task of recovering La-Ferté-Bernard and the other places in Maine taken by the Armagnacs would fall to John Talbot, who was then relatively unknown in France but would become one of the key men in the fight to maintain the English kingdom. Famously short-tempered, he did not suffer fools gladly, but his bravery, boldness and exceptional talent as a soldier and leader inspired his compatriots and his battlefield prowess struck terror into the hearts of the French. A Knight of the Garter, married to the eldest daughter and heiress of Thomas, earl of Warwick, Talbot was one of the richest men in England. Now in his early forties, he had spent his entire life in arms, playing a leading role in the suppression of rebellions in Wales and Ireland, where he had learned the military arts of speed and surprise which would inspire such fear in his opponents. He had served in France only once before, during the last two years of Henry V's life, returning with Bedford in March 1427 for what was supposed to be a six-month contract but would become a lifelong commitment.

Talbot began his campaign in the spring of 1428 by unexpectedly launching a punitive raid into the west of Maine and capturing Laval, a town which had never fallen to the English before. With that safely under his belt he proceeded to mop up all the pockets of resistance in the east of the county. On 25 May, however, the capital, Le Mans, was betrayed by some of its citizens to La Hire, who took the town and began a siege of the castle, into which the English garrison had retreated. Talbot was then thirty-two miles away at Alençon but in the early hours of 28 May he arrived at the head of three hundred soldiers and retook Le Mans by storm. La Hire's men were trapped between the relieving force and the garrison, who, on hearing Talbot's war-cry in the streets, threw stones on their besiegers and then rushed out to join in the slaughter. So many prisoners were taken that a special court of chivalry had to be set up, under the presidency of lord Scales, to decide disputes between their captors, and one especially complicated case, involving Talbot himself, John Popham, William Oldhall, Thomas Rempston and William Glasdale, was appealed to the *parlement* of Paris.[40]

Talbot's swift recapture of Le Mans and the savage retribution he exacted on those who had betrayed the town to the enemy established his reputation as 'the English Achilles', one of the most feared of English captains. Bedford too recognised his talents, rewarding him with generous gifts of land and summoning him to attend his council in Paris.[41] Talbot had earned his place as one of the senior English commanders in the major new campaign planned for the forthcoming summer.

PART TWO

JEHANNE D'ARC

CHAPTER SEVEN

The Pucelle

Bedford had now been regent of France for five and a half years. Throughout that time he had successfully pursued a policy of gradually extending and consolidating his nephew's kingdom and to that end he had done everything in his power to preserve good relations with Philippe of Burgundy, whose alliance underpinned all that the English had achieved in France. In 1428 all this was to come under threat. The catalyst once again was Humphrey, duke of Gloucester.

On 9 January 1428 the pope had ruled that his marriage to Jacqueline of Hainault was invalid and that she was still legally married to John of Brabant. Jacqueline herself was forced to end her three-year war against Burgundy and accept his humiliating terms, recognising him as her heir, ceding authority to a regency council appointed primarily by him and sharing the revenues of the three states with him.[1]

Gloucester tried to make up for the failure of his continental ambitions by making a bid for greater power in England. Taking advantage of the absence of both Bedford and Cardinal Beaufort, he demanded that parliament redefine his role and refused to attend until it did so. Again he was robustly rebuffed:

'we exhort and require you to be satisfied with the . . . declared power with which my lord of Bedford, your brother, the king's eldest uncle, was himself satisfied; and that you desire no greater power', he was told.[2]

Gloucester had, however, found an unlikely new ally in Thomas, earl of Salisbury, perhaps the longest-serving and most experienced of all the English commanders in France. Salisbury had returned to England to recruit a new army and on 24 March 1428 contracted to serve for six months 'in France, Normandy, and other marches and frontiers' with six hundred men-at-arms and eighteen hundred mounted archers. The contract was unusual in several respects. It allowed Salisbury latitude to substitute archers for men-at-arms at his discretion and to include in their ranks four master gunners (*canoniers*), together with ten miners as archers. It also specified the expenditure of 1000 marks (£350,000) on 'cannons, stone cannon-balls, wagons, carts, iron pincers, ropes and other necessities for cannons.' More importantly – and ominously – the contract gave Salisbury unprecedented independence from Bedford's authority as regent of France.[3]

To pay for the expedition, parliament granted the first direct tax of Henry VI's reign: levied only on churches and knights' fees, it raised £12,291 (£6.45m), less than a normal subsidy, but still a generous sum for a country which, since the Treaty of Troyes, was under no obligation to pay for the war in France.[4]

The decision as to how to deploy Salisbury's army should have rested with Bedford and in May he had presided over a meeting of the council in Paris which decided that it should be sent to capture Angers, the capital of Anjou. The following month a meeting of the estates-general voted 60,000*l.t.* (£3.5m) for this purpose, including the purchase of munitions sufficient for a four-month siege. When Salisbury landed in France in July, however, he headed not for Angers but straight for Orléans, 130 miles to the east. Bedford would later complain that this was done 'God knows by what advice' but the finger of suspicion pointed plainly at Gloucester, who shared Salisbury's preference for a decisive military strike against the dauphin rather than Bedford's slow but steady approach to conquest.[5]

The choice of Orléans as a target was provocative. Strictly speaking, it was illegal: Charles, duke of Orléans, was an English prisoner and his lands should therefore have been hors de combat because they provided the revenues to finance his ransom. A siege of Orléans was also against the interests and wishes of Philippe of Burgundy, which would have worried Bedford but may have been an added incentive to Gloucester and Salisbury, who, for different reasons, were both hostile to the duke.[6]

Salisbury began his campaign in such spectacular style that by 5 September he was able to write to Gloucester's loyal supporters in London that he had already taken thirty-eight strongholds. A month later he had captured the Loire river crossings at Meung and Beaugency to the west of Orléans and Jargeau to the east.[7] Orléans itself lay on a plain on the north bank of the Loire, at the top of a loop in the river, making it the closest point to Paris, which lay just eighty miles away. One of the largest and most populous towns in France, it was enclosed by ancient walls with eight heavily fortified gates and more than thirty towers. On the south side of the river, but separated from the bank by a drawbridge, stood the Tourelles, a small fortress guarding the access to the twelfth-century stone bridge whose nineteen arches spanned the Loire, taking in an island between the two shores.[8]

By a curious twist of fate the captain charged with the defence of the town was Raoul, sire de Gaucourt, a loyal servant of Charles d'Orléans and a formidable opponent. In 1415 he had incurred the wrath of Henry V by bringing reinforcements into Harfleur under the king's nose and, despite enduring heavy bombardment, starvation and disease, holding out for five weeks before being forced to surrender. As a consequence of his defiance Henry had refused to ransom him and, on his deathbed, had forbidden his release during Henry VI's minority. Gaucourt had endured ten years of imprisonment in England and had only been set free in 1425, when he was exchanged for John, earl of Huntingdon, who had been captured at Baugé.[9] There can have been few Frenchmen more motivated or better qualified to defend Orléans against the English.

On 12 October 1428 Salisbury laid siege to the city from the south, concentrating his attention on capturing the bridge. Gaucourt had prepared for this by demolishing the convent of the Augustinian friars, which, standing directly opposite the Tourelles, would have offered a vantage point for bombarding the fortress. He had also constructed a massive earthwork, or 'boulevard', in front of the main gate to inhibit cannon-fire and direct assaults. The English nevertheless trained their guns on the fortifications and began to mine beneath them. On 21 October they attempted to storm the fortress but were repelled with boiling water and burning coals and oil, which the women of Orléans prepared for the defenders to shower on their attackers below. Three days later the French withdrew across the bridge into the city, leaving Salisbury in possession of the Tourelles.

It proved to be a hollow victory. For while the English had been attacking the boulevard and fortress, workmen from Orléans had secretly undermined the bridge, waiting only until the garrison had withdrawn before demolishing the final two arches.[10] Salisbury was now stranded on the south bank of the Loire with 380 yards of deep and fast-moving water still separating him from his objective. His position was vulnerable, for, with winter approaching, he was not only on the wrong side of the river to receive supplies from the north but also potentially exposed to attack from the dauphin's heartlands: Bourges and Tours were both only seventy miles away.

Rather than withdraw, Salisbury decided to dig in for a long siege. He set up his headquarters and battery in the Tourelles, training his guns on the city walls, and began to rebuild and extend the boulevard, which would eventually become a massive fortification, 65½ feet long and 85 feet wide, surrounded by a ditch over 26 feet deep. On 27 October 1428, as Salisbury surveyed the city from an upper window of the Tourelles, he was struck by debris from a stone cannon-ball fired from Orléans, which shattered against the window frame and tore away much of his lower face. Mortally wounded, he was carried to Meung, where he died a week later, aged forty.[11] Though one has to question his motives and judgement in diverting his forces from

Angers to Orléans, his death undeniably removed an able soldier, 'the most ingenious, expert and fortunate in arms of all English princes and captains'.[12]

Salisbury's death left Bedford with the unpalatable choice of either abandoning a siege of which he disapproved or committing more resources to bring it to a successful conclusion. Ten days later he appointed William, earl of Suffolk, to replace Salisbury, issued orders for the siege to continue and called up more troops to reinforce the blockade. Suffolk too was a highly experienced soldier: though only thirty-two, he had served continuously in France since the invasion of 1417 and had fought at both Agincourt and Verneuil. A capable commander rather than a brilliant one, he was about to face his nemesis, an experience that would permanently change the course of his life and career.

Until the arrival of the new forces at the end of December, the siege fell into abeyance and Gaucourt seized the opportunity to strengthen his defences. The twelve watermills between the bridge and easternmost tower which Salisbury's cannon had targeted and destroyed were replaced by horse-driven mills within the city walls: out of the range of the English guns, they ensured that a regular supply of flour for bread was maintained. Vulnerable gates and towers were blocked up and the extensive suburbs outside the walls were burned and cleared away: at least twenty-three churches and chapels were demolished, together with many fine houses and buildings belonging to wealthy Orléannais. The citizens were drilled in preparation for manning the defences, and weapons, armour, artillery and victuals were solicited from neighbouring towns and stockpiled for a siege. Finally, just before lords Scales and Talbot arrived with their reinforcements, Gaucourt was able to welcome a force of twelve to fourteen hundred soldiers to add to his garrison. These were elite troops, commanded by some of the most potent names among Armagnac captains: the Bastard of Orléans, La Hire and Poton de Xaintrailles. It was the Bastard, as the dauphin's lieutenant-general, who now took overall charge of the defence of his half-brother's city.[13]

Scales and Talbot brought around 2500 soldiers with them,

many of whom must have been needed simply to replace
Salisbury's men, whose six-month contracts of service ran out at
the end of December. Even with the arrival of fifteen hundred
Burgundians there was not therefore necessarily a great increase
in available manpower, so that the besieging forces were still
unable to surround Orléans completely. Instead, over the next
few months, they built a series of bastilles, or small fortresses, at
the four points of the compass, each controlling access to one of
the city's main gates. To the south and west, five boulevards
(one of them on an island in the Loire) were also erected, to prevent the Armagnacs at Blois from bringing in supplies or
reinforcements along the river. Each of these would have been
surmounted by wooden palisading to protect a gun emplacement
and the men stationed there. The north-eastern corner of the
city, perhaps because it had no gate through which the enemy
could enter or exit in any number, was left unblockaded.[14]

The siege dragged on through the winter, marked only by sorties and skirmishes which the chronicler Monstrelet feelingly
dismissed as 'too long and boring' to describe in detail.[15] The
intention was clearly to starve the Orléannais into submission
rather than take the place by assault, but the length of the supply
line from Paris meant that the besiegers also suffered from
shortages.

On 12 February 1429 a convoy of several hundred carts and
wagons containing flour, herrings and other foodstuffs appropriate for the forthcoming season of Lent was ambushed at
Rouvray, on its way from Paris to Orléans. Forewarned of an
approaching enemy force, the military escort, commanded by Sir
John Fastolf and Simon Morhier, the provost of Paris, quickly
drew up the wagons into a circle, hammered in their anti-cavalry
stakes across the two entrances and placed the Parisian archers
and crossbowmen on one flank and the English archers on the
other. The civilians, who numbered almost a thousand, were
corralled with the horses in the further side of the circle.

The attackers were led by the count of Clermont, at the head
of a relief force from Blois, and a substantial detachment from
Orléans which had managed to slip through the English lines.

This latter force included the Bastard of Orléans, La Hire, Xaintrailles and the remnant of those Scots who had survived Cravant and Verneuil, led by John Stewart of Darnley. Together they outnumbered the English force by at least two to one.

In the time-dishonoured fashion, the Armagnac captains could not agree among themselves on how to proceed. The Scots wanted to fight on foot, the French on horseback, so in the end they each did as they pleased. The English and Parisian archers, protected by the wagons and their stakes, were free to shoot volley after volley without fear of returning fire. In the resulting confusion the horses of the cavalry, maddened by the barrage of arrows, turned back and ran into their own advancing troops or, pressing on, were disembowelled by the archers' stakes. The Scots line was broken and then overwhelmed by the English men-at-arms advancing from within their circle of wagons. It was a textbook English victory won by archers and men-at-arms working in concert. More than four hundred Armagnacs were left dead on the field, including Darnley and his son; hundreds more were taken prisoner. The English lost just four men, one of them Simon Morhier's nephew. Marshal Lafayette had knighted several Armagnacs, including the count of Clermont, before the battle in anticipation of success; the English celebrated their victory by conferring knighthood on those who had distinguished themselves.[16]

The 'battle of the Herrings' as it became known, in reference to the content of the wagons, was the last Armagnac engagement in which the Scots played a significant role. The dauphin had been anxious to renew the 'auld alliance', offering to marry his son and heir to James I's infant daughter and to give James a French county in return for the services of six thousand Scottish troops. Darnley had been sent to Scotland to negotiate the deal in April 1428; it had been confirmed at Chinon in October and the betrothal had formally taken place in December, with James's envoy, Patrick Ogilvy, standing in for Margaret of Scotland. The bride was to be sent to France the following year, together with the promised army. When Darnley was killed at the battle of the Herrings, the dauphin offered his post as constable of the Scottish army in France to Ogilvy, who had stayed on as a volunteer at the siege of Orléans. James I not only opposed this appointment but also peremptorily ordered Ogilvy back to Scotland: he was drowned at sea on his way home.

James, it seems, was playing a double game, for even as his daughter was betrothed to Louis of France he was negotiating with his own wife's uncle, Cardinal Beaufort, to marry another of his daughters to Henry VI of England. And the Scottish army never materialised, despite the dauphin's need for its aid to relieve Orléans.[17]

Help would come, but it was from a totally unexpected quarter. At the end of February 1429, a mere fortnight after the battle of the Herrings, a seventeen-year-old village girl arrived at Chinon, where the dauphin's court had taken up residence for the winter. She had travelled three hundred miles from her home in Domrémy, a small village at the most eastern corner of France, on the borders of the duchies of Bar and Lorraine, and her name was Jehanne d'Arc.

The story of 'Joan of Arc' is so well known that it is sometimes easy to forget that it is also extraordinary almost beyond belief. Her youth, her sex, her background, all militated against what she became: the companion of princes, inspirational military leader, martyr for faith and country. Her brief but dazzling career is recorded in exhaustive detail, most importantly in her own words, through the records of her trial in 1431, and in those of the people who knew her, through their depositions for the process of nullifying the judgement against her in 1456. Yet because she became, and remains, such an iconic figure, any discussion of her life is inevitably mired in controversy. Were her voices genuine or simply delusional? Was she on a divinely inspired mission or merely the political tool of others? Was she the saviour of France or just an enemy of the English? Some of these questions cannot be answered: they are a matter of personal religious faith or instinctive patriotism.

What ought to be possible, however, is an objective analysis of how and why she behaved as she did and the consequences of that behaviour. There is no doubt whatsoever, for instance, that she absolutely believed that she had been called to restore the dauphin to the throne of France by God, speaking through the saints Michael, Katherine and Margaret, who appeared to her in visions. Whether this was true or not is irrelevant: the fact that she believed it to be so is what matters. In the same way, Henry V's conviction that God had been on his side and would therefore restore to him his 'just rights and inheritances' in France was far more potent in determining his actions than the simple legality or equity of those claims.

A further complicating factor in the records of Jehanne d'Arc's life is that they are biased to an unusual degree. It was not just that she was illiterate and therefore reliant on others to put her words into writing, but that those recording her words and actions were doing so for entirely partisan reasons: in 1431 to secure her conviction as a heretic and sorceress and in 1456 to reclaim her as the innocent victim of the hated English who had only recently been driven out of France. Both sides had every reason to twist the evidence for their own political and patriotic ends.

Jehanne herself would have cared little for such niceties. She had begun to hear voices when she was thirteen, she later told her interrogators, but they had at first simply told her to be good. So she had gone to church regularly, taken a vow of virginity and conducted herself well, incurring her parents' wrath on only two occasions, first when she refused to marry a man from Toul and had to defend a court action for breach of promise and secondly when, commanded by her voices, she had left Domrémy to go 'into France'.[18]

Though it was not recognised by Jehanne herself, the defining moment in her life seems to have been a Burgundian raid on her village in July 1428, when she and her family were forced to flee to the safety of the nearest walled town, Neufchâteau, and returned to find their church and village burned and their fields devastated.[19] The experience left Jehanne with an abiding hatred of the Burgundians and, by association, the English. It seems to have prompted her earliest public action, the first of what would be three visits to Robert de Baudricourt, the Armagnac captain of Vaucouleurs, twelve miles north of Domrémy, from whom she demanded the provision of an escort 'into France' so that she could 'raise the siege positioned around Orléans'.[20]

Baudricourt, not surprisingly, did not respond kindly to such instructions, telling Jehanne's uncle that he should take her home and beat her. Yet in both Domrémy and Vaucouleurs she impressed others with her sense of mission. 'Have you not heard this prophecy,' she would ask, 'that France will be destroyed by a woman, and restored by a virgin from the marches of Lorraine?'[21] The prophecy was later identified by witnesses at the nullification trial as one made by a female recluse from Avignon, Marie Robine, whose story bears a strong resemblance to that of Jehanne. In 1398 Marie had a vision in which a voice told her to go to the king of France and tell him how to end the schism in the church. At Charles VI's court she had, in the presence of Master Jean Érault, a future professor of theology, described her visions of the desolation of the kingdom and the calamities that it would have to endure:

> in particular she saw a quantity of armour which had been presented to her; she was terror-stricken by this, fearing that she would be forced to accept these suits of armour; then she was told not to be afraid, that she would not have to bear these arms; but that after her, a Pucelle would come who would bear these arms and deliver the kingdom of France from the enemy.[22]

Érault was later convinced that Jehanne d'Arc was indeed the Pucelle, or Maid, whose coming Marie Robine had prophesied.

The phenomenon of the female visionary and prophetess had arisen in a world where women were denied a formal role within the church hierarchy. The Avignon papacy and the Great Schism had prompted an exponential increase in their numbers, as many pious women, deeply distressed by the chaos and corruption at the heart of the church, sought a direct relationship with God and to bring about reform. The most famous of these were Bridget of Sweden (1303–73) and Catherine of Sienna (1347–80), who were canonised in 1391 and 1461 respectively, but there were many less well-known figures, such as Ursuline Venerii, a simple girl from Parma who went to Avignon and, in a personal interview with Clement VII, urged him to resign in favour of his Roman rival. Marie Robine (d. 1399) and Jeanne-Marie de Maillé (1331–1414) similarly took their divine revelations directly to the king of France, threatening apocalypse if he did not intervene to end the schism.[23]

Jehanne therefore had much in common with women such as these, including, in the cases of Marie Robine and Jeanne-Marie de Maillé, a direct connection with the Angevin court. Jeanne-Marie had been godmother to one of the children of Louis I, duke of Anjou, and his wife, Marie. She was also a personal friend of Yolande of Aragon, the wife of Louis II, duke of Anjou. Yolande's husband had secured Jeanne-Marie's introduction to the king in 1395 and held long, private consultations with the prophetess. Yolande herself would later testify at Jeanne-Marie's canonisation process in 1414. Her mother-in-law, the duchess Marie, also knew Marie Robine and was present when she had one of her visions in 1398.[24]

The significance of the Angevin family interest in religious visionaries is that Jehanne's home village, Domrémy, was in the duchy of Bar, which belonged to Yolande's younger son, René d'Anjou, by right of his marriage to Isabella, the daughter of Charles, duke of Lorraine. Robert de Baudricourt was captain of Vaucouleurs on René d'Anjou's behalf and served him not only as a soldier but also as a councillor, chamberlain and witness to his documents. And it was Charles of Lorraine who, hearing rumours about Jehanne, ordered her to be brought to him at Nancy so that he could question her about his poor health. In her usual forthright manner she told Charles she knew nothing about that but she told him of her mission and offered to pray for him, if he would send René d'Anjou to escort her into France.[25]

The duke declined, but he did give her his safe-conduct and some money, both of which must have considerably enhanced Jehanne's reputation. It was becoming increasingly difficult to ignore her and it was perhaps at this point that either the duke or, more probably, Baudricourt, decided to contact the dauphin and inform him of Jehanne's self-appointed mission. This is suggested by the otherwise inexplicable presence of Colet de Vienne, a royal messenger from the heart of the Dauphiné, in the small military escort that Baudricourt finally assigned to Jehanne. Someone in the dauphin's innermost circles must have sent Vienne to Vaucouleurs with orders to bring her back to Chinon for personal interrogation. And who more likely than Yolande of Aragon, friend and patron of female visionaries, mother-in-law of the dauphin, and one of the most powerful people at the royal court? She was the natural person to whom Baudricourt would write concerning Jehanne d'Arc.[26]

The inhabitants of Vaucouleurs rallied round Jehanne to provide her with a suit of male clothing, specially made for her so that she could travel more comfortably and safely through the Burgundian lands barring her way to Chinon. The church considered it sinful to wear the clothing of the opposite sex but Saint Thomas Aquinas had ruled that there were exceptions: 'this may be done without sin due to some necessity, whether for the purpose of concealing oneself from enemies, or due to a lack of any other clothing'. Jehanne also had a recent respectable precedent in Jacqueline of Hainault, who in 1425 had dressed as a man to escape the duke of Burgundy when he put her under house arrest at Ghent.[27]

Before she left, Baudricourt gave her a sword and a horse and made those accompanying her swear to guide her well and safely, but his parting words were hardly encouraging: 'Go, depart and let what may happen, happen.' The little party, only seven strong, travelled mainly by night to avoid encountering English and Burgundian soldiers on the road and arrived at Chinon eleven days later. That the journey should have been without incident is surprising for, if the Bastard of Orléans is to be believed, rumours even reached him, besieged within Orléans, that 'a certain young girl, commonly called the Pucelle, had just passed through Gien and claimed to be going to the noble dauphin in order to have the siege of Orléans raised and to take the dauphin to Reims for his coronation.'[28]

Jehanne's arrival at Chinon placed the dauphin in a delicate position. If she really had been sent by God, to rebuff her would be sacrilege. On the other hand, if she were delusional or, worse still, a schismatic, a sorceress or a heretic, then he risked being tainted by association. His councillors were divided on the wisdom of allowing him to meet Jehanne but she insisted that her message was for his ears alone and a few days later she was brought into the great hall of Chinon castle, which was packed with courtiers and soldiers, and picked the dauphin out from the crowd. Raoul de Gaucourt later testified that he witnessed this momentous meeting: 'he saw her when she presented herself before the king's majesty with great humility and simplicity, like a poor little shepherdess; and he heard her say the following words in this way: "Most illustrious lord dauphin, I come, and am sent, from God to give assistance to you and the kingdom."'[29]

Whether the dauphin actually wanted that assistance was debatable. His position in the spring of 1429 was nothing like as calamitous as Jehanne d'Arc's cheerleaders have claimed. The greater part of southern France was still in his hands; the truces with the duchy and county of Burgundy were holding and offered the prospect of a negotiated peace. Neither of Jehanne's stated objectives was high on his agenda: the loss of Orléans to the English would be a blow, but not a catastrophe, and a coronation at Reims, though desirable, was not essential. He was, however, temperamentally drawn to those who said they could predict the future. Senior clergymen had already had cause to rebuke him for his reliance on astrology and some years earlier he had received Jehan de Gand, who had prophesied the birth of his heir and the expulsion of the English.[30]

The dauphin was no fool. Well aware of Jehanne d'Arc's potential to help or, conversely, to embarrass his cause, he put her to the test. Her virginity was critically important: it equated her with the saints and gave her a moral authority denied to married daughters of Eve. She deliberately drew attention to it by calling herself 'La Pucelle', the maid or virgin, perhaps initially because it explicitly identified her as the virgin of the prophecy, though it also asserted her femininity in contrast to her male garb and the male role to which she aspired. A physical examination carried out by Yolande of Aragon and her ladies proved that Jehanne was indeed a virgin; a witness at the nullification trial claimed that she never menstruated.[31]

More difficult to prove was Jehanne's orthodoxy, especially given her male clothing and her devotion to the controversial cult of the name of Jesus, which put faith in the miraculous power of repeated invocations of Christ's name and was endorsed by the anti-pope.[32] Over the space of several weeks Jehanne was interrogated a number of times, both at Chinon by clerical members of the dauphin's council, and at Poitiers by former students and teachers of theology at the University of Paris who had fled the Burgundian coup of 1418. No record exists of any formal doctrinal examination but both groups of 'theologians' had good political reasons for endorsing Jehanne. A document allegedly summarising their conclusions was circulated for propaganda purposes by the dauphin, but it was notably cautious in its endorsement. There was no mention of her voices. It confirmed that 'no evil is to be found in her, only goodness, humility, virginity, devotion, honesty and simplicity', and suggested that 'in light of her constancy and her perseverance in her purpose, and her insistent requests to go to Orléans, in order to show the sign of divine aid there', she should be allowed to do so. In other words, if she successfully raised the siege of Orléans, then her mission was demonstrably divinely inspired: a particularly convenient conclusion if, as seems likely, the document was drawn up after the event.[33]

Jehanne's arrival at Chinon could not have been more opportune for the court faction, headed by Yolande of Aragon and her two sons, which was opposed to any accommodation with the duke of Burgundy and wanted decisive military action. Those in favour of reconciliation with Burgundy, led by Georges de la Trémoïlle and Regnault de Chartres, archbishop of Reims, were in the ascendancy and had just begun an attempt to detach the duke from his English alliance. Poton de Xaintrailles had led a delegation, including representatives of the city of Orléans, to the duke with a proposition: if the siege was raised they would

deliver the city into his hands and allow him to appoint its governors. Effective control would therefore lie with him, but the city
revenues would be divided equally between Charles d'Orléans
and Henry VI. Ever keen to acquire more lands, Burgundy
accepted, only to be denied his prize by Bedford, who insisted
that the Treaty of Troyes had decreed that all conquests were to
become crown lands. Burgundy retaliated by withdrawing his
troops from the siege.[34]

Cautious to the last, the dauphin waited to learn that these
negotiations had failed and Burgundy had decided to withdraw
before unleashing Jehanne on Orléans.[35]

CHAPTER EIGHT

The Siege of Orléans

In the last week of April 1429 Jehanne d'Arc set out from Blois at the head of an armed convoy of several thousand men escorting wagons laden with supplies for the relief of Orléans. It must have been an extraordinary sight, calculated to inspire her own troops and strike terror into the English. In front of the column walked a group of priests under a standard painted with the image of Christ crucified, which had been made for them on Jehanne's instructions: as they walked they sang the great ninth-century invocation to the Holy Spirit, '*Veni creator spiritus*', a hymn more usually associated with the coronation of popes and kings. In recent memory only Henry V, who also believed God was on his side, had given the clergy such a prominent role in his military campaigns.[1]

Behind them came the Pucelle herself, riding on a charger. Slight but unmistakably feminine in figure, with her hair cropped in the unflattering above-the-ears pudding-bowl style favoured by gentlemen of the time, she wore a suit of plate armour made for her at Tours, on the dauphin's orders, at a cost of 100*l.t.* (£5833). She carried in her hand her white standard which, as her voices had commanded, depicted Christ in judgement, one hand holding the world and the other blessing the lily of France, proffered to him by angels on either side, and emblazoned with the sacred names 'Jhesus Maria'.[2]

At her waist she bore the sword of Charlemagne's grandfather which her voices had told her would be found behind the altar of the chapel at Sainte-Catherine-de-Fierbois. The chapel had been founded by Charles Martel as an act of thanksgiving for his crushing defeat of Muslim invaders at the battle of Tours in 732 and had become a popular place of pilgrimage, especially for wounded soldiers. Jehanne, prompted by her devotion to Saint Catherine, had visited the chapel on her way to Chinon in February 1429, attending masses and staying in the hospital and almshouses for pilgrims built in 1400 by Marshal Boucicaut, who had been captured at Agincourt and died a prisoner in England in 1421. She had not then asked for the sword but, after receiving the dauphin's seal of approval for her mission, she sent word to the clergy of the chapel telling them where they could find it and asking them to give it to her.

It is unclear whether the monks already knew of the legend that Charles Martel had also donated his sword or indeed that it was missing, but the sequence of events, together with Jehanne's curious choice of an armourer as messenger and the fact that she had to describe the sword, with its five engraved crosses, so that it could be identified, all suggest that its miraculous discovery owed more to human intervention than divine. The magical uniting of a sword with its destined owner was, after all, a commonplace of medieval chivalric literature. Charles Martel's sword was not Excalibur, but it had been sanctified in a Christian victory over Muslims and was therefore the ideal weapon for another saviour of France to wield against impious invaders. The discovery was especially opportune as the more evocative alleged sword of Charlemagne, which had been used in the French coronation rites at Reims since 1270, was in English hands at the abbey of Saint-Denis, near Paris.[3]

Whatever the truth of the story, it was rapidly circulated, adding considerably to the Pucelle's reputation as a prophetess. Rumours that her own coming had been foretold were also assiduously cultivated by Armagnac propagandists, even to the extent of rewriting one of the typically obscure prophecies attributed to Merlin to make it explicitly fit Jehanne's mission.[4] That the dauphin ordered and paid for her armour to be made by his master-armourer also suggests a deliberate attempt to identify her with the armour-wearing Pucelle foretold by Marie Robine, especially as the initiative to adopt armour, rather than simply male clothing, does not appear to have come from Jehanne herself.[5]

Jehanne also played an active part in the creation of her own legend. On 22 March, 'the Tuesday of Holy Week', she dictated a letter to the English. It began with her trademark invocation '+Jesus Maria+', and continued:

> King of England, and you, Duke of Bedford, who call yourself Regent of the kingdom of France; you, William de la Pole, Earl of Suffolk; John Lord Talbot; and you, Thomas Lord Scales, who call yourselves lieutenants of the said Duke of Bedford, make satisfaction to the King of Heaven; surrender to the Pucelle, who has been sent here by God, the King of Heaven, the keys of all the good towns that you have taken and violated in France . . . And you too, archers, companions-at-arms, gentlemen and others who are before the town of Orléans, go back to your own country, by God. And if you do not do this, await news of the Pucelle who will come to see you shortly, to your very great harm. King of England, if you do not do this, I am commander of war, and in whatever place I come upon your men in France, I will make them leave, whether they wish to or not. And if they do not wish to obey, I will have them all killed; I have been sent here by God, the King of Heaven, to drive you out of all France, body for body. And if they wish to obey, I will show them mercy.[6]

Jehanne always insisted that she had personally dictated this and all her letters, though before being sent they were shown 'to certain men among her party'. It was also circulated far afield, appearing in French, Burgundian and German chronicles (though not in English ones), and a copy was produced by her judges at Jehanne's trial in Rouen.[7]

Evidently the dauphin had put the full weight of his propaganda machine behind the Pucelle. Was it effective? Certainly, and most importantly it seems to have convinced the men she led to Orléans and beyond. In the time she spent at Blois preparing for the expedition she mixed freely with the troops and had no qualms about reproving them for their sins 'because God would then allow the war to be lost on account of the[se] sins'. Just like Henry V, she tried to drive prostitutes away from the army, even chasing one off with a drawn sword which broke as she did so. She was also 'very irritated' when she heard the men-at-arms swear and 'reprimanded them vehemently', regardless of rank. She even tamed both the duke of Alençon, who 'often' blasphemed, and, more remarkably, La Hire, 'who was accustomed to use many oaths and to use God's name in vain'; Alençon admitted that, after being rebuked, he curbed his tongue altogether in her presence and La Hire, who could not, was persuaded to swear on his staff of office instead.[8]

La Hire seems to have undergone something of a transformation under Jehanne's tutelage. The Gascon's most famous prayer hitherto had been 'God, I pray that you will do today for La Hire as much as you would wish La Hire to do for you, if he were God and you were La Hire'; now, 'at the instigation and admonition' of the Pucelle, he was actually persuaded to go to confession and encouraged those in his company to do likewise. It was perhaps no wonder that, as one witness later declared, the ordinary soldiers 'regarded her as a saint, because she bore herself so well in the army, in words and in deeds, following God, so that no one could reproach her'. [9]

Fighting under a saint's command and working with her were two entirely different matters, as the Armagnac captains were soon to discover. Jehanne had been expecting to launch an immediate attack on Talbot as soon as she arrived at Orléans, and fight her way into the city; the Bastard of Orléans, Gaucourt, La Hire and Loré had already decided that their forces were too small to take on the English army and therefore chose a 'better and safer' course of action. Travelling along the south bank of the Loire, they went six miles beyond Orléans to meet the Bastard at Chécy, where boats were waiting to transfer the supplies into the city. Only one English stronghold, the bastille of Saint-Loup, stood on this side of Orléans, and its attention was diverted by a pre-planned sortie from the city. Jehanne, however, was furious. 'You thought to deceive me,' she stormed at the Bastard, 'and you are the more deceived yourselves, because I bring you better help than has ever been given to any soldier or city, the help of the King of Heaven.' At that moment, the Bastard later testified, the wind miraculously changed direction, enabling the boats, now laden with supplies, to sail unhindered into Orléans.[10]

This was still not enough to persuade such experienced military leaders to give way to Jehanne's demands. When she refused to enter the city without her soldiers, who were 'confessed, penitent and right-minded', her captains mutually agreed to leave her alone at Orléans and go back to Blois. There they could gather reinforcements, cross the Loire and return on the north bank ready to take on the English and raise the siege. Jehanne clearly did not understand that the benefit of the supplies would have been lost if the army bringing them had entered the town and become reliant on them too. Nor had she realised that she was only escorting a supply convoy, not bringing an army, to the relief of Orléans.[11] Her role, the dauphin's advisers had already decided, would be as a figurehead to rally the city until that relieving army arrived.

Pre-empted by, and excluded from, this decision, Jehanne had little choice but to enter Orléans as the Bastard urged. On the evening of 29 April 1429, accompanied only by a small group, including the Bastard himself and La Hire, she sailed across the Loire and rode into the city on a white horse, fully armed and with her white standard flying. Her reputation had gone before her and the crowds went wild with excitement, 'rejoicing as much as if they had seen God descend among them'. Convinced that their deliverer had come, they pressed forward to touch her, and even her horse, as if they were sacred relics. In the crush a torch-bearer accidentally set fire to a pennant, providing Jehanne with the opportunity to demonstrate her horsemanship by spurring forward to extinguish it, 'as if she had extensive military expertise; the men-at-arms considered this a great marvel'.[12]

The next day, eager for action, Jehanne went to see the Bastard and was greatly put out to learn 'it had been decided not to stage an assault that day'. Her annoyance can only have increased on learning that La Hire had led a sortie which briefly captured the 'Paris' boulevard until English reinforcements drove him off. Jehanne had to content herself with trading verbal insults with the English, threatening to drive them out and being called in reply 'cow-herd', 'witch' and 'whore'.[13]

Such unimaginative abuse at least demonstrates that they knew who she was, but there is nothing to suggest, as the French later claimed, that her arrival immediately caused widespread panic and desertion among the English. On 15 April the council in England had received letters from Bedford, urging the recruitment of two hundred men-at-arms and twelve hundred archers to replace those from the earl of Salisbury's retinue who had abandoned the siege at Orléans.[14] This might be seen as evidence of a mass desertion, but it should be emphasised that this was the normal recruiting season for a new expedition to France and that the earl's men had been contracted to serve only until December 1428: they were under no obligation to stay beyond that date and though some may have done so, the indications are that the siege was scaled back for the winter, as was normal practice. Their 'abandonment' was therefore unlikely to have been desertion through fear of the Pucelle.

Bedford needed reinforcements from England because he could not spare soldiers from Normandy. His forces there were fully committed to a new blockade of Mont-Saint-Michel, for which both the estates-general and the clergy had again granted heavy taxes. John Harpeley, the *bailli* of the Cotentin, had spent the winter building a new bastille at Genêts, directly opposite the island on the northern coast of the bay, and it was now garrisoned with twenty men-at-arms and one hundred mounted

archers. On the same day that the English council received
Bedford's request the regent authorised the French treasury to
send money to England to hire men and ships for the blockade
of Mont-Saint-Michel.[15]

Though Bedford's long-laid plans were focused on the reduction of Mont-Saint-Michel, he had not lost sight of the problems
at Orléans. Despite his initial misgivings, he had personally contributed 117,000*l.t.* (£6.83m) to ensure its successful conclusion
but he could not tighten the siege without more men.[16] The lack
of English manpower, particularly after the departure of the
Burgundians, had already allowed the Bastard to slip in and out
of the city several times, most notably to fetch Jehanne. On 4
May 1429 the second detachment of the relieving army arrived
at Orléans. Its approach had been observed the night before by
watchmen placed in the city bell-towers, so the English, who had
their own scouts and watch, must have known that it was on its
way. Yet they allowed the column to pass unchallenged and
more supplies to enter the city. French sources attributed this to
the Pucelle's divine protection but it suggests that the besiegers
were too stretched to mount an attack.[17]

Later that day, bolstered by this success, the Orléannais forces
made a sortie against the bastille of Saint-Loup, the isolated
church-based fortress on the eastern side of the city. Again
Jehanne knew nothing of this until she was roused from her bed
by the cries of the townsmen that they were being defeated.
Jehanne armed, seized her standard, took a horse from a page
boy in the street and rode out of the Burgundy gate, just in time
to rally the troops who had been repulsed with many casualties.
Her appearance at this critical moment put fresh heart into the
assault, the fortress was overwhelmed and the 150 or so men of
its garrison were either killed or captured. There could be no
doubting the Pucelle's contribution to the first victory of the
Orléans campaign, though the fact that another well-organised
and well-timed sortie prevented Talbot sending reinforcements
to the bastille was just as important.[18]

The following day there was a suspension of hostilities
because it was the Feast of the Ascension. While the Bastard,

Gaucourt, La Hire, Xaintrailles, Loré and other captains held a council to decide their next move, Jehanne wrote another letter to the English:

> You men of England, who have no right in this kingdom of France, the King of Heaven orders and commands you through me, Jehanne the Pucelle, to abandon your strongholds and go back to your own country. If not, I will make a war cry that will be remembered forever. And I am writing this to you for the third and final time. I will not write anything further.
> Jesus Maria.
> Jehanne the Pucelle.

Unable to entrust the letter to her herald, Guienne, who had been taken prisoner by the English when delivering the previous one, she had it tied to an arrow and fired by an archer into the English camp.[19]

With Saint-Loup captured and the eastern side of the city secured, the next logical strategic step was to clear the south bank of the Loire and retake the bridge. The English had two bastilles on this side of the river: the fortified church of the Augustins, which they had rebuilt opposite the Tourelles, and Saint-Jean-le-Blanc, half a mile to the east. Early in the morning of 6 May the Orléannais crossed to an island in the Loire and made a pontoon to the southern shore by lashing two boats together. By this means they were able to make a concerted advance on Saint-Jean-le-Blanc, only to discover that it had been abandoned by the English, who had retreated to the greater security of the Augustins.

Rather than risk assaulting the combined garrisons in this much stronger fortress, the captains decided to place Gaucourt and the cream of their forces as a garrison in Saint-Jean-le-Blanc, and withdraw the rest back to Orléans. Gaucourt had orders to ensure an orderly retreat and prevent an attack by the English. As he stood guard at the gates he was harangued by Jehanne, who told him that the troops all wanted to attack the Augustins and that he was a 'bad man' for trying to prevent it. 'Whether you wish it or not, the men-at-arms will come, and they will win as they have won before.' Jehanne and La Hire (who could be equally rash) then mounted their horses and rode with couched lances towards the English who had begun to emerge from the Augustins to attack the retreating Orléannais. Their example spurred on the rest of their troops to follow, the English were beaten back and the Augustins taken by assault.[20]

The victorious forces camped there overnight and early the next morning began an assault on the boulevard before the Tourelles. Jehanne said at her trial that she was the first to place a scaling ladder against the ramparts, an action that, with her standard, made her an obvious target for the English archers. An arrow struck her between the neck and shoulder, passing cleanly through her body, so that the deadly arrowhead was not lodged in her flesh.[21] According to her confessor, Brother Jean Pasquerel, some of the soldiers wanted to perform an incantation over the wound, but she refused, saying she would prefer to die rather than offend God by such a sin. Pasquerel was a particularly partisan witness at the nullification trial: he had a strong personal interest in securing recognition that her mission was indeed divinely inspired and in overthrowing Jehanne's conviction for heresy and sorcery, which reflected badly on his spiritual guidance.

Nevertheless, there was a fine line between orthodoxy and heresy, and medieval soldiers often did use 'enchantments' to protect them in battle. Many of them inscribed 'Jesus of Nazareth' or his monogram 'IHS' at vulnerable points in their armour, especially their helms, to ward off fatal blows. The Charlemagne prayer, which repeatedly invoked the cross as a charm against sudden death, was also very popular among soldiers, including Talbot, who added it to his personal Book of Hours. Given Jehanne's own regular use of the sacred names, it does not seem likely that she would have refused what her confessor called an 'incantation' on her behalf.[22]

With or without such aid, Jehanne was soon back in the thick of the battle, urging on the men as they tried to take the boulevard in fierce hand-to-hand fighting which lasted until evening. The Bastard later admitted that he was about to give the order to withdraw, when Jehanne begged him to wait, retired to pray for a few minutes, then returned and set her standard on the edge of the ditch. Inspired to a last effort by this action, a final surge gave the Orléannais the victory. The English were pushed back towards the Tourelles but, as they retreated, the drawbridge broke beneath them and, weighed down by their heavy armour, they drowned in the Loire. Among those who were killed was the captain of the garrison, Sir William Glasdale, *bailli* of Alençon and a veteran of Cravant and Verneuil. This gave Jehanne's supporters considerable satisfaction as he had been 'the one who spoke most offensively, dishonourably and scornfully to the Pucelle'.[23]

The loss of the Tourelles and with it control of the bridge over the Loire was the last straw for the English. They had lost between six and eight hundred men and their depleted forces could no longer maintain the siege. The next morning, 8 May 1429, Suffolk, Talbot and Scales gathered their remaining forces and withdrew to their fortresses along the Loire, leaving behind the cannon and artillery which were too cumbersome to take with them.[24]

Jehanne had triumphantly fulfilled the first part of her mission but when the dauphin wrote to inform the major towns of 'the virtuous deeds and wondrous things' performed by his soldiers, he mentioned her just once, and then only to say that she 'has always been present at the accomplishment of all of these deeds'. A few days later he granted her an interview during which she urged him 'very insistently and frequently' to delay no longer but march to Reims for his coronation. Charles gave her a fine suit of clothes as an expression of his gratitude, but he would not be rushed into a rash decision. Reims lay over 150 miles to the north-east, in the heart of Anglo-Burgundian Champagne. Initially at least, it made more strategic sense to capitalise on the relief of Orléans by reclaiming the Loire.[25]

For a month Jehanne was forced to kick her heels while men, equipment and supplies were raised for the new campaigning season. Since the dauphin declined to lead the army personally, he gave the overall command to the twenty-year-old duke of Alençon. This was a curious choice. Although Alençon could perhaps claim the office of right, as the premier duke, he had played no part in the relief of Orléans and had little military experience, having spent several years as a prisoner of the English after Verneuil. He was, however, a patron of astrologers, dabbler in necromancy and one of the Pucelle's most ardent supporters. She could command him (unlike the Bastard of Orléans or Raoul de Gaucourt) at will.

On 11 June 1429 Alençon, with Jehanne at his side and an army several thousand strong, laid siege to Jargeau, a small walled town with a fortified bridge over the Loire, eleven miles east of Orléans. Having taken the suburbs easily, they set up their guns and the following day began a bombardment which soon brought down the largest tower. The earl of Suffolk, who had retreated to Jargeau after withdrawing from Orléans, now offered to surrender the town in fifteen days unless relieved in the meantime. Suffolk must have been aware that an English army commanded by Fastolf was on its way from Paris and hoped that it would arrive in time to save him. Nevertheless, his terms were refused. Ostensibly this was because he had negotiated with La Hire rather than Alençon himself, but such a refusal was a breach of chivalric convention and the normal practice of war. A second attempt by Suffolk to negotiate a surrender during the assault that followed was also ignored because, Alençon implausibly claimed later, 'no one heard'.[26]

The refusal to allow a negotiated surrender can perhaps be attributed to the Pucelle. There is no doubt that she wanted a fight. Unlike the professional soldiers, she was unencumbered by the baggage of the chivalric code and, with the moral authority of the divinely chosen, it seems she was able to persuade the duke to do as she wished. The slaughter of prisoners that followed the assault, which was also against the laws of war, since they posed no threat to the victors, may also perhaps be attributed to Jehanne's enthusiasm for the utter destruction of the enemy. Several hundred English were killed in the assault, including the captain of Jargeau, Sir Henry Biset, and Suffolk's brother, Alexander. Another brother, Sir John de la Pole, was captured, as was Suffolk himself. Before he surrendered, the earl insisted on knighting his captor to avoid the humiliation of being taken prisoner and having to give his faith to a man of lesser rank. (Such punctiliousness had not prevented him fathering a daughter on a French nun, Malyne de Cay, the night before his surrender.)[27]

Having captured Jargeau, the Armagnac army now marched west of Orléans to take Beaugency-sur-Loire. On the way they passed the English stronghold of Meung, taking the bridge but bypassing the massive fortress where Talbot and Scales had made their headquarters. On 15 June 1429 they laid siege to Beaugency, where Talbot's lieutenant, Matthew Gough, was in command. Gough's exploits in France made him feared and renowned in equal measure. The son of a Welsh bailiff, he had fought at Cravant and Verneuil, captured the Savoyard soldier of fortune, the Bastard of Baume, and in 1427 distinguished himself in the recapture of Le Mans, where he had coolly taken a break from the fighting to fortify himself with some bread and wine. With him was Sir Richard Gethin, another veteran of Cravant and Verneuil, who, like Gough, was a Welshman who had become a career soldier in France.[28]

The day after the siege began Arthur de Richemont arrived unexpectedly with some twelve hundred troops. Two years earlier he had been banished as a result of the factional quarrels that regularly tore apart the dauphin's court. That sentence of banishment had not been revoked and Richemont had defied it to come unbidden from Brittany to offer his aid in the campaign. Both he and the Pucelle were protégés of Yolande of Aragon, suggesting that the duchess may have had a hand in bringing together these two powerful advocates of aggressive war against the English, but his arrival caused consternation among the captains gathered at Beaugency, who were unsure whether to risk the dauphin's anger by accepting his help. No doubt the opportune announcement by La Hire's scouts that an English army, four thousand strong, had been sighted near Meung and was bearing down on Beaugency was a factor in their decision to do so.[29]

The knowledge that relief was so close was denied to Gough, who was convinced by the arrival of Richemont's troops that further resistance was useless. In return for being allowed to evacuate his men he agreed to surrender on 18 June and not to engage in combat for ten days afterwards. An hour after the garrison marched out of Beaugency news arrived in the Armagnac camp that the English army had withdrawn from Meung and was retiring northwards towards Paris. Alençon may have dithered, but Richemont, La Hire, Xaintrailles and Loré did not need Jehanne's encouragement to decide that they should set off immediately in pursuit.

Their unusual unity of purpose was in strong contrast to the divisions that bedevilled the English army. Fastolf was in nominal command, having been sent by Bedford from Paris with three thousand men to relieve the Loire towns, but he had joined forces with Talbot and the remnants of the army which had besieged Orléans. Fastolf was instinctively cautious and reluctant to risk a battle against numerically superior forces; the more impulsive Talbot, who had rapidly built a successful career upon daring initiatives, wanted an all-out strike to relieve Beaugency. 'If he had only his own men and those who were willing to follow him,' he declared, 'he would go and fight the enemy with the help of God and Saint George.' It was only when news came through that Beaugency had capitulated that Talbot reluctantly conceded to Fastolf's demand for a managed retreat.

On the day of the surrender, 18 June 1429, the English had only reached the village of Patay, fifteen miles north-west of Orléans, when they learned that the Armagnac forces were hot on their trail. There was nothing for it but to stand and fight. Fastolf drew up his men in a defensive position on a ridge while Talbot prepared an archer ambush from a flanking position but then, apparently dissatisfied with this first choice, moved his men further back. Before the archers had time to hammer in their defensive stakes, La Hire and the heavily armed cavalry of the vanguard were upon them. Caught by surprise, they were overwhelmed and slaughtered, without having had the chance to unleash their usual deadly volleys of arrows. Unimpeded, the cavalry then hurtled on to the ridge, crushing all who stood in their path and pursuing those who fled in the rout that followed. Over two thousand were killed and every one of the senior English captains was captured, apart from Fastolf, who alone had remained on horseback and was able to escape from the carnage with a portion of his men. They fled to the nearest English garrison at Janville, fifteen miles away, only to discover that the citizens had overpowered their English captain and shut the gates against them. It was after midnight before the exhausted survivors, including the Burgundian chronicler Jehan Waurin, found shelter at Étampes, almost forty miles from the battlefield.[30]

Patay was a disaster to outrank any other English defeat since Baugé and its consequences were much more far-reaching. Fastolf was temporarily stripped of the Order of the Garter while an inquiry was held into his conduct. Though he was apparently cleared, since he was restored to membership, he would never be able fully to shake off the charges that he was a 'fugitive knight' and guilty of cowardice, 'the worst accusation that can be made against a knight'.[31]

More seriously for the fate of the English kingdom of France, some of its most able defenders were now prisoners in French hands. Scales would appear to have been freed fairly quickly but Talbot would not be released until the spring of 1433 and then only after paying a huge ransom and being exchanged for his captor, Xaintrailles, who had himself been captured in August 1431. Sir Thomas Rempston, an eminent captain but one of the poorest knights in Nottinghamshire, spent seven years in 'hard and strait prison' because he could not raise his 18,000 écus (£1.31m) ransom.[32]

Sir Walter Hungerford died in February 1433, just as the final instalment of his ransom was paid by his family. A court case over the rights to his ransom, heard before the parlement of Poitiers in 1432, reveals the remarkable fact that his captor was Philip Gough, a relative of Matthew Gough. In 1427 he had been one of the leaders of a band of thirty archers from the English garrison of Sainte-Suzanne who had surprised the Armagnac castle of St-Laurent-des-Mortiers and taken its captain captive. Yet just two years later he was fighting at Patay in Alençon's company and making his fortune by taking five English prisoners, including Hungerford. Whether he had changed sides for purely mercenary motives or because he had himself been captured and, unable to pay his ransom, had agreed to serve the enemy, remains a mystery.[33]

There is no question but that the English defeat at Patay was a far more significant event, both militarily and historically, than the relief of Orléans. The English army was annihilated and its most important captains captured, leaving the way open for Jehanne to fulfil the second part of her mission, the coronation of the dauphin at Reims. The English failure to take Orléans, on the other hand, was relatively unimportant: as the several abortive attempts to take Mont-Saint-Michel had shown, such frustrations were not uncommon and were not in themselves catastrophic.

Yet the relief of Orléans has entered popular mythology in a way that the victory at Patay has not, for the simple reason that the Pucelle played no part in the battle. Patay was La Hire's triumph, not the Pucelle's. For the beleaguered citizens of Orléans, however, she was the heroine who had saved them, not just from the English but also from the dauphin's apathy. She had fought their corner and they would fight hers. Within six years there was a 'Mystery' or play of the siege: composed in part, and underwritten financially, by Gilles de Rais,[34] a marshal of France who had fought in Jehanne's company, it celebrated her role and was performed annually to commemorate the relief of the city. The citizens also commissioned a journal recounting the siege to celebrate the nullification of the verdict against Jehanne and campaigned tirelessly for her canonisation. It was their efforts which ensured that the names of the Pucelle and their city would go down in history as for ever linked and that the relief of Orléans would be remembered as an iconic moment in French history.[35]

CHAPTER NINE

A New King of France

On the same day that the battle of Patay was lost the council in England granted Cardinal Beaufort permission to
recruit 500 men-at-arms and 2500 archers. The councillors were
so out of touch with the pace of events in France that this was
not a belated response to Bedford's repeated requests for aid, but
a new initiative to raise an army for the cardinal to lead on a
crusade against the Hussite heretics of Bohemia.[1]

As a result troops were already assembling at the southern
ports when news of Patay arrived, and Beaufort was faced with
the unenviable choice of betraying either his papal commission
or his family and country. Dynastic loyalty proving stronger, he
agreed to divert his army to France, thereby forfeiting papal
favour and with it any chance of taking the place on the world
stage he had schemed and worked so long to achieve. The council agreed to take over financial responsibility for the army,
which was mobilised so swiftly that, on 25 July 1429, just five
weeks after Patay, it marched into Paris with the cardinal at its
head.[2]

Galvanised by the successes of his army, and goaded by
Jehanne, the dauphin had finally been persuaded to take to the

field in person. Though some of his advisers had argued for a strike into Normandy, Jehanne's determination to go to Reims overrode all their objections. The dauphin issued the usual summons to all the nobility and major towns to attend his coronation 'on pain of forfeiture of body and goods' while the Pucelle ordered all 'good and loyal Frenchmen . . . to be ready to come to the consecration of the gentle King Charles at Reims, where we shall shortly be; and come before us when you hear that we are approaching'.[3]

The march to Reims turned into something of a triumphal progress. With no hope of a relieving army coming to their rescue, terrified of Armagnac reprisals and mesmerised by the Pucelle's reputation, the Burgundian towns needed little persuasion to make their submission. Only Troyes, where the treaty laying the foundations of the Anglo-Burgundian alliance had been signed in 1420, made a half-hearted attempt at resistance. As the enemy approached, the townsmen sent a Franciscan friar to meet Jehanne, 'saying that they questioned whether [she] was not a thing sent from God'. Brother Richard had recently been expelled from the Faculty of Theology at the University of Paris for preaching that the Antichrist had been born, the end of the world was at hand and that the year 1430 'would see the greatest wonders that had ever happened'. His five- and six-hour sermons had daily attracted a crowd of six thousand in Paris, whipping up a frenzy of weeping and penitence, but their potentially subversive nature had resulted in his expulsion by the city authorities. Now, as he approached Jehanne, he made the sign of the cross and sprinkled holy water, fearing that she was the devil incarnate. He was soon won over to the extent that he attached himself to her entourage and followed her in the months to come.[4]

On 16 July 1429 the dauphin was welcomed into the city of Reims. The Burgundian garrison had withdrawn, the townsmen had opened the gates and the crowds lined the streets to greet him with cries of 'Noël!' The next day he made his way to the cathedral of Notre Dame, where he was knighted by the duke of Alençon and crowned Charles VII, king of France, by Regnault de Chartres, archbishop of Reims and chancellor of France. He was unable to wear the traditional coronation regalia, including the crown, because they were in English hands at the abbey of Saint-Denis, near Paris. He was, however, anointed with the holy oil which, according to legend, an angel in the form of a dove had brought to Saint-Rémi so that he could baptise Clovis: the phial containing the oil was preserved in the abbey of Saint-Rémi at Reims. The significance of the anointing was that it was a holy sacrament of the church, literally making the king God's anointed, and conferring the ability to cure scrofula. Only a few days later Charles would publicly demonstrate his new status by making the customary pilgrimage to Saint-Marcoul-de-Corbény to touch for the king's evil, as it was popularly known.[5]

Jehanne and her precious standard were accorded a place of honour at the altar in the cathedral among the nobles of church and state, the royal captains, councillors and officials who witnessed the coronation. When she was asked at her trial why her standard had been preferred above those of the other captains, she replied, 'It had borne the burden, it was quite right that it receive the honour.' Not all of the twelve lay and ecclesiastical peers customarily summoned to attend were present, the most notable absentee being the duke of Burgundy. Also absent was Arthur de Richemont, who as constable of France should have played an important role in the ceremony, but, despite his role at Patay, his banishment had not yet been revoked and he was excluded on the new king's orders. Two people were present who could never have imagined that they would ever attend the coronation of 'the most Christian king'. The Reims account books reveal that the Pucelle's parents were there and that they were provided with accommodation in an inn at the city's expense. What they made of their daughter's triumph can only be guessed.[6]

The coronation was an emotional moment for all those who had fought for almost a decade to overturn the Treaty of Troyes: the disinherited heir had reclaimed his birthright, increasing the pressure on those whose loyalties were ambivalent to acknowledge him as their duly crowned king. For the followers of

Jehanne it proved that her mission was divinely inspired: she had done the impossible and fulfilled her second mission. Now they all looked to her to achieve the third: to drive the English out of France.

On the very day of the coronation Jehanne dictated a letter to the duke of Burgundy reproaching him for not responding to her summons to attend the ceremony and urging him to make 'a firm and lasting peace' with Charles VII:

> Prince of Burgundy, I pray, beg, and very humbly request, rather than demand, that you no longer wage war on the holy kingdom of France, and swiftly and in a short time withdraw your people who are in some places and fortresses in this holy kingdom . . . And I would have you know . . . that you will not win any battle against loyal Frenchmen, and that all those who wage war against the holy kingdom of France, wage war against King Jesus, King of Heaven and of all the world.[7]

This was a change from the usual belligerent tone of Jehanne's letters and it reflected the fact that, far from taking advantage of the momentum she had created to launch an attack, Charles and his advisers had decided to use the coronation to make another attempt to detach the duke of Burgundy from his English alliance. They have been almost universally criticised for this, by both contemporaries and historians, who condemn the negotiations as signs of indecision and weakness on Charles's part, treachery on that of Georges de la Trémoïlle (whose brother, Jean, was the duke's chamberlain and councillor) and ultimately a betrayal of the Pucelle. Viewed objectively, however, the unpalatable fact is that a final peace could not be achieved unless and until Burgundy changed allegiance. And the coronation, following so quickly on the military successes in the Loire valley, was as good a point as any to offer Burgundy the olive branch.

No one was more aware of this than Bedford. On Sunday 10 July 1429, in a carefully choreographed show of unity, Philippe of Burgundy was formally welcomed into Paris and treated to a

general procession and a sermon at Notre Dame. Later he was
escorted to the *palais*, where the leading citizens and royal officers had gathered in force, to hear the reading out of a 'charter
or letter' which recounted in detail how the duke's father, 'desir-
ing and longing for this kingdom's pacification', had humbled
himself to go to Montereau 'and there on his knees before the
dauphin he was treacherously murdered as all men know'. The
reading had the desired effect: 'there was a great uproar and
some who had been closely allied to the Armagnacs began
instead to hate and detest them.' In the face of the supernatural
hysteria surrounding the Pucelle, it was a sober and timely
reminder of the earthly origins of the Anglo-Burgundian alliance.
Whether Burgundy was a party to the reading, or had it sprung
upon him by Bedford, he had no choice but to endorse the message. Similarly, when both dukes then called for a show of hands
from all who would be loyal and true to them, the outcome was
entirely predictable.[8]

Bedford did not rely solely on propaganda to bolster his position: he also immediately ordered Burgundy to be paid 20,000*l.t.*
(£1.17m) from the revenues of Normandy to raise troops in
Burgundy, Picardy and Flanders. (The treasury auditors, relying
on protocol rather than responding to the crisis, initially refused
to approve the payment on the grounds that the Burgundian
troops could not be mustered and reviewed to prove that the
money had been properly spent. Bedford had to force it through
and pawn his own jewels as security for further payments.)[9]

Bedford had also made extensive military preparations of his
own. In Normandy the siege of Mont-Saint-Michel was suspended and the soldiers returned to their garrisons. Pontorson,
where the captured lord Scales had been captain, was demolished and its defenders reallocated to Avranches and
Tombelaine. Financial measures were also taken to provide for
the payment of soldiers' wages and extra security for castles and
the port of Harfleur. Throughout lower Normandy the *baillis*
were ordered to recruit and muster reinforcements for each garrison, the necessary numbers and ratios of men-at-arms to
archers being determined by the king's council in the duchy.[10]

In Paris a strict twenty-four-hour watch was enforced, the walls were strengthened and the ditches outside them were cleared of the rubbish that always accumulated in peacetime. Wooden barriers were erected inside and outside the city and the armoury at the Bastille was plundered for weapons. Large numbers of cannon and other artillery were mounted on the walls and one contractor alone supplied 1176 gun-stones for those on the gates. The defence of the city was committed to the sire de l'Isle-Adam, who had enjoyed enormous popular support in Paris since leading the Burgundian coup in 1418: in an important gesture of solidarity, he was appointed captain of Paris jointly by Bedford and Burgundy.[11]

The great frustration for Bedford was that he had realised the threat posed by the Pucelle almost as soon as she appeared on the scene, in particular her boast that she would take the dauphin to Reims for his coronation, which had drawn attention to the fact that his seven-year-old nephew was also as yet uncrowned and therefore unconsecrated. When Bedford wrote to the English council in April 1429 requesting reinforcements, he had also urged that Henry should be crowned and sent to France as soon as possible: a second coronation could then take place at Reims so that all the French nobility would be obliged to give their homage and fealty to the new king in person, binding them more closely to the English regime.[12]

On 16 July, the day the dauphin entered Reims, Bedford dispatched Garter king-of-arms to London with specific instructions to inform the council that the dauphin was in the field, that several places had fallen to him without a fight and that he was expected to arrive in Reims that very day, where the inhabitants would open the gates to him and he would be crowned. His coronation would, Bedford predicted, be followed by an assault on Paris. Once again Bedford pleaded that his nephew should be crowned and sent to France 'in all possible haste' with another army.[13]

As town after town offered up its keys to Charles VII – Soissons, Laon, Senlis, Compiègne, Beauvais – the Armagnacs were gradually building up a semicircle of fortified towns on the eastern side of Paris, causing panic in the city. It was Bedford's decisive action that saved the day. On 25 August he returned to Paris from Normandy, where he had been gathering his forces; with him rode Cardinal Beaufort and the 2500 Englishmen who had been diverted from the Hussite crusade, and l'Isle-Adam, with seven hundred Picards recruited by Burgundy with English money.[14]

A few days later Bedford took to the field, protecting Paris by circling round and keeping his army between the city and the advancing Armagnacs. On 7 August he was at Montereau-sur-Yonne and seized the opportunity to issue a challenge to 'Charles of Valois, who are accustomed to name yourself dauphin of Vienne, and now without cause entitle yourself king'. Since this was not just a personal invitation to choose a site for battle but a public exercise in propaganda which would be circulated round Europe, he sought to reclaim the moral high ground which Charles, with Jehanne at his side, had so effectively usurped.

The murder of Jean, duke of Burgundy, was committed 'through your fault and connivance', Bedford informed Charles. 'Because of the peace that you broke, violated and betrayed' all Frenchmen had been 'absolved and acquitted from all oaths of fealty and of subjection, as your letters patent, signed in your hand and by your seal, can clearly reveal'. Charles's treachery and duplicity were self-evident in his current campaign:

> . . . leading the simple people to believe that you are coming to give them peace and security, which is not the fact, nor can it be done by the means that you have pursued and are now following. And you are seducing and abusing ignorant people, and you are aided by superstitious and damnable persons, such as a woman of disorderly and infamous life, dressed in man's clothes, and of immoral conduct, together with an apostate and seditious mendicant friar, as we have been informed. Both of them are, according to holy scripture, abominable to God.[15]

For all his righteous appeal to the judgement of God in battle, Bedford was not prepared to risk everything on a single engagement. There were several skirmishes between outlying forces but the nearest they came to a pitched battle was on 15 August, when the two armies met at Montépilloy, five miles east of Senlis. Bedford had seen the Armagnac army approaching and placed his men in a strong defensive position between it and Senlis, with the river to their rear. Both sides expected battle the next day but overnight the English dug themselves in, surrounding their camp with stakes and ditches and setting their carts and wagons along their front. Alençon drew up his battle lines and Jehanne, who was in the van with her standard, tried to provoke the English into combat by offering to withdraw until they could put themselves into battle order. They resisted the temptation and, since their position was too strong to attack, there was stalemate. After a stand-off that lasted all day, both sides withdrew, with only some desultory skirmishing to show for their encounter.[16]

After Senlis and Beauvais made their submissions to Charles VII, Jehanne and the hawks among his councillors argued for an attack on Paris itself. Charles, however, was reluctant, possibly because he feared overreaching himself but certainly, at least in part, because he still hoped to persuade Burgundy to join him. The day after Montépilloy, Regnault de Chartres and Raoul de Gaucourt were received at Arras, charged with offering the duke spiritual reparation and financial compensation for the murder of his father, territorial concessions and the promise that the duke would not have to pay personal homage to Charles for all the lands he held in France.

These were generous terms for a peace between them, especially as most of the towns taken in the current campaign were Burgundian, but neither carrot nor stick was enough to persuade the duke to change alliance. Philippe still demanded that Charles should formally apologise for the murder and hand over the murderers, both of which he refused to do. Nevertheless, the negotiations did achieve an important step forward: a four-month truce covering all territory north of the Seine between

Honfleur at the river mouth and Nogent-sur-Seine to the east of Paris. Although it excluded all towns on the Seine, and specifically Paris, it protected Normandy from attack and left the door open for further concessions.[17]

Though not in the main arena of war, Normandy was also in turmoil, necessitating Bedford's immediate return. An Armagnac army had laid siege to Évreux, forcing it to agree to surrender on 27 August unless relieved in the meantime. Bedford hastily threw together what men he could spare, including the marines from his warship on the Seine, and, leaving Paris under l'Isle-Adam's command, dashed across country to Évreux, arriving on the very day it was due to surrender. This Herculean effort saved the town, allowing Bedford to withdraw to Vernon, which lay halfway between the capital and Rouen. From this point he was well placed to return to Paris, if need be, but also to deal with the problems in the duchy.[18]

The Cotentin peninsula had always had a high incidence of highway robberies and numerous brigands operated in the woods. The previous year major efforts had been made to improve the safety of travellers by clearing the trees and shrubs, which provided cover for robbers, from either side of the main road between Carentan and Saint-Lô. The road was still so dangerous that in August 1429 a pair of messengers had to be sent between the two towns because no one could be found who was willing to travel alone.[19]

The flat, heavily wooded terrain also lent itself to covert operations by soldiers from Mont-Saint-Michel, which had recently become more frequent because the English had not been able to renew the siege and were preoccupied elsewhere. Detachments from the garrison had raided deep into the Cotentin. Saint-Lô had been attacked several times and as its captain, the earl of Suffolk, was still an enemy prisoner, Bedford appointed in his stead a Norman lord, Raoul Tesson, with an extra company of forty archers or crossbowmen, to improve its defences.[20]

More sinister was a carefully planned raid in August 1429 in which two groups of Armagnac soldiers joined forces to launch a night attack on Carentan. They set fire to the lodgings of the gatekeepers, killed some of the guards and escaped with a large amount of booty. This might be dismissed as simple opportunism, except for the fact that in the same month Jean Burnel, the Norman *vicomte* of Carentan, was pardoned for a compromising correspondence with a member of the garrison of Mont-Saint-Michel. Burnel had accepted a safe-conduct from the garrison captain, but for fear of this coming to the knowledge of the English, he had requested that it should be kept at Mont-Saint-Michel until he sent for it, and he referred to it by a code name in his letters. Although the pardon does not detail the content of the correspondence, the implication has to be that Burnel was required to earn his safe-conduct, perhaps by betraying Carentan. That was certainly how the *bailli* interpreted it, arresting and imprisoning Burnel, and his lieutenant at Saint-Lô, and confiscating all their lands and goods.[21]

Plots to deliver towns to the Armagnacs were on the increase in this period, no doubt inspired by the Pucelle's victories and Charles VII's coronation. Again the proximity of Mont-Saint-Michel seems to have been a factor. An attempt to take Vire that year failed, though a man from Domfront, who had sold the town and castle to the enemy, advising where they could enter at night, was captured and executed. In the best tradition of medieval romance it was a wandering minstrel, Phélippot le Cat, who, inspired by ballads of the Pucelle which were already in circulation, plotted to deliver Cherbourg to the garrison of Mont-Saint-Michel and was beheaded for his pains on the day of Charles VII's coronation. In upper Normandy successful plots by their inhabitants resulted in both Étrépagny and Torcy falling into Armagnac hands.[22]

August seems to have been a significant month, for Ambroise de Loré was then apparently in touch with traitors in Rouen, though plans to take the town fell through. At the same time a group of wealthy conspirators in Louviers fled when their plot was discovered: they escaped with their lives, but their property and goods were seized and distributed to loyalists. In a bizarre twist to this story the captain of Louviers, Guillotin de Lansac, and some of his men were in Rouen to receive the garrison's overdue wages when 'certain news' arrived that the enemy was preparing to take Louviers 'by treason, assault or otherwise'. Lansac refused to leave until the wages were paid, and the treasurer despairingly noted in his accounts that he scraped together an advance of 80*l.t.* (£4667) 'because it was necessary that he should return in all haste'. An agreement signed at the end of the month arranged for Lansac to be paid the additional wages due to him for the reinforcements placed at Louviers out of the receipts from the forfeitures of the conspirators. Despite the failure of this plot, Louviers remained in English hands only until December 1429, when it was surprised and taken by La Hire.[23]

The greatest threat, however, was to Paris, the capital of the English kingdom of France. On 26 August Alençon and Jehanne had captured Saint-Denis, to the north of the city, with such ease that its townsmen would later be heavily fined for their failure to resist. With Saint-Denis as their base, they had raided right up to the gates of Paris, though Charles VII, mindful of the possibility of alliance with Burgundy, had distanced himself, quite literally, from their actions.[24]

Bedford responded to this crisis by issuing a general call to arms for the relief of Paris, backing it up with an extraordinary personal plea to his officers which, unusually, was written in English:

We pray you heartily and also charge and command you straitly, upon pain of all that you may forfeit . . . that you come unto us in all haste possible . . . And do not fail in this, as you love the preservation of this land, and as you will answer to my lord and us for it in time coming. And know for certain that it never lay in our power, since we had the regency of France, so well as it does now, both of lordships, lands and other, to reward men. The which thing we promise you faithfully to do generously to all that come to us at this time.[25]

Before the army had time to gather, the Pucelle launched her assault on Paris. She chose to do so on 8 September, the church

festival celebrating the birth of the Virgin Mary. She had 'summoned' Gilles de Rais and Raoul de Gaucourt to her assistance
and together they made a concerted attack on the Saint-Honoré
gate.

Jehanne, as always, was in the forefront of the action. The
citizen of Paris, who was probably a priest, gave a graphic
description in his journal of this 'creature in the form of a
woman, whom they called the Maid – what it was, God only
knows' standing on the edge of the moat with her standard.
'Surrender to us quickly, in Jesus' name!' she shouted to the
Parisians: 'if you don't surrender before nightfall we shall come
in by force whether you like it or not and you will all be killed.'
'Shall we, you bloody tart?' a crossbowman responded and shot
her through the leg. Another crossbowman shot her standard-
bearer through the foot and, when he lifted his visor so that he
could see to take the bolt out, he was shot between the eyes and
killed.

A constant bombardment from the Parisian walls kept the
attackers at bay and a hoped-for revolt within the city did not
take place. It was not until ten or eleven o'clock at night that the
assault ceased. Gaucourt, recognising that the day was lost, went
out under cover of darkness to rescue Jehanne from the ditch
where she had lain for hours, immobilised but her spirit untamed,
as she urged her men on; ignoring her protestations, he carried
her off to safety. The next day, though she and Alençon were desperate to resume the assault, they were forbidden to do so and
ordered back to join their king at Saint-Denis. A day later men
were sent under safe-conduct to collect their dead and the herald
who came with them stated on oath to the captain of Paris that
they had suffered at least fifteen hundred casualties, of which a
good five hundred or more were dead or mortally wounded.[26]

The failure to take Paris marked the end of Charles VII's coronation campaign. He had probably realised that such an attempt
was futile and he had no wish to break the fragile bridges he had
built with Burgundy. He therefore retreated to the kingdom of
Bourges and on 21 September 1429 he ordered his army to
disband. More importantly, the failure to take Paris both sowed

the first seeds of doubt about the Pucelle's invincibility among
her supporters and endangered her position as the messianic
heroine who would save France. She had served her purpose
but she had already fatally demonstrated that she was not only
fallible but unpredictable and uncontrollable: her future role
was already in question.[27]

Alençon may have wanted her to accompany him on a
campaign to recover his lost duchy of Anjou but Charles's
councillors, fearful of her influence over him, were now anxious to keep them apart. They wanted to keep Jehanne
occupied but their options were limited by the truces with
Burgundy. In the county of Nevers, however, there were several
royal enclaves controlled by a mercenary captain, Perrinet
Gressart, who was in the happy position of receiving wages
from both Burgundy and Bedford. Since the latter paid more
promptly and in full, Gressart was more inclined to obey
English orders than Burgundian, though he was not above
playing them off against each other when it suited him. The
only two fixed principles to which he adhered were his hatred
of the Armagnacs and, more importantly, his determination to
keep La Charité-sur-Loire, which he had captured by surprise
at Christmas 1423 and regarded as his personal fiefdom.
Dominated by a vast stone abbey built by the Cluniacs in 1059,
and surrounded by heavily fortified walls, La Charité was just
thirty miles from Bourges and controlled a major bridge over
the Loire.

Gressart had long been a thorn in the flesh of the Armagnacs,
raiding deep into their territory to pillage and levy *appâtis*,
ignoring truces and waging war for his personal gain rather than
any political cause. He had even had the audacity to blockade
Charles VII at Bourges and to take prisoner an Armagnac
embassy, led by his bitterest enemy, Georges de la Trémoïlle,
whom he had terrified by threatening to hand him over to the
English, thus securing a princely ransom of 14,000 *écus*
(£1.02m).[28]

Since Gressart's fortresses could be considered English, they
were not covered by the truces between the Armagnacs and

Burgundians and were therefore a legitimate target for attack. La Trémoïlle's half-brother, Charles d'Albret, was appointed lieutenant-general for this campaign and the Pucelle was dispatched to aid him. They began well enough, with a siege followed by an all-out assault which won Saint-Pierre-le-Moûtier, an outpost thirty miles south of La Charité held by Gressart's nephew, François de Surienne.

At the end of November 1429 they laid siege to La Charité itself. Despite Jehanne's presence, like so many before and after them, they would find the place impregnable. They attempted an assault but it was repelled. Struggling in the depths of winter, having to beg gunpowder, saltpetre, sulphur, arrows, heavy crossbows and other military supplies from neighbouring towns, and running out of money and food, they were only able to maintain the siege for a month. Just before Christmas they withdrew, 'shamefully' abandoning their huge cannon, known as bombards, which the resourceful Gressart promptly acquired. The reason why they were left behind is indicated by the fact that when Gressart made a present to the duke of Burgundy of one of them, 'the Shepherdess', a bombard from Orléans named after the Pucelle which she had also used at Jargeau, it had to be dismantled into two pieces. Even then it required a team of seven horses to pull one and twenty-nine the other, and the bridges and roads had to be strengthened as they passed. Such logistical demands could not be fulfilled when breaking up a siege.[29]

The mercenary had successfully seen off the Pucelle, whose reputation was further tarnished by this failure. Her king was not ungrateful for what she had achieved. In December 1429, for instance, he raised her to the ranks of the nobility and, in a unique homage to her sex, the grant was made hereditary in either the male or female lines. Nevertheless, for the next few months she would remain at Charles's court, excluded from his councils and possibly even his presence. Unemployed and increasingly sidelined, she chafed at her inability to return to her mission. Since her king would not allow her to fight against the English, she toyed with the idea of leading a crusade against the Hussite heretics of Bohemia. 'Like the Saracens you have

Henry V, king of England, heir and regent of France: a fifteenth-century portrait by an unknown artist. (National Portrait Gallery, London/Bridgeman Art Library)

The tomb of John the Fearless, duke of Burgundy, whose murder at Montereau by the dauphin and his supporters in 1419 prompted the Anglo-Burgundian alliance upon which the English kingdom of France was founded. The elaborate carvings, including the alabaster figures of the duke and his duchess Margaret of Bavaria, took decades to complete and the finished tomb, which had been commissioned in 1443, was not installed in the choir of the Charterhouse at Dijon until 1470.

(Musée des Beaux Arts, Dijon/Bridgeman Art Library)

The thirteenth-century choir and great nave, with its spectacular thirteenth/fifteenth-century stained glass, of the cathedral of Saints Peter and Paul at Troyes in Champagne. It was on the altar here, on 21 May 1420, that the Treaty of Troyes was sworn and signed, making Henry V the heir to Charles VI of France, and here too that he was formally betrothed to Katherine of France. (Giraudon/Bridgeman Art Library)

The dauphin, whom Jehanne d'Arc took to Reims for his coronation as Charles VII in 1429. He eventually expelled the English from northern France in 1450 and from Gascony in 1453. This life-size portrait was painted in c.1445–50 by the French portraitist and illuminator Jean Fouquet. (Giraudon/ Bridgeman Art Library)

John, duke of Bedford, regent of France 1422–35, kneeling before Saint George, patron saint of England, who wears the Garter insignia on his cloak. From the Bedford Missal, produced by French artists for Bedford and his wife Anne of Burgundy, and presented by the duchess, with her husband's permission, to Henry VI at Rouen on Christmas Eve 1430. (© University of Hull Art Collection, Humberside/Bridgeman Art Library)

Philippe, duke of Burgundy, kneels to worship at the Nativity in this centre panel of a triptych painted as an altar-piece for a church in the Flemish city of Middelburg by Roger van der Weyden in 1445–50. (Scala)

A genealogy, in the form of a fleur-de-lis, shows the royal lineages of England and France descended from Saint Louis and united in Henry VI. A copy of this genealogy was commissioned in 1423 by the duke of Bedford and hung in the cathedral of Notre Dame in Paris as part of a propaganda campaign to support his nephew's claim to the throne of France. This version is from a book of French romances and works on chivalry written and illuminated at Rouen in 1444–5; it was commissioned by John Talbot and presented to Margaret of Anjou on her marriage to Henry VI. (British Museum)

· MAY·M[...]

Wednesday 18 May 1429. Entry in the register of the *parlement* of Paris describing the raising of the siege of Orléans by Jehanne d'Arc. The clerk, Clément de Fauquembergue, has drawn a sketch of Jehanne in the margin. It is the only known representation of her made during her lifetime, but it is purely imaginary, as Fauquembergue had never seen Jehanne; note that he assumes she wore female dress and had long hair. (Giraudon/ Bridgeman Art Library)

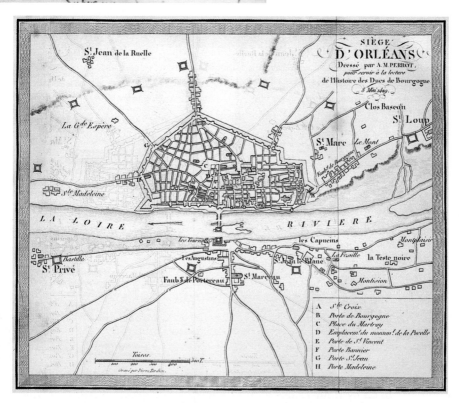

Plan of the English siege of Orléans in 1428–9. (AKG)

Jehanne d'Arc, a miniature painted in a fifteenth-century manuscript book of poems by Charles, duke of Orléans. Though painted after her death, it is the most accurate contemporary portrait of her, showing her wearing full armour and male attire and bearing her famous banner. (Archives Charmet//Bridgeman Art Library)

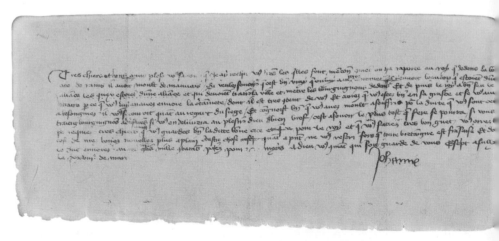

Jehanne's last letter to the people of Reims, dated 28 March 1430. The letter was dictated to a clerk, but the signature, which is in a different hand, may be Jehanne's own. (AKG)

A crossbowman from a fifteenth-century playing card. He carries a quiver by his side and a spare bolt in his hat ready for use. His crossbow is made of steel and to enable him to span it (bend it into the firing position), he uses a strap-and-roller device that can be seen tucked into his belt. The maximum range of a crossbow at this period was 370–80 yards, though the effective aim was probably only 220 yards. (Kuntshistorisches Museum, Wien)

Château Gaillard, one of the strongest fortresses in France, was built in 1197–8 by Richard I of England to defend the Norman frontier. Standing on a cliff overlooking a bend in the river Seine at Les Andelys, it dominated the countryside for miles around and was considered impregnable. When it fell to La Hire in 1430, liberating the sire de Barbazan who had been held prisoner there for ten years, its captain, Sir William Bishopton, was severely punished by the duke of Bedford. (Topfoto)

Medieval Rouen, capital of the duchy of Normandy, showing the ships on the Seine, the walls, castle and cathedral. (Granger Collection/Topfoto)

The coronation of Henry VI as king of France in Notre Dame cathedral, Paris, on 16 December 1431. From a fifteenth-century manuscript of Jehan Waurin's *Anchiennes Cronicques d'Engleterre*. (AKG)

blighted the true religion and worship', she wrote to them on 23 March 1430:

> What rage or madness consumes you? . . . As far as I am con-
> cerned, to tell you frankly, if I was not occupied with these
> English wars, I would have come to see you a long time ago.
> But if I do not learn that you have reformed yourselves, I
> might leave the English and set off against you, so that, by the
> sword if I cannot do it any other way, I may eliminate your
> mad and obscene superstition and remove either your heresy
> or your lives.[30]

It was all mere bombast. She no longer had either the means or the moral authority to make good her threats. Her usefulness was apparently at an end.

CHAPTER TEN

Capture

Bedford, assisted by his duchess and Cardinal Beaufort, had worked hard to ensure that Burgundy's dalliance with Charles VII did not mature into a closer relationship. He invited the duke to meet them in Paris and there, on 13 October 1429, after lengthy consultations with members of the university and *parlement*, Burgundy was appointed Henry VI's lieutenant in France, with authority to govern Paris and the counties to the east and south of the city. In practice this was just a recognition of the status quo but conferring the formal title was an important public recognition of the duke's importance to the alliance and to the English kingdom of France. In a sense it was an acknowledgement that it had been a mistake not to allow him to accept Orléans's offer to surrender to him. By making this concession to his pride and ambition Bedford also publicly bound him more closely to the English regime. Furthermore, it was a politically astute way of encouraging the loyalty of the Parisians, who mistakenly believed that this was an absolute division of power and the kingdom, and that Bedford would henceforth concern himself only with Normandy.[1]

In the duchy, Bedford was keeping up the pressure to ensure

that every stronghold and town was properly defended and on the alert for signs of disaffection within. The treasurer's accounts for the financial year 1428–9 reveal a threefold increase in the amount of money spent on messengers sent by the council in Rouen as a direct result of the military crisis. A messenger had to be sent to Argentan in October, for instance, to warn the lieutenant that the inhabitants were plotting to betray the town and castle to the duke of Alençon and ordering him to step up his security measures. The insecurity of the roads meant that messengers sometimes had to be sent in pairs for their own safety, travelling together or by different routes so that the letters got through. Women were often employed in this role, though their sex did not necessarily protect them: Agnès la Royne, who was regularly employed by the English, was set upon, beaten and had her letters stolen by brigands on one of her missions in 1429.[2]

The crisis also placed considerable strain on the military resources of the duchy. In August Bedford had to issue orders prohibiting any English, Welsh or other men-at-arms from going overseas because he needed all the skilled manpower he could get. In the wake of so many plots to betray towns and castles to the enemy, this had to be balanced with the need to employ only those who were trustworthy. In October, therefore, a new clause was introduced into the contracts of garrison captains prohibiting them from recruiting anyone who had previously fought for the Armagnacs or had only recently come into the king's obedience.[3]

The controller of Évreux, who was responsible for taking the daily roll-call, records the difficulties his captain faced in keeping his garrison up to strength. In just two months, January and February 1430, eighteen soldiers went absent without leave and did not return, four 'traitors' went off to join the enemy and thirteen were taken prisoner on a single day. The prisoners had their wages paid, since they had been captured in the king's service and were held for only a week, but Richard Aynsworth forfeited his month's wages because he was absent from the muster, having been imprisoned for two days by his captain for picking a quarrel with a fellow soldier.[4]

The vital importance of not only keeping garrisons fully manned but also being constantly vigilant was brought home in dramatic fashion on 24 February 1430. Château Gaillard was one of the strongest castles in France. Built by the English king Richard the Lionheart, it stood on a cliff jutting out into the Seine at Les Andelys, twenty miles north-east of Évreux. The castle could only be approached from the landward side and along a narrow strip of land which was defended by a bastion with five towers surrounded by a ditch. The great keep, with walls over sixteen feet thick, was protected by two sets of outer walls and ditches; the inner circle of walls was built in a distinctive scallop-shell form with nineteen semicircular protrusions to deflect bombardment and discourage the use of scaling ladders. Even if attackers succeeded in getting beyond the bastion and outer walls, the only entrance to the inner court faced out over the river, forcing them to run the length of the castle to gain entry.

The English captain of Château Gaillard was the highly respected and long-serving Sir William Bishopton. He and his garrison had earned unusual praise from the local *vicomte* for guarding the castle 'carefully' and for 'buying their supplies daily like simple country people, never seizing or demanding anything from the people'. The only blot on their copybook had occurred some eight years earlier, when they had caught and summarily executed a man who had been involved in the murder of their lieutenant when he was out on patrol against brigands.[5]

Perhaps because Château Gaillard's natural and man-made defences were so strong, and because the small garrison of five men-at-arms (three mounted and two on foot) plus fifteen archers had received twenty-one reinforcements in September 1429, complacency had set in. The Armagnacs had already made one attempt to take the castle by treason: a member of the garrison was imprisoned and forfeited his goods for failing to inform the captain that he had seen one of his company with letters from the enemy.[6]

La Hire, who had taken Louviers by assault a few weeks earlier, was also responsible for the capture of Château Gaillard, though it is not entirely clear whether it was betrayed to him by treason or simply taken by surprise. Two men were later executed because the castle had been captured 'through their fault, guilt and means': Colin le Franchois, who was on night-watch, and an Englishman, Thomas Surych, who had married into le Franchois's family and was absent without leave that night.[7]

William Bishopton escaped execution but he paid dearly for his 'negligence, carelessness or feeble resistance'. Bedford imprisoned him at Rouen for thirty-two weeks and only released him on compassionate grounds because he was losing his sight. To obtain his pardon Bishopton had to pay the wages of his garrison for three months out of his own pocket and a fine of 2000*l.t.* (£116,667) which, with a nice irony, was to be paid to the captain of Le Crotoy to cover the cost of that garrison's wages for six months. In addition Bishopton had to find the enormous ransom demanded by La Hire, for which his son was being held hostage, as the price of his own freedom.[8]

Bishopton's punishment was so harsh because he had lost not only an important stronghold but also one of the regent's most valuable prisoners, the sire de Barbazan, who had been held since the surrender of Melun to Henry V in 1420. La Hire had released him, but, as Bishopton and the garrison were marching out of the castle, Barbazan had recalled him and asked him formally for absolution from his obligations as a prisoner so that he was free to take up arms again. This he did to such good effect that Charles VII made him his lieutenant-general in Champagne and a short time afterwards, with the aid of a monk who let him and his men in through a postern gate, he seized Villeneuve-le-Roi from Perrinet Gressart, who narrowly escaped capture only by jumping from the walls and fleeing back to La Charité.[9]

The most damaging consequence of Barbazan's unexpected release was its timing. The English had just agreed to exchange him for Talbot, who had been captured at the battle of Patay on 18 June 1429. That deal was now no longer possible and as a result one of the most effective English captains would remain out of action for another three years.[10]

In England, in a belated response to Bedford's pleas, Henry VI was crowned king of England on 6 November 1429. The ceremony was performed at Westminster Abbey by Cardinal Beaufort and it marked the end of Gloucester's formal role as protector. He would still be chief councillor of England, but the reins of power had now, officially at least, passed to his nephew. In practice, as Henry was not quite eight years old, the council remained in control with its duties and personnel unchanged. Of the three major officers of state, John Kemp, archbishop of York, and Walter, lord Hungerford, had been appointed chancellor and treasurer respectively in 1426, while William Alnwick, bishop of Norwich, had been keeper of the privy seal since shortly after Henry V's demise. Together with Gloucester and Henry Chichele, archbishop of Canterbury, they formed the core of the council, providing experienced and able continuity of administration.[11]

In December parliament made an exceptionally large grant of direct taxation: two whole subsidies, one of which was to be collected on 14 January 1430, an unusually short period of notice, and the other on 30 December 1430. Each subsidy was payable on the value of movable goods at the customary rates of one-fifteenth in the countryside and one-tenth in the towns. Only those with movable goods worth less than 10s. were exempt from paying the tax.[12]

The purpose of these grants – the first English subsidies levied for the prosecution of the war in seven years – was to fund both an expedition to France which would retake all that had been lost since the relief of Orléans, including Reims, and the coronation, in suitable style, of Henry as king of France. In January an advance force of 3199 soldiers crossed the Channel under the command of Henry's cousin the Bastard of Clarence, and in February a further 4792 men were recruited to accompany the king. This would be the largest army sent to France during Henry VI's reign and it was unusual in two ways: the proportion of men-at-arms to archers was much higher, at one to three, than the one to five which had become the normal English practice, and the contracts of service were for a year, instead of the customary six months. Together the two forces represented England's heaviest commitment to France since the invasion of 1417.

These arrangements reflected the magnitude of the task ahead, the importance of putting on a display of wealth and power to impress Henry's French subjects and the necessity of providing him with a suitable household, court and administration. Twenty-two peers would accompany him, including the eighteen-year-old duke of York, making his first visit to the kingdom which he would later rule as the king's lieutenant-general, and three senior bishops, Bath and Wells, Norwich and Ely. More than half the indentures, or contracts of service, were made by members of the royal household, ranging from the great officers of state to minstrels, chaplains and surgeons, but John Hampton, the king's master of ordnance, also signed up to go with a company of eighty-nine, and was given £2222 17s. 11d. (£1.17m) to spend on artillery. (His purchases included two large guns, bought at Calais, one weighing 6780 pounds and the other 7022; in deference to the boy-king, the smaller one was named 'Henry'.)[13]

Every effort was also made to involve the duke of Burgundy, whose presence at the coronation would be an important rallying call to any subjects whose loyalty had wavered after the consecration of Charles VII. On 7 January 1430 Philippe married Isabella of Portugal, a significant choice since both his previous wives had been Armagnacs: Michèle (d. 1422), Charles VII's sister, and Bonne of Artois (d. 1425), whose husband had been killed at Agincourt. Isabella was a niece of Cardinal Beaufort and half-cousin of Henry VI, with whom she had spent a month in England before travelling to Flanders for her marriage. The wedding was marked with the usual extravagant feasting, pageantry and jousts in the market square of Bruges, but also a more permanent memorial in the foundation of a new order of chivalry, the Order of the Golden Fleece. Based on the English Order of the Garter, this would consist of twenty-four knights of irreproachable reputation and noble, legitimate birth drawn from the Burgundian empire.[14]

On 12 February Cardinal Beaufort, who had followed his niece to Flanders to secure the duke's military aid for the forthcoming campaign, persuaded him to sign a contract to serve the young king with fifteen hundred soldiers in return for 12,500 marks (£4.38m). A month later the county of Champagne was ceded to Burgundy and his male heirs, to give him an incentive to recover it from the Armagnacs: one of his new knights of the Golden Fleece, Hue de Lannoy, an ardent advocate of the English alliance, then drew up a convincingly argued strategy for which preparations were put in place. The execution would have to wait until the expiry of Burgundy's truces with Charles VII in April.[15]

One of the terms of those truces had been that Compiègne, which had submitted to Charles a month after his coronation, should be surrendered to Burgundy. Despite being ordered to do so, the inhabitants of the town had refused to hand it over. On the contrary they had stockpiled food and weapons and strengthened their defences in anticipation of a siege. Their fore-sight was rewarded when Burgundy and his captain, Jehan de Luxembourg, together with the earls of Huntingdon and Arundel, newly deployed from England, arrived in force before the town.

Compiègne was protected by walls and towers and sur-rounded by a moat which had been created by diverting the waters of the Oise. A single bridge, fifty feet long and lined with houses, spanned the river, just as at Orléans. The besiegers built a series of bastilles around the town, just as they had done at Orléans, and began a heavy bombardment which was returned by the artillery on the walls. And just as had happened at Orléans, Jehanne d'Arc came to the rescue, slipping into the town in the early hours with a small troop of two hundred men.

This time, however, she did not come with the blessing of Charles and his court; nor was she escorted by princes of the royal blood. Angered and frustrated by her king's refusal to employ her in the field, she had left the court without his leave (a treasonable offence) and made her own way to Compiègne. The men she had with her were mercenaries led by Bartolomeo Baretta, a Piedmontese soldier of fortune.[16]

That same day, 23 May 1430, towards evening, the Pucelle decided to make a sortie from the town. Guillaume de Flavy, the garrison captain, ordered the town gate leading on to the bridge to be opened and she rode out, with her standard, at the head of several hundred armed men. They cleared the bridge and the boulevard guarding its access on the opposite bank, and began to attack Jehan de Luxembourg's troops. Twice they drove the Burgundians back to their camp but on the third assault they were intercepted by the English, who cut off their retreat. As they tried to make their escape across the fields the Pucelle was pulled from her horse, surrounded and taken prisoner. Some four hundred of her men were killed or drowned and her brother and the master of her household were among those captured. The exulting Burgundians, who had 'never feared or dreaded any captain or war leader as much as they had this Pucelle', paraded their captive before the duke, who came specially to the front line to see her and had a conversation with her which Monstrelet, an eyewitness, disingenuously claimed not to recall. The duke, however, marked the occasion by writing a triumphal letter to the major towns that very day announcing that 'she who is called the Maid' had been taken prisoner.[17]

Although neither Jehanne herself nor any of the eyewitnesses blamed her capture on anything other than being caught between the two forces and overwhelmed by numbers, accusations of treachery have circulated for centuries. Guillaume de Flavy, a half-brother of Regnault de Chartres, is accused of having deliberately shut her out of the town by closing the gates against her. Only one contemporary, Perceval de Cagny, writing eight years after the event, suggests that Flavy raised the drawbridge and shut the gates. Cagny was not an eyewitness but he was master of the duke of Alençon's household: given that the duke was one of the Pucelle's most ardent supporters, it is not surprising that his own apologist might seek to blame treachery, rather than human fallibility, for her failure at Compiègne. Even Cagny, however, does not suggest malicious intent on Flavy's part, explaining that he acted as he did to prevent the English and Burgundians, who were already on the bridge, getting into the town.[18]

Jehanne was consigned to the custody of Jehan de Luxembourg, who sent her to his fortress of Beaulieu-les-Fontaines in Picardy;

when she attempted to escape she was transferred to the tower of his castle at Beaurevoir, where Luxembourg's wife and aunt were both in residence. Their presence did not prevent Jehanne suffering the indignity of having to fend off the attentions of one of the count's knights, who later testified that 'many times . . . in sport, he tried to touch her breasts, trying hard to put his hands on her bosom', though she always pushed him away as hard as she could. He cannot have been the only one and Jehanne lived in constant fear of sexual assault, even rape, her much-vaunted virginity evidently being a challenge to her male captors and guards. This was the reason she would give at her trial for refusing to wear female clothing, even when pressed to do so by the Luxembourg ladies, though she also insisted that her voices had told her it was not yet time to abandon her male attire. Her voices also daily warned her to submit to her fate and not to attempt another escape, but in desperation she eventually jumped from the tower, injuring her hips and her back. Recaptured immediately, she would return to her prison until the end of November.[19]

News that the Pucelle had been captured at Compiègne travelled fast. Only two days afterwards the University of Paris wrote to Philippe of Burgundy requesting that his prisoner should be sent to them 'to appear before us and a procurator of the Holy Inquisitor' to answer charges that she was 'vehemently suspected of many crimes smacking of heresy'. Two months later, after no response, the university 'required' Burgundy, Luxembourg and the Bastard of Wandomme, to whom Jehanne had surrendered, to deliver her to the church authorities: her suspected crimes were now enumerated as casting spells, idolatry and invoking devils.[20]

The principal mover in the attempt to prosecute Jehanne was Pierre Cauchon, a former rector of the University of Paris and ardent partisan of the Anglo-Burgundian alliance. He had been one of the leaders of the pro-Burgundian Cabochien revolt in Paris in 1413, which resulted in a massacre of Armagnacs, and had been exiled from the city as a result. The duke of Burgundy and his father had showered him with church offices as a reward for his loyalty, including making him chaplain of the ducal chapel at Dijon and engineering his appointment as bishop of Beauvais in 1420. A negotiator of the Treaty of Troyes, he had been entrusted with numerous important diplomatic missions by the English administration and was a senior member of the king's council in France.[21]

Cauchon had bitter first-hand experience of the Pucelle, having been forced to flee before her army as it advanced first into Reims, where he was then living, then into Beauvais, expelling him from the seat of his own bishopric. He had taken refuge in Rouen, where the English had compensated him financially for his losses, but he now had his eyes on the ultimate prize, the archbishopric of Rouen, which had just fallen vacant owing to Jean de la Rochetaillée's promotions to the rank of cardinal and see of Besançon. As both a royal councillor and a senior churchman, Cauchon owed much to the English regime and expected more from it. Jehanne had been captured in his diocese of Beauvais, so he was able to claim that the right to try her fell within his jurisdiction and for the next four months he worked unremittingly to persuade the Burgundians to hand her over to him.[22]

The removal of the Pucelle from the scene was a relief to Bedford, but it was secondary in importance to the recovery of the places lost during her campaigns. In November 1429 the estates-general of Normandy had granted him 140,000*l.t.* (£8.17m) specifically for the payment of garrison wages and to lay siege to Torcy, Aumâle, Conches and other troublesome neighbouring fortresses, 'and not elsewhere' – a stern reminder that there should be no repetition of the diversion of funds which had seen those intended for Angers go to Orléans. An additional grant in March 1430 of 70,000*l.t.* (£4.08m) was an acknowledgement of the strain that so many operations were putting on the finances of Normandy.

Miners and labourers were already working at the siege of Torcy, halfway between Beauvais and Dieppe, in January 1430; local taxes were levied to pay their 'reasonable and competent' wages promptly, together with those of the men-at-arms who, by the following month, were installed in bastilles round the town. A siege for the recovery of Château Gaillard was also in progress, though by April, John Lunberry, the under-marshal of the army there, was in despair because he could not obtain payment for the wages of his workmen: he had been forced to advance money out of his own pocket just to give them a subsistence allowance and they were now threatening to leave if not paid in full. Elsewhere in the duchy, even a reasonably secure place such as Lisieux was so alarmed by the Armagnac revival that it sought permission to levy local taxes to pay for the 'fortification, enclosure and defence of the town'.[23]

The new military effort was in preparation for the long-awaited arrival in France of Henry VI. On 23 April 1430 he landed at Calais, his voyage having been carefully planned so that he would arrive auspiciously on Saint George's Day and could celebrate the feast of England's patron saint on French shores. The difficulty now was what to do with him. One proposal had been for him to go straight to Reims for his coronation but this was impossible: not only Reims itself but many other places to the east and north of Paris were in enemy hands. He could not even go to Paris because the Armagnacs blocked his route by holding Louviers. His councillors, fearful of exposing the eight-year-old to any danger, decided to sit tight in Calais until the army arrived from England and cleared the way for him to venture further inland. It was not until the end of July that it was considered safe enough for him even to go to Rouen, where he would remain for the next sixteen months.[24]

The English council had decided that Bedford's role as regent should end on Henry's arrival in France. From that moment all military appointments and letters of gift were taken out of his hands, together with responsibility for payments from the Norman treasury. Until Henry returned to England the effective administration of France rested with the 'great council', an amalgamation of those English councillors who had accompanied Henry to France and the members of the council in France. This was only a temporary arrangement and it was understood and expected that Bedford would resume his role as regent on

Henry's departure. In the meantime he had to content himself with the title of 'formerly regent'. Though he could have claimed a place as 'chief councillor', as his brother had done in a similar situation in England, he rarely attended great council meetings, instead devoting his energies to directing the military reconquest. By accident, or perhaps by design, it was Cardinal Beaufort, president of the great council and a constant presence in Rouen, who now assumed the reins of government.[25]

With the aid of the reinforcements now arriving in batches from England, Bedford was able to make slow but steady progress: Château Gaillard was starved into submission in June and Aumâle and Étrépagny were retaken in July. Pushing doggedly on towards and beyond Paris, he deployed the duke of Norfolk and the earl of Stafford to capture twelve fortresses round the city within a month and by the second week in July they were at Corbeil. Torcy fell to the Bastard of Clarence in August but the siege of Louviers stalled, despite renewed and generous grants from the estates-general of Normandy. Another setback was the death of lord Roos, a twenty-four-year-old who had arrived in Paris 'with more ceremony than any knight ever did, who was not a king or a duke or an earl' and was drowned two days later in the Marne when he missed the ford as he chased after a band of raiding Armagnacs. His more experienced men successfully completed the mission, capturing the captain of Lagny, who had been a thorn in the flesh of the Parisians, and recovering all the prisoners and booty they had taken. Roos's replacement, the earl of Stafford, arrived in Paris at the beginning of September: appointed constable of France, he began a successful push to retake the towns and fortresses of Brie.[26]

The citizen-diarist of Paris had little sympathy with these comings and goings. 'Not a man of all those now under arms, whichever side he belongs to, French or English, Armagnac or Burgundian or Picard, will let anything at all escape him that is not too hot or too heavy', he complained. Nothing was sacrosanct. The Armagnacs had captured and pillaged the abbey of Saint-Maur-des-Fossés, but when the English retook it they ransacked it for a second time 'whether their commanders liked it or not . . . They stripped it so clean that they did not even leave a spoon standing in a saucepan.' The citizen at least recognised that the English were better soldiers, tartly recording in his journal that 'three hundred Englishmen got more done in matters of war than five hundred Picards' even if they were 'shocking thieves and always jeering at people', but he was daily disappointed by the duke of Burgundy's failure to take Compiègne and come to the relief of his Paris.[27]

Burgundy was preoccupied with his own problems. The siege of Compiègne dragged on and he was forced to withdraw some of his troops to redeploy in the north, where war had broken out between his county of Namur and the city of Liège. The ending of his truces with Charles VII in May 1430 also led to a resumption of border warfare in the south: though it was essentially opportunistic and intermittent, it drained men and money from any façade of a joint campaign with the English. On 11 June 1430 a twelve-hundred-strong Burgundian army, which had invaded the Dauphiné under the command of the prince of Orange, was ambushed by Raoul de Gaucourt and the notorious Castilian mercenary Roderigo Villandrando at Anthon, sixty miles east of Dijon. The Burgundians scattered in panic and were cut down as they fled, though the body of one unfortunate man-at-arms, who had hidden in a hollow oak and was trapped by his armour, was not discovered until the tree was chopped down in 1672. The prince himself escaped but he was badly wounded and was later expelled from the Order of the Golden Fleece because, like Fastolf at Patay, he had abandoned the field after unfurling his banner.[28]

At the beginning of November Xaintrailles and an Armagnac army made a feint attack which successfully drew the besiegers away from Compiègne, allowing the town to be resupplied. Jehan de Luxembourg and the earl of Huntingdon therefore decided to cut their losses and raise the siege. The much-maligned Guillaume de Flavy, by his steadfast refusal to surrender during more than five months of blockade, had done what the Pucelle had failed to do and saved his town.[29]

A few weeks later, at Guerbigny in Picardy, Xaintrailles surprised another Burgundian force, which had foolishly been travelling without sending scouts ahead, killing fifty or sixty and taking up to a hundred prisoners, including the Englishman Sir Thomas Kyriell, who had been detached to join them. A disastrous year for the Burgundians ended in defeat at the hands of the sire de Barbazan in a pitched battle near Bar-sur-Seine, in which much of their famed artillery was lost.[30]

Philippe of Burgundy laid the blame for his military failures squarely on the shoulders of the English. Writing to Henry VI two days after his army left Compiègne, he protested that he had undertaken the siege 'at your request and command . . . though this was contrary to the advice of my council and my own opinion'. He had been promised 19,500*l.t.* (£1.14m) a month to keep his men there, together with the cost of his artillery, but his payments were two months in arrears and he had personally had to find 40,000 *saluts* (£3.21m) to fund the guns. He had lost the services of the earl of Huntingdon, who had been forced to withdraw because his men's wages were unpaid and he could no longer afford to keep them at the siege. 'I cannot continue', Burgundy complained, 'without adequate provision in future from you . . . and without payment of what is due to me.'[31]

The English administration had financial problems of its own. Though the coronation expedition army had contracted to serve for a year, the soldiers had only been advanced six months' wages before they left England. The rest of their wages should have been paid monthly in advance but the money was not forthcoming and many decided to return home early. Sir William Porter, for example, had arrived with a company of eighty but by the end of October only fifteen men remained in his service. The great council, under Cardinal Beaufort's leadership, tried to remedy the situation by appointing at least twenty-three retinue leaders to the captaincies of Normandy garrisons, thereby transferring the costs to the duchy treasury. Such sweeping changes of personnel in some of the most strategically important fortresses were militarily questionable, especially as they led to some highly inappropriate appointments: the cardinal himself, for instance, became captain of Honfleur at Michaelmas 1430.[32]

At the end of December, with the prospect of Henry's coronation in Reims no closer despite the unprecedented resources poured into the campaign, the great council decided to send the cardinal and Sir John Tiptoft to England to seek more money and men for a new campaign. They arrived in time for Beaufort to give the opening address in the new parliament which met at Westminster on 12 January 1431. He chose as his theme the very apt 'The throne of his kingdom will be established' and parliament responded by granting a subsidy of one-fifteenth and one-tenth, to be collected by 11 November, together with a third of another whole subsidy to be paid by 20 April 1432.[33]

The cardinal was equally successful in recruiting men, though possibly only because he applied family pressure: his two nephews, Thomas and Edmund Beaufort, signed up to lead an expedition totalling 2649 men, more than two thousand of whom would accompany them to France early in March. At twenty-five Thomas had spent much of his life in France but only because he had been captured as a teenager at Baugé in 1421; released in the summer of 1430, he had spent the rest of the year on campaign, returning to England with his uncle in December. His younger brother Edmund, the future first duke of Somerset, would become one of the most important figures in the history of the English kingdom of France. At the age of twenty-one he had been seriously compromised by an indiscreet love affair with Henry V's widow but had redeemed himself by continuous military service since leading the cardinal's crusader forces to France in July 1429; Bedford had appointed him constable of the army and captain of several important fortresses, as well as entrusting the sieges of Étrépagny and Château Gaillard to him. Both men had extensive landholdings in France, Thomas as count of Perche and Edmund as count of Mortain, giving them strong personal reasons for defending English interests in France. Another of the cardinal's nephews, Richard Neville, who had inherited his father-in-law's earldom of Salisbury when the latter was killed at the siege of Orléans in 1429, would bring a further force of eight hundred men in the summer of 1431. The total cost of the wages and shipping for these expeditions would rise to £24,000 (£12.6m), over half of which was funded by personal loans from the cardinal. No one could doubt the Beaufort commitment to the English kingdom of France: the question was whether that commitment was ultimately in the interests of the kingdom itself.[34]

CHAPTER ELEVEN

Trial and Execution

Bedford remained active throughout the winter with the limited forces at his disposal. On 30 January 1431 he shepherded into Paris a convoy of 'at least' fifty-six boats and twelve barges, all laden with much-needed victuals. His feat was much applauded in the city because it was accomplished both against the current and in the teeth of raging winds and three weeks of heavy rain which had swollen the Seine beyond recognition; unlike several previous convoys, he had also evaded every Armagnac ambush set along the route from Rouen. By March, when the weather had eased and his first reinforcements had arrived from England, he was out in the field again, recapturing several strongholds on the Marne around Lagny, but failing to take Lagny itself.[1]

Despite Bedford's heroic efforts, Armagnac raids from their fortress-bases surrounding Paris constantly disrupted the supply chain, causing prices to soar and an exodus of poor from the city: twelve hundred adults were said to have left in a single day in April. The insecurity meant it was not practical to bring the young king, with his huge entourage, into his French capital, causing administrative problems because all the major institutions of state were based in Paris, but the king and the great council remained at Rouen. Officials such as the chancellor, Louis de Luxembourg, whose presence was required in both places, were obliged to spend much of their time on the road, shuttling between Rouen and Paris.[2]

Another consequence of the insecurity in and around Paris was that the trial of Jehanne d'Arc, which the university had wanted to stage in the capital, also had to be relocated to Rouen. The duke of Burgundy, hard pressed for money, had finally agreed to sell the Pucelle, and the estates-general of Normandy set aside 10,000*l.t.* (£583,333) out of a tax of 120,000*l.t.* (£7m) granted in August 1430 'to purchase Jehanne la Pucelle, who is said to be a witch, a "war person" leading the armies of the dauphin'.[3]

It is worth considering what might have happened to Jehanne had Burgundy not handed her over to the English. Would he have succumbed to the demands of Cauchon and the university and put her on trial for heresy? Would he have ransomed her to the Armagnacs if the sum offered was high enough? Would he have kept her as a potential bargaining tool for his future negotiations with Charles VII? Or would he have left her to rot as a prisoner at Beaurevoir? In the event his decision to take the money and pass the problem on to his allies proved to be astute.

The same options were available to the English. Obviously they would not have wished to ransom her so that she could return to the field against them, but there was no reason why they could not have simply sent her into perpetual imprisonment in England: after all, the dukes of Bourbon and Orléans, who had both been captured more than fifteen years earlier at Agincourt, were still incarcerated in English prisons without hope of ransom. As she was a prisoner of war who had never taken the oath of allegiance to Henry V or VI, there was no requirement to try Jehanne in a civil court.

Why, then, allow her to be tried before an ecclesiastical tribunal? To modern eyes it seems a convenient way of getting the church to do the state's dirty work. In fact in the medieval mind there was no great distinction between heresy and political

subversion, especially during this particular period, when rad-
icalism in religion and politics walked hand in hand. In England
the Lollards had been closely associated with plots and rebellion
against the monarchy for a generation and in Bohemia the
Hussites were actually at war against their Catholic Emperor,
who had launched five successive crusades against them between
1420 and 1431. Ironically, as we have seen, the Pucelle also
wanted to lead a crusade against the Hussites and dictated a
letter challenging them to return to the faith or face her sword.[4]
Cardinal Beaufort, who had attempted to lead the crusade of
1429, had attacked heretics for undermining 'not only the faith
but all political rule and governance, stirring the people to rebellion and disobedience to their lords and governors'. Jehanne's
trial for heresy was neither an isolated nor an unusual event: in
both England and Burgundy the church was actively prosecuting
large numbers of suspected heretics during this very period. In
the Norwich diocese alone sixty men and women were tried in
1428 and three were burned at the stake; in Lille twenty suspected heretics were arrested in 1429 and 1430, of whom at
least eight were burned.[5]

Cauchon's motives for trying the Pucelle for heresy have been
rightly questioned but also much maligned. As both a bishop
and a royal councillor, he had a duty to uphold the authority of
church and state. Jehanne's flagrant defiance of the church's
teachings on a woman's dress and conduct, and her insistence
that these had been determined by divine revelation, made
redundant the church's role as the sole conduit between God and
mankind. And as her messianic ability to inspire the populace to
resist and overthrow their Anglo-Burgundian masters had
demonstrated, she also posed a serious threat to secular authority. For Cauchon and the theologians of the University of Paris
she did indeed fulfil prophecy, but it was the words of Christ
himself: 'False prophets will arise and show great signs and wonders, so as to lead astray, if possible, even the elect.'[6]

There was a risk, of course, that the heresy trial might find
Jehanne innocent – which is why, when the great council issued
its letter in Henry VI's name authorising Cauchon to proceed,

they informed him that 'it is our intention to retake and regain possession of this [Jehanne] if it comes to pass that she is not convicted or found guilty of the said crimes, or those of them concerning or touching our faith'.[7]

The chance that the Pucelle might be found guilty, however, was a risk worth taking. If she was convicted of heresy, then her claim to have been sent by God was discredited and her victories in the field could be ascribed to the work of the devil. More importantly, her conviction would taint Charles VII by association: 'I'm talking to you,' one of her interrogators would say to her, 'and I tell you that your king is a heretic and a schismatic.'[8] Jehanne's public condemnation would undermine the validity of Charles's consecration as king and pave the way for the coronation of Henry with the blessing and authority of the church.

Jehanne arrived in Rouen under an English military escort on 23 December 1430 and was committed to Rouen castle, where she was to be held in a room, chained and guarded by three English esquires and half a dozen soldiers. Strictly speaking, since she was being tried by the church she should have been held in the archbishop's prison, or under house arrest in a convent, where she would have been guarded by women. Imprisoning her in Rouen castle was not in itself evidence that her trial was politically motivated, as later commentators have suggested, but a practical recognition that she was too valuable a prisoner to be held in any of the ordinary prisons, ecclesiastical or civil, where she might escape or be rescued. The castle was the most secure place in Rouen, but it was not neutral ground. It was also the seat of Norman government and Henry VI and his court were in residence at the time. In terms of public perception, therefore, the decision to hold her and try her within the castle precincts was ill conceived, since it indelibly associated her trial with the English regime and raised justifiable doubts about its impartiality.

Those witnesses who were involved in the proceedings, and then had to give evidence twenty-five years later at the nullification process, made extravagant efforts to vindicate themselves and blame 'the English' for manipulating and running the trial.

Yet of the 131 judges, assessors and other clergy involved in the process only eight were English and of those eight only two attended more than three of the fifteen or more sessions. The rest, including Cauchon, were Burgundian partisans, two-thirds of them graduates of the University of Paris.[9]

All the due forms of a trial for heresy were observed. The chief inquisitor of France, who was detained at a trial elsewhere, appointed a Dominican friar, Jehan le Maistre, to represent him and join Cauchon as the second judge. An investigator was sent to Domrémy to question Jehanne's family, friends and neighbours; his evidence was used as a basis for many of the questions asked in the ensuing interrogations but it was not cited directly to prove or disprove the charges, as such testimony was in other contemporary heresy trials. Detailed records were kept of the entire process, including the interrogations, so that the inquisitors could demonstrate that they had acted fairly and that Jehanne had convicted herself out of her own mouth. She had no advocate to defend her but this was not exceptional for the times and she apparently refused assistance when it was offered on 27 March. When the possibility of torturing her was proposed, as was commonplace, twelve assessors were consulted but they decided against by a majority of nine to three.[10]

Between 21 February and 3 March 1431 she was questioned in six 'public' sessions in the castle chapel: the audience was entirely composed of theologians and canon lawyers who were there in an advisory capacity. A further nine interrogations were carried out privately in her cell between 10 and 17 March, with up to eleven people present, all, except her guard on the last occasion, being interrogators or notaries. There is no discernible difference in tone or subject matter between the public and private sessions, though there is no way of knowing what was omitted from the official record as this was not a verbatim account of the proceedings.

Guillaume Manchon, one of the notaries who produced a French transcript of the trial and later collaborated on its translation into Latin, would claim at the nullification process that other notaries had not recorded Jehanne's answers in full, leaving out anything that exonerated her; that she was spied on by Cauchon and the earl of Warwick when she was making confession; and that her confessor had revealed all she had told him to her interrogators. His claims may well have been true, but clearly he was also desperate to avoid censure or punishment for his own role in the original trial. He had to be 'forced' to hand over his notarial records in 1456 and insisted that he had participated against his will and out of fear of the English regime. There is a somewhat hollow ring to his protestation that 'he knew and firmly believed that, if he had been on the side of the English, he would not have treated [Jehanne] in this way, and he would not have put her on trial in this way'. He even claimed he had spent his wages for the trial on a missal 'in order to remember her and to pray to God for her'.[11]

Despite all the fallibilities of the evidence at both trials, what emerges indisputably and triumphantly is the Pucelle's absolute faith in the divine origin of her mission and her utter conviction that her voices were real. Honest and artless, stubborn and direct to the point of rudeness, this nineteen-year-old illiterate village girl held her own against some of Europe's most eminent professors of theology and canon law, but in her refusal to accept their opinions and deny her own, she set herself in defiance of the church. In the eyes of the law she was therefore guilty of heresy and schism. And just like the hundreds of Protestant and Catholic martyrs who found their faith in conflict with the prevailing orthodoxy, she was required either to admit publicly that she was wrong or suffer the ultimate penalty of being burned at the stake.

On 24 May she was taken to the cemetery of the abbey of Saint-Ouen in Rouen and placed on a public scaffold. The site was chosen not for its intimidating associations with death but because it was a large, open space where crowds too big to meet within a church regularly gathered to hear sermons, especially those by visiting friars. A sermon was preached at Jehanne, exhorting her to reject her errors and return to the unity of the church. She was offered the chance to abjure three times and refused but, when Cauchon began to read out her sentence, her courage gave way. In the presence of a vast crowd which had gathered to witness these events, she repeated after Cauchon the renunciation of her 'crimes and errors'

> in falsely pretending to have had revelations and apparitions from God, His angels, Saint Katherine and Saint Margaret; in leading others astray; in believing madly and too lightly; in making superstitious divinations; in blaspheming God and His saints; in contravening divine law, holy scripture and canon law; in wearing a dissolute, shameful and immodest outfit, against natural decency, and hair cut in a circle in a masculine fashion, against all decency of womankind; also in bearing arms most presumptuously; in cruelly desiring the shedding of human blood; in saying that I did all these things at the command of God, His angels and the saints named before, and that I acted properly in these matters and did not err; in despising God and His sacraments, encouraging insurrections and practising idolatry by adorating[12] and invoking evil spirits. I also confess that I have been schismatic and that I have strayed from the faith in many ways.[13]

By making Jehanne personally deliver this comprehensive public rejection of all that she had believed, said and done (and much that she had not), the trial achieved its purpose to discredit her and her king. Her punishment was to be committed to perpetual solitary confinement and ordered to adopt women's clothing. Two days later she changed her mind, saying that promises that she should be allowed to go to mass and be freed from her chains had not been kept and she would rather die than endure the pain of imprisonment any longer. She admitted that her voices had spoken to her again – 'the fatal reply' someone noted in the margin of the record – resumed her male clothing and insisted that her renunciation was not genuine but had been entirely motivated by fear of the fire. Her voices had told her that she had damned herself eternally merely to save her life.[14]

This was the worst possible outcome both for Jehanne herself and for the English. Her public renunciation had enumerated and advertised her 'errors' to a broader, popular audience and now, as she was a relapsed heretic, there was no alternative but to burn her. There could be no more effective way to draw attention to her belief in the righteousness of her mission than her willingness to die for it. And on 30 May 1431 that was what she did. She was taken to the Old Market, the traditional place of public execution in Rouen. Cauchon gave a final sermon and pronounced her sentence before handing her over to the secular authorities. Geoffroi Thérage,[15] the royal executioner, then dragged her to the stake, placed on her head a mitre emblazoned with the words 'heretic, relapse, apostate, idolater' and lit the fire. A sympathetic Englishman had made her a small cross of wood which she placed at her breast and a Norman cleric, who had served as an usher at the trial, took the parish cross from the church of Saint-Sauveur and held it aloft so that she could see it as she was consumed by the flames. Several times she called out 'Jesus!' and it was his name that she invoked with her last breath.[16]

After she was dead Thérage raked back the fire to expose her naked body 'to take away any doubts from people's minds' that she was a woman. When the watching crowds had stared long enough he rebuilt the fire so that her body was reduced to ashes, which were then thrown in the Seine to prevent them becoming objects of veneration. For it was already clear from the reaction of some of the crowd that they believed 'that she was martyred, and for her true lord'. Even Thérage, it was later claimed, had said that 'he greatly feared to be damned for he had burned a holy woman' – though not so much that it persuaded him to give up his gruesome occupation. At least two witnesses at the nullification process claimed that Thérage had told them that he had been unable to destroy Jehanne's heart, which, in the manner of saintly relics, had resisted his best efforts to burn it, using oil, sulphur and charcoal, and had remained intact. Thérage himself was conveniently unable to verify this as he had died many years previously.[17]

The public burning did not prevent the circulation of rumours that Jehanne had escaped the fire. In 1436 a woman calling

herself 'Jeanne du Lys' appeared at Metz and was 'recognised' as
the Pucelle by Jehanne's brothers; showered with gifts, she made
her way to Cologne and then in 1439 to Orléans, where she was
fêted by the townsmen and presented with money 'for the good
which she did the town during the siege'. She was brought to
Paris on the orders of the university and *parlement* and there
exposed as Claude des Armoises, the wife of a knight of
Lorraine; her only similarity to Jehanne was that she claimed to
have dressed as a man and fought as a hired soldier in the papal
army. She disappeared from view in 1440 after her exposure, but
another impostor, Jeanne de Sermaize, spent three months in
prison at Saumur until she was pardoned by René d'Anjou in
1457.[18]

It was just this sort of story that the authorities in Rouen had
sought to stamp out. On 28 June letters were addressed in Henry
VI's name to the pope, cardinals and Emperor Sigismund, as
well as to other kings, princes and dukes outside France, giving
the official version of the career, trial, recantation, relapse and
sentence of the 'false witch'. The letters suggested that such a
detailed account was necessary because popular report had carried tales of Jehanne's deeds throughout 'almost the whole
world', but there can be little doubt that the great council was
also using the opportunity subtly to denigrate Charles VII. There
was no reference to the political aspects or context of Jehanne's
role, simply a vague description of her having boasted that she
had been sent by God, worn men's clothing, borne weapons of
war and taken part in battles where men were slaughtered. What
was emphasised repeatedly was that Jehanne's behaviour had
offended the Christian faith and that she had been tried and
sentenced by an ecclesiastical court. Any secular power which
dared to challenge her conviction therefore laid itself open to the
charge of defying the church.[19]

Similar letters, copied to the nobility and the major towns of
France, were written to the French bishops with a request that
the material be used in public sermons for the benefit of the
populace 'who have been deceived and abused for a long time by
the works of this woman'. One of these sermons was given in

Paris at the beginning of July by no less a person than Jean Graverent, the chief inquisitor of France, who had delegated his powers during Jehanne's trial. Unlike the more measured tone of the circular letters, it was an emotionally charged and occasionally vicious tissue of lies and half-truths. He accused Jehanne of dressing 'as a man' from the age of fourteen: 'after that her father and mother would have liked to kill her if they could have done so without guilt, and . . . she had therefore left them, in the devil's company, and had ever since been a murderer of Christian people, full of blood and fire, till at last she was burned.' Her saints, he declared, were devils who had deluded her and led her to her death.[20]

What is particularly interesting about Graverent's sermon is that he denounced not only Jehanne but also three other women, Pieronne the Breton, her unnamed companion and Catherine de la Rochelle. All four, Graverent claimed, had been manipulated by Brother Richard, the Franciscan friar who had been expelled from Paris in May 1429 for his subversive preaching, which had attracted vast crowds and led to public bonfires of the items he denounced as vanities. He had persuaded many Parisians to wear a tin medallion bearing the name of Jesus as a symbol of repentance, only for them to cast if off again (and resume their cards and dice) when they learned that he had joined Jehanne and the Armagnacs and was persuading Burgundian towns to renounce their allegiance. By drawing their attention to how easily Brother Richard had deceived them, Graverent forcibly reminded the Parisians that they should trust the church's judgement and not allow other false prophets to exploit their credulity.[21]

The story of the Pucelle seems to us so extraordinary and iconic that we tend to forget that, to contemporaries, she was by no means unique. As Graverent pointed out, she was just one of four women linked to Brother Richard who had come to the attention of the authorities. Pieronne the Breton and her companion were both penitent followers of Brother Richard; they had been with him and Jehanne at Sully-sur-Loire and were captured at Corbeil in the spring of 1430. The companion was released after interrogation but Pieronne had stoutly defended

Jehanne, saying that 'what she did was well done and was God's will'. She too was tried for heresy: like Jehanne, she had received communion from Brother Richard more than once in a day, which was in breach of canon law. More importantly, she insisted that God had appeared to her repeatedly in human form, dressed in a long white robe over a red tunic, and talked to her 'as one friend does to another'. She refused to recant and was also burned at the stake as a heretic, just a few months before Jehanne, on 3 September 1430 in Paris.[22]

Catherine de la Rochelle was arrested in Paris in December 1430 and actually gave evidence against Jehanne, telling her interrogators that the Pucelle 'would escape from her prison with the devil's aid if she were not well guarded'. The two women had met under Brother Richard's aegis at Jargeau and Montfaucon but had soon fallen out. Like Jehanne, Catherine believed she had a divinely appointed mission, revealed to her in visions by a white lady dressed in cloth of gold. The lady told her that Charles VII would give her heralds and trumpeters to accompany her on a journey through the major towns of France, proclaiming that anyone who had hidden gold, silver or treasure should bring it to them immediately: if they refused or kept it hidden, Catherine would discover its whereabouts by means of divine revelation. In this way, Catherine claimed, she would raise the money to pay for Jehanne's men-at-arms.

With an irony that was not lost on the judges at her trial, Jehanne, who had never thought to prove that her own revelations were real, insisted on putting her rival visionary's claims to the test, spending two nights watching over her as she slept, but failing to see the white lady with her own eyes. Brother Richard had been keen to set Catherine to work but Jehanne was scornfully dismissive, telling them both, and Charles VII as well, that her own saints had informed her that Catherine's visions were 'all nothing' and 'just madness'. Catherine, she said, should return to her husband, do her housework and look after her children, which is presumably exactly what she did do when she abjured and was released in June 1431, shortly after Jehanne's execution.[23]

There was an additional irony in that Brother Richard was

also in prison during the Pucelle's trial, but not in the English kingdom of France. Despite his advocacy of the then dauphin during the coronation campaign and his closeness to the queen, Marie d'Anjou, on 23 March 1431 the *parlement* of Poitiers granted the request of the bishop of Poitiers and the inquisitor for orders to place him under house arrest in the local Franciscan convent and to prohibit him from preaching anywhere within their jurisdiction. The arresting officers were authorised to seize him, 'even if he was in a sacred place', and he was duly taken on the very day Charles VII made his formal entry into Poitiers. The imminent arrival of their king had clearly frightened the authorities into removing Brother Richard from the scene for fear that his powerful oratory might be unleashed publicly on behalf of the Pucelle and, worse still, that he might appeal personally to Charles to save her. Such an embarrassment could not be countenanced.[24]

The sad truth was that the Pucelle had served her purpose and the Armagnacs had washed their hands of her. The church authorities were the first to distance themselves. Regnault de Chartres had never really approved of her because she championed the view that 'peace would not be found except at the end of a lance'; he had already written to his bishops informing them that God had allowed Jehanne to be captured 'because she had puffed herself up with pride and because of the rich garments which she had adopted, and because she had not done what God had commanded her, but had done her own will'.[25]

Charles made no such excuses but he did nothing whatsoever to assist his champion. He could have offered a huge ransom to obtain her release: he did not. He could have ordered Regnault de Chartres, as archbishop of Reims, to exercise his superior authority over Pierre Cauchon so that the trial could be transferred to Armagnac jurisdiction: he did not. He could have appealed on Jehanne's behalf to the new pope, Eugenius IV, elected on 3 March 1431, eleven days after the death of Martin V: he did not. Charles had always known that there would be risks in associating himself with someone as unorthodox as Jehanne.

He would not, and could not, help her now because to do so would implicate him as the harbourer and supporter of a heretic. It would also draw attention to the fact that 'the most Christian king of France' owed his coronation not to God but to a woman accused, and later convicted, of being in league with the devil. For these reasons he maintained a discreet distance from the proceedings in Rouen and never once, in the twenty years following her capture, commented on the Pucelle and her fate.[26]

In any case, as Regnault de Chartres callously remarked when Jehanne was first captured, the Armagnacs had already found her successor, a young shepherd boy from the Auvergne 'who talks just as well as Jehanne ever did'. Guillaume le Berger, as he was popularly known, 'caused people to idolise him' because, like Saint Francis, he bore the stigmata, bloody marks on his hands, feet and side which reproduced the five wounds Christ received on the cross. This literally marked him out as a holy man and he too claimed that he had been sent by God. Unlike Jehanne, who rode astride her horse like a man, the shepherd rode side-saddle, like a woman, and, as both friend and foe alleged, was either insane or a simpleton.[27]

There seems little doubt that the Armagnacs deliberately set out 'to exalt his reputation, just as, and in the same way that, they had previously done with Jehanne the Pucelle'. It was therefore something of a triumph for the English when he was captured before his career could properly begin. In August 1431 an Armagnac force from Beauvais was lured out of the town and ambushed in what would appear to have been a joint operation by the earls of Warwick and Arundel. Guillaume le Berger was one of those taken prisoner, together with an altogether more significant figure, Poton de Xaintrailles. For Warwick this was an especially lucky chance, since his own son-in-law, John Talbot, was Xaintrailles's prisoner, enabling negotiations for an exchange of the two men to begin.[28]

The execution of the Pucelle seems to have changed the fortunes of the English, for Xaintrailles was not the only feared Armagnac captain to lose his liberty this summer. In the very

week that Jehanne was burned, 'the worst, cruellest, most piti-
less' of them all, La Hire, was captured and committed to the
castle of Dourdon, close to La-Charité-sur-Loire. A few weeks
later, on 2 July, the sire de Barbazan, whom La Hire had rescued
from his long incarceration at Château Gaillard the previous
year, was killed in a battle against Burgundian forces at
Bulgnéville, twenty miles south-west of the Pucelle's home village
of Domrémy. René d'Anjou, Charles VII's brother-in-law and
confidant, was taken prisoner in the same battle, temporarily
ending his struggle to assert himself as duke of Bar by right of his
wife.[29]

The capture of La Hire deprived Louviers of its captain and
may have been connected with the siege which began at the end
of May. Louviers was a fortified town just eighteen miles south
of Rouen, on the south bank of the Seine. It had been in
Armagnac hands since December 1429 and, as we have seen, the
garrison had plagued English shipping, preventing convoys of
supplies getting upriver to Paris. The siege therefore began with
an ingenious attempt to lure the Armagnacs out from behind
their walls so that they could be ambushed. Two ships fully
laden with wheat were dispatched from Rouen without a military escort or an enemy safe-conduct, but the garrison did not
fall for the ruse and so a full-scale siege was implemented.[30]

The estates-general of Normandy, meeting in June 1431, allocated a third of its 150,000*l.t.* (£8.75m) tax-grant for the
recovery of Louviers, with an extra 20,000*l.t.* (£1.17m) to pay
the wages of the four hundred men-at-arms and twelve hundred
archers from the duchy in the army there. Men had been withdrawn from garrisons all over Normandy for the siege, including
a quarter of those stationed at Honfleur; they had the gratifica-
tion of taking their revenge for the fact that, some months earlier,
La Hire had led a raid from Louviers and burned the suburbs of
their town.[31]

So many men were committed to the siege that providing
provender for all their horses in the immediate locality became a
major problem. Some of the archers and valets were therefore
employed to take the horses further afield to graze. Their

captains later complained that the treasury, adhering to its usual strictly literal interpretation of 'being at the siege', refused to pay their wages, even though the reason for their absence was marked on the musters.[32]

It would take five months to force Louviers to surrender and the English captain, Thomas Beaufort, died there three weeks before it did so, but on 25 October 1431 the garrison was allowed to leave with full honours and Louviers once more became English. Not that this prevented the soldiers from looting the town or the authorities from razing the walls, a measure designed both as a punishment for the citizens' treachery, which had allowed La Hire to seize it in the first place, and to prevent it becoming an Armagnac fortress again.[33]

The recapture of Louviers opened up the route to Paris, making it possible for Henry VI to pay his first visit to the capital of his French kingdom. Just as his landing in France nineteen months earlier had been carefully timed to take place on Saint George's Day, so his arrival in Paris was choreographed for maximum effect. He arrived with his entourage to pay the customary royal visit to the abbey of Saint-Denis, where his mother's ancestors lay buried, on 30 November 1431, which was Saint Andrew's Day, the patron saint of the Burgundians. Two days later, on the Sunday which was the first day in Advent, he made his ceremonial entry into Paris. He was escorted into the city by Simon Morhier, the provost, and a group of aldermen who carried a blue canopy, spangled with the fleurs-de-lis of France, over his head. All the government officials came to greet him, wearing their colourful red and blue robes of state, led by Philippe de Morvilliers, the first president of the *parlement*.[34]

Every ceremonial entry to a town was accompanied by extravagant pageantry designed to impress the king with the loyalty of his subjects and persuade him to look favourably upon them. Often there was an overtly political message behind the visual displays but in this instance it was curiously lacking. Perhaps in deference to the king's age, the citizens who organised and paid for the proceedings chose entertainment, rather than propaganda, as the theme. The king's procession was therefore led by the Nine Worthies,[35] the greatest warriors the world had ever known, and their female counterparts, though it also included the unfortunate Guillaume le Berger, bound with rope 'like a thief', who would disappear at the end of the day, supposedly having been thrown into the Seine to drown. At various points along the way the king was treated to tableaux and plays which included mermaids, wild men and a stag hunt, as well as a representation of the arms of Paris (a ship containing three people symbolising the church, university and citizens), the martyrdom of Saint Denis and the usual biblical scenes.

The only overtly political tableau was staged in front of the Châtelet, the seat of the provost of Paris. It was not paid for out of municipal funds, suggesting that it had been arranged and sponsored by Simon Morhier, possibly acting on behalf of the great council, of which he was a leading member. The scene was a physical representation of the Treaty of Troyes: a boy about Henry's age, clothed in fleurs-de-lis and wearing two crowns on his head, supported on one side by the duke of Burgundy and count of Nevers, and on the other by the duke of Bedford and the earls of Warwick and Salisbury, each presenting him with a shield bearing the respective coats-of-arms of France and England.[36]

On 16 December 1431, the third Sunday in Advent and ten days after his tenth birthday, Henry VI achieved the ambition for which his father had fought and died. He was crowned and consecrated king of France.[37]

PART THREE

WAR OF ATTRITION

CHAPTER TWELVE

A Year of Disasters

The coronation of Henry VI should have been a triumphant moment in the history of the English kingdom of France. Never before had the two crowns been united in one person, nor would they ever be again. Yet the whole episode was somehow shabby, rushed and unsatisfactory. Only six months earlier the English council had still anticipated that the ceremony would take place, as tradition demanded, in Reims. Instead, because Reims was still in Armagnac hands, Henry was crowned in Paris – not even at Saint-Denis, where Pepin the Short had been crowned by Pope Stephen II in 754 in the presence of the future Charlemagne, but in the cathedral of Notre Dame.

At almost every stage of the proceedings the English managed to cause offence to their French subjects. The bishop of Paris was aggrieved that Cardinal Beaufort usurped what he felt was rightfully his role within his own church by crowning the king and singing the mass. The canons were annoyed because the royal officials failed to give them their customary offering of the gilded cup used in the service. Officials from the municipality, university and *parlement* were offended because they were not treated with the dignity they expected at the coronation feast: worse still

for Frenchmen, the English had cooked the food four days earlier and it was 'shocking'. The traditional celebratory jousts were
a small-scale affair and did not give rise to the usual distribution
of largesse. The new king also failed to grant the customary
release of prisoners and abolition of certain taxes. These were all
petty quibbles, but they were symptomatic of a wider discontent.
As the chronicler Monstrelet noted, everything concerning the
coronation was carried out 'more in accordance with the customs of England than of France'. The citizen of Paris concluded
that it was 'probably because we don't understand what they say
and they don't understand us' but there must have been many
who felt that this lack of sensitivity to French concerns was
simply the arrogance of an English conqueror.[1]

The 'Englishness' of the coronation was underlined by the
absence of most of the peers of France, in particular Philippe of
Burgundy. In the preceding weeks the Parisian authorities had
daily announced that his arrival was imminent 'but all this was
only to keep the people quiet'.[2] His failure to put in an appearance was a major disappointment to the Parisians but more
especially to the English. His alliance had made the English
kingdom of France possible: his absence at what was literally its
crowning moment was therefore a significant and very public
political statement. Burgundy had always liked to keep his
options open. Throughout the entire period of Henry's residence in France he had never once met the young king in
person, thereby avoiding the otherwise inevitable requirement
that he should give his oath of allegiance with his hands
between those of the king himself. It was one thing to make a
king, but quite another to give his sacred vow of obedience to
him.

But there was also a more worrying reason for Burgundy's
absence. Just three days before the coronation he had agreed a
six-year general truce with Charles VII. Writing to inform Henry
the day before he signed the treaty, so that, 'because of this, you
do not conceive any suspicion or imagine anything sinister
against me', he claimed that he had been forced into accepting
the truce. And once again he laid the blame squarely at the feet

of the English, who had failed to give him the money and assistance he needed to maintain the war and protect his lands. The future burden of defending the English kingdom would now rest entirely on the English themselves.[3]

At this juncture a gesture of commitment from the English would have been politic and welcome to Henry's French subjects, but no sooner had the new king arrived in Paris than he was whisked back to Rouen. He had spent just three weeks in the city, leaving the citizens with nothing to show for his visit but a bill for 2297*l.t.* (£133,992) for staging the formal entry. The unseemly haste with which he left Paris was matched only by the speed with which he then left Rouen. Pausing only to mark his coronation by confirming the foundation of a new university at Caen (thereby offending that of Paris), he departed from Rouen on 12 January 1432, arrived in Calais fourteen days later and by 9 February was back in England. He had spent only twenty-one months in his kingdom of France and he would never set foot on French soil again.[4]

The coronation of the ten-year-old king was a natural and probably necessary reaction to that of Charles VII. As Bedford had argued, doing homage and taking the oath of loyalty to a consecrated king would bind Henry's French subjects more closely to the English regime. The problem neither he nor anyone else had foreseen was that it also committed the English more fully to supporting what was now Henry's divinely sanctioned right to the French crown. An uncrowned and unconsecrated king might, at some future date, have been able to renounce his claim in order to secure peace on advantageous terms but an anointed king had a sacred duty to uphold the crown God had bestowed upon him. The possibility of a diplomatic rather than a military solution to the future security and survival of the English kingdom of France had just become more difficult to achieve.[5] The coronation, combined with the king's first visit to his French capital, had offered a unique opportunity to whip up enthusiasm for the English regime which was completely thrown away. It is difficult to believe that Bedford would have acted so high-handedly or insensitively, but throughout the period of the king's residence in France he had been sidelined. All real power had been in the hands of the great council and its president, Cardinal Beaufort, who not only ran the government but also bank-rolled it with his loans. And mistakes had been made.

One of the reasons military wages were so badly in arrears was that the treasury had been ordered to pay soldiers individually instead of through their captains, a policy which had to be reversed when Bedford resumed the regency because it was so impractical. Beaufort was also responsible for a huge increase in gifts of lands and captaincies to Englishmen, many of them his supporters who had come over on the coronation expedition: this caused resentment among long-serving English and Norman captains and, more seriously, created a problem for the future by putting the military infrastructure in the hands of those who would not reside permanently in France.[6]

Beaufort had also quarrelled personally with Bedford, who on 12 October 1431 had been forced to accept, under protest, that in future he would hold the office of regent as a commission from the king and council, rather than as his birthright, a change which introduced the possibility that he could be dismissed from office. Beaufort was undoubtedly behind this restriction on the regent's office, which was in line with the assertion of conciliar supremacy over Gloucester's role as protector of England. His reasoning for doing so at this juncture was probably because he was thinking of remaining behind once Henry VI returned to England. Since his arrival in France in 1429 he had worked hard to create a new power base for himself there. As president of the council in France he had effectively controlled administrative and diplomatic affairs there, confining Bedford's role to the military sphere. He therefore had little incentive to return to a marginalised position in England. If he wanted to retain his own powers in France he needed to limit those of Bedford once the latter resumed the regency on the king's departure, hence the issuing of a formal commission for the office. Though Bedford was forced to accept this, because he needed his uncle's money to shore up the war effort, he was not prepared to concede what was effectively a sharing of the regency. When the king left France Bedford made a small but significant change to his title: henceforth he would be 'Governor and Regent', emphasising the all-embracing nature of his appointment.[7]

Beaufort had dominated the coronation, which perhaps explains why it was so badly handled as far as the Parisians were concerned. He may also have been responsible for the abrupt ending of the king's residence in France because his own position in England was once again under serious attack. In November 1431 Gloucester, who was determined to prevent his uncle resuming public office in England, had brought a prosecution against him for becoming a cardinal without resigning his see of Winchester: if Beaufort did not appear in person to defend himself within two months, he was liable to forfeiture under the statute of praemunire. Returning with the king would obviously offer him some protection, which is why they set out for England together so soon after the coronation.

When they reached Calais, however, Beaufort's courage deserted him. Pleading a summons from the new pope, he obtained permission to go to Rome but instead stayed in Calais to await the arrival of his gold and jewels, which he had ordered to be shipped over to him. He had done this in secret and in contravention of laws controlling the export of precious metal, so when Gloucester found out, he had the perfect excuse to confiscate it all. And as his treasury was the security for his loans, Beaufort was now not only penniless but powerless too.

Unable to resist going for the kill, Gloucester dismissed all Beaufort's supporters in the English government and prepared to indict his uncle for treason. This proved to be a step too far for those who feared Gloucester's despotic tendencies and parliament intervened once again to impose a settlement. Beaufort was fined £6000 (£3.15m), refundable within six years if he proved his innocence, and required to make a loan of a further £6000: in return all the charges against him were dropped and his treasury was restored. Nevertheless, his influence over the king and the council, which he had been rebuilding since 1429, was at an end. Excluded from political power in both England

and France, he was forced to fall back on his diocesan duties, which must have been a novel and frustrating experience for him.[8]

While Henry was being welcomed back to London with lavish pageantry and by cheering crowds, Rouen was in the grip of the most serious attempt ever made to take the city during English rule. Marshal Boussac had assembled a force of six hundred men-at-arms at Beauvais and hidden them in the woods near Rouen. On the night of 3 February 1432, 120 of them, under the command of Guillaume de Ricarville, were sent on foot to the castle, where they were secretly admitted by Pierre Audebeuf, a Swiss traitor in the garrison. The sleeping English were completely taken by surprise and fled as best they could: the captain of Rouen, the earl of Arundel, who was trapped inside the great tower, made a dramatic escape by having himself lowered over the walls in a basket. With most of the castle in his hands, Ricarville went back to Boussac to bring the rest of the men, as agreed, only to find that they refused to help him and set off back to Beauvais.

Abandoned and unable to defend the entire castle without reinforcements, Ricarville's men retreated into the great tower with as many supplies as they could find. The English hastily called in reinforcements and weaponry, including one hundred gun-stones sent from Vernon; surrounding the tower, they began a bombardment that would last thirteen days and inflict such damage that it became indefensible, forcing Ricarville's men to surrender. Geoffroi Thérage was said to have executed 105 of them in a single day, including Audebeuf, who, as a traitor, was beheaded and quartered: his limbs were then displayed on the town gates and his head on a lance.[9]

That such a bold attempt was possible, and so nearly succeeded, in the heart of the English administration just weeks after the coronation was a remarkable indictment of the missed opportunity to encourage unity and loyalty presented by that occasion. It was also an indication that the Armagnacs regarded their general truce with Burgundy as an opportunity to exploit the weaknesses in the Anglo-Burgundian alliance. With the duke's troops removed from the field, the military burden fell entirely on the English, though some Burgundians, including l'Isle-Adam and Jehan de Luxembourg, continued to serve in English pay. English garrison forces being stretched to the limit increased the potential for Armagnacs to take strongholds by surprise. And in this they were aided by the fact that the Armagnac-Burgundian truce had hugely raised the hopes of the civilian population that a full peace settlement would follow. In the circumstances it is not surprising that the attempted betrayal of Rouen was only the first of nearly a dozen recorded conspiracies in 1432.

The most spectacular and successful occurred early in the morning of 12 April 1432. Two merchants from Chartres, who had been captured by the Armagnacs and persuaded to change sides, brought a dozen carts laden with barrels from Orléans into their home town. The gates were opened for them because they were well known, had safe-conducts and allegedly brought salt, which was in short supply. Yet once most of the wagons were safely through the gates the 'carters' blocked the drawbridge by killing the horse in the shafts of the next wagon and a number of soldiers leapt out of the barrels in which they were hiding. They killed the guards at the gate and secured the gatehouse. The Bastard of Orléans, Raoul de Gaucourt and La Hire (who was back in the field having just escaped from his prison at Dourdon) were waiting a short way off with an army and, at the agreed signal, charged into the town. They met with little resistance because their collaborator (and, if Monstrelet is to be believed, the man who conceived the plan), a Dominican friar, had arranged to preach an important sermon at the farthest end of the town, so that all the citizens would be gathered there. The town was taken before most of the startled citizens were even aware that the enemy was inside their gates. The Burgundian bishop of Chartres was killed in the street trying to fight his way out and all those who had 'governed for the English' were beheaded the following day.[10]

Another Dominican friar was the ringleader in a conspiracy to deliver Argentan to the neighbouring enemy garrison of

Bonsmoulins. An unfortunate merchant, Guillaume du Val, was also arrested because he had made regular trips to Bonsmoulins to negotiate the ransom and release of a trading partner held prisoner there. His visits were entirely legitimate because he had obtained permission to make them from Henry VI's lieutenant in Normandy. Nevertheless, under torture so severe that he lost the use of an arm and a leg, du Val revealed that the French had failed to persuade him to assist them in taking Argentan. He also confessed that he had recognised a man from the garrison at Bonsmoulins dining in disguise at the house of the Dominican. Implicated by his association with the traitors, as well as for not informing the authorities of his suspicious encounters, du Val was fortunate to escape with his life. It was only the fact that he had taken his place as a defender on the town walls when the alarm was eventually raised that secured him his pardon.[11]

Friars were particularly active as spies and enemy agents because their itinerant life and religious habit allowed them to travel from place to place and across political boundaries without raising suspicion. Charles VII regularly employed them as messengers and spies. One, known by the code-name *Samedi passé*, was sent 'many times' to Calais and other places 'to discover the enterprises of the English'; captured and tortured seven times, he spent twelve years in an English prison before he managed to escape, but was ultimately rewarded for his services by becoming a pensioner of the French crown. In Paris in September 1432, however, the unlikely traitors were the abbess of Saint-Anthoine-des-Champs and some of her nuns, who were arrested and taken into custody for plotting with the abbess's nephew to kill the gatekeepers at the Porte Saint-Anthoine and betray the city to the enemy.[12]

Not even Englishmen could always be trusted. At the beginning of June 1432 several Englishmen were executed at Pontoise for plotting with the citizens of the town to betray it to the Armagnacs. Later in the year Thomas Gernes and his companion were captured by the garrison at Domfront. For reasons which were not explained, but perhaps because they had settled on the land or had been captured and were unable to pay their ransoms, they had joined the enemy garrison at the castle of Gontier-sur-Orne. Before they were executed as 'Englishmen, traitors, thieves, brigands, enemies and adversaries' the two confessed that they had also committed a 'certain treason . . . which, quite simply, without having had this confession, could not have been discovered'.[13]

The surest method of preventing such betrayals was to offer peace, security and a plentiful supply of the necessities of life. None of these things was in Bedford's gift. Even the elements conspired against him. The winter of 1431–2 had been exceptionally long and hard. In January the Seine froze to a depth of two feet all the way upriver from Paris to Corbeil, stopping all the watermills in the city; ships on their way from Rouen to the capital were unable to pass beyond Mantes, so their much-needed cargoes of perishable food rotted. Constant frost, hail and bitter cold throughout the spring destroyed the buds and flowers of fruit and nut trees, ruining the prospects for the autumn harvest. Heavy rains and floods in July were followed by scorching heat in August which burned the vines and made the corn crop fail, creating a shortage of bread but also prolonging the scarcity by ensuring that there would be no stocks of seed corn to plant the following year. Famine and disease always went hand in hand but it was young people and small children who fell victim to the epidemic sweeping through Paris.[14]

Bedford did what he could to alleviate the situation, concentrating his efforts on trying to prevent Armagnac raids, which disrupted trade and destroyed the countryside, by recapturing their bases. After retaking Louviers he had, at the request of the estates-general of Normandy, kept three hundred men-at-arms and nine hundred archers in the field under the command of lord Willoughby. His specific remit was to recover several fortresses on the Norman frontier within a twenty-mile radius of Sées, including Bonsmoulins and Saint-Cénéry, and substantial sums had been granted to support his campaign.[15]

The reason for targeting these strongholds as a priority was that their captain was Ambroise de Loré, marshal of the duke of Alençon, and on 29 September 1431 he had led seven hundred men in a daring raid from Saint-Cénéry. They had managed to travel undetected for fifty-five miles through the heart of Normandy, the last ten of them with the aid of guides who led them through valleys and covert ways to the outskirts of Caen. Their objective was the annual Michaelmas fair which was always held in the open fields between the town and the abbey of Saint-Étienne.

Their attack came out of the blue. The terrified merchants and citizens abandoned their stalls and goods and fled back towards the town in such numbers that the gatekeepers were unable to open or close the gates for the press of the crowd. Soldiers from the garrison tried to make a sortie to rescue them, but were beaten back so decisively that the Armagnacs were almost within the walls themselves. Loré knew, however, that he did not have enough men to take the town and had the presence of mind to draw his troops back. He had achieved what he wanted, striking terror into the heart of Normandy and gaining a rich haul of merchandise, horses and prisoners. Many of those taken captive were wealthy merchants and citizens of Caen, who were brought back to Bonsmoulins to be held until ransomed: the demand for Guillaume du Val's business partner alone was 2000 *saluts* (£160,417) in cash, two lengths of silver cloth and other, more minor items.[16]

When news reached Loré that Willoughby had laid siege to Saint-Cénéry with a huge artillery train, he obtained permission from the duke of Alençon to attempt a relief operation, and set up camp fifteen miles away in two villages either side of the river Sarthe connected only by a single bridge. Getting wind of this, Matthew Gough led a detachment out from the besieging army under cover of night: at dawn he fell upon those in Vivoin, catching them by surprise and overwhelming them.

The cries of those being attacked attracted the attention of those lodged at Beaumont-le-Vicomte, who saw the English standards already flying around Vivoin. Despite being heavily outnumbered, Loré launched a counter-attack with the small force of bowmen available to him, to buy time for the soldiers on the other side of the river to cross over to join him. After several hours of indecisive fighting, during which the Armagnacs were constantly reinforced by those from Beaumont-le-Vicomte filing steadily over the bridge, they eventually carried the day.

The English fled, leaving Matthew Gough a prisoner in enemy hands. It was all the more frustrating that they had actually captured Loré himself, who had been badly wounded, only for him to be rescued before the day was out. Worse still, his men were so infuriated when they mistakenly thought he had been killed that they massacred all their English prisoners in an act of revenge which breached the laws of war. The next day Willoughby abandoned his siege of Saint-Cénéry, leaving behind several of the great guns and siege engines in his haste to withdraw without further losses.[17]

Bedford, meanwhile, was equally unsuccessful. At the beginning of May he had begun his second attempt in two years to relieve Paris by taking Lagny-sur-Marne. Despite throwing several temporary bridges across the Marne and building a fortified encampment surrounded by ditches which was larger than Lagny itself, his troops made no headway. They had to endure floods and a heatwave so powerful that some of the men-at-arms died from heatstroke because they were encased in armour: Bedford himself was said to have collapsed with exhaustion. And long-promised reinforcements from England failed to arrive.

Early in August the Bastard of Orléans, Raoul de Gaucourt, Gilles de Rais and Roderigo de Villandrando brought a large army to the relief of Lagny garrison. While the rest drew up in battle formation and kept the English busy with diversionary skirmishes and attacks on their encampment, Gaucourt slipped into Lagny from the other side with reinforcements and desperately needed supplies. The rest of the Armagnac army then withdrew towards Paris, still in battle formation, forcing Bedford to choose between continuing his siege and pursuing them to prevent an attack on the capital. When Bedford sent a message offering to fight them in a pitched battle, he was told in no uncertain terms that 'they had done what they came to do' and there was therefore no need for battle. Without the twelve hundred reinforcements, who were only just embarking from England, Bedford did not have enough men both to maintain the siege and protect Paris. On 20 August 1432 he therefore reluctantly raised his siege and returned to the capital, much to the disgust of its citizens, who were too afraid of the resurgent Armagnacs to venture into the countryside for the grape harvest, so that a shortage of wine was added to the lengthening list of their miseries.[18]

With the Lagny garrison free to continue raiding several times a week up to the gates of Paris and disrupting essential supplies of food and firewood into the capital, the Parisians would continue to suffer the consequences of Bedford's failure for years to come. Their problems were compounded by the epidemic which continued to rage in the city and, on 13 November, claimed its most important victim. Anne, duchess of Bedford, was twenty-eight years old. Her marriage was childless but her quiet and unobtrusive diplomacy had done much to bolster relations between the two dukes personally and in the wider context of their supporters. 'She was good and beautiful,' the citizen of Paris lamented. 'The Parisians loved her . . . and with her died most of the hope that Paris had, but this had to be endured.' Her funeral exemplified the union of French and English customs which she and Bedford had promoted. Parisian priests led the processions wearing black stoles and carrying candles. Then, as her body was lowered into the grave, the English took over, singing most movingly, 'in the fashion of their own country', the polyphonic music for unaccompanied voices which had been pioneered in the royal chapel and become famous throughout northern Europe.[19]

The severing of this link opened another small but significant crack in the Anglo-Burgundian alliance. The strains were beginning to tell. Burgundy's announcement of his six-year truce with Charles VII in 1431 had raised popular hopes and expectations that a general peace might follow, especially as it was widely known that the new pope, Eugenius IV, was determined to broker an end to the conflict and had sent his envoy, Cardinal Albergati, to France to mediate a settlement. None of the parties involved had requested or even wanted this intervention but neither could they afford to offend the head of the universal church by refusing to cooperate with his initiative. Their unwillingness to engage in any meaningful way with the peace process doomed the talks to failure.

In November 1432 Albergati chaired a three-way conference at Auxerre between the English, Burgundians and Armagnacs. It soon became clear that nothing concrete could be achieved. All the arguments that would be rehearsed so many times over the coming years were trotted out on this occasion. The English had already decided as long ago as May 1431 that they could not commit Henry VI to a peace treaty while he was still legally a minor, but they were willing to accept a truce. The Armagnacs insisted that the French prisoners held in England since Agincourt should be a party to the proceedings: this was not unreasonable as the dukes of Orléans and Bourbon and the count of Eu were all Armagnac and no lasting peace could be made unless they were reconciled with the Burgundians. They refused, however, even to consider a peace unless Henry first surrendered his claim to the French throne, which was unacceptable to the English.

Philippe of Burgundy, who was in the happy position of being able to play the two sides off against each other, sought only the best possible deal for himself. What he wanted from the Armagnacs, apart from an apology and compensation for the murder of his father, was the cession to him of the county of Champagne. In the end all that could be agreed was that they should meet again in March 1433 and the Agincourt prisoners should be involved. When the commissioners returned to Paris the citizen noted in his journal that they had 'done nothing except spend a great deal of money and waste their time', a bitter but accurate description of the intransigence on all sides.[20]

A miserable year for Bedford and the English kingdom of France ended with the unexpected rebellion of a Norman who had been an important supporter of the regime from the beginning of the conquest. Raoul Tesson, sire du Grippon, had submitted early to Henry V and in April 1422 had been rewarded with the gift of all the land and property confiscated from his brother, Jean, who had left Normandy for Armagnac territory and never returned. On 21 August 1429, in the crisis caused by the Pucelle's victories, Tesson had been appointed captain of Saint-Lô, replacing the earl of Suffolk, who had been captured at Jargeau. It was a significant display of trust in him, for the town was strategically important and had recently been subjected to a number of raids by the garrison of Mont-Saint-Michel. During Henry VI's sojourn in Rouen Tesson had come to swear his oath of loyalty in person to the young king, and in June 1432 he had personally served at the siege of Lagny with a large contingent of twenty-one men-at-arms and sixty-three archers, almost half of whom he had had to find himself.[21]

Six months later, however, Tesson was a 'traitor and disobedient'. The earl of Arundel was forced to take most of his garrison from Rouen and race to Saint-Lô to resist and repel 'by battle or otherwise' the duke of Alençon's army, which had entered Normandy to take the town by means of Tesson's treachery. Perhaps as a result of Arundel's diligence, the attempt to take Saint-Lô failed. Tesson withdrew with his family and household to Mont-Saint-Michel, where in 1433 they participated in a sea raid on Granville, the rocky peninsula at the northernmost point of the bay, capturing several English ships and bringing them back to the island. Tesson's extensive possessions were confiscated and lands, worth an annual 875*l.t.* (£51,042), were granted in March 1433 to Richard Merbury, the English captain of Gisors.[22]

Another long, hard winter, with frosts nearly every day until Easter and long periods when the Seine was again frozen, preventing the shipment of supplies into Paris, did nothing to raise spirits. 'There was no bread eaten in Paris except such as used to be made for dogs', the citizen complained, 'and even that was so small that a man's hand would cover a fourpenny loaf.' In Calais the garrison became so desperate when the English government failed yet again to pay their wages that they mutinied: they seized the wool belonging to the merchants of the Staple, the company which held the monopoly on the export of English wool, and forcibly ejected Sir William Oldhall, Bedford's deputy in the town.[23]

For Bedford these setbacks were made worse by the knowledge that he could expect little or no aid from England, where Gloucester's government was teetering on the brink of bankruptcy. The previous year had seen only one English expedition sent to France: led by lords Camoys and Hungerford, it had consisted of only twelve hundred men and its departure had been delayed until August because no money was available to pay its wages until Gloucester and Cardinal Beaufort had settled their quarrel, reopening the stream of loans from Beaufort. Once again it had been too little too late, and as a consequence Lagny-sur-Marne had been lost.[24]

The situation had not improved over the winter and Bedford faced the prospect of beginning a new campaigning season without substantial support from either England or Burgundy. It was perhaps for this reason that he decided to align himself more closely with one family which had remained steadfastly loyal and supportive. Louis de Luxembourg, bishop of Thérouanne, was a former president of the *chambre-des-comptes* in Paris, a member of the Norman council and, since 1424, chancellor of France; his brother, Jehan de Luxembourg, count of Guise and Ligny, had consistently provided military support in the field and served in person regularly with the Anglo-Burgundian army. Their brother, Pierre, was count of Saint-Pol, in Artois, and it was his daughter, Jacquetta, that Louis de Luxembourg suggested Bedford should marry.

The marriage meant that Bedford could continue to rely on the military support of the house of Luxembourg but it also had political advantages. It strengthened ties with the Low Countries, where England had substantial trading and economic interests, and with the Emperor Sigismund, who was Jacquetta's cousin. It also rejuvenated Bedford's own territorial ambitions in Artois, which had been thwarted by the death of Anne of Burgundy and the birth of a legitimate son and heir to her brother.[25] His new bride, who was just seventeen, 'frisky, beautiful and gracious', might provide the forty-three-year-old Bedford with a legitimate heir. (He already had two bastards from liaisons before he married Anne.) After all, Philippe of Burgundy had had two childless marriages yet his third wife, Isabella, was now expecting his second son. (Philippe allegedly managed the prodigious feat of fathering twenty-six bastards, though only one of his three legitimate sons survived infancy.)[26]

The marriage was celebrated in Artois on 20 April 1433 at Louis de Luxembourg's episcopal seat of Thérouanne. Whatever political advantages Bedford may have hoped to gain by it were nullified by the reaction of the duke of Burgundy. Philippe was offended by both the haste of the remarriage and the fact that the count of Saint-Pol had not sought his permission for it, as he was bound to do because the duke was his feudal overlord. It was a further affront to Burgundy's dignity that the wedding had taken place within his own county of Artois, albeit in a royal enclave that was not subject to his jurisdiction.[27]

Cardinal Beaufort, who had always enjoyed a good personal relationship with Burgundy, was so concerned about the situation and its potential to split the Anglo-Burgundian alliance that he organised a special meeting between the two dukes at Saint-Omer at the end of May. His object was to effect a reconciliation but he had not counted on the depth of personal pride and pique involved. Both dukes arrived in the town but neither would make the first move to accept the subservient role of visiting the other: Bedford claimed precedence as regent; Burgundy refused to cede it because Saint-Omer was in his territory. Nothing Beaufort could do or say would persuade them to put aside their differences and they left Saint-Omer without having met. It was, like the coronation, another opportunity lost, for they would never meet again.[28]

CHAPTER THIRTEEN

Recovery

By the spring of 1433 it had become clear that the English kingdom of France was under serious threat. As a direct consequence of Philippe of Burgundy's truces with Charles VII and his subsequent withdrawal from an active military role, the burden of defending the realm now fell entirely on the English, stretching Bedford's military and financial resources to the limit. The regent had been unable to prevent Armagnac captains raiding deep into the heart of Normandy or closing in on Paris itself. Plots to betray major towns and fortresses to the enemy were rife and required constant vigilance. And the strained state of relations with Burgundy raised the spectre of an irrevocable breach between the allies which could only exacerbate Bedford's difficulties. Without substantial and regular aid from England, the regent was acutely aware that his position in France was unsustainable.

In April 1433 Bedford therefore convened a crisis meeting at Calais. It was attended by Gloucester and Cardinal Beaufort, together with representatives of both the councils of England and France, and its purpose was to agree a strategy to safeguard the future of the English kingdom of France. The choice of venue was significant, coming only a few weeks after the mutiny of the Calais garrison, which Bedford had ended by promising to pay the soldiers' overdue wages from the local customs. His first actions on entering the town, however, were to withdraw his promise and order the arrest of the mutineers. One hundred and twenty of them were evicted from Calais but, when Bedford returned to the town after his wedding, he personally supervised their trials, in which four men were sentenced to death and a further 110 banished. Though mutiny could not be tolerated, his actions were seen as vindictive and unnecessary, further souring his relations with Calais, but also with his brother Gloucester, who had always championed the town.[1]

The two brothers were already at loggerheads, each disapproving of the other's handling of affairs within their respective jurisdictions. Bedford blamed Gloucester for the abysmal state of England's finances, which had deprived him of the men, money and goodwill he needed to defend the English kingdom of France; Gloucester, who had always believed he could do a better job than Bedford in prosecuting the war, blamed him for the reverses of the previous year.

When they met in Calais, therefore, it was no surprise that they were unable to agree and Bedford's demands for an increased commitment from England did not receive a sympathetic hearing. All that he was able to secure was another loan of 10,000 marks (£3.5m) from Beaufort, to finance the recapture of Saint-Valery, a Burgundian stronghold in Picardy which had just been taken by the Armagnacs. The loan purchased the cardinal's way back into favour with his nephews but it must have given Bedford further cause for alarm that the English treasury was unable to find any stream of income from which Beaufort could be repaid: the only security he could be given was letters of obligation provided by sympathetic members of the council.[2]

It was an indication of the depth of Bedford's concern that he decided he would have to go to England in person to rally support for the cause in France and to investigate the true state of English finances. On 24 May 1433 he ordered writs to be sent out summoning a parliament to meet at Westminster on 8 July and early in June he sailed for England with his new bride.[3] His arrival meant that Gloucester had to give up his authority as protector to his elder brother, enabling Bedford to make sweeping changes in the government and administration.

He began in parliament with a passionate speech to the king, lords and commons defending his own conduct in France:

> he had heard from the report of several persons how a false and perverse belief was being put about and spread among very many people in the realm of England, namely that the damage and loss which our aforesaid lord king had sustained in his realm of France and in his duchy of Normandy must have resulted from the negligence and carelessness of the duke himself, which was to the scandal of his person and to the grave damage of his name, reputation and honour, but also to the sadness and sorrow of his heart.

Bedford then challenged anyone, of whatever rank, who wished to uphold such a charge against him to repeat it before the king in parliament and offered to prove his innocence in a judicial duel 'according to what the law of arms demands and requires'. Though Bedford undoubtedly meant what he said when he offered to fight his accuser to the death, he must have known that it was extremely unlikely that anyone would take up his challenge and that his emotionally charged rhetoric would elicit a public vote of confidence. This he duly received. The king, Gloucester and members of the royal council all denied knowledge of any such scandalous rumours and the eleven-year-old king gave his 'most special thanks' to 'his true and faithful liege and his dearest uncle . . . for his good, laudable and fruitful services expended in many ways'.[4]

Having obtained the royal endorsement and stamped his authority on parliament, Bedford set about taking personal control of the English government. It was clear to him that the best interests of neither country were being served by Gloucester, whose lack of judgement, jealousy and quarrelsome nature were creating friction and faction among the aristocracy, or by the royal council, whose independence and narrow interests were at odds with the wider concerns of his nephew's two kingdoms. Bedford began by securing for himself a twelve-year appointment as lieutenant of Calais and captain of all the fortresses in the Calais marches: only Guînes, where Gloucester was captain, was excluded and that was to be handed over to Bedford in 1436 when Gloucester's term of office ended. This meant that Calais, which had always been ruled and funded directly from England, would retain this special status but its interests would no longer be considered separately and independently: Bedford would now be able to incorporate it into his overall strategy for the defence of the English kingdom of France. In return he conceded the partial reversal of his judgement against the mutineers of the Calais garrison: parliament was allowed to restore the wages, lands and rents of those who lived in the town.[5]

This was followed by the removal from office of Gloucester's nominees, including the treasurer, who was replaced by Ralph, lord Cromwell. It was immediately clear that the exchequer was empty and that all its revenues for the next two years were already assigned to repay loans to the crown. Within two days of his appointment Cromwell instituted reforms and economies to address the situation and began an audit so that he could present its results to the king in the next session of parliament. It revealed that 'all the revenues and profits, ordinary and extraordinary, certain or casual, which pertain to you for any reason are insufficient for the burden and satisfying of your ordinary annual charges by the sum of £35,000 [£18.38m] per year and more'. And that was without including any expenditure on the war in France.[6]

This was a powerful argument in favour of a peace settlement with Charles VII but the negotiations mediated by Cardinal Albergati had already foundered. The representatives of the three parties had reconvened in March 1433 at Seine-Port, a deserted village between Corbeil and Mantes. The English, in a gesture of goodwill which they hoped would lead to a lengthy truce, had then offered to bring their Agincourt prisoners to Dover and provide facilities for them to confer with the

Armagnacs, if the conferences were relocated to Calais. In anticipation of the delegation's arrival the dukes of Bourbon and
Orléans were moved to Dover, and Bedford, Gloucester, Beaufort
and members of the councils of both kingdoms stayed on in
Calais until 23 May. Their wait was in vain for the Armagnacs
refused to come.

Albergati succeeded in bringing them all back to the table at
Seine-Port in June, but the most he could persuade the Armagnacs
to offer was a four-month truce, which even their own ambassadors conceded would be of little effect, saying that 'if their master
had a hundred thousand écus [£1.46m], he could not enforce it,
because only foreigners served in his war, he had abandoned the
country to them, and they would not obey him in this'. The
English rejected the offer outright, seeing it as merely an opportunity for the Armagnacs to provision their strongholds and
prolong English expenses in besieging them. They would consider
nothing less than a truce for twelve months. Albergati gave up and
went to Basle to report his failure to the general council of the
church meeting there.[7]

The Parisians had no hesitation in blaming their own chancellor, Louis de Luxembourg, for this unsatisfactory result. It
was noted that he had spent the time between the two peace conferences at Corbeil gathering troops in Normandy which he
brought to Paris in the first week of July. Perhaps as a result of
Armagnac propaganda, the citizen-diarist believed that Albergati
and Regnault de Chartres, the principal Armagnac negotiator,
had already agreed and signed a peace treaty: it was only Louis
de Luxembourg, 'a man of blood' whom Bedford had left in
charge in his absence, who refused to sign it. The people therefore detested him: 'It was said secretly – and openly too, often
enough – that if it were not for him France would be at peace, so
that he and his accomplices were more hated and cursed than
ever the Emperor Nero was.'[8]

This was unfair, for what the Parisians did not yet know was
that there had been a seismic shift in Armagnac policy. Despite
Jehanne d'Arc's intervention on his behalf, Arthur de Richemont
had never been readmitted to Charles VII's presence and it was

no secret that he hated Georges de la Trémoïlle, who had procured his banishment and reigned supreme as court favourite.
Knowing this, Bedford had offered to 'cede' the county of Poitou
to Richemont's brother, the duke of Brittany, and a number of
lordships, including La Rochelle, and all Trémoïlle's possessions
in Poitou to Richemont himself, in the hope of winning his support for a closer Anglo-Breton alliance. The offer was a hollow
one, since none of these places was actually in English hands, but
it was meant to give Richemont an incentive to conquer them
and revenge himself on Trémoïlle.

Richemont, however, was more interested in acquiring his
hated rival's lands by less strenuous means and had been plotting
with the Angevin party to overthrow their mutual enemy. In
June 1433 Raoul de Gaucourt's lieutenant at Chinon secretly
opened a postern gate at night to admit a band of armed conspirators, including the Bretons Prégent de Coëtivy and Pierre de
Brézé. They seized Trémoïlle at sword-point from his bed,
wounding him in the process, and, when questioned by a terrified Charles VII, who thought they were about to commit
regicide, informed him that they had done it 'for his own good
and for the good of the realm'.

The tables were now turned. Trémoïlle was charged with
financial irregularities, removed from office and exiled to his
castle of Sully. The queen's brother, Charles d'Anjou, became the
new court favourite and Richemont returned in triumph. The
Angevin-Breton party was now back in power, bringing with it
a return to the pro-war policies of the Jehanne d'Arc era.[9]

The possibility of securing a lasting peace, which had always
been remote, had now been removed altogether and the renewed
belligerence of the Armagnacs did what diplomatic efforts had
failed to do: it persuaded the Burgundians that the English
alliance was still in their best interests. For, despite the six-year
general peace that had been agreed in 1430, Burgundian territories were everywhere under attack, from Saint-Valery in
Picardy to Pacy-sur-Armançon in the duchy of Burgundy itself.
Clearly the Armagnac ambassadors had been correct when they
admitted that Charles VII could not enforce a binding truce on

his foreign mercenaries who lived off the land and had nothing to gain by peace.

In the summer of 1433 Philippe sent an embassy to England to test English opinion. It was led by the Anglophile Hue de Lannoy, but even he detected a certain frostiness in the atmosphere, which the earl of Warwick explained in forthright fashion: 'We English, to tell you the truth, are exceedingly displeased and disappointed that, whilst the king was in France, my lord of Burgundy, your master, has neither seen him nor visited him.' Bedford was more emollient, seeking to heal the personal breach between himself and Burgundy: 'By my faith, I promise you that it displeases me much that my brother-in-law has such a bad opinion of me; for I do not hate him; he is one of this world's princes whom I have always loved the most. And I know well that the way we have conducted ourselves is greatly prejudicial to my lord the king and to the public good.'[10]

In the dispatches he sent home Lannoy was able to reassure Burgundy that the English were not, as he had feared, intending to make a separate peace with the Armagnacs, though he picked up rumours that 'certain persons' were pushing for a marriage between Henry VI and one of the infant daughters of Charles VII. This is the first real indication we have that there were those among the young king's councillors who had begun to look beyond the stated English objective of a mere truce towards a more permanent settlement. This was not, as some historians have characterised it, the emergence of a 'peace faction' as opposed to a 'war faction', which is a simplistic view that does not take into account the fact that both 'parties' were equally committed to the preservation of the English kingdom of France but sought to achieve that aim by different means. Though opinions became more entrenched with the passing years there was never an explicit division along party lines. Gloucester was a die-hard opponent of any concession to the French and unswerving in his belief that the military option was the only way forward, but in this he was virtually alone. On the other side, even Cardinal Beaufort and the earl of Suffolk, who are generally seen as leaders of a 'peace faction', were not inclined to support anything more than limited concessions to secure a lasting peace and both did more than most to support the war effort: Beaufort was its chief financier and Suffolk, with thirteen years of continuous military service in France already under his belt, would return to arms again in the crisis of 1436. With the exception of Gloucester, probably every person of any influence in the royal council believed that a lasting peace could not be achieved without diplomatic engagement with the enemy. The only point at issue was the price by which peace could be purchased.[11]

In 1433 the earl of Suffolk was already one of those looking to a long-term and peaceful resolution of the war. His capture at Jargeau had brought an abrupt and permanent end to his military career. He had earned a swift release at the beginning of 1430 by promising to pay his captor, the Bastard of Orléans, an enormous ransom of £20,000 (£10.5m) and, more significantly, to endeavour to secure the release of the Bastard's two half-brothers, Charles d'Orléans and the count of Angoulême. This gave him a personal interest in a negotiated settlement and, as part of the process, in the summer of 1432 he acquired custody of the captive duke. Together, he hoped, they could act as intermediaries between the English and the Armagnacs.

Suffolk was undoubtedly one of those members of the royal council who promoted the idea of a marriage between Henry VI and a Valois princess and he freely admitted to Hue de Lannoy in the summer of 1433 that he now had greater hopes of a general peace than he had ever had before. He permitted Lannoy to meet Charles d'Orléans in his presence but it was an uncomfortable occasion. Charles told Lannoy that he was 'in good bodily health but he was unhappy that he was spending the best years of his life as a prisoner'; he indicated his eagerness to serve as an intermediary for the cause of peace but made it clear by his gestures that he did not dare to say what he really wished and he was not allowed to write a personal letter to Burgundy. So desperate was Orléans to obtain his freedom, after almost eighteen years in captivity, that a few weeks after this opportunity eluded him he agreed to recognise Henry VI as the true king of France and his supreme lord, even in unconquered Mont-Saint-Michel.

The duke of Bourbon had made a similar submission in 1429 but neither man regained his liberty.[12]

The official purpose of Lannoy's mission was to present Henry VI with letters urging him either to make peace or a long general truce, or alternatively 'to make such and so terrible a war that the pride of the enemies may be humbled and, by this means, they may be forced to come to the said peace or truce'. This was, of course, a polite way of saying that Burgundy wanted more money and men to defend his own interests, obliging the king's councillors to point out the quite astonishing level of their commitment to the English kingdom of France: the English were currently paying for four months the wages of 9700 soldiers: 1600 were besieging Saint-Valery with the count of Saint-Pol and 500 men in Burgundy's pay; 1200 were in the field to safeguard the lower marches of Normandy with the earl of Huntingdon; 900 were in the field in Alençon and Maine under the earl of Arundel; added to which there were 'more than 6000' serving in garrisons in France, Normandy, Anjou and Maine.[13]

These surprising figures are borne out by other independent evidence. Arundel's contract for service, for instance, obliged him to recruit two hundred men-at-arms and six hundred archers, but it often happened that the overall numbers exceeded the contractual requirement, particularly if there was difficulty in obtaining sufficient men-at-arms, in which case several archers might be accepted in lieu of each missing man-at-arms. An audit of soldiers serving in garrisons from Michaelmas 1433 to Michaelmas 1434 reveals that 488 mounted men-at-arms, 523 foot men-at-arms and 2925 archers, or 3936 men in total, were employed in Normandy and the counties of Alençon and Maine alone. A further 2000 in garrisons in France does not therefore seem unreasonable.[14]

Lannoy's mission to England was not successful in terms of mobilising an immediate surge in troop numbers, but it did renew military cooperation between the two allies, both of whom had an interest in weakening the Armagnac grip on the Gâtinais area south of Paris. In June 1433 Perrinet Gressart and his nephew by marriage François de Surienne were able to capture Montargis, a stronghold some seventy miles south of Paris, by means of a barber in the town who was bribed by the woman he wished to marry into showing them where to scale the castle walls. His treachery cost Gressart and Surienne 2000 *écus* (£145,833) but they still turned a handsome profit, having been promised 10,000 *saluts* (£802,083) by Bedford for taking Montargis. Surienne, who always wore the red cross of England even when fighting in Burgundian pay, became captain of Montargis, providing him with the excuse he needed to withdraw from the Burgundian army and turn Montargis into a second La-Charité-sur-Loire.[15]

The capture of Montargis opened the way for Philippe of Burgundy to begin a major campaign on the border of his duchy for the recovery of places lost to the Armagnacs in 1431. From July to November Philippe led his armies in person, spending over 150,000 *francs* (£8.75m) of his own money in the process. Lord Talbot, newly released from his four-year captivity since the battle of Patay, was dispatched from Paris at the head of sixteen hundred soldiers to assist in this campaign, helping to retake Pacy-sur-Armançon and many of the Burgundian towns on the river Yonne. In the meantime lord Willoughby and Bedford's father-in-law, the count of Saint-Pol, were operating in Picardy, recovering Saint-Valery for the Burgundians on 20 August 1433 after a three-month siege. Eleven days later, while making preparations to lay siege to Rambures, the count died suddenly, so it was left to his brother, Jehan de Luxembourg, and the new count, who confusingly shared his uncle's name, to continue the campaign.[16]

The twenty-five-year-old earl of Arundel, acting as lieutenant in the lower marches of Normandy, was also making headway in Maine. On 10 March 1433 he issued a pardon to the churchmen and inhabitants of Sées, which he had just recaptured from the Armagnacs in the town's fifth change of ownership since 1418. He also successfully targeted the neighbouring fortresses, belonging to Ambroise de Loré, which Willoughby had failed to take the previous year. Bonsmoulins surrendered relatively quickly and its fortifications were demolished to prevent its use by the enemy again. Saint-Cénéry proved a more difficult nut to crack, not least because Loré's wife and children were in the castle and the defenders were determined not to let them fall into English hands. They held out for three months but Arundel's great bombards succeeded in making a huge breach in the wall and most of the Armagnac leaders, including Loré's lieutenant in charge of the castle, were killed attempting to defend it. Since Loré himself did not come to their rescue in time, the remaining besieged had no choice but to surrender and were allowed to leave on foot but without any of their possessions. It was a measure of Saint-Cénéry's strategic importance that the treasurer of Normandy, John Stanlawe, was personally sent to supervise its demolition in February 1434.[17]

Arundel himself moved thirty-six miles south-west, to the other side of Alençon, to besiege Sillé-le-Guillaume, which agreed to surrender in six weeks' time if no relief arrived. The army that Loré had raised to help Saint-Cénéry was now commandeered by the duke of Alençon, Arthur de Richemont and Charles d'Anjou and diverted to Sillé-le-Guillaume. Arriving just before the deadline, the relief force squared up to Arundel's army and some skirmishing took place, but neither side was prepared to commit to battle. Nevertheless, the Armagnacs sent their herald to Arundel, demanding the return of the hostages given for the surrender on the grounds that a relief force had indeed been brought, according to the terms of the capitulation. Arundel conceded the point, handed over the hostages and made as if to withdraw. As soon as the Armagnacs had dispersed, however, he returned to Sillé-le-Guillaume and, catching the garrison unawares, took the place by assault.[18]

Despite these military successes, there was still no security for the civilian population as the Armagnacs kept up the pressure elsewhere. In September La Hire led a raid from his base at Beauvais, forty-five miles north-west of Paris, into the heart of Artois and the region round Cambrai, over eighty miles away, rounding up peasants for ransom, plundering and burning houses, mills, churches and villages with impunity.[19]

The combination of renewed Armagnac aggression so close to Paris and frustration at the failure of Cardinal Albergati's peace talks led to two major conspiracies to betray the capital to the enemy. The two plots were apparently independently conceived and both were planned for the last week of September. One involved a number of wealthy citizens, who had arranged for several thousand Armagnacs to be stationed in quarries and other hiding places outside the city. In a variation on the sub-terfuge which had tricked Verneuil into submission in 1429, two hundred Scots would enter Paris wearing the cross of Saint George and pretending to be English soldiers escorting a hun-dred 'prisoners' who were, in fact, their fellow countrymen. They would enter the gates at noon, when the gatekeepers were eating their dinner, kill them, capture the gates and fortresses, and admit the armies waiting outside.

The second plot involved secretly bringing a number of soldiers in small boats into the city along the moats between the Saint-Denis and Saint-Honoré gates, where there were no houses for them to be observed. They intended to launch their attack on the feast of Saint-Denis, when the Parisians could be caught off-guard at their patron's celebrations and massacred. Both conspiracies were discovered and those involved beheaded as traitors.[20]

In November there was widespread panic in lower Normandy when the garrison of Avranches learned through six captured soldiers from Mont-Saint-Michel that the duke of Alençon had entered the duchy with a large army the previous day to seize one of four towns which had been sold to the enemy. The *bailli* of the Cotentin wrote 'in haste' to warn Caen, Bayeux, Saint-Lô and Neuilly l'Évêque that they were all at grave risk of betrayal and attack, urging them to pay special attention to their watches by day and night and adding the no doubt heartfelt prayer, 'may Our Lord have you in his holy safe-keeping'.[21]

It was a sign of the times that, on the cusp of the new year, the abbot of Saint-Ouen in Rouen received royal permission to hold its courts of forest pleas within the abbey precincts, as he could not find a justice who was prepared to go out into the forest because of the war and fear of being attacked by enemies and brigands. A couple of weeks later, on 13 January 1434, a former *vicomte* of Pont-Audemer was excused having to travel in person to attend the *chambre-des-comptes* in Paris 'for fear of the dangers both by water and by land.'[22]

The council of Normandy wrote to the *bailli* of Caen about the same time, informing him that rumours were again circulating that the Armagnacs were assembling ready to capture certain towns in Normandy and telling him to have it proclaimed throughout his *bailliage* that no one from the countryside carrying weapons (even a simple wooden staff) or wearing armour should be allowed to enter a town unless they left them outside. Hot on the heels of this letter came another, ordering him to inform the captains of Falaise, Bayeux and Avranches to be on the alert as their towns had been sold to the enemy.[23]

On 29 January La Hire attacked a convoy of some two thousand pigs, together with large quantities of cattle and sheep, which was being driven to Paris. Not content with killing the escort, seizing the beasts and holding the merchants to ransom, La Hire's men returned to the scene of the ambush to search the field: 'and they cut the throat of every man, alive or dead, who wore an English emblem or who spoke English'. The following week they carried out a night attack on Vitry, a few miles outside Paris, sacking and burning it, and then La Hire's brother, Amado de Vignolles, established a base a mere twenty miles north of the capital at the castle of Beaumont-sur-Oise, which had supposedly been dismantled. It was no wonder that the Parisians felt abandoned. 'There was at this time no news of the Regent', the citizen of Paris noted in his journal, adding bitterly, 'No one governed, except the Bishop of Thérouanne, a man whom the people detested.'[24]

Bedford had not abandoned the English kingdom of France, though he must have been sorely tempted. On 24 November 1433 the House of Commons had presented the king with a lengthy petition which lavished praise on the way in which Bedford, 'through his great wisdom and valour, with long and continuous personal labour, peril and danger', had 'nobly done his duty' in preserving the French kingdom:

and as often as the matter required it, he has subjected his person to the deed and to the danger of war as the poorest

knight or gentleman who was there in the king's service, and
undertaken many great and noble deeds worthy to be held in
remembrance forever; and in particular the battle of Verneuil,
which was the greatest deed undertaken by Englishmen in our
time, save for the battle of Agincourt . . . in addition, the said
commons consider that the presence and residence of my said
lord of Bedford in this realm since his arrival has been most
beneficial, and that the peaceful rule and governance of this
realm has thereby greatly grown and been increased by both
the noble model and example that he has given to others . . .
and also in assisting through his great wisdom and discretion
by means of advice and counsel to the king and to the said
rule and governance.[25]

In short they begged the king to 'will, pray and desire' Bedford
to stay in England, a petition that the lords seconded. Such a
ringing personal endorsement must have been music to Bedford's
ears, especially given the reasons that had brought him to
England in the first place, but he believed it was his sacred duty
to bear the burden of governing France that his brother had laid
upon him.

After considering the matter for several weeks he put his own
proposals to parliament, setting out the terms under which he
would spend more time in England, until his nephew came of
age. These included his right to be consulted upon the appointment of members of the English council, officers of state and
bishops, and upon the dismissal of secular appointees; that
before any parliament was summoned he should be informed of
the potential date and place, 'wherever I shall be in my lord's
service'; and that a book should be kept of the names of all
those 'old and feeble' servants who had spent their lives in his
grandfather's, father's and brother's service, so that they might
be rewarded with appropriate offices and annuities whenever
these fell vacant. He also asked that he should be paid £500
(£262,500) for his expenses in crossing the Channel as required
but offered to accept a salary of only £1000 (£525,000) a year,
payable proportionately for the amount of time he spent in

England. This was a direct reproach to his brother, Gloucester, who had raised his own annual salary as protector to 8000 marks (£2.8m), despite the financial difficulties of the realm.[26]

Indeed the entire package was implicitly critical of Gloucester, whose position was now reduced to that of a senior member of the king's council. What the new arrangement cleverly succeeded in doing was to make Bedford the highest authority in both kingdoms during the king's minority, but without undermining the principle of their separate governance set out in the Treaty of Troyes.[27] Bedford would not actually be ruling England from France, but it was now enshrined in law that the most important decisions in England could only be taken after consulting him and bearing in mind his advice, even if he was in France. It was Bedford's intention that, in future, the two realms would be working with a common purpose.

Parliament responded to Bedford's acceptance of a greater role by granting a tax of a fifteenth and a tenth and extending duties payable on imports and exports. Recognising that cloth was becoming a more valuable export than raw wool and that a new stream of income would be needed as collateral for loans, parliament also introduced a new tax of twelve pence in the pound on the value of all exported cloth. This financial package was less than Bedford had hoped for, but it was as much as the realm could afford.[28]

The estates-general of Normandy, meeting at the same time, granted 160,000*l.t.* (£9.33m) expressly for the maintenance of the garrisons. This too was not considered sufficient, and a number of extra direct levies were made, including a duchy-wide tax of 20,000*l.t.* (£1.17m) to finance a new siege of Mont-Saint-Michel and local impositions to fund the demolition of Saint-Cénéry and repay loans Bedford had made to pay for the earl of Arundel's campaigns in Maine.[29]

Bedford himself would remain in England until July, trying to scrape together cash and loans for the new campaigning season, but in February John, lord Talbot, signed up to lead just under a thousand troops to France. They mustered in preparation for embarkation on 11 March 1434 and made their way first to

Rouen, then to Paris, capturing the small fortress of Jouy, between Gisors and Beauvais, as they did so. Talbot, with the ruthlessness which was to become his hallmark and would make him feared throughout France, hanged all the garrison.[30]

In Paris, after consultations with the French council, he joined forces with the earl of Arundel and the sire de l'Isle-Adam and went to lay siege to Beaumont-sur-Oise. They arrived to find that it was deserted: Amado de Vignolles had learned of their approach and removed himself, his men and their property to the more secure fortress of Creil, fourteen miles further upriver. Pausing only to destroy Vignolles's new fortifications at Beaumont, Talbot followed him to Creil and surrounded the town. The besieged defended themselves vigorously at first but Vignolles was killed by an arrow during a skirmish and his death sapped morale. When Louis de Luxembourg arrived with reinforcements, some six weeks after the siege began, the defenders came to terms: on 20 June 1434 they were allowed to leave, taking their belongings with them.[31]

On the same day that Creil was taken Bedford held his final meeting of the English council at Westminster to urge upon the king's councillors the importance of observing the terms of the agreement he had made the previous December. He cannot have been confident that they would do so, for Gloucester had not waited for him to return to France before making another attempt to undermine his authority. This time he did not merely foment rumours. On 20 April he presented a formal memorandum to the council which was extremely critical of recent mismanagement of the war. He followed this by offering to lead a huge army to France in person to win so decisive a victory that there would no longer be any need to levy taxes in England to support the war.

Bedford was deeply angered but he could not afford to dismiss these proposals out of hand because, however unrealistic, they had won enthusiastic popular support and raised expectations among hard-pressed tax-payers. A carefully worded response had to be composed to prevent 'murmur and grouching' among the populace. 'My lord of Gloucester's offer . . .

should, with God's grace, have been of great avail . . . if it had been, or were, possible to put it into execution', he was told. An expedition on this scale would cost between £48,000 and £50,000 (£25.2m and £26.25m) and, as the treasurer informed him, recent experience had proved that it was impossible to raise even half that amount.[32]

Bedford's practical alternative to his brother's grandiose scheme was to offer to maintain two hundred men-at-arms and six hundred archers at his own cost, if a similar force was funded out of the Lancastrian estates of the crown and the garrisons of Calais and its march were placed at his disposal for the defence of the whole English kingdom of France. It was not enough, but it was the best he could do. With a heavy heart he informed the king that his subjects in France, especially the Parisians, could not last much longer without greater assistance. He called God to witness 'how great a pity it were to lose that noble realm for the getting and keeping of which my lord that was your father, to whose soul God do mercy, and many other noble princes, lords, knights and squires and other persons in full great number have paid with their lives'. Then he returned to France to dedicate the rest of his own life to the service of his king and country.[33]

CHAPTER FOURTEEN

Disorder and Defeat

Despite the pessimism in England, the war in France was going through one of its more successful phases. Having captured Creil on 20 June 1434 and installed an English garrison, Talbot advanced eight miles further up the Oise valley to besiege Xaintrailles's nephew, Guillon de Ferrières, at Pont-Sainte-Maxence. Ferrières put up only a token resistance, surrendering after a few days, so Talbot moved on to clear up the remaining Armagnac fortresses in the vicinity, including Crépy-en-Valois, which had to be taken by assault, and Clermont, where yet another member of La Hire's family, his half-brother, the Bastard of Vignolles, had established himself. Talbot ended his campaign with a final flourish by flaunting his victorious army before the walls of Beauvais, but prudently withdrew without laying siege to this powerful Armagnac stronghold. Talbot's actions had cleared the Armagnac garrisons from the area north of Paris and, in recognition of this, Bedford created him count of Clermont on 24 August.[1]

Arundel was also in the field that summer, capturing fortresses in the Mantes and Chartres regions to the west and south-west of Paris while lord Willoughby and a force of some five hundred

English were assisting Jehan de Luxembourg in Picardy, among other places recapturing Saint-Valery for a second time, it having fallen to the Armagnacs through lack of an effective night-watch. In June lord Scales, who was then captain of Domfront, launched an assault on Mont-Saint-Michel; the garrison drove them off, wounding Scales in the process, but this was just a pre-liminary skirmish before the siege began in earnest. Yet another bastille was built, this time at Saint-Jean-le-Thomas, between the existing bastilles of Granville and Genêts on the coast across the bay. Together with the garrisons at the bastilles of Ardevon (eighty men-at-arms and 240 archers) and Tombelaine (twenty-six men-at-arms and seventy-eight archers) this represented a massive investment of money and men in the siege.[2]

Yet even the existing garrisons were finding it difficult to retain men. When Makyn of Langworth, the lieutenant of Tombelaine, gave his receipt for his garrison's wages on 14 December 1433, he noted that 12*l*. 11*s.t.* (£732) had been deducted by the treasurer for men who were absent from the monthly musters and a further 150*l.t.* (£8750) for ten archers 'who are of nations which, according to his contract, ought not to receive wages'. This meant that Langworth had recruited archers who were not English, Welsh, Irish or Gascon, indicating that he had had difficulty fulfilling his quotas from those nations. (The nationality of another archer called Pleuron was unclear, though his wages were paid 'because he is said to be English'.)[3]

The non-payment of wages became a real issue as the siege of Mont-Saint-Michel dragged on. In July William Cresswell and three other Englishmen, who were among the extra one hundred men-at-arms and three hundred archers stationed by lord Scales at Ardevon, deserted because they had run out of money on which to live. They made their way to the Saint-Lô area, where they committed a number of petty thefts and extortions, though, if Cresswell's pardon is to be believed, they took only as much money as they needed and when one of them robbed a country-man of his shoes he replaced them with his own, which were not as good. Eventually they were seized by the local people and taken before the *vicomte* of Coutances, who threw them all into prison. Perhaps recognising that this was a case of genuine necessity rather than wilful crime, Cresswell obtained his pardon on 19 August 1434 and was released. The authorities were certainly aware that wages were not being paid and the following month ordered the levying of local taxes which would enable the Ardevon garrison to be paid in full and for three months in advance.[4]

Cresswell and his friends were only a very minor manifestation of a problem that was spiralling out of control. There had always been problems with renegade soldiers, usually deserters from the expeditionary armies sent over from England, who found it easier and more profitable to prey on the civilian population living in the countryside than to serve in the field or in garrison. As early as October 1422, within weeks of Henry V's death, Bedford had stamped his authority on such men by ordering all soldiers to attach themselves to a captain and forbidding them from pillaging, extorting or imprisoning civilians. On 1 August 1424 he ordered his officers in the Cotentin to stop deserters taking ship for England and to arrest all those living on the land or committing pillage, robbery or extortion. Similar orders were issued in May and August 1429 and again in May, June and December 1430.[5]

Individuals could be dealt with in this way, but the problems escalated when deserters banded together and, in imitation of Armagnac captains like La Hire, Xaintrailles and Loré, made their living by levying *appâtis*, taking hostages for ransom and seizing goods without payment. In July 1428 two hundred Welsh and Irish freebooters were apparently operating in the region of the river Touques and troops had to be commissioned to suppress them. Nine members of another Welsh band preying on the countryside round Valognes were arrested and imprisoned in June 1433.[6]

The summer of 1434, however, saw probably the largest company acting independently within the English kingdom. It was led by Richard Venables, a man-at-arms who had come to France in the earl of Salisbury's expeditionary army of 1428 with a retinue of three men-at-arms and twelve archers. Perhaps having withdrawn from the siege of Mont-Saint-Michel, which was not far away, he set up his headquarters at the twelfth-century fortified abbey of Savigny-le-Vieux, which lay on the disputed Norman-Breton border, halfway between Saint-James-de-Beuvron and Domfront. Within a short time, it was said, he had attracted up to twelve hundred men to his standard and for four months he waged a successful private war against the Armagnacs in the area.

The sires de Loré, Lohéac and Laval therefore decided to make a concerted attempt to destroy him. They attacked Savigny-le-Vieux at dawn, killing and capturing two hundred of his men, but the remainder put up such a spirited resistance that after four hours they withdrew to Fougères. A short time afterwards, learning that Venables's men had left the security of the abbey and were out in the field, Loré and Lohéac ambushed them and, though their leader escaped, he was said to have lost some three hundred of his band.[7]

Ironically, it was not the enemy which ended Venables's career but his own side. His depredations against the local Norman population had brought an avalanche of complaints to the English authorities. Bedford had always been a stickler for discipline and he attached huge importance to the suppression of this illegal and oppressive operation. Instead of relying on local officials he sent the king's secretary, Jean de Rinel, and other royal officers from Rouen on 3 September to apprehend Venables and disperse his men. The English esquire, Thomas Turyngham, who captured Venables, was given not the customary bounty of 6l.t. (£350) but 1000 *saluts* (£80,208) 'as recompense for his great labour, travail and great diligence'.

Though Venables may have hoped that his unauthorised military actions against the Armagnacs would count in his favour, he was tried, sentenced and beheaded as a thief and a traitor. This exemplary punishment of one of their own by the English authorities was incomprehensible to the Armagnacs, who put it down to 'envy, because they saw that he was a great entrepreneur in the conduct of the war'. Venables's men were apparently

pardoned on condition that they return home, as Norman captains were warned the following January that four hundred of
them were on their way to the coast and they were not to be permitted to enter any town on the way there.[8]

Venables was operating illegally as a freelance captain but
similar crimes against the local population were being committed by members of established garrisons. On 2 August 1434
probably the most shameful episode in the entire history of the
English kingdom of France occurred when soldiers in English
employment and pay massacred a large number of Normans at
Vicques, a village between two English garrisons, Falaise, eight
miles to the south-west, and Saint-Pierre-sur-Dives, some five
miles to the north-west. The *baillis* had always encouraged
ordinary civilians to arm themselves according to their estate so
that they could be used as a local militia to seek out and arrest
wrong-doers and to protect their communities from pillaging
by brigands and deserters. Though they were no match for professional soldiers, lacking their superior armour, weaponry and
training, they performed an important, if subsidiary, military
role.

On this occasion some two thousand of these militiamen had
been called out to deal with English soldiers who, contrary to
royal edicts, were pillaging and foraging in lower Normandy.
They successfully drove them out of their towns, arresting some
and killing others in the process. As the militia retired they were
secretly followed, ambushed and slaughtered in a revenge attack
by a group of English, Welsh and Norman soldiers led by
Thomas Waterhouse and Roger Yker, the 'chiefs, captains and
instigators' of the whole affair. Around twelve hundred were
killed.[9]

The Waterhouse affair stretched the loyalties of the Norman
population to breaking point, even though Bedford reacted
swiftly to what official documents unhesitatingly labelled a 'horrible murder'. A commission of inquiry was set up with orders to
report to the council at Rouen and as a consequence four of the
most important knights in the duchy, John Fastolf, grand-master
of the regent's household, John Salvein, *bailli* of Rouen, William

Oldhall, *bailli* of Alençon, and Nicholas Burdet, lieutenant of Rouen castle, were sent to Falaise to apprehend the murderers. Waterhouse and several of his accomplices were arrested, tried and executed as traitors; not all of them were English, for at least one Norman, Jehan le Maçon, from Écorcheville, admitted numerous 'larcenies, pillages and robberies', as well as taking part in the murder of the 'nobles and common people' at Vicques, before his execution.[10]

The incident was clearly so serious that it had to be dealt with at the highest levels, but the four commissioners may also have been appointed because they were from outside the area and therefore above suspicion of involvement. The results of the inquiry certainly implicated members of the Falaise garrison. It is unclear whether Waterhouse and Yker were employed there (or indeed at Saint-Pierre-sur-Dives) or were unattached deserters, but at least three of those called to account were Englishmen in the garrison at Falaise. John Plummer and William Tintal were arrested and imprisoned at Caen and Bayeux respectively, rather than Falaise itself, where they no doubt had sympathisers. A further inquiry was launched into the conduct of Richard Porter, 'so-called buyer for Falaise castle', who had been accused of numerous 'seizures, thefts and abuses' against the king's subjects. Some months later the under-age children of one of the victims of the 'horrible murder', who had gone to live with distant relatives, had to seek a royal injunction against Philippin le Cloutier, lieutenant of the *vicomte* of Falaise, to prevent him entering a judgement against them in their enforced absence. While not necessarily evidence of wrong-doing, this bears out the sense of popular grievance against royal officials at Falaise.[11]

Bedford followed up the inquiry into the Waterhouse affair by introducing a series of military reforms designed to prevent a recurrence of such abuses. He had already accepted some of the improvements introduced by the great council in 1430, including the idea of springing an unannounced duchy-wide muster and allowing garrison archers to pursue relevant military trades, such as being gunners or fletchers, so long as they remained in residence rather than migrate into the towns. (Captains had always been banned from employing those living or trading in the local town, even if they were Englishmen, for the simple reason that the garrison needed to be permanently up to strength. Many English archers set up taverns, often after marrying a Frenchwoman. The problem this could cause was graphically illustrated by one who had done so at Honfleur and was living there, instead of in the barracks, when La Hire attacked the suburbs: his house was burned down and both he and his son were taken prisoner, so he was absent from the muster on 26 September 1433.)[12]

Bedford's reforms, introduced in October 1434, took these measures to their logical conclusion. For the first time the contracts for all captains would begin on the same day, 20 October, last for two years and contain identical terms. The obligation to employ only English, Welsh, Irish or Gascon archers was removed, but no more than an eighth of an entire garrison was to be French.

Another innovation was the inclusion in the same contract of both the regular garrison and the *creue*, an additional force of mounted soldiers which was always ready for service in the field. The *creues* had been introduced as a temporary measure in the crisis of 1429 but they had become an essential part of the military organisation, their flexibility and mobility enabling them to be sent out as armed escorts, field armies and siege reinforcements without compromising the strength of the regular garrison. Their virtues could also make them a liability, however, especially if they were owed wages and careering round the countryside. Bedford now ordered that they were to continue to be paid quarterly like the rest of the garrison when in residence, but monthly when they were in the field, so that they could buy their provisions regularly instead of having to make their wages last three months and thereby increase the temptation to pillage. A clause was also inserted into all captains' contracts specifically prohibiting the recruitment by Norman garrisons of anyone involved in any way with the 'horrible murder' by Waterhouse and his accomplices.[13]

Bedford's reforms were well intentioned but, as far as the

local population were concerned, purely academic. In addition to the problem of unpaid soldiers preying on the countryside, civilians had to contend with enemy raids from Mont-Saint-Michel and Beauvais and also from Clermont, where La Hire had quickly re-established himself by the simple expedient of seizing its captain during a 'friendly' meeting and forcing him to hand it over at sword-point. They were also facing massive taxation. Bedford had personally attended the meeting of the estates-general at Vernon in September to plead for generous grants not only to pay the ordinary wage bill for the Norman garrisons, which had risen to 250,000*l.t.* (£14.58m) annually, but also to repay the costs incurred in the campaigns of the summer. In all, 344,000*l.t.* (£20.07m) was to be raised from the civilian population, plus further levies for local defences, such as the 22,000*l.t.* (£1.28m) imposed on lower Normandy to help build the new bastille at Saint-Jean-le-Thomas.[14]

These impositions fuelled the economic hardship of a country that, having suffered a run of long, hard winters, was now in the grip of the worst winter of the century. On 30 November (ironically the feast of Saint Andrew, patron saint of the Burgundians) 'it began to freeze extraordinarily hard. This frost lasted a quarter of a year, less nine days, without ever thawing, and it snowed as well for forty days without stopping night or day.' In England the Thames and its estuary froze, so that wine ships from Bordeaux had to be unloaded at Sandwich. In wealthy Arras the citizens amused themselves by competing to build the most elaborate snowmen, with subjects from the *Danse Macabre* to Jehanne d'Arc at the head of her men.[15]

In lower Normandy, and especially in the Cotentin, the peasantry starved. Guy de la Villette, *vicomte* of Rouen from 1434 to 1438, pointed out that many parishes were simply unable to pay the charges imposed on them: 'because they are set in the middle of an area where the enemies and adversaries of the king pass through most often, and for this reason, the parishioners have fled, most of them no one knows where, the others are dead, so these parishes remain uninhabited and depopulated . . . the people are so impoverished that they can no longer afford to pay any levies'. The village of La Roche Tesson, near Saint-Lô, was a case in point. From a population of eighty inhabitants it had dropped to just three by July 1433, the rest having fled to Brittany, probably for fear of the consequences after the treasonable defection of their lord, Raoul Tesson, six months earlier.[16]

At the turn of the new year, 1435, the area between Falaise, Carentan and Bayeux erupted in the first popular uprising in the history of the English kingdom of France. The authorities were in no doubt that it had been instigated 'by the false and evil persuasion' of various nobles and the local officials responsible for organising the militias, but the fact remained that several thousand ordinary people took up arms, stormed the abbey of Saint-Étienne and laid siege to Caen. Messengers were dispatched in all haste to lord Scales at Domfront, begging him to come with all the might he could muster and a general call to arms was also issued from Rouen, where the earl of Arundel was put in charge of a second force and sent to Caen.[17]

Even before the relieving forces arrived, however, the garrison of Caen had repelled its besiegers, successfully ambushing them in the suburbs and killing large numbers, including Jean de Chantepie, one of their leaders. Disheartened by this failure, and no doubt suffering from exposure to the biting frosts and snow, the rest withdrew towards the abbey of Aunay-sur-Odon, halfway between Falaise and Saint-Lô. There they were met by Ambroise de Loré, who was under orders from the duke of Alençon to bring them to the abbey of Savigny-le-Vieux, the former headquarters of Richard Venables. The timing of the revolt and Loré's intervention both suggest that the duke encouraged the uprising to divert English forces away from Mont-Saint-Michel so that he could launch an attack that would break the siege there.

The progress of the rebel army was carefully monitored as it made its way through Normandy and the English knew not only that the location of the assembly point with Alençon was at Savigny-le-Vieux but also that Ardevon was the intended target. Scales therefore took the decision to demolish Ardevon completely rather than let it fall into enemy hands and on 20 January 1435 the homeless garrison of 80 men-at-arms and 240 archers marched out to join him in the field.

Thwarted in this objective, Alençon laid siege to Avranches, where the size and disposition of his army were duly observed and reported to the English authorities by two women spies. Armed with this information, Scales joined forces with Arundel and set off to relieve Avranches. The news that they were on their way was sufficient to persuade Alençon to lift his siege and decamp but the whole bay region remained on high alert. Spies reported that Alençon intended to set up his headquarters permanently at Savigny-le-Vieux, so Hugh Spencer, *bailli* of the Cotentin, was sent to demolish it, pulling down the vaults and fortifications, so that it could not be used as a fortress again. In April 70 men-at-arms and 210 archers from Ardevon were transferred to the new bastille of Saint-Jean-le-Thomas with a brief to keep the depredations of the Mont-Saint-Michel garrison in check.[18]

While Alençon and his marshal, Loré, were breaking the siege of Mont-Saint-Michel and carrying the war to the English in the south-west of Normandy, La Hire was continuing to retake the fortresses in Picardy which he had lost to Talbot the previous year. Not only was Saint-Valery back in his hands but so was Rue on the opposite coast, endangering Le Crotoy and English access to the mouth of the river Somme, and enabling the Armagnacs to raid as far north as Étaples.

Arundel, who had overseen the dispersal of the Norman rebels back to their homes or into Breton exile, was therefore recalled and sent to recover Rue with a force of eight hundred men. When he reached Gournay, however, he learned that La Hire was refortifying an ancient castle at Gerberoy, just seven miles north-east of this important English garrison and only thirty-seven miles east of Rouen. To allow La Hire to extend his reach so much further from Beauvais could not be contemplated, so Arundel diverted his army as a matter of urgency, arriving with the vanguard at the castle at eight in the morning. While he waited for his foot soldiers and artillery train to arrive, he set about preparing his lodgings and defences ready to besiege

Gerberoy. What he did not know was that both La Hire and Xaintrailles were in the castle with several hundred men at their disposal.

From their vantage point the two captains could see the main body of Arundel's army approaching and this persuaded them that their only chance to avoid siege and capture was to launch an immediate assault. While some of the garrison sallied out on foot to attack and distract Arundel's men, La Hire led a desperate sortie with his cavalry which intercepted the advancing column, catching the troops by surprise. They broke, scattered and fled, with La Hire in hot pursuit across the countryside.

He returned to find the tables had turned: Arundel had taken refuge in the enclosure he had begun to build and the besiegers were now the besieged. With only hedges to cover their backs and wooden stakes to protect their front, they were no match for the reunited Armagnac forces and were swiftly overwhelmed; a few were able to escape with their lives, but most were killed or taken prisoner. What turned a defeat into a disaster was the fact that Arundel himself was mortally wounded. A shot from a culverin, a medieval version of the musket, had shattered his leg above the ankle. He was captured and carried to Beauvais, where his leg was amputated in an attempt to save his life (he was, after all, worth a massive ransom), but he died of his injuries on 12 June 1435.[19]

Arundel's death, at the age of twenty-seven, deprived the English of one of their youngest, most able and dedicated military leaders but it was not the end of his story. Contemporary chroniclers believed that, because he had died in enemy hands, his body had been buried in the Franciscan church at Beauvais. However, the will of Fulk Eyton, a Shropshire squire who died in 1454, proves that the earl's bones were then in his possession: his executors were ordered to ensure that they were buried in the family chapel at Arundel, as the earl had wished, but only on condition that the current earl settle the debt he owed Eyton 'for the bones of my lord John his brother, that I brought out of France; for the which carriage of bones, and out of the Frenchmen's hands deliverance, he oweth me 1400 marks [£507,500]'.[20]

Eyton had personal links to the earl, holding the office of constable of Oswestry castle in the Welsh marches by his grant, but he was also a professional soldier and a hard-headed businessman who was not prepared to part with the bones till he had been 'reimbursed', probably at a profit to himself. When and how he acquired them are a mystery. He may have paid a ransom for the corpse before it was buried, in which case he would have had to perform the customary unpleasant task of having it quartered and boiling off the flesh so that the bones could be more easily transported back to England. Such an eventuality would mean that Eyton had effectively held the dead earl hostage, hanging on to the remains in vain for almost twenty years.

The alternative is that Eyton made his gruesome acquisition much later, probably in 1450 when he left France himself, though, as a respected English captain, it is possible he could have returned later with a commission to secure Arundel's disinterment and repatriation. A later acquisition of the remains is likelier, for when the earl's tomb at Arundel was opened in the mid-nineteenth century a six-foot-tall skeleton, intact except for a missing leg, was found, indicating that he had not been dismembered shortly after death.[21]

Arundel's death was just the latest in a series of disasters to strike the English. The Armagnacs were turning the screw on Paris. The Bastard of Orléans recaptured Pont-Sainte-Maxence; and, most seriously of all, in the early hours of 1 June twelve hundred of his men surprised and captured Saint-Denis. In both cases the 'English' garrison was slaughtered without mercy, together with any English natives found in the town.[22]

The loss of Saint-Denis was especially significant, since even the English recognised its importance as the symbol of France. It was also on the outskirts of Paris itself. 'The consequences were very bad,' the citizen recorded in his journal:

Paris was now blockaded on all sides, no goods could be brought in by river or any other way. And they came every day right up to the gates of Paris; everyone belonging to the

city that they found going in or out they killed, and the
women and girls they took by force; they cut the corn all
round Paris; no one stopped them. Afterwards they made a
habit of cutting the throats of all whom they captured, working men or whatever they were, and used to leave their bodies
lying in the middle of the road; women too.[23]

The military resurgence of the Armagnacs, and the increasingly brutal tactics they employed, were part and parcel of a
campaign of terrorism which was planned to coincide with the
renewal of peace talks. Pressure for these had been building on
all parties for some time and the death in England of the
Agincourt prisoner, Jean, duke of Bourbon, on 5 February 1434
had brought a new figure into the equation. The new duke, his
son Charles, count of Clermont, was married to Philippe of
Burgundy's sister Agnès, though this had not prevented him
waging war against his brother-in-law, nominally as Charles
VII's lieutenant, but actually in the hope of annexing the county
of Charolais for himself. After a disastrous campaign in the
summer of 1434, however, he agreed a three-month general
truce with Burgundy in December. Of greater consequence was
the fact that the two men agreed to meet again at Nevers in
January 1435 for further discussions.[24]

The significance of this meeting was that it was no longer
confined to Burgundy and Bourbon. Both men were also brothers-
in-law to the constable of France, Arthur de Richemont, whose
wife was Philippe's sister Margaret, and he was also present.
Richemont too had been in negotiation with Burgundy and in
September had secured a six-month truce for north-eastern
France between the Armagnacs and Burgundians. This family
summit (with the notable absence of Bedford, whose remarriage
had excluded him) was joined by Regnault de Chartres, archbishop of Reims. The presence of the archbishop, who was both
Charles VII's chancellor of France and a leading member of the
peace party at his court, was an early indication that more was
afoot than simply renewing truces.

And so it proved. After all the feasting and dancing to

celebrate the family reunion, the heads of an agreement were drawn up. The parties all agreed to meet again to discuss a general peace on 1 July 1435 at Arras, in the Burgundian Low Countries, and Burgundy personally undertook to notify Henry VI and urge him to attend. If the English refused to accept Charles VII's 'reasonable offers', Burgundy promised to break with them and join the man whom he now, for the very first time, called 'King Charles'. His reward would be the gift to him of all the crown lands on either side of the Somme, including the county of Ponthieu. The pope would be asked to mediate and the general church council, meeting at Basle, would be asked to send representatives. Burgundy's demands for an apology and compensation for his father's murder, and for the punishment of those involved, which had always been the stumbling block in previous negotiations, were quietly dropped.[25]

It was left to an unnamed Burgundian knight to say what must have been in the minds of many who were present on that day. Speaking in a loud, clear voice that was meant to be heard, he remarked to no one in particular, 'Between ourselves, we have been very badly advised to risk and put in peril our bodies and souls for the capricious whims of princes and great lords who, when it pleases them, are reconciled to each other, while . . . we are left impoverished and ruined.'[26]

The bitterness of the iconic unknown soldier was not entirely shared by the civilian population, which gave a hero's welcome to Philippe of Burgundy when he arrived in Paris on 14 April promising peace for his time. The university did a presentation before him on the subject and a delegation of women appealed to the duchess to use her influence in the great cause. Having created an overwhelming sense of expectation that peace was nigh, Burgundy moved on to Arras, without having seen the one person whose opinion really mattered. Bedford had retired from Paris to Rouen on learning of the agreement reached at Nevers. He made no effort to return to Paris during the week that Burgundy was in residence and Burgundy did not seek him out. There was little point in doing so, for Bedford had made his position clear and nothing would move him from it. Until his nephew was of an age to be able to take responsibility for his own decision, Bedford would defend the English kingdom of France to his dying breath.[27]

CHAPTER FIFTEEN

The Treaty of Arras

In the spring of 1435 the Isle of Wight and most of the counties along the south coast of England were put on alert against the threat of French invasion. It was the first time that this had happened in many years and it was a direct response to the parlous military situation across the Channel. The rebellion in lower Normandy, the losses in the bay of the Somme and around Paris and the death of the earl of Arundel had all undermined the English kingdom of France to the point where it was no longer able to serve as a buffer against enemy attack. The situation had to be retrieved, not only to preserve English possessions in northern France but also to protect the borders of England herself.[1]

In Normandy the estates-general met in May at Bayeux and granted 40,000*l.t.* (£2.33m) to fund a new field army of up to eight hundred men-at-arms and 2300 mounted archers. In England, where a parliamentary grant was out of the question, £21,813 (£11.45m) was raised in loans from wealthy individuals, led by Cardinal Beaufort and his nephew John, earl of Somerset. This sum was allocated to pay for a new expeditionary army of over 2500 men recruited and led by lords Talbot and Willoughby.

Talbot's army sailed to France in July and made straight for Paris, relieving Orville, near Louviers, before travelling on to lay siege to Saint-Denis.[2]

The departure of this military expedition from England coincided with that of the deputation appointed to attend the Congress of Arras. The whole question of English involvement in these peace talks had been fraught with difficulty, not least because, on the face of it, the instigator and coordinator of the process was not the papacy, as before, but the duke of Burgundy. He had conducted the preliminary meetings, was hosting the congress at Arras, the capital of Burgundian Artois, and had issued the invitations to attend. He had done all this without prior consultation with his English allies and, as they complained, in breach of the Treaty of Troyes, which prohibited either party negotiating unilaterally with the Armagnacs. Burgundy's role was of such concern to the English that they even approached the pope to find out whether the duke had asked to be freed from his oath to the treaty. Eugenius reassured them that he had not, but he added his own ominous injunction that the English should show a more conscientious desire for peace than they had previously done.[3]

Burgundy had played his cards well. The English were the last of the main parties to receive their formal invitations and, since Charles VII, the pope and the church council at Basle had already accepted and appointed delegates, the pressure on them to participate was increased. Representatives from Sicily, Spain, Portugal, Denmark, Poland and Italy were also invited, ensuring that the eyes of all Europe would be upon the outcome.

The English had difficulty in appointing the leaders of their delegation. Their first choice was Philippe of Burgundy but this was nothing more than a political gesture designed to demonstrate that Anglo-Burgundian interests were synonymous and that the alliance remained strong. It can have been no surprise when he flatly refused the role on the grounds that he was an independent party. Cardinal Beaufort was a more obvious choice but he too declined the office, preferring to exert his influence behind the scenes, uninhibited by diplomatic protocol. Louis de

Luxembourg, bishop of Thérouanne and Henry VI's chancellor of France, was a third powerful figure who was appointed but did not, in the end, go to Arras.

By comparison with Charles VII's embassy, which was led by three of the most important people at his court, Charles, duke of Bourbon, Arthur de Richemont, constable of France, and Regnault de Chartres, archbishop of Reims and chancellor of France, the English delegation that eventually went to the congress was relatively low-key. It was led by John Kemp, archbishop of York, a close colleague of Cardinal Beaufort and member of the English council, who had been Henry V's first chancellor of the English kingdom of France. He was accompanied by the bishops of Norwich and Saint David's and William Lyndwood, keeper of the privy seal. The secular representatives were – ominously for any prospect of peace – all distinguished for their military service against the Armagnacs: the earls of Suffolk and Huntingdon, Walter, lord Hungerford, and Sir John Radclyf, seneschal of Gascony. Two Norman members of Bedford's council in France also joined the delegation: Raoul le Sage, whose years of loyal service had been rewarded with the grant of letters of naturalisation by the English parliament in 1433, and Pierre Cauchon, bishop of Lisieux, who had played such a prominent role in the trial of Jehanne d'Arc.[4]

The English delegates were formally empowered to negotiate for peace but in reality their ambitions were limited to securing a twenty-year truce. The hope was that such a prolonged period of abstinence from war might stabilise the situation, allowing the economies of both kingdoms to recover from the burden of war and depriving Burgundy of any excuse to break his oath to the Treaty of Troyes. The ambassadors had authority to treat for a marriage alliance with Charles VII in return for a lengthy truce but one topic was entirely outside their remit: the Treaty of Troyes itself. The foundation stone on which the English kingdom of France had been built would remain inviolate and with it Henry VI's right to the crown of France.

And that, of course, was the Gordian knot at the heart of the peace negotiations. The English had no option but to stand by the Treaty of Troyes. To renounce all, or even part, of it would invalidate the legal basis of their claim to the French throne and deprive them of any justification for their continued presence in northern France.[5] For the Armagnacs there could be no question of peace unless and until the English accepted Charles VII as the true king of France: their ambassadors had instructions to refuse any English offer which did not include a renunciation of the French crown. With the question of sovereignty unresolved, there could be no compromise and no diplomatic solution to the war.

As a forum for a general peace settlement between England and France the Congress of Arras was therefore bound to fail. All three parties knew this but the whole process was brilliantly stage-managed to place the onus for the failure on the English. Throughout August 1435 the Armagnacs gradually raised their offers. They began by repeating the derisory terms which Henry V had rejected as inadequate in July 1415. Since these did not even take account of the Agincourt campaign, let alone the English conquests which had changed the face of northern France from 1417, there was no prospect of their being accepted. By contrast, therefore, their final offers seemed munificent: they conceded the whole of the duchy of Normandy, together with certain places in the marches of Picardy, and a marriage with a French princess, in return for a full and final renunciation of the French crown, which could be deferred for seven years until Henry VI came of age, and the release of the duke of Orléans, for whom a reasonable ransom would be paid. In the meantime, however, the English were to surrender all other places they occupied and restore to their lands and property in Normandy all those who had been expelled by their conquest.[6]

It was impossible for the English to accept such terms. Their apparent generosity obscured the fact that the English were effectively being required to give up everything they had acquired in France since 1415, including Paris itself, so that their king could exchange his crown for an empty dukedom from which his own supporters had been expelled and which he would hold subject to Charles VII. However bad the military situation, it did not warrant the acceptance of such a settlement. Since there was nothing more to be said, archbishop Kemp withdrew his embassy from Arras and returned to England, thereby handing the propaganda victory to the Armagnacs. The English, they declared, were proud, obstinate and unreasonable; they had refused to make any concessions and, by walking out of the negotiations, had declared themselves the enemies of peace. One cannot imagine that Henry V, a master tactician in the field of diplomacy as well as that of battle, would have allowed himself to have been so wrong-footed.

The Congress of Arras had been carefully choreographed to provide Philippe of Burgundy with the excuse he needed to break with the English. It had given him an international forum in which to demonstrate his own personal commitment to securing a general peace and the intransigence of the English. They had refused to accept the Armagnacs' 'reasonable offers' and therefore, in accordance with the terms of the agreement he had reached at Nevers with his brothers-in-law, Philippe would transfer his loyalties to Charles VII. Cardinal Beaufort made a last-ditch intervention, breaching diplomatic protocol to obtain a private interview with Philippe in which he pleaded so passionately for him to remain loyal that the sweat ran from his brow. On 6 September Beaufort admitted defeat and left Arras with his entourage, each one of whom was dressed in the cardinal's vermilion livery with the word 'honour' embroidered on his sleeve. It was a fitting reproach to the duke, who had been Beaufort's personal friend and colleague for so many years.[7]

Four days later, on the sixteenth anniversary of the murder of John the Fearless at Montereau, a solemn requiem mass was held for the duke at Arras. (A similar anniversary mass for the death of Henry V on 31 August had been boycotted by all except the English.) Afterwards Philippe of Burgundy gathered all the remaining delegates together and sought their opinion as to whether he should proceed unilaterally to make peace with

Charles VII. Naturally they voted with one accord in favour. The only remaining stumbling block was Burgundy's sacred oath to the Treaty of Troyes, which had been sworn at the altar, but Cardinals Albergati and Lusignan, the papal and conciliar legates who had presided over the congress, had already helpfully commissioned lawyers to see if it could be annulled. Their opinion had declared it legally invalid on the twin grounds that it had endangered Burgundy's immortal soul by committing him to bloodshed and that Charles VI had no power to disinherit his own son. The cardinals now endorsed this opinion and undertook to free the duke from his obligations.[8]

On 21 September 1435 the Treaty of Arras was concluded in a ceremony held at the abbey of Saint-Vaast. The cardinals formally absolved Burgundy from his oath to the Treaty of Troyes; the duke of Bourbon and Arthur de Richemont offered a public apology at the altar on behalf of their king for the murder of the duke's father; and Philippe swore a new oath of peace with, and loyalty to, Charles VII. The terms of the new treaty, which were widely circulated and appear in many chronicles of the time, were extraordinarily generous to the duke. In addition to punishing his father's murderers by exiling them and confiscating their property, Charles promised to expiate the crime by funding religious foundations and masses in the duke's memory. He confirmed Philippe in possession of all the lands the English had granted him and ceded to him all the French crown possessions on the Somme. Finally he exempted the duke personally from having to do homage to him and his subjects from having to do military service to the crown. Unlike the Treaty of Troyes, Burgundy was not required to commit himself to war against his former allies, only to seek to include them in the peace.[9]

The Congress of Arras had been a triumph for Philippe of Burgundy. He had extricated himself with honour from his English alliance, won major concessions from his new sovereign and emerged as a dominant figure on the world stage. What he did not know was that he was merely a puppet whose strings had been pulled by the Armagnacs. Charles VII had no intention of honouring the terms of the Treaty of Arras. He had bought the duke by its overt promises but, more insidiously, he had also bought those whom the duke trusted most. Sixty thousand *saluts* (£4.81m) had been paid out in bribes on 6 July 1435 to Nicolas Rolin, the chancellor of Burgundy, who drafted the treaty, and eight members of the ducal council, 'bearing in mind that this peace and reconciliation is more likely to be brought about by our cousin's leading confidential advisers, in whom he places his trust, than by others of his entourage'. Even the duke's wife, Isabella of Portugal, had been won over. As Beaufort's niece she might have been expected to support the Anglo-Burgundian alliance but had instead exerted her influence and negotiating skills on behalf of the Armagnacs, and the following December was rewarded by Charles VII with an annual rent of £4000 (£2.1m) for her services in negotiating the 'peace and reunion'.[10]

Such widespread deception and corruption did not bode well for the future of the new alliance, but for the English the Treaty of Arras was a disaster. They were now completely isolated. That perennial waverer the duke of Brittany had already made his peace with Charles VII the previous year; so had Sigismund, the Holy Roman Emperor. The defection of Burgundy was the final blow. And at this critical moment the one man who might have been able to salvage something from the wreckage was lying on his deathbed.

Bedford had been ailing for some time. The heavy burden he bore in maintaining his brother's legacy in both the field and the council chamber had taken its toll on his physical strength and the reverses of the preceding months seem to have hastened his end. As he lay dying he knew that Burgundy had deserted and that the future of the English kingdom of France was in jeopardy as never before, but there was nothing more he could do. He died on 14 September 1435, aged forty-six, at Rouen castle, in the heart of the realm to which he had devoted so much of his life. Unlike most Englishmen in France, he chose to be buried there. On 30 September he was interred 'magnificently' near the high altar in Rouen cathedral, close to the tombs of his ancestors Rollo, the Viking founder of the duchy of Normandy, and Richard I of England, whose 'Lionheart' had been buried in Rouen.[11]

Bedford's contribution to the English kingdom of France cannot be over-emphasised. Like his brother Henry V, he led by example, providing energetic and decisive military leadership and never fearing to risk his own person in combat but also demonstrating a considerable political ability to reconcile and unite disparate interests. Though he undoubtedly acquired enormous wealth and extensive lands because of his position, he never abused his power and often financed campaigns out of his own pocket rather than allow them to fail. He showed a genuine commitment to his French subjects, endeavouring always to administer justice even-handedly and, in strong contrast to Charles VII, refusing to countenance their exploitation or oppression by the military.

More than this, however, he had actually made his home in France, not only acquiring a number of properties in Rouen and Paris but also building his own house at Rouen to which he gave the heart-felt, if suburban-English-sounding, name Joyeux Repos. Though often wrongly blamed for acquiring Charles VI's magnificent library on the cheap and breaking it up, he had been a munificent patron and promoter of French artists and scholars, commissioning many of the most important illuminated liturgical manuscripts of the period and translations of secular and religious texts: under his patronage Rouen became a major centre of book production to rival Paris, and Caen acquired its university. Bedford had also been a generous benefactor of the church, giving valuable plate and vestments which he commissioned from French craftsmen, founding a Celestine monastery at Joyeux Repos and in his will leaving many bequests to churches in Rouen. In recognition of his piety and munificence, in 1430 the cathedral chapter at Rouen had formally admitted him as a canon, even though he was not a clergyman.[12]

Bedford had his critics ranging from the humble Robin le Peletier of Valognes, who accused him of 'being good for nothing except levying taxes and oppressing the people', to his brother Gloucester. On the whole, however, his contemporaries admired

him and even those historians who think that he should have
dedicated his talents to a better cause believe that his motives
were good and he had done the best he could. The citizen of
Paris considered his 'nature quite un-English, for he never
wanted to make war on anybody, whereas the English, essentially, are always wanting to make war on their neighbours
without cause'. Among his adversaries he was widely respected
as 'noble in lineage and virtues, wise, generous, feared and
loved' and, more succinctly, 'wise, humane and just'.[13]

Bedford's death and Burgundy's defection dealt a crippling
blow to the English kingdom of France from which it would
never recover. Within a single week its twin bulwarks had gone,
and there was no one of their stature to replace them. And just
ten days after Bedford's demise the third architect of the Treaty
of Troyes, Queen Isabeau, widow of Charles VI and mother of
Charles VII, died in Paris. Though her death was insignificant
compared with that of Bedford, it was a further loosening of the
bonds of alliance and its timing must have seemed to contemporaries further proof that God had set his face against the English.

Isabeau died on 24 September. That same day the Armagnacs
who had held Saint-Denis for almost four months finally agreed
to surrender after a five-week siege by an Anglo-Burgundian
force, led by lords Willoughby and Scales and the sire de l'Isle-
Adam. There had been heavy casualties, including Sir John
Fastolf's nephew Sir Robert Harling, who was killed in an
unsuccessful assault which cost more than eighty English lives,
but the town's recapture enabled Queen Isabeau to be buried
alongside her husband in Saint-Denis. Nevertheless, it was still
too dangerous to allow the funeral cortège to travel by land and
it was instead conveyed with all due honour by boat down the
Seine.

The recovery of Saint-Denis turned out to be the last occasion
on which English and Burgundian troops fought side by side but
it provided no relief for the beleaguered citizens of Paris. The very
night of the capitulation, in what was surely a coordinated
attack, the Armagnacs took Meulan, twenty-four miles west of
Saint-Denis, with the aid of two fishermen, who hid a ladder in

their boat and entered the town by climbing up the sewers which emptied into the Seine. The English garrison and their captain, Sir Richard Merbury, were caught by surprise and the Armagnacs took possession of the bridge. The main Parisian supply route from Normandy was now controlled by the enemy and as a consequence the price of essential foodstuffs soared. To compound the city's sufferings the fifteen hundred Armagnac soldiers allowed to leave Saint-Denis under the terms of the capitulation took to the field, looting, pillaging and kidnapping around Paris with impunity.[14]

Without Bedford's steadying hand at the helm the whole of the English kingdom of France seemed about to founder as the Armagnacs took advantage of the withdrawal of Burgundy to launch an all-out campaign against the English. Matthew Gough and Thomas Kyriell set out from Gisors with a force to retake Meulan but they were intercepted and defeated by Ambroise de Loré and Jean de Bueil; Gough himself was taken prisoner. While Arthur de Richemont and the Bastard of Orléans tightened their grip on Paris, the constable unleashed his dogs of war, giving the mercenary captains who had previously operated independently against Burgundy in the east of France free rein to attack Normandy.

As a result, at the end of October Dieppe fell to Charles Desmarets and Pierre de Rieux in a dramatic coup: Desmarets and six hundred men secretly scaled the walls on the harbour side before dawn, then broke open the gates facing Rouen to admit the marshal and his men. Not only the town but all the ships in the harbour fell into Armagnac hands, giving them an enormous haul of plunder and prisoners. The fall of Dieppe, just thirty-six miles from Rouen, was an enormous shock: as Monstrelet put it, 'all the English generally throughout Normandy were very deeply distressed, and not without cause, for this town of Dieppe was remarkably strong and well protected, and situated in one of the good areas of Normandy'. If Dieppe could fall, where else was safe?[15]

Worse was to come. Desmarets established himself as captain of Dieppe and was soon joined by Xaintrailles and a number of other freelance captains, notably Anthoine de Chabannes and the two Bastards of Bourbon, who were commonly known as the *écorcheurs*, or flayers, because of their unspeakable savagery: a report into their excesses in the county of Burgundy in 1439 includes 'people crucified, roasted on spits and hanged'. Their arrival was the catalyst for a second popular revolt, this time in the Caux region of upper Normandy. Several thousand Normans, some of them well armed, others simple peasants with make-shift weapons, put themselves under the command of a man named Le Caruyer and went to Dieppe to offer their assistance against the English.[16]

The strategy of the campaign that followed was to capture the coastal towns, which allowed the English to control the Channel and to ship foodstuffs, men, weapons and ammunition into the English kingdom of France. If these supply lines could be cut off, then Normandy, but more importantly, Paris, could be isolated and starved into submission. The combined Armagnac forces, led by Marshal de Rieux, but including Le Caruyer's people's army and many dispossessed Norman noblemen, such as Jean d'Estouteville and Guillaume de Ricarville, who had led the coup at Rouen, first made their way to Fécamp, which surrendered on Christmas Eve; two days later Montivilliers capitulated without a fight. Harfleur proved a stronger nut to crack: the English garrison, under the command of William Minors, repelled an assault and killed some forty attackers but he too was obliged to surrender when a band of inhabitants (later mythologised as the 'One Hundred and Four' who had been dispossessed by Henry V's capture of the town and barred from the privileges of citizenship) opened the town gates to the Armagnacs. Minors, the garrison and some four hundred Englishmen within Harfleur were allowed to leave, taking their goods with them. Within fifteen days seven or eight other towns and fortresses were also taken and a large part of the Caux region was now in Armagnac hands. Significantly this included Tancarville and Lillebonne, as the enemy army pushed down the Seine towards Rouen. By the beginning of 1436 some two to three thousand Armagnacs were garrisoned in upper Normandy.[17]

A disaster on an epic scale was unfolding yet the English authorities seemed paralysed by indecision and lack of leadership. The most senior figure in the kingdom was the chancellor, Louis de Luxembourg; though he did not let his clerical status as bishop of Thérouanne stand in the way of active military service, it effectively disqualified him from taking command in the field. He might have looked for military assistance to his brother Jehan de Luxembourg and nephew Jehan, count of Saint-Pol: neither of them had yet sworn to observe the Treaty of Arras but their position as subjects of Philippe of Burgundy made it difficult for them to lead a campaign against the duke's new allies.

Bedford had perhaps foreseen these difficulties. In June 1435, when his own health was failing, Arundel had just met his death at Gerberoy and Saint-Denis had been captured by the Armagnacs, he had revived the post of seneschal of Normandy, which, under the terms of the Treaty of Troyes, he had been obliged to abolish on the death of Charles VI. The seneschal was the chief military officer of the duchy, with a role comparable to that of the constable of France. To revive the office at this particular moment suggests that Bedford recognised that an independent English military command might be needed in Normandy and he entrusted the post to Thomas, lord Scales, one of his longest-serving and most trusted captains, who had previously acted as his regional lieutenant.[18]

Scales's authority, however, did not extend beyond Normandy and in any case as captain of Domfront he was fully occupied maintaining that dangerous frontier against the resurgent Armagnacs and the Bretons, who, his spies reported, were prefabricating bastilles in preparation for shipping them to the coast to set up a fortress between Coutances and Granville.[19] Unless and until a new regent was formally appointed by the English council, it was difficult for anyone to coordinate and lead a military response to the new Armagnac offensive. And without men and money from England the situation might be irretrievably lost.

In desperation the estates-general, meeting at Rouen, sent a petition to Henry VI which was presented to him at Westminster on 3 December 1435. In it they expressed as strong a criticism as they dared of the English rejection of Charles VII's offers at the Congress of Arras. They had rejoiced on learning that Charles would concede the duchy of Normandy 'because between England and Normandy there is not only alliance but unity of blood and common origin'. A speedy and definitive peace was essential after twenty years of suffering warfare and if Henry wished to reject peace against the wishes of his Norman subjects, then he must prosecute the war with vigour under the leadership of a prince of the royal family who would be able to impose his authority on the duchy and especially on the military.[20]

Henry's response was concerned and conciliatory: he informed them that parliament had decided to send a great army of at least 2100 men-at-arms and nine thousand archers to stay as long as was necessary to force the Armagnacs to suspend their hostilities. Since Henry himself was only just fourteen and his uncle, Gloucester, had no intention of leaving his power base in England, the army would be led by Richard, duke of York, an unlikely choice in such a crisis, given that he was just twenty-four and a military novice; moreover he had very little knowledge of France, having visited the country only once before, as part of Henry's retinue for the coronation expedition of 1430. He was, however, of royal blood, being descended from Edward III through both his parents (an inheritance that would later lead him to challenge Henry VI's right to the English throne), and was married to Cecily Neville, the king's cousin. He would be accompanied by two of his Neville brothers-in-law, Richard, earl of Salisbury, and William, lord Fauconberg, and their cousin, Edmund Beaufort. The significance of these associates was that all three were nephews of Cardinal Beaufort, who would personally fund the forthcoming campaign with loans to the tune of some £28,000 (£14.7m). The only senior member of the company who had extensive military experience was William, earl of Suffolk, who had served in France from 1417 until his capture by Jehanne d'Arc in 1429; despite his peaceful proclivities since then, he had no qualms about returning to arms in this crisis.[21]

Henry had promised that, weather permitting, the advance party would set out before the end of December and the rest of the army by the end of January. The Norman ambassadors, waiting to cross the Channel with the first contingent, became increasingly desperate as news arrived of the fall of Harfleur and the Caux rebellion and the weeks ticked by without action. They appealed again to the English council, warning of the dangers of delay, and even to Gloucester himself, urging him to take personal control of affairs in France. On 16 January Sir Henry Norbury and Richard Wasteneys, who were leading the advance party and had not been able to assemble enough shipping to cross together, were ordered to go separately: 'Praying you both, and straightly charging you, that you speed thitherward in all goodly haste that you may, for the more comfort of our said true subjects and to the rebuke of our enemies.'[22]

The first contingent of 970 soldiers finally set sail at the end of January; storms at sea delayed the departure of Sir Thomas Beaumont with his company of eight hundred men until the end of February and York's 'great army', reduced to a mere 4500, of whom nearly four-fifths were archers, did not even embark for Normandy until the end of May.[23] Such a dilatory response could not keep pace with the course of events in France.

As the Armagnac forces in Normandy advanced down the Seine towards Rouen, lord Talbot stepped up to the mark, taking over the captaincy of Rouen and sending his lieutenant, Fulk Eyton, with reinforcements to defend Caudebec, the last remaining stronghold still in English hands between the capital and the rebel army. With over four hundred men at his disposal Eyton did not hesitate to launch a sortie when the rebels approached the town, successfully driving them off and scattering them. Talbot immediately followed this up with sorties of his own from Rouen in which he deliberately set about a scorched-earth policy, driving all livestock into Caudebec and Rouen and destroying whatever he could not take with him. This had the desired effect, stripping the locality of anything which might provide sustenance or support for the enemy and preventing them living off the land round Rouen.[24]

Although the insurgents and most of the Armagnac captains were thus forced to retire, Rouen was not yet out of danger. At the end of January La Hire and Xaintrailles, at the head of six hundred soldiers, set out from Beauvais and Gerberoy with the intention of taking the city by surprise. Perhaps because they failed to make contact with the conspirators inside Rouen, or they were warned that reinforcements had arrived and it was too well guarded, they retired to the village of Ry, ten miles to the east. In the early hours of 2 February 1436 Talbot, Scales and Kyriell led a thousand men from the garrison and, catching them unawares, attacked them before they could get to their horses. Many were killed and a great number of prisoners, horses and supplies were taken; La Hire and Xaintrailles managed to escape, though they were pursued for many miles and La Hire received a number of serious wounds.[25]

This bold and decisive action, so characteristic of Talbot, ended the immediate threat to Rouen, but the popular rebellion had now spread to lower Normandy. On 25 January the *vicomtes* of Mortain, Avranches and Vire were ordered to enquire secretly and report back immediately as to why one Boschier, 'a captain of the common people', had held a 'huge gathering' in that area. Every loyal subject was ordered to wear the English red-cross badge, on pain of being treated as a rebel, and expressly prohibited, regardless of rank, from going armed or gathering in arms unless ordered to do so by the king's officers. The *vicomtes* were commanded to stock all walled towns and fortresses with provisions and military equipment in preparation for a siege.

Letters and spies passing between the frontier fortresses and the council in Rouen in the spring of 1436 confirmed that Boschier was indeed leading a popular insurgency and that his objective was thought to be the Cotentin region, suggesting that he was in touch with the Armagnacs of upper Normandy. Attempts to dissuade the rebels from taking up arms by offering them redress for their grievances were rejected and ultimately the insurgency had to be put down by force. On 28 March lord Scales issued a summons to arms to all the nobility of the *bailliage* of the Cotentin and took to the field. The rebels were routed in a pitched battle at Saint-Sever, eight miles west of Vire, in which Boschier himself and around a thousand of his followers were killed.[26]

CHAPTER SIXTEEN

The Fall of Paris

The first contingent of the 'great army' promised from England had been sent to the relief of Normandy, where at least three hundred soldiers, under the command of Richard Wasteneys, were allocated to the defence of Rouen and its environs. The second contingent, consisting of eight hundred men led by Sir Thomas Beaumont, was dispatched to the aid of Paris, where the situation was now critical. Richemont was steadily closing in on the city: Corbeil to the east and Saint-Germain-en-Laye to the west both fell to his advancing armies and on 19 February 1436 Bois-de-Vincennes, just four miles to the south-east, was captured when a Scottish agent infiltrated the watch and, with the assistance of the abbess of Saint-Anthoine-des-Champs, admitted Richemont's forces.[1]

On 20 February yet another strategically vital outpost fell. The citizens of Pontoise, nineteen miles north-west of Paris, shut the gates of the town against the English garrison after the greater part left on a routine foraging expedition. They then seized the few remaining soldiers from their lodgings, meeting no resistance except from the lieutenant, Sir John Rappeley, who with two others barricaded himself into one of the gatehouses, from which vantage point he bombarded the crowds below with any missiles that came to hand. One of many Englishmen who had married a Frenchwoman, he was eventually persuaded to extricate himself from a hopeless situation by surrendering into the hands of a leading citizen who was related to his wife. Having taken control of Pontoise, the citizens invited the sire de l'Isle-Adam to become their captain on behalf of Charles VII. His acceptance of this role was of the greatest significance for it could not have been done without the permission of his liege lord, Philippe of Burgundy. And although Burgundy had made his peace with Charles VII, he was not yet at war with England.[2]

Since December 1435, however, he had been conducting negotiations so secret that their purpose was not even noted in his own financial accounts. These involved two of his most loyal supporters, l'Isle-Adam himself, who had been captain of Paris since 1429, and Jean de Belloy, who had been the city's sheriff from 1422 to 1429. Their role, it soon became clear, was to deliver Paris to Charles VII. The last time Charles's troops had attempted to take the city had been in September 1429: Jehanne d'Arc had then received the first check in her military career when, as we have seen, the citizens had risen to the occasion, uniting with the garrison to repel their attackers and wounding the Pucelle herself.[3]

The situation was now very different. Paris was a Burgundian city and the English had held it only because the duke was their ally and allowed them to do so. Though the kingdom's administration was based in the city, most of its employees were French and few native Englishmen had actually taken up residence there. Like most immigrants, those who had done so had mostly settled in a ghetto in the Saint-Anthoine district, near the Bastille, leaving large areas of Paris untouched by any obvious English influence. All the municipal offices and most of the military and ecclesiastical ones continued to be held by Frenchmen of the Burgundian party. The veneer of Englishness was spread very thin.

Since the Treaty of Arras the citizens of Paris had found

themselves in an anomalous position. Their city remained the official capital of the English kingdom of France, yet their natural allegiance lay with its enemies. Louis de Luxembourg and his administration tried to rally support, as they had done in the past, by publicising Charles VI's letters condemning the murderers of John the Fearless as traitors, but they were flogging a dead horse. Even Clément de Fauquembergue, the civil servant responsible for maintaining the registers of the *parlement* since 1417, decided Paris was a lost cause after the treaty and decamped to Cambrai. On 15 March 1436 the chancellor informed a general assembly of leading officials and citizens that anyone who wished to leave would be allowed to do so: those who remained, however, must take the oath of loyalty, wear the red cross and stay away from the walls and gates. So great was the fear of treachery that the canons of Notre Dame, whose houses backed on to the river, were ordered to seal their doors.[4]

As the price of corn quadrupled owing to the blockade, and the supply of herrings (the staple food throughout Lent) ran out two weeks before Easter, popular discontent reached fever pitch. There was talk of rescuing an Armagnac prisoner, Guillaume de la Haye, from the royal prisons and turning him into a 'chief and captain' of the mob. Ironically, then, it was not the civilians, with their notorious reputation for murderous rampages, who revolted, but the military. The supply of money had dried up even faster than that of food, and the garrison's wages had not been paid for months on end. On 4 April four hundred of its soldiers deserted their posts: a day later they were still stealing all the food and goods they could find from the houses and churches in the parish of Notre-Dame-des-Champs, outside the city walls.[5]

The arrival a few days later of Sir Thomas Beaumont, with his eight hundred troops from England, could not have been more opportune. A veteran of the siege of Orléans and captain of Château Gaillard since 1430, he brought military experience that was as welcome as his reinforcements. For it had now become clear that Burgundy had indeed abandoned his neutral stance. On 3 April the three armies of Arthur de Richemont, the sire de l'Isle-Adam and Philippe de Ternant, a knight of the Golden Fleece and the duke's own chamberlain, had joined forces at Pontoise for an assault on Paris.

Duplicating Talbot's tactics at Rouen, the English had already made preparations for a siege, destroying crops, seizing all available foodstuffs and burning the villages on the Seine between Paris and Pontoise; officials had also been sent out within Paris itself to find out what quantities of corn, flour and dried pulses each household held. To the citizen of Paris writing his journal, these activities were indistinguishable from the looting by the deserters. He reported with justifiable outrage that English soldiers, in their desperate search for items which could be turned into hard cash, had even sacked the abbey of Saint-Denis, stealing the reliquaries for their silver and impiously snatching the chalice from the hands of the priest during mass. Such blatant sacrilege was certainly a far cry from the days when Henry V had assembled his whole army to observe the hanging of one of his own soldiers as punishment for a theft from a church.[6]

Learning that the enemy was approaching Saint-Denis, where all the fortifications, except for a single tower adjoining the abbey, had already been dismantled when it was retaken from the Armagnacs the previous year, Beaumont decided to intercept them. As he approached the stone bridge at Épinay-sur-Seine he encountered the advance forces of the Armagnac-Burgundian army and, after a fierce struggle, was overwhelmed. Beaumont himself was taken prisoner and at least four hundred of his men were killed. Some of those who escaped managed to get back to Paris, but others, including the sire de Brichanteau, nephew of Simon Morhier, the provost of Paris, took refuge with the English garrison in the tower at Saint-Denis, where l'Isle-Adam promptly laid siege to them. When they made an attempt to escape at daybreak they were caught and executed, Brichanteau's body being publicly exposed outside the abbey for a day before it was buried. This brutality had the desired effect, persuading the rest of the garrison to surrender to save their own lives. L'Isle-Adam had taken Saint-Denis for the second time in six months, but this time for the other side. Saint-Denis was in Armagnac hands once again.[7]

The defeat of Beaumont's force and the loss of Saint-Denis were the last straw for those Parisians whose loyalty to the current regime had only ever been purchased by Burgundian persuasion and English military success. The enemy was literally at the gate. The English armed forces were defeated and demoralised; the administration was bankrupt; the population was starving. And l'Isle-Adam, the great Burgundian hero who had rescued Paris from the Armagnacs in 1418, was ready and waiting to deliver the city from the English. He had with him a general pardon from Charles VII, sealed with his great seal, which the duke of Burgundy had procured on behalf of those Parisians who would immediately change their allegiance. Armed with this knowledge, l'Isle-Adam's friends and contacts among the leading Parisian citizens were already at work preparing for his return. A message was smuggled out to him, telling him to be at the Saint-Jacques gate in the early hours of 13 April 1436.

L'Isle-Adam arrived at the rendezvous with Richemont, the Bastard of Orléans and several thousand troops. Shown the general pardon, the guards at the gate offered no resistance, the conspirators let down ladders and l'Isle-Adam led the way into the city. So it was that the man who had forced Charles VII, as dauphin, to flee the city in 1418 was now responsible for his restoration, as king, seventeen years later. L'Isle-Adam had the gates flung open and, to the cleverly chosen cry of 'Peace! Long live the king and the duke of Burgundy!', his army swept down the streets into the university district, where Burgundian loyalties had always been strong and least resistance could be expected, then across the Île-de-la-Cité into the main part of the city.

When the alarm was raised the English formed into three companies, one of which, under Jean l'Archier, the lieutenant of the provost, 'one of the cruellest Christians in the world . . . a fat villain, round as a barrel', was sent to secure the Saint-Denis gate to the north. Making his way through the deserted streets shouting the rather less persuasive rallying cry of 'Saint George! Saint

George! You French traitors, we'll kill the lot of you!', he arrived only to find that the citizens had got there before him. They had already secured the gate and turned its cannon on him, forcing him to join the general retreat of the loyalist forces into the Saint-Anthoine district. Lord Willoughby, captain of Paris since the defection of the Burgundians, and Louis de Luxembourg had been equally unsuccessful with their companies, finding that the citizens had used against them the chains that were usually strung across the streets to hinder attackers and coming under a hail of missiles from a civilian population which scented the end of a hated regime. Outnumbered and outmanoeuvred, the English fled without taking a stand and took refuge in the Bastille.[8]

'Immediately after this', the citizen recorded in his journal, 'the Constable and the other lords made their way through Paris as peacefully as if they had never been out of the city in their lives.' Richemont publicly reiterated Charles VII's general pardon for the Parisians and issued proclamations prohibiting his men from lodging in any civilian house without the owner's permission or from insulting or robbing anyone except natives of England and mercenaries. 'The Parisians loved them for this and before the day was out every man in Paris would have risked his life and goods to destroy the English.'[9]

So many Englishmen and members of their administration were packed into the Bastille that their situation was untenable but Richemont too had no desire for a siege. Willoughby and Luxembourg were therefore allowed to negotiate a heavy ransom to obtain their freedom and on 17 April they led the last Englishmen left in Paris out of the city. With them went all those who had been so compromised by their association with the regime that they could not remain, from the greatest, such as the members of the royal council, down to the door-keeper of the *chambre-des-comptes*, whose activities as an informer against his Armagnac neighbours made his future residence in Paris impossible. They left for Normandy with the jeers of the newly liberated population ringing in their ears. When they had gone the Parisians celebrated by ringing the church bells, singing the *Te Deum* and holding thanksgiving processions.[10]

They would soon discover that they had little to rejoice about, for they had simply exchanged one oppressive master for another. The currency, bearing Henry VI's insignia, was devalued, huge 'loans' were demanded from every household, the shortage of food continued and the soldiers of the new French garrison did nothing to resist the incursions of the English but raided the neighbouring towns and villages for all the provisions they could seize. The return and restoration to office and property of those Armagnacs who had fled Paris in 1418 was also a source of conflict and grievance since it inevitably dispossessed some who had legitimately taken their place.[11]

There is a poignant footnote to the 'liberation' of Paris which reveals its human cost. Many families were divided by the civil war. For some this was a pragmatic arrangement. Georges de la Trémoïlle, for example, had joined the Armagnacs in 1418 while his brother, Jean, sire de Jonville, remained loyal to the Burgundians. As a consequence they were able to keep their family estates intact since Georges was given the lands confiscated from Jean and vice versa. This was by no means a unique arrangement. However, for others, separation from their families was forced upon them. Arnoul Turgis, for example, remained in Paris after the expulsion of the English and became an officer of the watch but his son Nicaise was one of eight royal secretaries obliged to leave and he continued in Henry VI's service.[12]

The saddest story of all was that of Jehanette Roland, whose parents owned a house in the 'English quarter' of the rue Saint-Anthoine, where she had met and fallen in love with an English herald, Gilbert Dowel, Wexford pursuivant to lord Talbot, when the latter was captain of the Bastille from 1434 to 1435. The pair had become formally betrothed just before the expulsion of the English, and afterwards Jehanette announced her intention of going to find her fiancé and marry him. Her parents and friends, afraid of the consequences in the light of the new regime, did their best to dissuade her but she declared that 'as long as she lived, she would have no other husband'. She remained adamant even when the *parlement* ordered her to be imprisoned to prevent her leaving Paris.

On 11 January 1437 she was remanded into the custody of her parents on bail of a hundred silver marks. Her fiancé, in the meantime, had remained equally steadfast and on 22 January he lodged a plea with the *parlement* demanding his right to marry her and take her with him. Two days later judgement was pronounced: 'The court will not permit Jehanette to go with the said Wexford and become English during the war and the division between the king and the English.' The case should rightly have been heard in the ecclesiastical courts, but canon law would have upheld their marriage, hence the intervention of the *parlement*. And since the issue was not within its jurisdiction the *parlement* had to invent a new justification for its decision: the marriage was acceptable in peacetime but allowing it to take place during time of war would add to the number of the king's enemies and was therefore not permissible.[13]

This heartless doctrine was more explicitly set out in the case of Denise Le Verrat, who married her man, a merchant from Lucca with strong English ties, at the beginning of 1436. When he was expelled a few weeks later, she obtained permission to join him but they were then both declared rebels and all their property in Paris was confiscated. Her mother tried to get the judgement overturned on the grounds that her daughter was bound by divine and canon law to obey her husband and go to him. In 1441 the *parlement* upheld the forfeiture, declaring Denise had a duty to obey her prince above her husband, that she had committed a crime in joining him and, as a consequence, joining the English and that she had aggravated that crime by having four children in Rouen, thus increasing the ranks of the king's enemies.[14]

To all intents and purposes the loss of Paris put an end to the English kingdom of France. Henry VI and his ministers did not drop his title or his claim to the crown but all the offices of state were, of necessity, transferred to Rouen. The duchy of Normandy and the enclave of Calais were now all that remained in English hands in northern France, and both were under threat. On 7 May Talbot dashed to the rescue of Gisors, which had been betrayed to La Hire and Xaintrailles, probably by John

Baedolf, an English member of the garrison; the town had fallen but the garrison had retreated to the fortress and held out for three days before Talbot's prompt arrival put the besiegers to flight. Perhaps as a reward for this feat, but certainly in recognition of his abilities in the field, on 9 May Talbot was appointed a marshal of France, raising him broadly to the same status as lord Scales, the seneschal of Normandy.[15]

At about the same time the council at Rouen received urgent messages reporting that the castle of Saint-Denis-le-Gast, eleven miles south of Coutances, had been captured by the sires de Lohéac, de la Roche and de Bueil, who were now raiding near the town, capturing supplies and threatening neighbouring Chanteloup castle. Enemy prisoners taken in the vicinity boasted that Coutances would fall but it was actually the bastille at Granville, isolated on its rocky peninsula on the edge of Saint-Michel bay, that was seized. A flurry of spies then reported that the Armagnacs were building extra fortifications and planning a raid on Saint-Lô.

Lord Scales, from his base at Domfront, issued a general call to arms throughout the *bailliage* on 22 May, together with an urgent order for the carpenters and labourers necessary for a siege; he also wrote to the Channel Islands requesting the aid of English ships based there for a blockade. With the marches of all lower Normandy at risk and desperate for more men, Scales took the unauthorised and unorthodox step of recruiting 'certain soldiers, not taking or being then on any wages, living and dwelling in the open countryside on our poor and loyal subjects'; since they were poorly armed he also supplied them with bows, strings and arrows at his own expense, later struggling to obtain reimbursement from the accountants of the treasury.[16]

The very fact that Scales was reduced to such measures was an indictment of the dilatory military response from England. The duke of York's 'great army' promised in December 1435 had still not sailed. It was not until 20 February that York eventually signed his contract to serve for a year with 500 men-at-arms and 2500 archers. Haggling over his title and powers delayed his appointment even further, for this was not to be merely the leadership of a military expedition but that of the English administration in France as well. There was not to be another regent, with independent powers, for no one could replace Bedford. Only Gloucester, the king's sole surviving uncle, had the rank to demand such a position but his behaviour as protector of England had convinced the councils on both sides of the Channel that he could not be trusted with untrammelled power in France. Fortunately Gloucester himself was reluctant to push his claim, fearing that he would lose all power and influence in England if he left the country.

With no obvious candidate to take Bedford's place, and the possibility that Henry might wish to make radical changes to the structure of the administration when his minority ended in a few years' time, the royal council was determined to limit the role of the next head of the government in France. York had no doubt wanted to be, like Bedford, 'regent and governor', but instead he had to settle for 'lieutenant-general', at a salary of 30,000*l.t.* (£1.75m). What is more, his period of office was limited to a year and he was denied Bedford's power to appoint to major military and civil offices or to grant lands worth more than 1000 *saluts* (£80,208). It was this emasculated role which would become the blueprint for future appointments, creating a conflict of interest and authority in the English kingdom of France which had not existed before. The greatest problem it caused was that, effectively, supreme authority on behalf of the king was no longer exercised by a single regent but by a lieutenant-general on a short-term contract, whose own appointment and powers were subject to the royal council in England. And that council was both too far away to understand or deal rapidly with affairs as they developed on the ground in France and also riven with faction, leaving the appointment of the lieutenant-general at the mercy of prevailing party politics.

It was a poor omen for the future prospects of the English kingdom of France that the lengthy debate over the office of the lieutenant-general delayed the sealing of York's formal commission until 8 May 1436 – by which time Paris had fallen and his sphere of authority had shrunk from a kingdom to a duchy.[17]

Despite the military imperative, York had refused to leave until his powers were settled. Even the council became frustrated with his failure to embark, 'praying you that, considering the great jeopardy that the said countries stand in . . . and also the great hurt and loss that daily falls upon us, without longer delay, with your retinue, take your passage into our said realm and duchy, to the consolation and comfort of our true subjects there'. The duke, like the leaders of the earlier contingents, blamed lack of available shipping – a direct result of the council's own lack of foresight in disbanding and selling off Henry V's navy. In a belated acknowledgement of this, and in an attempt to protect both English shipping and the southern coast, the council encouraged ship-owners to become privateers, relaxing Henry V's stiff penalties for breaking safe-conducts and allowing them to keep any booty or ships they might acquire.[18]

Since every other port on the Channel coast between Harfleur and Calais now belonged to the enemy, York was obliged to disembark at Honfleur, the nearest port to Rouen still left in English hands. Some of his troops were mustered there on landing on 7 June but, all told, the combined army of York and the earls of Suffolk and Salisbury, who accompanied him, amounted to only 4500 men. Even if the 1770 already sent in the advance forces were added to this, England had provided 6270 men, rather than the 11,100 Henry VI had promised. And York's army, unlike the earlier contingents which had contracted to serve for two years, was committed only for a year.[19]

York made his way straight to Rouen, where he took up residence in some style for the next three months. He seems to have interpreted his role as being administrative rather than leading from the front in the field and had the good sense to entrust the active military campaigns to those most experienced and capable, whom he appointed his own lieutenants-general for the waging of war. Scales would continue to hold the marches of lower Normandy against the threat from the Bretons, the duke of Alençon and the garrison of Mont-Saint-Michel. Talbot, ably assisted by William Neville, lord Fauconberg, who within the next twelve months would be given his own independent command in the central marches based at Évreux and Verneuil, set about the recovery of the Caux region with the aid of York's reinforcements. By the end of the year a large part of what had been lost to the Armagnacs was back in English hands, though no attempt had been made to lay siege to either Harfleur or Dieppe, and Fécamp, which had been recaptured, was lost again a few days later when the expelled garrison gained access to the town by removing the iron grate through which a stream flowed out under the town walls.[20]

The castle of Lillebonne, a few miles east of Tancarville, was retaken by a clever, if risky, stratagem devised by Fulk Eyton, Talbot's captain at neighbouring Caudebec. He persuaded a captured member of the Lillebonne garrison, who was unable to pay the ransom demanded, to collaborate in return for his freedom. He was told to go back to his garrison and act as though nothing had happened. To allay suspicions he was to continue taking part in nightly raids from Lillebonne, returning there with Englishmen from Caudebec whom he claimed to have captured, thus building up a contingent within the castle. This he did until finally he came back with a party of several horses and men 'disguised as prisoners'. Once they were on the bridge they abandoned their pretence, seized the porter, gained entrance and promptly made themselves masters of the castle and those within it. For this 'signal service', which ended the disruption to traffic on the Seine, Eyton was rewarded with the gift of 3510*l.t.* (£204,750), which was levied as a tax on the inhabitants of the duchy.[21]

While the English were distracted by the loss of Paris and the need to defend Normandy, Philippe of Burgundy decided that this was an opportune moment to seize Calais. This was a logical extension of his long-term plan to annex all the Low Countries which, ironically, he had been able to carry out so far because his English allies had kept the Armagnacs occupied elsewhere. The fulfilment of this objective had been one of the reasons why he had defected, leaving Calais and its marches isolated from Normandy and vulnerable. As the home of the Staple, which had the monopoly on the export of wool, England's most valuable commodity, to the continent, Calais was vital to the financial interests not only of England, but also those areas of the Low Countries, in particular Flanders, which depended on the supply of high-quality wool to make cloth. The Flemings deeply resented both this monopoly, which arbitrarily drove up their own costs, and the increasingly successful trade in home-produced English cloth, which undercut their products. The Treaty of Arras had freed the duke to place a ban on English imports into his dominions and the resulting stockpile of unsold wool at Calais was a tempting prospect to Flemish merchants and weavers.

Philippe of Burgundy's defection had raised feeling against him in England to fever pitch: his ambassadors were arrested and the London mob pillaged the houses of Flemish merchants. Gloucester also continued to harbour resentment towards the duke for thwarting his own ambitions in Hainault in 1424. Always an advocate of Calais, whose lieutenancy he had resumed on his brother's death, when English spies reported that Burgundy was preparing an assault on the town, he leapt into action with an alacrity that had been noticeably lacking in his support for the English kingdom of France. He had the backing of both parliament and the city of London, where the mercantile interest was powerfully represented.[22]

As part of his price for financing the campaigns of 1436, Cardinal Beaufort had procured a two-year independent commission in Anjou and Maine for his nephew, Edmund Beaufort, so that he could protect Bedford's inheritance in those counties and his own interests in Mortain. Beaufort had recruited two thousand men, sixteen hundred of them archers, in preparation for what was intended to be a field campaign, and they were ready to sail in April. At the last minute, however, because these were the only forces available, Gloucester diverted Beaufort to the defence of Calais, where his field army was so effectively deployed in raids into Flanders that he was rewarded with election to the Order of the Garter. John Radclyf, the lieutenant of Calais, meanwhile kept both citizens and garrison on their toes, having the alarm bell rung to signify an attack 'but there was none; for Sir John Radclyf did it for a sport, because it was Saint George's Day, and for that he wanted to see how [quickly] soldiers would buckle and dress themselves in their armour'.[23]

The attack was slow in coming but it was made by one of the biggest and best-equipped armies fielded in recent years. The wealthy Flemish cities of Ghent and Bruges, in particular, provided men from their civil militias and guns of every description. Three huge cannon were even sent from Burgundy on a journey that took forty-nine days and required roads and bridges to be reinforced: at Châlons-sur-Marne they had to be loaded on to boats as they could not cross the bridge. The smallest was none other than the Shepherdess, which had accompanied Jehanne d'Arc from Orléans to the siege of La-Charité-sur-Loire, where it had been acquired by Perrinet Gressart, who had presented it to the duke of Burgundy. A larger cannon, Prussia, was carried on a cart pulled by a team of thirty horses while the largest, Burgundy, was so heavy that it required two separate carts hauled by forty-eight horses to pull the barrel and thirty-six the chamber. In all, the duke's records reveal he had access to ten bombards, around sixty *veuglaires* and fifty-five *crapaudeaux* (both smaller versions of the cannon), 450 culverins or hand-guns, several thousand cavalry lances and 450,000 crossbow bolts.[24]

Despite this wealth of artillery, Burgundy would later claim that he never fired a shot at Calais. He entered the Calais marches in the middle of June and captured Oye, Marck, Balinghem and Sangatte in swift succession, only Guînes, five miles south of Calais, holding out under bombardment from his 'great brass gun'. By 9 July he was encamped before the town itself, employing several artists to paint a vista of the salient points to plan his attack and waiting for his fleet to arrive to complete the blockade. He had some thirty-five ships of varying sizes and different nationalities, including nine small Breton boats, prepared to sail from Sluis, in Zeeland, and fourteen hundred marines on his payroll, but what he did not have was a prevailing wind. So he had to sit there, seething with frustration, while the contrary winds which kept his fleet pinned into its harbour blew English ships daily into Calais.[25]

It was not until 25 July that Burgundy's fleet finally arrived but, to the dismay of the Flemish militias on shore, all it did was scuttle a few ancient boats in the harbour to prevent English ships entering or leaving, and then depart. Since they had misjudged the depth of the water, the people of Calais were able to go out at low tide, dismantle the boats for firewood, remove the stones for building work in the church of Saint Mary and open up the harbour for business again.

On 28 July the English garrison sallied out, destroyed the wooden bastille of the men of Ghent and killed its defenders; that night the remaining Ghenters panicked when they heard reinforcements from England disembarking in Calais, packed their bags and decamped. The next morning the men of Bruges, discovering that they had been abandoned, deserted too. They left behind their provisions and much of their renowned artillery. The whole débâcle was so shameful that the duke (who blamed the Flemish) later claimed that he had never fired a shot or summoned the inhabitants to surrender: since these were the two requirements for formally commencing a siege, he could therefore comfort himself with the thought that he had merely 'lodged before' Calais, rather than 'laid siege to' it and failed.[26]

In the meantime, anxious for revenge on his old adversary, Gloucester had determined to lead an army to the relief of Calais in person. In a remarkable display of what could be done if the political will was there, he raised an army of almost eight thousand men and set sail for Calais, arriving on 2 August. He was cheated of his moment of glory, for the Burgundians had already gone. He vented his wrath, as he had done a decade before, in leading his men on an eleven-day raid into Flanders, burning towns and crops and driving a great haul of cattle back into Calais. It was poor compensation for being deprived of the opportunity to inflict a crushing defeat on Burgundy and, in the process, make good his claim to the county of Flanders, which Henry VI had granted to him just before he crossed the Channel.

Nevertheless, the most serious threat to Calais in decades had been averted and Burgundy and the Flemish humiliated: such things were music to the ears of Londoners, and Gloucester returned in triumph to a hero's welcome.[27]

PART FOUR

THE SEARCH FOR PEACE

CHAPTER SEVENTEEN

Defending Normandy

On the eve of Saint Andrew, 29 November 1436, a hard frost set in which would last until 12 February 1437. It brought with it the heavy snows that had been a feature of the decade and caused such hardship in towns and countryside alike. The harsh weather also provided the opportunity for a bold enterprise by Talbot. Having secured Rouen and recovered much of the Caux region of upper Normandy, including Fécamp, he had now undertaken to regain control of the upper reaches of the Seine and the eastern marches of the duchy. In January he left Rouen with a detachment of two hundred men-at-arms and six hundred archers from the troops York had brought to Normandy, and took Ivry after a short siege.[1]

On 13 February 1437 his men recaptured the important town of Pontoise, which had been in French hands for a year. A company of them camouflaged themselves with white bed-sheets so that they could creep across the outlying snow and frozen town moats without being seen. They then took up their positions, in hiding, at the foot of the walls to await their prearranged signal. In the meantime a small detachment had disguised themselves as peasants coming to market. Under the leadership of John Sterky, a man-at-arms from Talbot's personal retinue, they boldly made their way to the town gates and were admitted by the guards on the bridge just before daybreak. Once inside, they raised the cry 'Talbot! Saint George!' At this signal the rest of the company waiting beneath the walls scaled the ramparts and burst into the town. The garrison and the sire de l'Isle-Adam, who happened to be in Pontoise at the time, had been celebrating Shrove Tuesday over-heartily the day before and were completely taken by surprise. They were forced to flee, breaking down the gate below the bridge to escape and leaving all their belongings behind them. A few gentlemen barricaded themselves into a gatehouse and sent to Paris and Saint-Denis for help but surrendered at sundown after none was forthcoming. The following Sunday a similar attempt was made on Paris itself but, aware of the events at Pontoise, the night-watchmen were on the alert and drove the raiders back across the frozen moats with cannon-fire.[2]

Over the next few weeks Talbot swept across the Vexin, capturing at least fifteen towns and the castle of Orville, near Pontoise, which commanded the roads into Paris from Flanders, Picardy and Brie. The garrison at Orville had refused to put up any resistance because its wages had not been paid, leading to the capture of the owner's wife as well as his castle. Once in English hands, it caused considerable inconvenience in Paris: the garrison of Saint-Denis had to be reinforced to guard the men bringing in the harvest but, as the citizen of Paris complained, 'really no one could decide which lot was the worse bargain', for the Armagnacs levied *appâtis* and taxes every three months and the English captured anyone brave enough to venture out beyond the walls and held them to ransom.[3]

Small, privately owned castles like Orville caused problems out of all proportion to their size and importance because of the ease with which they could be captured by the enemy. In Normandy Talbot and York had initiated a policy of demolishing any fortress of this kind once it had been recaptured. This was not an innovation in itself, but the scale of it was new. In April, for example, John Salvein, the *bailli* of Rouen, paid out 1089*l.t.* (£63,525) in wages to workmen for demolishing at least eight, including castles at Préaulx, Rouvray and Saint-Germain-sous-Cailly.[4]

York's year of service was now drawing to a close. He had overseen the recovery of much of Normandy and dealt sympathetically with the grievances of the Normans, especially their complaints about abuses committed by the military. He had, however, found it difficult to extract the money owed to him for his salary and for the loans he was obliged to make out of his own pocket to finance certain sieges. (He was still owed £18,000 (£9.45m) in 1439.) He was therefore anxious to return to England but the council asked him to remain in France until his successor was in place. York agreed, a decision he came to regret because his replacement did not arrive until November. For six months, therefore, he was in the anomalous position of exercising an authority he no longer possessed. This undermined him and caused administrative problems, particularly with the service contracts of garrison captains, which ran out in June. The power of reappointment lay with York's successor, but the payment of garrison wages was dependent on production of a valid contract, so monthly extensions had to be issued until the new lieutenant-general arrived, causing uncertainty and confusion.[5]

This had a direct impact on the summer campaigns of 1437. On his return from the Vexin Talbot was commissioned to stamp out the remaining pockets of resistance in the Caux region. York agreed to call out a further three hundred men-at-arms and nine hundred archers from the garrisons to add to Talbot's existing company for this purpose, but many captains were reluctant to let their men go, fearing that the wages of these absentees would be deducted from their payrolls and that their own fortresses would be placed in jeopardy. Guillaume de Broullat, captain of the outpost at Dreux, for instance, did not send the ten men-at-arms and thirty archers demanded of him because Armagnac field armies were operating in the vicinity and a large stretch of the ancient castle wall had tumbled down, leaving a breach which required all his manpower to guard. (This may, of course, have been a lie: Broullat had made the same excuse in 1431 and his seventeen years as captain were remarkable for his having had no deductions made by the treasury because, uniquely, he recorded no absences from muster and no gains of war. The following year he surrendered Dreux in return for a large bribe.) To enforce his demands for men York was obliged to impose heavy financial penalties on captains who failed to comply, effectively the deduction of six months' wages.[6]

Talbot needed such a large army because the recovery of Tancarville, the huge fortress on the Seine between Caudebec and Harfleur, could not be put off until the arrival of the new lieutenant-general. Several smaller places had already been captured, either by assault or by freeing prisoners in exchange for their capitulation: all had been demolished. The siege of Tancarville began in August and dragged on until early November, a frustrating but necessary exercise requiring huge numbers of men and William Gloucester, master of the king's ordnance, to bring it to a successful conclusion.[7]

Tancarville's recapture was possibly hastened by the arrival of Richard, earl of Warwick, who landed at Honfleur on 8 November 1437. Warwick had spent a lifetime in the service of the crown and had only reluctantly agreed to accept the office of lieutenant-general, complaining that it was 'full far from the ease of my years, and from the continual labour of my person at sieges and daily occupation in war'. It was a measure of how politically charged the appointment had become that it was engineered to prevent the obvious candidate, Humphrey, duke of Gloucester, taking up the position. Gloucester's role as protector of England was coming to an end as his nephew approached the age of majority, when he would personally take up the reins of government. It was natural that he should wish to seek a new sphere of authority, but neither Cardinal Beaufort and his faction, nor Louis de Luxembourg, who travelled to England to express his opinion in person, wanted Gloucester to step into Bedford's shoes.

Warwick was not of royal blood, but he had been Henry VI's personal governor and tutor, and his distinguished military career made him an acceptable compromise candidate. Though he was persuaded to accept the post of lieutenant-general in April, he was not prepared to sign his contract until his terms and conditions had been fully determined and he had been repaid the sums he was owed by the crown, including £12,656 8s. 1½d. (£6.64m) from his tenure as captain of Calais between 1423 and 1427. It took almost three months of haggling before the formal appointment was eventually made on 16 July, but then, despite attempting to sail seven times in eleven weeks, he was forced back by violent storms at sea and so arrived late in Normandy.[8]

Though Warwick had enjoyed a long and respected career in arms, he was now almost fifty-six and not in the best of health. Like York, therefore, he was content to remain in Rouen and leave the defence of Normandy in the capable hands of Talbot, Scales and Fauconberg. Warwick had not been at the helm for a month when news arrived that Philippe of Burgundy, in an attempt to salvage his wounded pride over his failure at Calais the previous year, had now laid siege to Le Crotoy, an important fortress on the north bank of the bay of the Somme. He had built a bastille outside the town and garrisoned it with a thousand soldiers, not craven Flemish militiamen this time, but men 'skilled and renowned in arms', including four knights of his Order of the Golden Fleece. Philippe himself was directing the operations but prudently did not expose himself beyond the mighty stone walls of Abbeville.

Talbot, with Fauconberg and Kyriell, swiftly came to the rescue, crossing the Somme on the famous ford at Blanchetaque under the noses of the besiegers. Instead of attacking the Burgundians directly, however, they merely skirted round Le Crotoy and began a ten-day raid into Picardy, terrorising the inhabitants and gathering a rich haul of prisoners, horses and other beasts. Terrified of an attack from their rear, the Burgundians abandoned their bastille, their guns and their siege and a mortified duke was forced to retreat to Arras.[9]

Talbot had scarcely returned to Rouen when he was ordered to go to the relief of Montargis, one of the few English enclaves left outside Normandy. Throughout the summer Armagnac forces had been trying to secure the region between Paris and the Loire to ensure that supplies could be brought safely into the capital. The town of Montereau-sur-Yonne, besieged since August, was taken by assault on 10 October and, although Scales attempted to raise a relief army, the English captain, Thomas Gerrard, was obliged to surrender the castle two weeks later. Château Landon and Nemours had also fallen, leaving Montargis isolated.

The captain of Montargis was François de Surienne, the Aragonese nephew by marriage of Perrinet Gressart. The wily captain of La-Charité-sur-Loire had finally – after thirteen years of successful evasion – surrendered his fortress and taken the oath to Charles VII on 6 October 1436, but only after being formally appointed its captain for life on an annual salary of 400*l.t.* (£23,333) and receiving a one-off payment of 22,000 *saluts* (£1.76m). Surienne, however, had joined the English, on whose behalf and in return for a large reward he had captured Montargis in 1433. Self-interest, rather than ideology, had kept him loyal. As heir to half Gressart's fortune, which included the Norman lordship of Longny, he avoided its forfeiture by allying with the English and until 1440, when Charles VII finally accepted that he could not be bought again, escaped the confiscation of the lands in Armagnac allegiance.[10]

Surienne had provided another important service for the English besides his capture of Montargis. After the fall of Paris he had maintained contact with four informants within the heart of the new Armagnac administration: three were lawyers in the *parlement* and the fourth a clerk in the *chambre-des-comptes*, their offices giving them privileged access to sensitive information. Thus they had learned that some clergymen and citizens of Meaux were plotting to deliver the town to Charles VII and that two prisoners from the garrison at Vernon had been persuaded to betray the place in return for remission of their ransoms. The informants were present when the plans and dates for the fruition of both plots were fixed and they had sent this information to Surienne via his pursuivant. As a result the two conspiracies had been foiled and those involved arrested and executed. The informants were unmasked, however, and on 26 March 1437 two of them were beheaded as traitors, together with the pursuivant; a third was spared death because he was a clerk in holy orders but committed to perpetual imprisonment in an oubliette. The following week the fourth informant, who had previously come under suspicion and had handed over his wife and two sons as pledges for his good behaviour, was arrested at Beauvoir and he and his servant were also executed.[11]

Shortly after these executions Surienne had taken it upon himself to go to London, ostensibly to secure payment for his outstanding wages as captain of Montargis, but as the money for this should have come from the Norman treasury it may have been a cover for confidential discussions with the English administration. When the estates-general met in December after his return, it granted 300,000*l.t.* (£17.5m) in taxes to pay garrison and field army wages for five quarters but also levied a further 10,000*l.t.* (£583,333) 'for certain secret purposes concerning the king's welfare'.

That same month the Armagnacs laid siege to Montargis, but, after discussions with their leader, Xaintrailles, Surienne agreed to negotiate a surrender if the besiegers withdrew. Charles VII undoubtedly hoped that Surienne could be detached from his English allegiance, as Gressart had been, offering him an enormous sum of money and restoration to his former office as *bailli* of Saint-Pierre-le-Moûtier if he surrendered Montargis and changed allegiance. Surienne falsely encouraged him to believe that this was possible, reaching an agreement in January 1438 that a truce would be observed at Montargis. Surienne would keep his garrison in the castle, buy his supplies from Orléans and other towns (rather than foraging or levying *appâtis*), allow the Armagnacs free access to the town and give four hostages, including his nephew, as a pledge for his surrendering the castle as soon as he was paid his money in full. It would take Charles VII the best part of a year to raise the cash but, when Regnault de Chartres and the Bastard of Orléans delivered it in person on 18 November 1438, Surienne duly led the 150 men-at-arms and 150 archers of his garrison from Montargis into Normandy. In the meantime, with a financial acumen and moral casuistry worthy of his mentor, in September he had renewed his

English contract to serve as captain of Montargis for another year from 1 October and accepted 3375*l.t.* (£196,875) as an advance on his wages. Needless to say, he did not reimburse the money when he left six weeks later.[12]

When Surienne agreed terms with Charles VII in January 1438, the army that Talbot and Fauconberg had raised to go to the relief of Montargis became redundant. Rather than simply disperse it, they spent the spring in and around Évreux, holding themselves in readiness to repel any renewed Armagnac attacks and occupying their time by recapturing and demolishing two small fortresses and leading an expedition round Paris to resupply Creil and Meaux.[13] This latter duty highlighted a problem that had worsened significantly in recent months. The harsh winters of the preceding years had steadily impacted on the ability to provide seed corn for the next planting, on the productivity of vines, fruit and nut trees and on the availability of foodstuffs for domestic animals. The summer and autumn of 1437 were exceedingly wet, leading to a failure of crops right across northern Europe and consequently such a shortage that wheat and corn prices doubled and then trebled.

In England, where the southern counties were especially affected, the scarcity would last for two years. In France the agricultural crisis was compounded by the war: punitive enemy raids, the garrisons, field armies and *écorcheurs* living off the land, and the scorched-earth policy to deter siege and rebellion had all taken their toll and both sides in the conflict suffered. Famine stalked the land. Every time an armed convoy escorted supplies into Paris it was accompanied by poor people from the countryside hoping to find better conditions there; when it left, several hundred starving citizens would leave with it, because they could obtain no food in the city and were dying of hunger. As always, disease went hand in hand with famine, especially in the close confines of the urban areas. The cities of Flanders were badly affected and thousands died in Paris, where the epidemic wiped out whole families and spared neither Charles VII's sister, the abbess of Poissy, nor the bishop of Paris. Wolves again came scavenging into the city, carrying off dogs and even a child.[14]

The worst-affected area in Normandy was the Caux, where the desolation was such that it was still evident to Sir John Fortescue a generation later. The value of rents fell by a half and a priest in the diocese of Rouen, prosecuted in 1438 for non-residence, claimed that there was not a single man left living in his parish, only five or six women.[15]

The scarcity of supply meant that it was difficult to maintain an army in the field. This was perhaps a contributing factor in Charles VII's decision to direct his main campaign of the year against the English in Gascony, where there was greater potential to live off the land than in the north. The diversion to this area of his mercenary captains, including Xaintrailles and Roderigo de Villandrando, also temporarily solved the problem of their depredations within his own lands.[16]

An inability to support the army in the field because of the lack of victuals and provender may account for the fact that neither side embarked upon a sustained or coordinated military campaign in northern France in 1438. The marches of lower Normandy were on high alert throughout the winter of 1437–8 as spies operating in Brittany reported intelligence that an invasion army was secretly assembling at Laval and Mont-Saint-Michel, and that Richemont had returned to the duchy and was rebuilding the dismantled border fortresses of Pontorson and Saint-James-de-Beuvron. At the same time reports that the duke of Burgundy was planning to besiege Guînes in the Calais marches prompted the council in England to contract Edmund Beaufort to go to its relief with a force of two thousand men. None of these threats really materialised. Burgundy did embark on a grand scheme to flood Calais and its marches by destroying one of the sea-dykes but was obliged to withdraw his workmen after it proved impracticable. In Normandy the market-place at Torigny-sur-Vire was captured by marauding Armagnacs and the early spring saw two sea raids on the Channel coast, one near Caen, the other near Bayeux: both were repelled and at least two of the perpetrators were captured and beheaded as traitors at Bayeux, suggesting that they were from Dieppe, rather than Brittany, the usual suspect where piracy was concerned.[17]

Dieppe was certainly the focus of some attention in the summer. The town was too strongly fortified to be taken except by a long and costly siege, so Talbot and Kyriell had to content themselves with reducing some of the neighbouring towns and fortresses. By July, however, they were in the vicinity of Harfleur, responding to an appeal from some Armagnac traitors in the garrison who were resisting the imposition of a new captain. On 3 May 1438 the final agreement had been signed for the exchange of two of the longest-held prisoners of the conflict: Charles d'Artois, the forty-one-year-old count of Eu, who had been captured at Agincourt in 1415, and John Beaufort, the thirty-five-year-old earl of Somerset, who had been captured at Baugé in 1421.

On his return to France the count had been appointed Charles VII's captain of Normandy between the Seine and the Somme. When he went to take possession of Harfleur some of Marshal de Rieux's men refused to accept him, barricaded themselves into a gatehouse and sent to Rouen for assistance. By the time Talbot's forces got there, however, they had already made their peace with the count and the opportunity had passed. An attempt to blockade Harfleur failed at the end of August when forty-two Armagnac ships apparently succeeded in getting through by the simple device of flying the English red cross.[18]

For Talbot, a choleric man at the best of times, the frustration of these events must have been intensified by the knowledge that, with more men at his disposal, he might have been able to retake Harfleur. Even more annoying was the fact that those men should have been available to him but were actually employed elsewhere serving the personal ambitions of their commander, who happened to be Talbot's brother-in-law.

When Edmund Beaufort had contracted to serve in France on 22 March he had done so as captain-general and governor for the king in Maine and Anjou, with a seven-year term of office. He had already raised an army of 346 men-at-arms and 1350 archers which he was able to muster within four days of his commission, so it was clear that his expedition had been in preparation long before the council sought his services. The Burgundian threat to Guînes passed before he set sail, so Beaufort reverted to his original intention of securing the lands in Maine that he claimed as the family inheritance from Bedford. He was able to do this only because his uncle, Cardinal Beaufort, financed his expedition to the tune of £7333 6s. 8d. (£3.85m), but that money was a loan which would have to be repaid by the English treasury. As Gloucester would later complain, it was a wilful misdirection of money and resources which could have been better employed elsewhere.[19]

Beaufort carried out a brief campaign on the Norman-Breton border, capturing La Guerche (and losing it again 'through misgovernance') before settling in Alençon, where he made a four-year truce, regulating the *appâtis* levied by each side, with the duke of Alençon and Charles d'Anjou, count of Maine. As his own castle of Mortain had been demolished in 1433 to prevent it being taken by the enemy, he made good his claim to Bedford's lordship of Elbeuf by building a fortress there.[20]

That Beaufort was able pursue his own agenda at public expense was an indication of the supremacy at the English court of Cardinal Beaufort. His independent commission meant that Warwick, despite being lieutenant-general of Normandy, had no authority to force him to deploy elsewhere; in any case, as Beaufort was his son-in-law, Warwick may not have wished to curb his territorial ambitions.

However, a new factor was coming into the equation which would profoundly affect the future of the remnants of the English kingdom of France. On 6 December 1437 Henry VI had attained his sixteenth birthday. Though this was not the usual legal age of majority, by common consensus he had reached an age at which he could begin personally to take up the reins of government. Since his accession as a nine-month-old baby, England had effectively been ruled by committee: power and influence had been won and lost by jockeying for position among relative equals. Henry's assumption of personal kingship changed all that: political authority and patronage would flow from the fountainhead of his throne alone. In future aspirant politicians would have to win the king's ear and his confidence if they wished to have any impact on the events of the day.

Henry had simply been a cipher up to this moment. Now he was to emerge from the shadows with an enormous weight of expectation on his youthful shoulders. Those who had expected him to be cast in the same mould as his father, or even his uncles, were to be disappointed. Henry lacked any real political ability.[21] Accustomed from birth to having decisions made on his behalf and being advised by others, he never acquired the independence, judgement and decisiveness of thought that medieval kingship demanded. He had little understanding of the deviousness of others, his naivety frequently leading him to accept what he was told at face value, to the detriment of himself and his country. He was easily influenced, susceptible to flattery, profligate with his gifts and overly lenient in the administration of justice. Perhaps worst of all was his inability to foresee the consequences of his own actions.

Henry showed no aptitude for, or even interest in, military affairs: despite the desperate plight of his French kingdom, he was said to have been the first English king who never commanded an army against a foreign enemy. It was symptomatic of his nature that he dissipated the proud and exclusively martial tradition of the Order of the Garter by bestowing membership on his friends and companions rather than on those who had earned this distinction by their exploits. He was insular to an extreme degree, the remoter regions of his realm beyond England exciting neither his curiosity nor sympathy: he did not repeat his one and only childhood sojourn in France; he never set foot in Ireland, let alone Gascony; even Wales, the birthplace of his father, merited only a single fleeting visit, in 1452.

Perhaps the only aspect in which he resembled his father was his deeply and sincerely held religious beliefs, though the ostentatious piety, bordering on saintliness, so often attributed to him owes more to Tudor propaganda than reality. Henry V's belief that God was on his side had led to Agincourt and the conquest of northern France; Henry VI's more compassionate faith convinced him that it was his God-given duty to bring peace to his war-ravaged kingdom of France. Though he lacked the strength of character to stand up to the more belligerent members of his council, from the moment of his assumption of personal rule the path to peace became more compelling than the old reliance on the sword.

It was therefore significant that one of his first actions was to appoint ambassadors to treat for peace with France. In this he had the full support of Cardinal Beaufort. As most of his loans to the crown were secured on the income from taxes on wool, the cardinal had, by default, become 'the chief merchant of wools in [the] land', with a vested interest in restoring good relations with Flanders. This meant a rapprochement with Burgundy, which Beaufort had also come to believe was in the best interests of the future security of English possessions in France. He had enjoyed good relations with the duke, until his defection in 1435, and in the duchess, his niece, he had an able and willing mediator. The duke of Brittany, never an enthusiastic ally or enemy of either side, was also keen to promote peace. Charles d'Orléans, despite the long incarceration in England which had deprived him of any personal influence he might have had at the French court, was regarded by all parties as a potential intermediary whose presence at any peace conference was absolutely essential; he too was eager to serve. The only senior figure adamantly opposed to a peace which would inevitably require some concessions to the French was Gloucester. In this he probably represented the views of most Englishmen and certainly those who held lands in France.

The young king's personal intervention ensured that the negotiations would go ahead. Orléans was brought to London in preparation for his voyage to Brittany, where the duke had offered to host the conference at Vannes. Though it duly opened at the end of May 1438, Orléans did not attend, probably because he could not finance his journey himself, as the English required him to do. His absence and the opposition of Gloucester and his faction on the council caused the collapse of the talks without any progress towards peace.[22]

Despite this, discussions between the English and Burgundian representatives continued in Rouen and elsewhere, leading to a summit meeting in the Calais marches between Cardinal Beaufort and the duchess Isabella of Burgundy in January 1439. Delegates from Flanders, Holland and Zeeland met representatives of London and the Staplers to draw up lists of mutual grievances and compensation which would enable a resumption of the all-important shipment of wool into Calais. At the same time the cardinal and duchess agreed to hold formal peace negotiations later in the year at Calais: Charles VII's representatives were to be invited to attend and Orléans would also be present.[23]

By the end of June 1439 all the delegates were gathered in or near Calais. This time there would be no mediation by the church: neither the papacy nor the council at Basle was represented; indeed the latter's offer to send a deputation was rejected outright by the English, who felt betrayed by the way that the legates at Arras had favoured the Armagnacs. As at Arras, Cardinal Beaufort was not a member of the English embassy but was to act as a 'mediator and stirrer to peace'. The duchess of Bedford and Charles d'Orléans would occupy similar roles, though none of them, and least of all Beaufort, could claim to be impartial.

Beaufort's ally, archbishop Kemp, led the English embassy, which included supporters of both Gloucester and the cardinal as well as four representatives from the Norman council. Charles VII's embassy was led by Regnault de Chartres, archbishop of Reims, and the Bastard of Orléans, who in this way met his half-brother, the duke, whose interests he had so loyally upheld, for the first time in twenty-four years. The Burgundians were nominally included in this embassy but the duke remained on hand and available for consultation twenty miles away at Saint-Omer.

To avoid a repeat of the débâcle at Arras, the English had a three-tiered set of instructions. In the first instance they were to make the usual bold assertion of the king's rights to the crown and full sovereignty, which, it was optimistically claimed, was 'the most reasonable means of peace'. If this failed, as it inevitably would, the minimum they were empowered to accept in return for a 'perpetual peace' was Normandy, Anjou and Maine, with an enlarged Gascony (as it had been in 1360) and Calais, all in full sovereignty. Finally, if Henry's title to the crown was the only obstacle in the way of peace, the ambassadors were to refer to Cardinal Beaufort 'to whom the king had opened and declared all his intent in this matter'. Beaufort's solution was to urge the French to accept historical precedent going back to the days of Charlemagne for a de facto division of the realm, with neither king claiming exclusive right to the crown except within their own territories.[24]

The French were equally hard-line in their opening gambit, demanding a total renunciation of Henry's right and title to the crown and to all the lands and lordships he held in France: those that he might be permitted to retain must be held of Charles VII and the original landowners restored; the duke of Orléans must be released without paying a ransom.

After several weeks of acrimonious exchanges and much coming and going between the different camps by Orléans and the duchess of Burgundy, a compromise was reached. In return for what they called a half-peace, which was a truce for between fifteen and thirty years, the French demands for Henry's renunciation of the crown and admission of Charles's sovereignty would be put in abeyance and they would recognise his right to hold Calais and its marches, his current possessions in Gascony and all of Normandy and its appurtenances, except Mont-Saint-Michel, for the period of the truce. Throughout that time Henry would have to refrain from using the title 'king of France', either verbally or in writing, restore all those driven out by the conquest and release Orléans without ransom, though he would have to pay the reasonable expenses incurred in his captivity.

While Beaufort remained in Calais to maintain appearances that the peace talks were ongoing, archbishop Kemp returned to England to put these terms to the young king and his council. The two clerics seem to have believed that the suspension of Henry's claims offered a genuine way forward: Gloucester would later say of Kemp that 'it was his single opinion and labour' to argue the case for acceptance but he failed to convince his compatriots. Several memoranda drawn up for presentation to the council give us an insight into the discussions. The most powerful argument for accepting was financial: constant warfare, famine, pestilence and emigration had halved the population of Normandy, so that it could no longer provide the level of revenue necessary to continue the war on its own; England was unwilling and indeed unable to support the burden.

On the other hand, acceptance would dishonour the memory of Henry V, 'who surpassed all mortal princes in his noble reputation for honour, wisdom, courage and every virtue'. More persuasively, if Henry stopped using the title 'king of France' over such a long period, it might be seen as an admission that he had no right to it, especially as Charles would strengthen his position by continuing to call himself king and exercising royal rights and prerogatives; pragmatically, even if the truce lasted only fifteen years, when it ended it would be impossible to resurrect and enforce Henry's claims and previous position. If Henry surrendered his conquests outside Normandy he would lose two counties and around fifteen towns while gaining only Harfleur, Montivilliers and Dieppe in exchange. Restoring those who had left Normandy would create a fifth column within the duchy and alienate those who had been given their lands for services to the English crown; if any form of restitution was to be made, the French should pay compensation to those forced to give up their property. It can have come as no surprise to anyone that Gloucester, when asked his opinion, replied that he would rather die than accept the terms on offer.[25]

When Kemp returned to Calais with news that the offers had been rejected, he found that the French had expected nothing less and had already withdrawn. This was not the end of the process. Charles called a meeting in October of his estates-general at Orléans, in the presence of representatives of the dukes of Burgundy, Brittany and Orléans, and it was agreed that the English should be invited to resume peace talks on 1 May 1440. Before he left Calais Cardinal Beaufort secured a three-year commercial truce with Burgundy which allowed the exports of English wool from Calais to recommence, reopened trade routes and guaranteed the safety of merchants and merchandise.[26] It was not the perpetual peace, nor even the long truce he had hoped to achieve, but it was a major step forward in Anglo-Burgundian relations. And the quest for a diplomatic termination to the war would continue.

CHAPTER EIGHTEEN

Gains and Losses

The case for peace had not been helped by the actions of Arthur de Richemont. Within a couple of weeks of the commencement of the peace talks he laid siege to Meaux, the last remaining English stronghold east of Paris. The timing and choice of objective were deliberately designed to goad the English: Meaux was an important bargaining counter and potentially one of the places in the Île-de-France which could be exchanged for Harfleur, Dieppe or Montivilliers.

Richemont was also under pressure to redeem himself after two important successes by Talbot. In November 1438, helped by a Scottish traitor in the garrison, Talbot had scaled the walls and captured the town and castle of Gerberoy from La Hire. Two months later he seized Saint-Germain-en-Laye, on the outskirts of Paris, with the aid of the prior of Nanterre, who befriended the captain, stole his keys and then admitted Talbot's men. The prior's reward for this service was 300 *saluts* (£24,062) from the English – and imprisonment in irons on nothing but bread and water for the rest of his life, from the Armagnacs, when he was arrested a few days later. Talbot installed François de Surienne as the new captain, an interesting appointment given that the Aragonese had just surrendered Montargis in return for money, but one that he would carry out in exemplary fashion.[1]

Richemont had been severely blamed for the loss of Saint-Germain; his Bretons had failed in their duty of guarding the place and his extortions had turned the people of Paris against him. He was, the citizen wrote in his journal, 'a very bad man and a thorough coward . . . he cared nothing for King, prince, or people, nor what towns or castles the English might take; as long as he had money, he cared nothing for anything or anywhere else'. Having begun and abandoned an attempt to take Pontoise in retaliation for Talbot's seizure of Saint-Germain, Richemont called in the *écorcheurs*. On 20 July 1439 they laid siege to Meaux and on 12 August took the town by assault. The garrison retreated to the stronghold of the market and sent urgent pleas for assistance to Rouen. Talbot, Scales and Fauconberg joined forces to go to their relief. When they arrived Richemont refused all provocation to fight a pitched battle but, in the skirmishes that ensued, he lost twenty boats laden with victuals and most of his siege works were destroyed.

Believing the market to be strong enough to hold out until he could come back with a second relief column, Talbot reinforced it with around five hundred men, commanded by Sir William Chamberlain, stocked it with supplies and left for Rouen. When he returned, later than expected, on 16 September, he discovered that the market had surrendered the day before. In his fury Talbot had Chamberlain arrested, imprisoned and charged with treason; his unfortunate lieutenant was only able to clear himself by pointing out that, although he still had supplies, he could not have withstood Richemont's artillery and, without relief, his position had been hopeless.[2]

Charles VII was in Paris when Meaux surrendered, paying only his second visit to the capital since the Treaty of Arras. He cannot have been blind to the impact of the famine and plague, nor to their consequences, which were horribly illustrated by the fact that fourteen people were killed and eaten by starving wolves in the streets between Montmartre and the Saint-Anthoine gate in the week before his departure on 30 September. No doubt Charles was also told in no uncertain terms about the sufferings caused by the *écorcheurs* stationed in and around Paris. It was not just that they stole all the crops and beasts which were intended to feed the local population but also that they made arbitrary demands for money which Richemont's regime supported or at least condoned. 'If you did not pay them the moment they appeared for the money, you at once had sergeants quartered on you, which was a great distress to poor people, for once these men were in your house you had to maintain them at great expense, for they were the devil's own children and did far more damage than they were ordered to.'[3]

When Richemont and his 'company of thieves and murderers' returned from their triumph at Meaux, Charles ordered them to leave Paris and take the war to the English in Normandy. This would have the twin benefits of relieving Paris of their racketeering and pillaging and reminding the English of the inevitable consequences of their failure to accept his terms for peace. Richemont joined forces with Jean, duke of Alençon, and the sires de Laval and Lohéac, and with more ambition than prudence laid siege to Avranches.

Perched on the top of its great cliff, the citadel was virtually impregnable; three or four weeks of bombardment by all kinds of artillery had left it unscathed, and a message to Rouen had brought Edmund Beaufort and lords Talbot, Scales and Fauconberg to the rescue at the head of a large army. They encamped at Pont-Gilbert, on the river Sée at the foot of the escarpment, with the river between them and the besieging army. A number of skirmishes took place but Richemont's men were able to hold the line of the river and prevent them crossing. On the night of 22 December, therefore, the English moved downriver and took advantage of the retreating tidal waters of the estuary secretly to cross the sands, skirt round the back of the cliff and enter Avranches from the opposite side. They then sallied out of the town en masse, catching the Armagnacs unawares, overwhelming them and seizing their bombards, artillery, victuals and personal possessions. It was a complete rout and by the next morning, as the well-named pursuivant Bonne Adventure reported gleefully to his masters in Rouen, the siege was raised because the enemy 'fled shamefully, to their great dishonour and embarrassment'. A subsequent inquest revealed that some people in the *vicomté* of Avranches had joined, or at least collaborated with, the enemy during the siege, obliging the whole region to purchase a general pardon: one of them, Perrin Fillepouche, was later beheaded at Avranches as a 'traitor, thief, brigand, arsonist of the church of Les Biards, enemy and adversary of the king'.[4]

The relief of Avranches was marred only by news that during the siege one of the duke of Alençon's companies, led by the sire de Bueil, had taken advantage of Edmund Beaufort's absence from Maine to capture the stronghold of Sainte-Suzanne, which lay halfway between Le Mans and Laval. A member of the English garrison who was on night-watch had sung a particular song as a prearranged signal to let the attackers know that he was there: he had then pulled their scaling ladders up to the ramparts, enabling them to enter the castle and seize the rest of the garrison in their nightshirts. Thus returned to Alençon's obedience, Sainte-Suzanne would again become a thorn in the flesh of the English.[5]

The days of the *écorcheurs* were numbered, however, but not because of their disgraceful flight from Avranches. For many years they had been a useful tool against the enemy, particularly when that enemy was Burgundy. Since the Treaty of Arras, however, they had become a liability, not just because their activities turned Charles's own subjects against him but because they owed loyalty to no one except their current paymaster (and sometimes not even to him). The duke of Bourbon, in particular, had strong family ties with some of the most notorious captains: the two Bastards of Bourbon were his own half-brothers and the Castilian Roderigo de Villandrando was married to their sister. He had employed them all for his own ends, including when he briefly rebelled against Charles VII in 1437.

Charles could no longer afford to ignore the complaints of his subjects or the danger that the *écorcheurs* posed to his allies and himself. The meeting of his estates-general at Orléans in

October–November 1439 endorsed a series of ordinances designed to stamp out their abuses and reform the military system in France. In future no one could claim to exercise military authority without royal approval; all captains were to be chosen by the king and held responsible for the discipline of their men whose misdeeds they were authorised to punish; any action against civilians would be treated as treason, and property, livestock and agricultural produce were to be protected; a fixed levy of 1,200,000*l.t.* (£70m) was to be imposed annually on the king's subjects to pay for the royal army, which in future would live in garrison rather than on the land. The combined effect of these ordinances was to outlaw freelance companies and create a single royal army subject to the control of the constable of France, Arthur de Richemont.[6]

Though these measures were generally welcomed by the civilian population, they were deeply resented by the princes of the realm, who were thus deprived of their right to own and command private armies. Most, like Burgundy, quietly ignored the ordinances and continued as usual. For some, such as Bourbon and Alençon, who had no liking for the constable anyway, the reforms were an act of despotism which had to be forcibly resisted. And in the sixteen-year-old dauphin, Louis, who intensely disliked his father and was anxious to throw off the constraints he had placed on him, they found a figurehead round whom they could rally.

The Praguerie revolt began in April 1440 when Bourbon and Alençon refused to expel the *écorcheurs* from their companies or muster before Richemont's deputies, Xaintrailles and Gaucourt, and took up arms against their king. They were joined by other disaffected courtiers, such as Georges de la Trémoïlle, and, of course, the *écorcheurs* themselves. It was a measure of the depth of feeling against Charles VII among his own nobility that even the Bastard of Orléans temporarily joined the revolt, because he was rightly suspicious of Charles's unwillingness to assist in securing the release of his brother. Once again, instead of fighting the English, the French were fighting among themselves. Though the dauphin was bribed into a reconciliation with his father in July, the rebellion lasted throughout the summer, and diverted important military resources to its suppression and the recapturing of places taken by the insurgents. Bourbon and the leading rebels were all subsequently pardoned, but Charles showed no mercy to those *écorcheurs* who refused to join his army: the Bastard of Bourbon was tried for his crimes, found guilty and thrown in a sack into a river to drown, an exemplary punishment which persuaded some other captains, including Villandrando, that they had no future in France.[7]

Charles VII's court had always been riven by faction but another powerful factor in persuading so many of the rebels to resort to arms, including Bourbon himself, was anger and dismay at the progress of peace talks with the English. The 'war party' in France was unable to reconcile itself to any concessions and particularly not the permanent loss of Normandy, irrespective of who ultimately retained sovereignty. In England there was a similar reaction by those who felt betrayed by those pushing for peace. Though it did not result in armed rebellion, it caused much dissension and a final bitter showdown between Cardinal Beaufort and Humphrey, duke of Gloucester.

At the opening of parliament in January 1440, after its adjournment from Westminster to Reading, Gloucester launched a ferocious attack on Beaufort and Kemp. Rehearsing all his old complaints against Beaufort, he now accused the two men of 'great deceits' in their peace negotiations at Calais, especially in their advocacy of Charles VII's offers and the release of Orléans. He also charged them with profiteering from the war, selling offices in France and Normandy to the highest bidder and furthering Beaufort family interests at the expense of those of the kingdom. 'It is not unknown to your highness', he told the king,

how often I have offered my service unto you, for the defence of your realm of France and lordships there, [but] have been prevented by the labour of the said cardinal, in preferring others of his singular affection, which has caused a great part of your duchy of Normandy, as well as of your said realm of France, to be lost, as is well known.

Gloucester ended his denunciation by seeking the dismissal of Beaufort and Kemp from the council, 'to the intent that men may be at their freedom to say what they truly think; for though I dare speak my truth, the poor dare not so'.[8]

Gloucester's appeal produced no response from the young king, whose own desire for peace naturally inclined him to support his conciliatory clergymen rather than his bellicose uncle. Henry allowed the duke to enter a formal protest 'that I never was, am, nor ever shall be consenting, advising, nor agreeing to [Orléans's] deliverance or being set free ... otherwise than is expressed in my said Lord my brother's last will'. Nevertheless, Henry felt obliged to publish his own justification for the policies carried out in his name, reciting his moral duty to find peace as well as the miseries of Normandy and the impossibility of financing a continuing war. He also added a stern injunction that he wished 'that it be openly felt and plainly known that that [which] he has done in the said matter he has done of himself and of his own advice and courage ... moved and stirred of God and of reason, as he fully trusts'.[9]

Henry would not allow Beaufort to be blamed for his own decision to release Orléans but he may have been influenced by Gloucester's belief that the duke would not fulfil his side of the bargain by working for peace once he had been set free. The terms eventually agreed included a ransom of 40,000 nobles (£7m) payable immediately, plus a further 80,000 (£14m) within six months; if the duke succeeded in arranging a peace within that time, the entire ransom was cancelled; if he failed and could not produce the money, he was honour-bound to return to captivity. This was as much as Henry was prepared to concede and Gloucester did himself no favours by storming out of Westminster Abbey during the public ceremony in which Orléans swore to observe the terms of his release.

As Charles VII was as uncomfortable as Gloucester with the idea of Orléans being released, he refused to contribute to his ransom and it was the redoubtable duchess of Burgundy who press-ganged the French aristocracy into raising the necessary sums. On 5 November 1440 Charles d'Orléans returned to

France as a free man: it was almost exactly twenty-five years since he had been taken prisoner at Agincourt. Though he demonstrated his reconciliation with Burgundy by accepting membership of the Order of the Golden Fleece and marrying Philippe's niece, Marie of Cleves, the high hopes entertained of his abilities as a peacemaker were not to be realised. In the wake of the Praguerie, Charles VII was so suspicious of the new alliance between the two former enemies that it would be over a year before Orléans was even admitted to his presence, let alone his councils, and the war continued. Gloucester's dire warnings that the cause of peace could not be served by releasing Orléans turned out to be correct.[10]

Gloucester had failed to prevent the duke's release but he did succeed in thwarting Cardinal Beaufort's ambition to raise his nephew to the highest position in France. Ever since Bedford's death in 1435 the cardinal had worked towards securing the appointment of John Beaufort, earl of Somerset, as his successor. As Somerset was then an Armagnac prisoner, the cardinal had immediately resumed negotiations for his release and persuaded the king to authorise his exchange with Charles d'Artois, count of Eu, even though the dying Henry V had expressly forbidden the latter's release until Henry VI came of age. When Somerset was eventually released towards the end of 1438 he was allowed to spend only a few months in England before being sent to Normandy, where his connections ensured him immediate appointment to the council of Rouen.[11]

Somerset was therefore well placed to succeed the frail Warwick, who died in office at Rouen on 30 April 1439. (Unlike Bedford, Warwick had chosen to be buried at home, where his magnificent gilded effigy adorning his tomb in Saint Mary's church, Warwick, is one of the glories of medieval England.) Until his successor could be appointed his powers were devolved to a governing council composed of four Norman clerics and five English laymen: Louis de Luxembourg, now archbishop of Rouen; Pierre Cauchon, bishop of Lisieux, chief prosecutor of Jehanne d'Arc; Gilles de Duremont, abbot of Fécamp, and Robert Jolivet, abbot of Mont-Saint-Michel; Somerset; his brother Edmund Beaufort; and the three field commanders, lords Talbot, Scales and Fauconberg. Though the least experienced of them all after seventeen years in prison – he had seen his first action since Baugé in 1421 at the relief of Meaux in August 1439 – it was Somerset whose rank entitled him to assume overarching military command.

In September 1439 Somerset returned to England to lobby his claims to be appointed formally as Warwick's and, more importantly, Bedford's successor. Initially his prospects looked good. The complicated arrangements for his release, which included his having to purchase the count of Eu from the crown in order to effect the exchange, had cost him £24,000 (£12.6m). On 12 December he petitioned the king for assistance with his ransom and was granted compensation from the London customs so that he might do 'better service to the king in this expedition'. The following day he contracted to serve in France for six months with four knights, one hundred men-at-arms and two thousand archers. This was a very large army, indicating that a major campaign was planned for the first time in three years. Somerset could not have funded it himself from his impoverished finances and it was, of course, Cardinal Beaufort who provided the loans necessary to create this command for his nephew.[12]

What Beaufort could not do, however, was secure the coveted prize of the lieutenancy-general for Somerset. That had now been claimed by Gloucester, who, dismayed by the course of recent events, was determined to revive his oft-repeated plan to go to France himself at the head of a large army. The council in Normandy was told to expect his arrival but, since the cardinal held the purse-strings and declined to open them for him, Gloucester was obliged to concede that he was not yet ready to go 'in such powerful array' as his status demanded. Almost by default, therefore, Somerset stepped into his shoes. When he left for France in January 1440 he did so on a salary of 600*l.t.* (£35,000) a month but his commission was to stand only until Gloucester's arrival and was limited to that of 'lieutenant-general and governor for the war', suggesting constraints on his civil powers.[13]

In the event Gloucester never did take up his appointment. His reasons remain a mystery. He may have got cold feet at the prospect of uprooting himself for another country at the age of almost fifty, thereby losing what little personal influence he could exert over the young king and his peace policies, or he may have been blocked by the cardinal and his supporters on the council. As his acting lieutenant Somerset was the prime candidate for the post, but Gloucester was determined that he should not have it. Once again therefore it was the compromise candidate who emerged as the victor. On 2 July 1440 Richard, duke of York, was again appointed lieutenant-general of Normandy with the explicit endorsements of both Gloucester and the cardinal.

York had driven a hard bargain before accepting the office, demanding the same powers as Gloucester 'had or should have had'. All the authority that Bedford had enjoyed thus devolved on him, though he would still be called 'lieutenant-general' since Henry VI was no longer a minor in need of a regent. In an ominous development for the Beauforts, and Normandy, he also sought and obtained powers to replace non-resident captains with his own men and to have no restriction on the value of lands he could grant, ensuring that he could reward his own men and build up a personal following in a duchy that was largely dominated by the Beaufort family interest. York's appointment would last five years and he was promised an annual payment from the English exchequer of £20,000 (£10.5m) to fund his troops, a sum far in excess of both his own previous salary and that of Somerset as lieutenant-general and governor.[14]

Despite these concessions, York demonstrated no urgent desire to take up his new post. It would be almost a year before he left for Normandy and in the meantime Somerset remained in command. He took the opportunity to further Beaufort interests, taking over a number of important captaincies, including those of Avranches and Tombelaine from the earl of Suffolk. Even Talbot lost all his captaincies, apart from Lisieux, so that the king had to pay him a compensatory pension 'to enable him to maintain himself in our service more honourably'.[15]

Somerset did not exactly cover himself with glory in his first military campaign in February 1440. In the hope of putting pressure on the duke of Burgundy to make peace, he launched a highly profitable raid into Picardy, the softest target on the Norman border. With a further twelve hundred troops from Normandy and Talbot by his side he captured three fortresses, installed an English garrison at Folleville and burned down the church in which the people of Lihons had barricaded themselves, which was an appalling war crime even by the standards of his own day. The remaining inhabitants of Lihons had to pay Talbot a ransom of 2500 *saluts* (£200,521) to escape the same fate.[16]

The main purpose for which Somerset had been sent to Normandy with such a large army was to retake Harfleur, Henry V's first conquest in France, which had been in Armagnac hands since 1435. From its vantage point at the mouth of the Seine, the garrison had preyed on English shipping, disrupting supplies to Rouen and forcing the authorities to employ a warship to patrol the river for their protection. The outbreak of the Praguerie rebellion against Charles VII provided the ideal opportunity for a major effort while enemy troops were deployed elsewhere. Perhaps fortunately Somerset delegated the command in the field to his more talented younger brother, Edmund Beaufort, and by June the town was under siege and the port blockaded.

While Beaufort, Talbot and Fauconberg ensured that nothing could get in or out of Harfleur, Somerset occupied himself in gathering supplies and recruiting more men to resist the relief army that was said to be on its way. Among those who joined the siege as it dragged on over several months was Matthew Gough, whose services Beaufort was so anxious to retain that he paid his wages out of his own pocket. Rather less welcome was François de Surienne, not because his abilities were not appreciated, but because on 19 October 1440 he had surrendered Saint-Germain-en-Laye to Charles VII, leaving the few remaining English outposts round Paris even more isolated and vulnerable. A temporary visitor to the siege was the Windsor herald, who arrived bearing the insignia of the Garter for Somerset and Fauconberg, both men having just been admitted to the order: his presence is noted only because he fell off his horse, breaking three ribs and his arm, and was therefore late claiming his wages.[17]

For at least some of the Armagnacs defending Harfleur there must have been an oppressive sense of familiarity. The captain was Jean d'Estouteville, whose father had held the same office in 1415 when Henry V laid siege to the town. The overall command had then been taken over by Raoul, sire de Gaucourt, who had brought a relief column into Harfleur under the nose of the English king, prolonging its ability to resist by several weeks. Gaucourt was now seventy but age had not dimmed his spirit. Responding to Harfleur's urgent pleas for assistance, he had joined the count of Eu, the Bastard of Orléans, La Hire and the Bastard of Bourbon (on one of his last outings before his execution) in bringing a relieving force to the town's aid. This time, however, he was in charge of the rearguard and, following the rest of the army as it left Eu, he was surprised and taken prisoner by Gryffydd Dŵn, the Welsh captain of Tancarville. Unlike his previous imprisonment at the hands of the English, which had lasted ten years, a ransom was swiftly accepted and his incarceration would be brief. Gaucourt's capture, however, spurred his colleagues into a determined attempt to break the siege of Harfleur.[18]

While the count of Eu launched an attack by sea, the Bastard of Orléans led his men on foot against the English encamped before the town. La Hire, because of his lameness, was entrusted with the cavalry to bring aid wherever it was needed. Despite heavy fighting and a sortie by the garrison, the Armagnacs could make no headway. The English were too well dug into their trenches and their camps too well fortified to be taken. The attack by land was repelled and the fleet was forced to withdraw after losing several ships. The count of Eu tried to mitigate this disaster by offering to fight for Harfleur in a duel with Somerset, or with one hundred of his champions against a similar number of Englishmen, but was rebuffed with contempt. The English knew that the town's supplies of food had run out and that its surrender was imminent. At the end of October Harfleur capitulated: the garrison was allowed to march out in the customary fashion, each man bearing a stick in his hand to signify that he was unarmed and a safe-conduct to allow him to withdraw into lands of his own allegiance. The duke of Burgundy, however, expressly forbade any of them to go through his territories for fear of pillaging and had his soldiers on stand-by to expel any who dared to trespass.[19]

The recapture of such an important town as Harfleur, with its valuable harbour, was a welcome success, especially as its neighbour, Montivilliers, surrendered as part of the terms of capitulation. Dieppe was now the only major stronghold in Normandy seized by the Armagnacs in 1435 which still remained in enemy hands. Elated by their success – and having overstayed the term of Somerset's six-month contract to see the job completed – the Beaufort brothers returned to England, leaving Normandy in the hands of its veteran defenders, lords Talbot, Scales and Fauconberg.

Even before a triumphant Somerset and his troops left Normandy the Armagnacs fought back with a vengeance, launching a concerted assault on the eastern marches of the duchy. Xaintrailles, Anthoine de Chabannes and a Spanish mercenary named Salazar, aided and abetted by collaborators within the town, took Louviers. In a sense this was retributive justice, for the English had demolished the fortifications and withdrawn the garrison when they recaptured it in 1431, leaving it defenceless. The priority of its new owners was to restore and rebuild the town's walls and towers, ensuring that Louviers remained in Armagnac hands for the duration of the war. The citizens petitioned Charles VII, reminding him of all that they had suffered because they had been his loyal subjects, 'wishing rather to choose death than return ever to the subjection of our enemies', and in 1442 were granted exemption from tax, assistance in rebuilding their fortifications and the rights to call the town 'Louviers the Free' and wear on their clothing a crown superimposed on the letter 'L'.

At about the same time as Louviers fell, Pierre de Brézé and Robert Floques took by assault the town of Conches-en-Ouche, twenty-three miles south-west of Louviers. The two strongholds thus created an Armagnac enclave which, like La Hire's Beauvais, would cause endless trouble to the neighbouring English-held districts.[20]

Talbot, the new captain of Harfleur, spent the winter fortifying strongholds in the vicinity of Conches and Louviers against the new threat but, with diminishing forces at his disposal, he could not afford to risk a siege, even though the Armagnac garrison of Louviers was building a bastille on the Seine to disrupt the vital passage of supplies downriver from Rouen to Pontoise.[21]

This was part of a concerted plan, for Charles VII's response to the loss of Harfleur and Montivilliers was to launch a summer campaign to recover the few remaining English outposts round Paris. Having cleared Champagne of the *écorcheurs* and executed the Bastard of Bourbon, on 8 May 1441 he laid siege to Creil, the town and castle on the Oise, thirty miles north of the capital and twenty-six miles north-east of Pontoise. To show that he meant business he had gathered an impressive army which included not only the king himself and his recently reconciled son, the dauphin, but also Constable Richemont, Admiral Prégent de Coëtivy, Charles d'Anjou, Xaintrailles and La Hire. Also with the king was his master of the artillery, Jean Bureau, and the huge artillery train of heavy guns for which he was responsible. These were deployed so effectively that a substantial breach was created in the walls in just over a fortnight. The garrison's soldiers, led in person by their captain, Sir William Peyto, sallied out to defend it but after hard hand-to-hand fighting they were forced to withdraw. The following day, 25 May, they agreed terms, surrendered their charge and left for Normandy.[22]

Charles now homed in on Pontoise, where between a thousand and twelve hundred English were said to be stationed, laying siege to the place on 6 June. He directed operations from the Cistercian abbey of Maubuisson at Saint-Ouen-l'Aumône across the river while his army spread out along the river plain below. Prégent de Coëtivy brought a flotilla of boats to create a pontoon bridge across to the abbey of Saint-Martin outside the town walls, which he then seized and made his headquarters. Fifteen days of heavy bombardment by Bureau's guns destroyed the bulwarks at the end of the town bridge, allowing the besiegers to take this position.

Before they could proceed any further they were stopped in their tracks by the arrival of Talbot with a relieving army. Anticipating a siege, Talbot had been sending supplies and artillery into Pontoise since the middle of May and had established a route into the town through the gate upriver. This gate the Armagnacs had neglected, or were unable, to besiege, allowing Talbot to send in victuals and reinforcements, a process he was able to repeat on five occasions over the next three months without any impediment. Before he left for the first time he installed lord Scales in the garrison to give new heart and additional weight to the defence.

'There was only one English captain who stood fast against the king and his forces,' the citizen of Paris wrote in his journal at this time. 'This was Talbot; and indeed, it looked from the way they behaved as if they were terrified of him. They always kept a good twenty or thirty leagues between him and themselves and he rode about France more boldly than they did. Yet the king taxed his people twice a year at least so as to go and fight Talbot, but nothing was ever done.'[23]

CHAPTER NINETEEN

Missed Opportunities

In June 1441 the members of the council at Rouen wrote an extraordinarily frank and dramatic letter to Henry VI. They complained that they had repeatedly sent him letters and messages without response. Now they were writing 'in extreme necessity, and we tell you that our malady is nearing death or dissolution and, as regards your lordship, very nearly total destruction'. For two years the king had encouraged them to believe that Gloucester was about to come to them; they had been disappointed in this, and in the arrival of the duke of York, which 'was promised by you and awaited in vain by us for so long that we despair of it. We now have no reason, cause or occasion to give or promise hope of comfort to [your people].'

They did not know what to do, they said. They felt abandoned 'like a ship tossed on the sea by changeable winds, without commander, without helmsman, without rudder, without anchor, without sail, floating, disabled and wandering in the midst of tempestuous waves, overburdened by agony, harsh fortune and every adversity, far from the safety of port and from human aid'. Fifteen days earlier Henry had received their letters telling him that Creil, 'one of the notable places and centres in

France', had fallen and that Pontoise would be next. Now they had to inform him that 'your chief adversary and his son' were indeed besieging Pontoise and how long it would hold out they could not say. Talbot was at Vernon gathering all the troops he could muster to go to its aid. 'It is a great injury to you, our sovereign lord,' they concluded, 'that the said lord Talbot does not have enough men, for he has a high and notable courage in his wish to employ himself on your behalf against your said enemies.'[1]

In fact, as Talbot led his relief column into Pontoise, the duke of York was finally making his way into Rouen. He arrived at the head of the largest army to embark for France in recent years: nine hundred men-at-arms, including a large noble contingent of two earls, four barons, six bannerets and thirty knights, and 2700 archers. Its military credentials were rather undermined by the fact that it was also accompanied by a significant number of well-born women who had chosen to accompany their husbands, among them the duchesses of York and Bedford (the latter, Jacquetta of Luxembourg, having secretly married Bedford's chamberlain, Richard Wydeville, just a year after the death of her first husband) and the countesses of Oxford and Eu.[2] The English holder of the title count of Eu was Henry, lord Bourgchier, who had just been appointed captain of Le Crotoy, at the mouth of the Somme. Just as Scales had been put into Pontoise, Bourgchier had been drafted into Le Crotoy to bolster the garrison and demonstrate its value to the crown. The previous captain, Walter Cressoner, had struggled against Armagnac raids and the indiscipline of neighbouring English garrisons and Le Crotoy was under constant threat of attack from the sea by Burgundians, Armagnacs and Bretons alike. Knowing that he was taking on a difficult and dangerous commission and mindful of the potential consequences of failure, Bourgchier obtained Henry's promise that he would not be held responsible for surrendering if a relief army was not sent to his aid within a month of being besieged. He then accepted a seven-year term of office on a salary of £1000 (£525,000) in war and £867 (£455,175) in peace. By March 1442 he had also been appointed governor-general of the marches of Normandy and Picardy, a newly created position supplementing those of Talbot, Scales and Fauconberg.[3]

Within three weeks of arriving in Rouen, York mounted a rescue mission to Pontoise, crossing the river at Beaumont-sur-Oise by means of boats he had brought with him in carts and bridges made from wood and cord. With the numbers at his command, it should have been possible to raise the siege completely, but once again, the Armagnacs refused to be drawn into battle. Having learned from the English at Harfleur the previous year, they had dug themselves in securely, surrounding their encampments not only with ditches but also with wooden palisades, stakes and carts, and installing cannon and artillery. To fight would mean abandoning, even temporarily, these defences and the captured strongholds of the bridgehead and Saint-Martin's Abbey, which the besiegers were not prepared to do. Even a diversionary raid on Poissy by Talbot failed to draw them out.

Frustrated of his main purpose, York resupplied Pontoise and installed new men in the garrison, including John, lord Clinton, who had accompanied him from England, and the veteran captain and director of the siege of Mont-Saint-Michel, Sir Nicholas Burdet. He then withdrew downriver, establishing a second bridge to enable him to return to Normandy and prevent supplies reaching the besiegers from Paris. Ambroise de Loré, however, in his capacity as provost of Paris, a post which he had obtained after the city's fall in 1436, succeeded in bringing at least one ship-load of victuals through to the admiral at Saint-Martin's. Apart from some skirmishing and much crossing and recrossing of the Oise in an attempt to cut off the besiegers, York was unable to do anything more and returned to Normandy, promising to return again with aid for the garrison of Pontoise.[4]

As soon as he had gone, however, Charles VII resumed his siege and ordered a major bombardment to begin. On 16 September the sires de Lohéac and de Bueil were commanded to lead an assault through the breaches in the wall and, in a bitterly fought assault, they seized the church of Notre Dame, killing twenty-four of the thirty Englishmen defending it. Three days later a general assault was launched in which both Charles VII and the dauphin personally took part. The first man to enter Pontoise was a Scot, who was rewarded for this feat with lands confiscated from the *écorcheur* captain Anthoine de Chabannes. The besieged put up a fierce resistance but were overwhelmed by superior numbers: in the bloodbath that followed the attackers lost very few men but between four and five hundred Englishmen were killed, including Burdet. Lord Clinton and hundreds more were taken prisoner; fifty-three people were captured sheltering in the Cock and Peacock inn alone.

Since Pontoise had been taken by assault rather than by agreeing to surrender, the laws of war authorised that the property of all the inhabitants was forfeit and their lives were at the king's mercy. They were treated with unusual severity. The citizen observed them being brought to Paris:

> It was a sad spectacle, for they took them away eating the bread of sorrow indeed, coupled together two and two with very strong rope, just like hounds being led out to the hunt, and their captors riding tall horses which went very fast. The prisoners had no hoods, all bareheaded, each wearing some wretched rag, most of them without shoes or hose – everything, in fact, had been taken from them but their underpants . . . All those who could pay no ransom they took to the Grève by the Port-au-Foin, tied them hand and foot with no more compunction than if they had been dogs, and drowned them then and there in the sight of all the people.[5]

With the capture of Pontoise the English lost their last remaining stronghold in the Île-de-France. It had taken Charles VII five years to expel them, an indictment of his lack of will rather than means, but also a tribute to the tenacity of the English. Things were changing, however, as Charles's military reforms, his building up of his artillery under the Bureau brothers[6] and his employment of new tactics at the siege of Pontoise all demonstrated. Ironically all these innovations, which turned him into a much more powerful adversary, had been learned from the English. And the military initiative had now passed to the French.

Four days before the fall of Pontoise the English lost another major town by more traditional means. Robert Floques, who had seized Conches-en-Ouche in Normandy the previous autumn, had established himself as its captain and begun to extend his sphere of influence within a twelve-mile radius of the town. In May he had bombarded the castle of Beaumesnil into surrendering, then stormed and taken the fortress of Beaumont-le-Roger. On 15 September he captured Évreux with the aid of two local fishermen, one of whom was performing the night-watch and looked the other way while his colleague, pretending to fish from a boat in the river, brought scaling ladders and a party of men-at-arms up to the walls. The town – head of its own *bailliage* – was swiftly taken by assault. A local man, Thomassin le Mareschal, 'one of the most senior leaders of the enterprise', who had 'secretly facilitated Robert Floques's exploit', was rewarded with a valuable tax-collecting office. Floques himself was reimbursed the 6000 *écus* (£437,500) it had cost him to take the town and acquired a new and more important captaincy; two years later his son would become bishop of Évreux, a sign that the capture of such a prominent place was still appreciated by his king.[7]

Perhaps the loss of Évreux alerted the English administration to the dangers posed by fishermen apparently going about their business, for in October they suspended the traditional facility offered to herring boats from Dieppe allowing them to put in to Calais. This had been left in place even after Dieppe fell into Armagnac hands in 1435 and was used by substantial numbers of fishermen. In the light of the loss of Évreux it was too much of a security threat to be permitted to continue.[8]

By the end of 1441 the successes of the previous year in recapturing Harfleur and Montivilliers had been more than outweighed by the loss of Creil, Pontoise and Évreux and the establishment of an aggressive Armagnac enclave based at

Louviers and Conches-en-Ouche. The arrival of York and his large army had failed to tip the balance in England's favour and Talbot's valiant efforts to save Pontoise had been futile.

It was left to François de Surienne to bring the only ray of light at the end of a depressing year. In December one of the English prisoners captured at Pontoise, who had been released on parole to find his ransom, told him that many of his fellow captives had been taken to Courville-sur-Eure, some twelve miles west of Chartres, and that the place was badly guarded. Acting on this prisoner's inside information, Surienne sent into Courville three or four of his men disguised as peasants carrying sacks of apples to market. They found part of the garrison absent and the rest sleeping, made their way to the captain's room and seized him from his bed. With him as their prisoner they were able to release all the English from Pontoise and open the gates to allow Surienne and his men into the town. Courville was captured and pillaged.[9]

The Aragonese thus won himself a valuable haul of booty and prisoners in addition to having the satisfaction of rescuing some of the miserable Pontoise prisoners. A grateful duke of York appointed him captain of Courville and suggested that he might like to apply his considerable talents to the capture of Gallardon, a fortress eleven miles east of Chartres. Surienne obliged and with the aid of Thomas Hoo, captain of Verneuil, raised a force of 120 men-at-arms and 380 archers, all mounted. The fact that this was a risky raid into enemy territory was recognised by encouraging the army to be aggressive: only half its wages would be paid by the king; the rest would come from levying *appâtis* and the gains of war, which Surienne and Hoo were allowed to divide equally between them. By mid-February 1442 Surienne was installed in Gallardon with a large garrison of 60 men-at-arms and 190 archers and busy restocking it with artillery and munitions shipped from Rouen to Mantes and then hauled the last thirty miles over land.[10]

Though heartening, Surienne's successes were insignificant compared with the loss of places of the magnitude of Pontoise and Évreux. The army York had brought with him having returned to England at the end of its six-month contract of service, the need for another expeditionary force to recover lost ground became imperative. It was a measure of the desperation felt in Normandy that when, on 15 February, a delegation from the council in Rouen sailed from Harfleur to plead for more aid, it was headed by lord Talbot, a man not noted for his diplomatic skills but whose record in the defence of the English kingdom of France was second to none.

York fully appreciated Talbot's military abilities. He had promoted him to lieutenant-general for waging war and reappointed him captain of Rouen, a position from which he had been removed by Somerset. Such was Talbot's commitment to the English cause in France that he had not set foot in his native land since 1435. His arrival was therefore bound to make an impact and was designed to coincide with the first meeting of an English parliament in over a year. As parliament was attended by all the great lords of the realm as well as many knights of the shire, it was a useful gathering at which to recruit a new army. It was also an opportunity for Talbot, in person, to put Normandy's needs to the decision-makers on whose grants of taxation the funding of any expedition would depend.

The England to which Talbot returned cannot have been much to his liking. Henry VI was more interested in building his twin foundations of Eton and King's College, Cambridge, than in prosecuting the war in France. His assumption of personal power meant that the old guard had seen their powers and influence much diminished. Cardinal Beaufort had continued his search for a permanent peace, toiling away in conjunction with the newly liberated duke of Orléans and the duchess of Burgundy but without success. Orléans had been as good as his word, persuading the dukes of Burgundy, Brittany, Alençon and later even Bourbon to push Charles VII for new peace negotiations with England, beginning in the spring of 1441. Charles was suspicious of their motives, however, fearing that this sudden union of old enemies might lead to another Praguerie, but also increasingly convinced by his military successes in both northern France and Gascony that a negotiated peace was not necessarily to his advantage. His refusal to appoint ambassadors led to the deferral of the negotiations to November and then May 1442. The English delegation duly arrived in Calais in February 1442 to prepare the ground for the May conference, but they waited in vain for Charles's ambassadors and in June they abandoned hope and returned home.[11]

As the tortuous peace process slowly ground to a halt, Beaufort's standing at court steadily diminished. His arch-rival Gloucester had also seen his influence wane since his angry protests at the release of Charles d'Orléans, and he was replaced as captain of Calais, a position which had always been close to his heart, at the beginning of 1441.[12] That summer, however, he was the victim of an attack which left him socially and politically ostracised and removed the last vestige of his authority and influence. Who was behind the plot was never discovered – it could have been any one of the many enemies Gloucester had made over the years, including the cardinal or the increasingly powerful William de la Pole, earl of Suffolk – but it was particularly cruel because it aimed to destroy him through his wife.

Eleanor Cobham had been Gloucester's mistress before she became his wife and their marriage, though childless, was happy. Beautiful and ambitious, she had revelled in her husband's position, particularly after the death of Bedford made him heir to the unmarried Henry VI. Like most of her class, she regularly consulted astrologers, a profession which required literacy and numeracy and was therefore usually practised by clerics. Astrology went hand in hand with medicine and was regarded as a respectable way of determining treatment and predicting recovery from illness. It could also be used to pinpoint favourable auspices for events: the sire de l'Isle-Adam, for instance, was said to have consulted an astrologer before choosing the date for his Burgundian coup in Paris in 1418. Jean, duke of Alençon, had his nativity cast by an astrologer to find out why his life had been so unfortunate and was given both an astrological talisman to bring him good luck and protect him from disease, and a powder which had the extraordinary ability to detect enemies and to give perfect intelligence of important questions in dreams.[13]

Alençon's use of such devices illustrates the fine line between astrology, which was respectable, and magic, otherwise termed necromancy or sorcery, which was not. The fifteenth century saw a number of high-profile individuals charged with witchcraft. In 1419 Henry V ordered the arrest of his stepmother, the dowager queen Joan, and her confessor-astrologer, Friar Randolf, on charges of trying to destroy him 'by sorcery and necromancy'. The queen was put under house arrest and forced to surrender her dowry and other revenues to avoid trial, conveniently increasing Henry's revenues by 10 per cent at a time when he urgently needed cash for his campaigns in Normandy. He tacitly admitted that the accusation was a false one by ordering her release and the restoration of her money when his conscience was needling him at the end of his life.[14]

Jehanne d'Arc was also convicted of making 'superstitious divinations', though the accusations of her witchcraft were subsumed in the greater crimes of heresy, apostasy and idolatry. One of the most infamous subjects of a sorcery charge, however, was her companion-in-arms, Gilles de Rais, who had financed the annual plays in Orléans to commemorate her memory. Rais kidnapped a cleric in a dispute with a local church and, as a result, was investigated by the bishop of Nantes and charged with a range of appalling crimes; his prisoner was forcibly rescued by Richemont and after ecclesiastical and secular trials Rais admitted invoking devils and the kidnap, rape, sodomy, torture and mutilation of a vast number of children between the ages of six and eighteen. He and his accomplices were executed at Nantes on 26 October 1440.[15]

Gilles de Rais was unusual in being a male accused of witchcraft, but, as with most of the alleged sorcerers, there was a strong political element in the charges brought against him. This was certainly true of the duchess of Gloucester, who had consulted two eminent astrologers, Thomas Southwell, her physician and a canon of Saint Stephen's at Westminster, and Roger Bolingbroke, principal of Saint Andrew's Hall, Oxford.

At her request they drew up Henry VI's horoscope and predicted that he would die from a serious illness in July or August 1441. This was just what Eleanor wished to hear, for she would then become queen, but 'imagining' or predicting the death of a king was treason.

How or why her activities came to the notice of the royal council is unclear but she was arrested, tried in the ecclesiastical courts and on 21 October 1441 found guilty of treasonable necromancy; although her life was spared, she was committed to life imprisonment and on 6 November forcibly divorced from her husband by Archbishop Chichele and Cardinal Beaufort. Her alleged accomplices were all condemned to death: Southwell was fortunate to die in the Tower before his execution, Bolingbroke was hanged, drawn and quartered and Margery Jourdemayne, the 'Witch of Eye', from whom Eleanor had bought potions to help her conceive Gloucester's child, was burned at the stake.[16]

Eleanor's trial, conviction and divorce caused a public scandal of epic proportions and they ruined and humiliated her husband, who became a pariah at court. Whatever his many faults, he had always been loyal to Henry VI and did not deserve to have his last years tainted by suspicion of sorcery and treason.

Gloucester's very recent downfall removed the one man to whom Talbot could have looked for assistance in drumming up support for his recruitment mission in the spring of 1442. On 24 March, just before the parliamentary session ended, Talbot contracted on York's behalf for an army 2500 strong to serve in France for six months. Traditionally a quarter of such an army would have consisted of men-at-arms, the military elite recruited from the ranks of the nobility and gentry who could afford to equip themselves with the expensive armour, weaponry and horses that this rank demanded. It was a measure of the war-weariness of these classes that they now refused to serve in anything like the numbers required. Even Talbot, newly elevated on 20 May 1442 to the earldom of Shrewsbury in recognition of his services in France, could not arouse their enthusiasm for war service: they sensibly preferred the safer and more profitable exercise of their civilian duties, upholding the judicial and financial administration of the shires, which could be carried out from the comfort of their own homes.[17]

When Talbot mustered his troops on 15 June after landing at Harfleur he had achieved the required goal of 2500 men, but only two hundred of them were men-at-arms and just three hundred of the archers were mounted. That he had been able to fulfil the quota at all was due to the fact that there was a much larger pool of archers to draw from than men-at-arms. Archery was a highly skilled craft, requiring physical strength and regular training just to pull the great longbow. By law every man in England between the ages of sixteen and sixty, regardless of status, was therefore obliged to practise at the archery butts every Sunday and feast day. Anyone who could not shoot a minimum of ten aimed arrows into a target in the space of a minute was regarded as unfit for military service. The problem with archers – particularly foot-archers – was that they were unable to withstand a concerted enemy attack, which is why a substantial proportion of men-at-arms was also needed to protect them. That so few archers among Talbot's recruits had horses was also a problem: such men were ideal for garrison duty but their lack of mobility made them less effective when employed on campaign. The poor quality of the army would hinder Talbot's capabilities in the field but it was still costly. Henry was forced to pawn the crown jewels to raise the £1500 (£787,000) necessary just to transport the troops over the Channel: 'us needeth in haste great and notable sums of money . . . for the setting over of the said army [or] . . . as far as the said jewels will stretch'.[18]

The summer campaign of 1442 was a saga of missed opportunities. Charles VII, the dauphin and the bulk of their forces were occupied in Gascony, drawn there by the urgent need to relieve the siege of Tartas before the sire d'Albret fulfilled the agreement he had made with the English seneschal, Sir Thomas Rempston, to hand over the town and swear allegiance to Henry VI. This disaster averted, Charles remained in the area, besieging and capturing Saint-Sever, Dax and La Réole and even threatening Bordeaux.[19]

Rempston himself was taken prisoner at Saint-Sever, a personal disaster for a man who had already spent seven years as a French captive after the battle of Patay because he could not pay the ransom demanded. Even though he had been able to obtain a prisoner-exchange to reduce his payment by half, his finances had not yet recovered and he was still in prison several years after his second capture. In March 1446 William Estfield, a London merchant, bequeathed him £10 (£5250) 'towards his ransom, if he is still alive'; his whereabouts throughout this period remains a mystery, though he was back in England by January 1449. Another eminent victim of this campaign was one of Charles VII's most successful captains and staunchest allies. Étienne de Vignolles, the great La Hire, was mortally wounded and eventually died, aged fifty-three, at Montauban on 11 January 1443. Such was his reputation even among his enemies that Guto'r Glyn, the Welsh poet, described him and his lifelong comrade-in-arms, Poton de Xaintrailles, as the Castor and Pollux of France: his name is still immortalised, somewhat inappropriately, as the Jack-of-hearts in a deck of French playing-cards.[20]

Before departing for Gascony Charles had left an army in the north under the command of the Bastard of Orléans with a watching brief over English activity. Talbot had decided his priority was to secure the eastern reaches of Normandy and in July 1442 he laid siege to Conches-en-Ouche. The Bastard responded by setting siege to Gallardon, where François de Surienne's garrison had just been depleted by the departure of twenty men-at-arms and eighty-three archers in the company of Matthew Gough. Talbot refused to be drawn away until Conches surrendered at the end of August, enabling him to go to the relief of Gallardon. The Bastard raised his siege on Talbot's approach but the continuing presence of his army in the region prevented Talbot from making an attempt on the more important strongholds of Louviers or Évreux and persuaded Surienne that there was no point in his continuing to hold Gallardon. On 30 October the Aragonese issued a joint receipt with Matthew Gough, Thomas Gerrard and Thomas Stones for 2900 *saluts*

(£232,604) from the Bastard as a down payment on 10,900 *saluts* (£874,271). For this sum the four captains had consented to evacuate both Gallardon and Courville, leaving no English presence in the region of Chartres. Gallardon, it was mutually agreed, would be demolished to prevent its being used again by either side. A curious footnote to this story reveals that the money received for the surrender might not have enriched the individual English captains but rather the Norman treasury. In March 1445 Thomas Hoo, by now elevated to the chancellorship of Normandy, issued a receipt to the Bastard for 1000 *saluts* (£80,208), paid in wines and silks, which was to be set against the debt he owed for the demolition of Gallardon and Courville.[21]

Talbot's campaign in the east having fizzled out with no major gains to justify the financial outlay involved in deploying so many men, he decided to tackle Dieppe, the last Armagnac stronghold on the Norman coast. By the time he did so it was already too late, for the six-month contract of service of the army he had brought from England was almost at an end: some were persuaded to stay on but the core of the besieging army was six hundred men drawn from the Norman garrisons. It was not until the end of October that sufficient men had gathered for Talbot to leave his headquarters at Jumièges and march on Dieppe.

The garrison of the outlying castle of Charlemesnil surrendered as his vanguard approached but Talbot's plan was not fully to blockade Dieppe by land and sea: he had neither the men nor the ships to do so effectively. Instead, on the heights of Le Pollet to the east of the town, overlooking the harbour, he built 'a very strong and huge bastille of wood, of great circumference' and installed Sir William Peyto with a garrison of five hundred men under his command, including Talbot's own bastard son, Henry, and many of his personal retinue. William Fforsted, master of the king's ordnance and a veteran over several reigns of campaigns in Ireland, Scotland, Wales, Gascony, Normandy and France, had apparently scouted out the site the previous year, personally accompanying Talbot 'to the parts of Dieppe' with 'secret ordnance of war'. Now he poured two hundred cannon, bombards, catapults and other artillery, great and small, into the bastille and began a bombardment of the walls, towers and houses of Dieppe.[22]

Just a week after the siege began, the English bastille at Granville, in the bay of Mont-Saint-Michel, was surprised and captured by Louis d'Estouteville. This was a flagrant instance of negligence by a garrison captain, for he had been warned two months earlier to pay special attention to his watch because intelligence had revealed that Estouteville was planning a secret enterprise against Granville and intended to make his assault from the sea using scaling ladders. This was precisely what happened. Had the captain been responsible to Talbot, he would undoubtedly have been prosecuted and severely punished; as he was the bastard son of lord Scales and responsible to his father, he escaped the consequences of his dereliction of duty.

Granville was a stronghold of enormous strategic importance. It had excellent natural defences, standing on a rocky peninsula so narrow that it was almost completely surrounded by sea. When the Armagnacs had first captured it, in 1436, the only building had been the parish church of Notre Dame, which had been a place of pilgrimage since ancient times because of the miracles said to have taken place there. After Talbot had recaptured it a major programme of fortification had been undertaken which had created a town and castle in the fields around the church, making Granville 'the strongest and most useful place, commanding all the country by sea and by land, that one could choose and find in order to hold the said country of Normandy and its neighbouring marches in subjection'. It was now occupied by the men of Mont-Saint-Michel.

All the neighbouring garrisons had to be swiftly reinforced to resist the threat they posed and in December Andrew Ogard, Simon Morhier and Pierre Cauchon were sent from the council in Rouen to discuss ways and means of retaking the fortress with lord Scales and Matthew Gough. The latter, who already had a company of sixty men-at-arms and 180 archers employed at the king's wages, was persuaded to extend their service until

Easter in return for a one-off payment of 1000*l.t.* (£58,333). Taxes were levied locally and duchy-wide to fund a recovery campaign and the *vicomte* of Caen was sent on a mission to the Channel Islands to hire ships and mariners to blockade the place. Despite all their efforts, they could find no way to regain it 'by force, by surprise or otherwise' and Granville was never recovered.[23]

The loss of Granville persuaded at least one Norman, Raoulet Fontaine 'called the Barber', to defect from the neighbouring garrison at Tombelaine and join that of Mont-Saint-Michel. It was a decision with fatal consequences for himself as he was later stabbed to death in a quarrel with another member of the garrison after they had returned from a pilgrimage together to Santiago de Compostela. Fontaine had previously been a loyal servant of the English crown, however, and his defection at this time is unlikely to have been the only one.[24]

Estouteville wasted no time in adding to the fortifications at Granville to prevent its recapture, installing a captain and introducing stocks of men, victuals and artillery. The isolation of the place, however, made it difficult to find enough civilians to man the watches, leaving it vulnerable to recapture by the English. It was a measure of Granville's strategic importance that in 1446 Charles VII responded to a petition from the captain and offered free houses and plots of land, together with exemption from all war taxes, as inducements to anyone prepared to settle there.[25]

CHAPTER TWENTY

A Last Military Effort

The capture of Granville placed added pressure on Talbot to bring his siege of Dieppe to a successful conclusion. This clearly could not be done without the assistance of a large expeditionary force from England. Summer campaigns in Normandy had long been dependent on the arrival of these reinforcements and York's deed of appointment as lieutenant-general had promised him £20,000 (£10.5m) annually to pay their wages. The exchequer had struggled to pay this from the start and by the end of 1442 he was already owed half the sum due for that year with no expectation of receiving it until the next instalment of a lay subsidy was collected in May 1443.[1]

York also faced increasing competition for the limited resources of England as a result of Charles VII's successful campaigns in Gascony. With intelligence reports that Charles was planning to resume his offensive with Castilian support in the spring of 1443 and that a concerted attack on Normandy was in the offing, the English council had to take a decision worthy of Solomon: whether to commit everything to the defence of one duchy and see off the threat decisively, but possibly lose the other altogether, or to divide what was available and risk losing one or both. Most of those present at the meeting when the matter was discussed on 6 February 1443 sat on the fence, unhelpfully advising that an army should be sent wherever it was most needed, but Cardinal Beaufort's ally, the treasurer, lord Cromwell, reminded them that the money sent to Normandy the previous year had been wasted. When the council reconvened on 2 March he told them that it would be financially impossible to send two armies and that the king, his lords and captains would have to take a decision one way or the other. In the meantime a small force under two West Country knights, Sir William Bonville, the captured Rempston's replacement as seneschal, and the veteran John Popham, set sail for Gascony in February, only to lose one of their ships and a third of their men to winter storms on the long sea voyage.[2]

In this crisis it was once again the Beauforts who stepped into the breach. John, earl of Somerset, had already offered the previous autumn to lead a major expedition to Gascony 'in all possible haste' but his appointment foundered when the council refused to cancel York's assignment on the lay subsidy in favour of Cardinal Beaufort, whose loans would finance the expedition. By the time the council met again, on 30 March, Somerset had once more agreed to serve but, possibly at his suggestion, a radical new strategy had been devised to solve the problem of choosing between Gascony and Normandy.

The failings of the past few years had dictated that it was 'full fitting and necessary that the manner and conduct of the war be changed' from the defensive to the offensive. Somerset would therefore lead the largest army to set out for France since Henry VI's expedition for his coronation in 1430; he would take the shortest route across the Channel, thus avoiding the fate of Bonville's fleet and allowing him to land at Cherbourg, where he was captain; he would pass through lower Normandy and cross the Loire into Armagnac territory, where he would wage the 'most cruel and mortal war that he can and may'. The primary objective was to draw Charles VII from Gascony, force him to battle, inflict on him a second Agincourt or Verneuil and so drive him in suppliant mode to the peace table. Even if these events failed to materialise, Henry VI rather lamely explained to York, the huge English army would act as a shield between Normandy and 'the adversary'.[3]

Such a policy had long had its advocates in England. Gloucester, for one, had consistently argued the need for a surge in troop numbers combined with a hard-hitting offensive instead of the piecemeal war of attrition conducted by both sides. The most eloquent proponent was lord Fastolf, who had fought as a humble esquire at Agincourt, was made a knight-banneret on the field of Verneuil and had defended in arms the English kingdom of France continuously since 1417. His knowledge, experience and commitment to the war, as well as his long service as master of Bedford's household and as a councillor of Bedford himself, York and Gloucester, entitled him to have his views heard. He had argued passionately against accepting the peace terms offered at Arras, urging instead, in words that found their echo in Somerset's commission, 'that the traitors and rebels must have another kind of war, and more sharp and more cruel war'. He was no friend of the Beauforts and his solution differed markedly from the policy they now initiated, but he too had advocated a scorched-earth policy on the Norman border and an end to siege warfare, unless a place 'be right prenable', that is, easily taken.[4]

Somerset's terms for conducting this campaign were remarkably bold. Before he signed his contract he must be elevated to a dukedom and take precedence over Norfolk (who had shown no interest in the war effort), so that he ranked behind only Gloucester and York; to support his new status he wanted 1000 marks (£350,000) of additional income, though this was whittled down to 600 marks (£210,000), which was to be drawn from the grant to him of Bedford's earldom of Kendal. His command was to be completely independent of York and he was to exercise full royal rights in any 'countries, lands, towns, castles, fortresses and places as he shall get within the said realm and duchy and elsewhere', including the right to acquire those places for himself and his heirs, dispose of them as he wished and appoint to all civil and military posts. He was also to have all the royal rights to gains of war, even down to the third of a third of their value which captains could claim from those who won them.

Somerset further demanded that, like his own contract of service, his brother's seven-year grant of office as captain-general and governor of Anjou and Maine should henceforth be held under the great seal of England rather than France, meaning that he would no longer be subordinate to York; when that term of office ended, or if York's council in Normandy successfully overturned the grant, as it was trying to do, then Somerset insisted that he should take his brother's place. And he wanted the county of Alençon too. As these terms suggest, Somerset was just as interested in personal aggrandisement and the old Beaufort scheme of acquiring Bedford's inheritance in France as he was in defending Normandy. Gascony does not seem to have featured at all in his thinking, other than as a subsidiary beneficiary of the plan to induce Charles VII to withdraw from the duchy to confront Somerset's army.

Somerset was well aware that his conditions for accepting leadership of this expedition went well beyond those ever sought by previous captains. They were also a direct challenge to the authority of York as lieutenant-general. Somerset had already warned that any powers granted to himself would be ineffectual, 'seeing that my said lord of York hath the whole power before of all the said realm and duchy' and he refused to serve unless he had York's goodwill and 'consentment'. (Neither he nor his brother had served in France since York's appointment as lieutenant-general, so this was not a threat to be taken lightly.) To make it more difficult for York to withhold that consent, Somerset persuaded the malleable king to write to him in person, telling him of the new arrangements.

As a sop to York, Somerset's own cumbersome title was to be that of 'lieutenant and captain-general of our duchy of Gascony and of our realm of France in the areas in which our very dear and beloved cousin the duke of York does not actually exercise the power given to him on our behalf'. This was so vague as to be meaningless. Did it mean that if Somerset recaptured Dieppe or Granville, for instance, these places would belong to him, rather than be restored to the duchy and York's authority? Somerset's trump card was the king's agreement to the independent status of his commission: no one 'neither in this realm nor beyond the sea' could command him to do anything which was contrary to his 'own will and intent'.[5]

One of the reasons why Somerset obtained such extraordinary concessions was that the twenty-one-year-old Henry was genuinely concerned to promote and strengthen the extended royal family. Unmarried and childless himself, with no legitimate cousins, the prolific Beauforts were his nearest blood relatives, though their illegitimate descent from John of Gaunt debarred them from the throne. Henry believed that Somerset's high birth entitled him to command, despite his lack of military experience. A more powerful reason was that Cardinal Beaufort was prepared to finance the expedition – if it was led by his nephew. In the three years since 1439 he had loaned just 13,000 marks (£4.55m); for Somerset's mobilisation he would lend £20,000 (£10.5m) to pay the army's wages for six months and £1167 (£612,675) to enable it to ship across the Channel. It was the largest amount of money he had ever loaned in a single year and it dwarfed the £5250 (£2.76m) which was the sum total of all other loans.[6] Henry's weakness of character had once again allowed the personal and factional ambitions of his courtiers to triumph over the needs of his kingdom overseas.

News of Somerset's appointment and the unusual latitude of his powers was received with consternation by York and the council in Rouen, which had not been consulted on this important issue so closely affecting the duchy. In June York sent a high-level delegation, led by Talbot, Andrew Ogard, the treasurer John Stanlawe and the royal secretary Jean de Rinel, to seek formal clarification of Somerset's authority and if necessary register a formal protest. Their concerns were not appeased when York sought the £20,000 which his contract had promised him and was urged to 'take patience for a time' because Somerset's expedition was very expensive and would leave little to spare for other enterprises. Clearly there would be no money or manpower available for the recovery of Dieppe, Granville, Louviers or Évreux, which was the duchy's own military priority. The deputation urged the king to reconsider, or at least limit Somerset's powers, but its pleas fell on deaf ears. Somerset's commission remained unchanged and Talbot, who should then have been reinforcing his siege of Dieppe, could only obtain a promise of a single light warship to aid his enterprise.[7]

Convinced that he could surpass the quality and quantity of the army which had accompanied York to Normandy in 1441, Somerset had offered to raise one thousand men-at-arms, of whom four would be barons, eight bannerets and thirty knights. The council wisely trimmed this back to eight hundred men-at-arms and in the event Somerset could only muster 758: his much-vaunted aristocratic contingent consisted of a single banneret, Sir Thomas Kyriell, and just six knights. Extra archers had to be drafted in to substitute for the missing nobility. His plans for embarkation were equally overambitious. When he signed his contract on 8 April the date for his muster and departure had been set at 17 June. Rightly appreciating the urgency, Somerset had twice suggested an earlier date, but he did not turn up even on 17 June or on a deferred occasion. The delay cost £500 (£262,500) daily and many of those who had mustered promptly deserted, taking the king's wages with them; others mustered twice in different places, enabling them fraudulently to claim two sets of wages. Observing this chaos and delay, the council finally lost patience on 9 July and ordered him to leave immediately, 'all excuses ceasing'. Even then it was not until the end of July that he set sail with an army whose final numbers were still in dispute but, according to the musters, consisted of one banneret, six knights, 592 men-at-arms and 3949 archers.[8]

A fleet of three hundred ships ferried this huge army to Cherbourg at the beginning of August, together with all its baggage, horses, supplies and a vast artillery train, including twenty cartloads of *ribauldequins* (a medieval version of the machine gun with up to twelve barrels firing a volley of shots at the same time), a new cannon and a bridge of barrels that Somerset had ordered to be made for him at the king's cost 'to pass the rivers that he shall find in his way'. Even before he got to his first river, Somerset encountered difficulties: he did not have enough carts and wagons to transport all his equipment. He therefore decided to levy a *charroy*, the local tax designed for such occasions, in the six *vicomtés* through which he passed: this enabled him to requisition all available transport, even from church property, and raise money to pay the wages of those accompanying them. Since he was armed with letters patent from the king ordering all royal officials in the realm of France and the duchy of Normandy to obey his commands diligently, they did so, but under protest, since the *vicomtés* were indisputably within York's jurisdiction and they had no authorisation from him.[9]

Details of Somerset's campaign are sketchy and confused. By 17 August he was at Avranches, seventy-three miles south of Cherbourg, ordering a *charroy* for the 120 carts he needed for the next stage of his journey. Then, according to plan, he marched through Maine and into Anjou, at some point being joined by his brother, Edmund Beaufort, and Matthew Gough. Like him, they both had significant landed interests in Maine. Having joined forces they ravaged and burned Anjou right up to the walls of Angers. And there they stopped. The river Loire was just two miles further south but they made no effort to cross it or invade into enemy territory. Instead they retreated thirty-nine miles north-west into northern Anjou to lay siege to Pouancé, a town belonging to the duke of Alençon. It is possible that, in reaching Angers, the army had run on too far and too fast in its campaign of devastation, for the order on 17 August for levying the *charroy* at Avranches had specified Pouancé as the destination for the wagons.[10]

Whatever the reason, the siege of Pouancé proved fruitless, unless its real objective was to draw out d'Alençon from his main stronghold at Château-Gontier twenty-five miles away. Certainly a relief army did gather there and, when spies brought this information to Pouancé, Matthew Gough was dispatched with a sizeable force to intercept them. Catching them by surprise, he succeeded in routing them and bringing back a number of prisoners. Though an undoubted victory, it was not another Agincourt or Verneuil, and no one of note was captured, least of all Alençon himself.[11]

When several weeks of siege had failed to persuade Pouancé to submit, Somerset decided to cut his losses and try somewhere else. Fifteen miles further north, just inside the Breton border, lay La Guerche, which also belonged to Alençon. Its Armagnac garrison had plagued English territories in Maine, including those belonging to the Beauforts; in 1438 Somerset's brother Edmund had captured it briefly and extorted a four-year truce from Alençon. That truce was now at an end. Somerset could also argue that a truce with Brittany which he himself, as lieutenant-general, had negotiated in June 1440 had also technically lapsed. Not only had the old duke died in August 1442 but also the existence of Alençon's garrison at La Guerche was in breach of the Breton undertaking not to shelter England's enemies.

Somerset therefore had no compunction in laying siege to the town: its inhabitants surrendered and those with Armagnac connections were arrested. Somerset's men pillaged the surrounding countryside while their captain, also acting like an *écorcheur*, demanded a ransom of 20,000 *saluts* (£1.6m) from the new duke of Brittany, François I, to release La Guerche and prolong the truce. Half that sum was paid on 16 October, with the remainder due after Christmas.[12]

Since Henry VI had ceded his royal right to the gains of war to Somerset, the latter had made himself a handsome profit. He had also created a major diplomatic incident. The furious duke, who had offered his services as a mediator for peace talks with Charles VII and actually had an embassy in England for that purpose at the time, protested through his ambassadors and demanded reparations. Henry VI was particularly mortified as the leader of the embassy, Gilles de Bretaigne, was the duke's brother and his own particular friend. He immediately disowned Somerset's actions, offered restitution and showered Gilles with gifts including a pension of 1000 marks (£350,000), two 'books of song for his chapel' which had belonged to the recently deceased Louis de Luxembourg and a gold cup containing £100

(£52,500). A formal reprimand was sent to Somerset from the council which even Cardinal Beaufort signed.[13]

From La Guerche Somerset retired into Maine, where he undertook the reduction of Beaumont-le-Vicomte, an important Armagnac fortress commanding the main road between Alençon and Le Mans, both places where his brother happened to be captain. Though the Beauforts had again expected that a relief army would be sent, none materialised, and the fortress surrendered. It was the last action of the campaign, for though Somerset's contract of service was for a year, the wages of his men had not been paid beyond the end of the six months that had already expired. Another clause in his extraordinary contract allowed him to return home if the payments fell into arrears, which is exactly what he chose to do. At the end of December he disbanded his army in Normandy, where some of the men joined the garrison at Falaise and others were left to live off their wits and the countryside, much to the distress of the local population. The infamous artillery train, whose transport had caused so many problems, was later discovered where Somerset had left it, with his lieutenant at Avranches.[14]

Somerset returned to England at the beginning of January 1444 to find that he was a disgraced man. His expedition had not been a complete failure but neither had it been the hoped-for triumph. The manner and conduct of the war had not been changed dramatically: despite the weight of expectation and the precious resources poured into it, his campaign resembled nothing so much as those that had always been waged on the frontiers. The Beauforts had benefited more than the realm or the duchy. More damaging was the deep offence he had caused to the dukes of Brittany and Alençon, driving them into the arms of Charles VII at a time when both were potential English allies.

Somerset's insistence on having full personal control of his expedition now came back to haunt him. He was held entirely responsible for its failure to achieve great things. Though no formal charges were laid against him, he may have been banished from court and council, as he retired permanently to his private estates at Wimborne in Dorset. He died there a broken man, at the age of forty, on 27 May 1444: rumour had it that he had committed suicide. Even before he died formal inquiries were launched into the 'crimes, murders, mutilations, abuses, robberies, pillages, exactions and other offences and evils' committed by the soldiers he had abandoned in Normandy. Posthumously he was accused of levying the *charroy* illegally and corruptly: in 1446 another inquiry revealed he had received just over 5210*l.t.* (£303,917) from it and his executors were pursued for monies he had obtained from the crown for his expenses and equipment.[15]

Somerset was emphatically not the right man to lead a major offensive, not just because of his lack of military experience but because he was in poor health even before he left England and was not fit for the rigours of campaigning in the field. Undoubtedly he embarked upon his expedition believing that it was in the best interests of England and Normandy – interests which he regarded as synonymous with those of the Beauforts and the preservation of their possessions in Maine. It was therefore ironic that the diversion of resources to his expedition and, even more, his insistence on his right to independent command, caused irreparable damage to Normandy.

From the moment of his landing at Cherbourg in August 1443 to his final departure five months later Somerset never once made contact with the duke of York or the council at Rouen. He therefore did not know that on 12 August the dauphin, the Bastard of Orléans, Raoul de Gaucourt and the count of Saint-Pol had entered Dieppe with a reinforcement of sixteen hundred men. This was the third and largest relief column to enter the town since Talbot had built his bastille there, and the captain, Charles Desmarets, already had several hundred men-at-arms at his service, including Guillaume de Ricarville, whose bold coup in 1432 had captured Rouen castle. The arrival of such a huge relief force, however, was a clear indication that an attempt was about to be made to break the siege.[16]

At eight o'clock on the morning of 14 August 1443 the dauphin had his trumpets sounded to launch an assault on the

English bastille. He had brought with him five or six wooden bridges on wheels and several cranes to assist in levering them into position over the ditches surrounding the bastille. By this means his men were able to rush the bastille walls, only to meet with a barrage of missiles and arrows from the garrison which killed up to a hundred of them and wounded several hundred more. Urged on by the dauphin, and encouraged by the arrival of between sixty and eighty large mechanical crossbows brought by the citizens of Dieppe, they renewed their assault and, after fierce hand-to-hand fighting, they carried the day. More than three hundred of the defenders were killed and the dauphin ordered all surviving native French-speakers to be executed as traitors: eight men-at-arms, four archers and two cannoneers were duly hanged. Sir William Peyto, Sir John Ripley and Henry Talbot were among the prisoners. The dauphin ordered that the bastille should be dismantled and all the artillery found there was carried into Dieppe to add to the town arsenal.[17]

This disaster could have been avoided if Somerset had diverted his army to Dieppe – and in taking on the dauphin he could have won the major victory which later eluded him in Anjou. Instead a siege which had lasted ten months was broken off and no attempt to reinstate it would be made again. Dieppe, like Granville, Louviers and Évreux, would remain permanently in Armagnac hands.

Somerset's determination to do things his own way meant that York and the council were not kept informed of either his whereabouts or his plans. Breton intelligence probably alerted them to his seizure of La Guerche, for, at the end of October, a messenger was sent from Lisieux to Brittany to locate him, find out about his army and report back to Rouen. The only contact between the English administration and Somerset was informal and at one remove: in December an ambassador of the duke of Orléans on his way for an audience with York at Rouen met and travelled with Somerset as he made his way home from Falaise to Caen.[18]

Though Somerset was answerable to the English government, his refusal even to communicate, let alone cooperate, with the

Norman administration was reprehensible. The disappointment in England over his singular lack of achievement in his campaign was as nothing to the bitterness in Normandy. The authority of York and his council had been undermined and Somerset's personal enrichment rubbed salt in the wound. York was still owed his £20,000 (£10.5m) for the year and the straitened finances were felt in all the military operations within the duchy. At the end of October 1443, for instance, lord Scales was personally owed 600*l.t.* (£35,000) for his own employment and more than ten times that amount for the unpaid wages of fifty-one men-at-arms and 318 archers he had withdrawn from garrisons elsewhere in the duchy for a field army to contain the depredations of the Granville garrison. Nothing more clearly illustrates the necessity of scraping together funds from all available sources at this period than the fact that, considering 'the present need and the slenderness of our finances, he liberally condescended' to accept a one-off payment of 3000*l.t.* (£175,000), two-thirds of which was to come from Norman sources but a third from York's (unpaid) money from England.[19]

Somerset's expedition did mark a turning point in the conduct of the war, but not in the way he had hoped. The Breton embassy which had arrived in England in August 1443 had brought an invitation from the duke to accept his mediation for a resumption of peace negotiations. Undoubtedly this came with the prior endorsement of Charles VII: the timing suggests that by reopening the diplomatic channels for peace, which he had kept firmly closed since the release of Charles d'Orléans, he was hoping to undermine, or even forestall, any military success by Somerset's army. Henry VI had leapt at the chance of peace when it was first offered but he had always been pacific by nature. Somerset's failure to impose a military solution persuaded even the most hawkish members of the council that a negotiated settlement was now the only way forward. Within weeks of Somerset's ignominious return the formal peace process began anew.

On 1 February 1444 the king and his council took the momentous decision to send William, earl of Suffolk, to France to treat for a peace or a truce with 'our uncle of France' and to discuss Henry VI's marriage with a French princess. Suffolk was now one of the most powerful figures at court, his star having risen as those of the elderly Gloucester and Cardinal Beaufort declined. As steward of the royal household he had gained influence over the young king by identifying with his interests, but he had astutely avoided polarising court opinion against him. His record of military service in France from 1415 to 1429, and finally in 1435 and 1436, and his participation in many previous peace embassies, including Arras, are symptomatic of his beliefs in the need to preserve England's French possessions by military force and in the benefit of seeking peace from a position of strength.

In the wake of Somerset's expedition, however, the English were not in a position of strength and Suffolk had strong reservations about assuming the leadership of a peace embassy, particularly as the French had specifically asked him to do so. Aware that he was setting himself up for a fall, and with Somerset's example of the dangers of personal responsibility still vividly before him, Suffolk protested against his appointment to the council. Ultimately, at the king's insistence, he accepted the role, but only after he received royal letters patent giving him absolute indemnity against being held to account for anything he did in good faith while carrying out the king's orders with regard to either the peace or the marriage. In other words, responsibility for the mission and its outcome began and ended with the king.[20]

Suffolk's reluctance to lead the embassy was genuine and well founded. It was an unenviable position. His instructions came from a king who was determined to have peace at almost any price and he was negotiating with another king whose very survival had depended on his guile. Suffolk had sought the appointment of experienced associates and in Adam Moleyns and Sir Robert Roos received them: Moleyns, in particular, was a professional lawyer and diplomat, keeper of the privy seal as of 11 February 1444, a noted humanist whose Latin 'was the best written in England since Peter of Blois' and in his spare time bishop of Chichester.[21]

On 15 March the English ambassadors landed at Harfleur. They made their way first to Rouen, presumably to consult with the lieutenant-general and council, then to Le Mans in Maine. Vendôme, where it had eventually been arranged that the first meetings would take place on 8 April, lay in enemy territory but roughly equidistant between English Le Mans, Orléans (whose duke would play a part in the proceedings) and Tours, where Charles VII regularly held court. From Vendôme they were escorted to Blois, where they were met by Suffolk's former prisoner, Charles d'Orléans, then on 16 April to Tours, where the dukes of Anjou, Brittany and Alençon were waiting to introduce them to Charles VII the following day. A Burgundian delegation made its way into Tours on 3 May but the duke himself did not attend: he was deliberately being marginalised by Charles, who, in what should have been a warning to the English, had reneged on the promises he had made at Arras. The last to arrive was the person who had absolutely no voice in the proceedings, but without whom there would be no peace: Margaret, the fourteen-year-old daughter of René, duke of Anjou, whom Charles had selected as Henry VI's bride.[22]

At what point Margaret's name had been put forward is not clear, but the speed of the settlement after her arrival suggests that it had been discussed and approved even before Suffolk left England. Quite why she should have been thought a suitable wife for the king of England and France is also unclear. She was a Valois princess in that she was the great-granddaughter of Charles V, but she was only the niece by marriage of Charles VII. Her father and uncle, René and Charles d'Anjou, enjoyed privileged and influential positions at court, having been brought up with Charles, but her grandmother, the formidable Yolande of Aragon, had died in November 1442. She had, more appropriately, already been touted as a potential bride for the counts of Saint-Pol, Charolais and Nevers but nothing had come of the negotiations, not least because of her father's slender means and inability to substantiate his claims to a glittering array of patrimonies – the kingdoms of Sicily, Naples, Aragon and (through his wife) Majorca and the duchies of Lorraine and Bar.[23]

THE SEARCH FOR PEACE

A more suitable bride, as far as the English were concerned, would have been one of Charles's own daughters. Catherine, the eldest, had already been married off at the age of eleven to Philippe of Burgundy's son, the count of Charolais, and the third, Yolande, had been betrothed to the prince of Piedmont before her second birthday. Joan, Jeanne and Madeleine, aged between nine and one, were all available and their youth did not make them unacceptable: after all, Richard II had been twenty-nine when, in pursuit of the same goal of peace with France, he had married Charles VII's six-year-old sister Isabelle. There were two objections to marriage with a daughter of Charles. The first, which could have been overcome, was that from the English point of view the Treaty of Troyes had disinherited that branch of the family and to marry one would implicitly reinstate the legitimacy of their claims. The second, which was insuperable, was that Charles himself had no intention of allowing a marriage which would inevitably lead to a formal partition of France and might even endanger the succession of his own son.[24]

So it was that the unfortunate Margaret became the sacrificial offering on the altar of peace. Except that it was not the permanent peace for which the English had hoped, nor even the 'half-peace', the twenty-year truce, which the French had offered before. Irrespective of the claim to the crown, neither side would concede the right to full sovereignty over Normandy, Gascony and Calais. All that could be agreed was a general military truce to last for just twenty-two months beginning on 1 June 1444 and ending on 1 April 1446. Two days later the marriage agreement was drawn up and two days after that, on 24 May 1444, the formal betrothal took place in the church of Saint-Martin at Tours.[25]

The ceremony was conducted at the altar by the papal legate and Suffolk stood in for Henry VI. It was witnessed by two putative kings, Charles VII and René d'Anjou, and a future undisputed king, the dauphin Louis, together with their wives and a host of the French nobility. A notable absentee was Regnault de Chartres, archbishop of Reims. Having lost three brothers at Agincourt and his father in the Burgundian seizure of

Paris in 1418, he had committed his life to the peace process, endeavouring to reconcile Armagnacs and Burgundians, English and French. He had come to Tours to assist in the negotiations but had collapsed and died just before they began in earnest.[26]

There was a second ghost at the feast. In the chapel behind the choir lay the body of Marshal Boucicaut, whose internationally celebrated life as the great chivalric hero of France had been abruptly cut short with his capture at Agincourt. Six years later, Boucicaut had ignominiously ended his days as an English prisoner in an obscure Yorkshire manor-house.[27] He had lived to see the Treaty of Troyes and the triumph of the English: now, in death, he was a witness to the event which would bring about their final destruction.

PART FIVE

THE TRUCE OF TOURS

CHAPTER TWENTY-ONE

A Truce and a Marriage

The Truce of Tours was greeted with euphoria throughout England and France. In Paris, where there had already been intercessory processions for peace, there were now thanksgiving processions, and the Saint-Martin gate, which had been blocked up since Jehanne d'Arc's attack on the city in August 1429, was reopened for the first time. In Rouen Suffolk was greeted on his way home with cries of 'Noël! Noël!' and on his return to England a grateful king, who had already granted him the valuable wardship of Margaret Beaufort, Somerset's infant daughter and sole heiress, four days after her father's death on 27 May 1444, promoted him to the rank of marquess.[1]

The universal rejoicing was a natural reaction to the first general truce in the war since 1420: war-weariness was endemic. Yet, in itself, the truce offered nothing more than a temporary suspension of hostilities on land and at sea: all territories would remain in the hands of their current possessors, no new fortresses were to be built and no old ones repaired and all soldiers were to live in garrison on wages instead of living off *appâtis* levied on the enemy.

Henry VI believed, and Suffolk hoped, that the Truce of Tours was just the first step on a path that would lead to permanent peace: the marriage was their warranty that negotiations would continue, that the truce would be prolonged and that the powerful Angevin faction at Charles's court, which had previously been for war, would put its weight behind any potential settlement. Charles VII undoubtedly encouraged these presumptions but for him the truce was just a breathing space in which to reorganise his armies and focus his energies elsewhere. Henry's marriage to Margaret had his blessing because it ended the possibility that the English king might ally himself with one of his recalcitrant nobles (the count of Armagnac had already made approaches on behalf of his own daughter) and planted his niece as his observer and advocate in the biddable Henry's court, chamber and bed.[2]

The truce and the marriage had been arranged with almost indecent haste compared with the tortuous and protracted negotiations which had always accompanied previous attempts to end the war. This was partly because Henry was now a twenty-two-year-old adult in control of his own destiny: as king he could take decisions that were impossible for his council to do during his minority and Suffolk, acting as his personal emissary, was responsible only to him for carrying out his wishes. In retrospect, however, the ease and speed with which Suffolk carried out his mission were regarded by his detractors as evidence that he was a traitor who had sold out to France – had even, it was alleged, been suborned by Charles d'Orléans, his former prisoner, and the Bastard of Orléans, his former captor, to become Charles's liegeman. His foolish errors in omitting the king of Aragon and the duke of Brittany from the list of Henry VI's allies in the truce and, worse still, in allowing Charles VII to include Brittany among his allies, were interpreted as a deliberate and sinister conspiracy to empower Charles at the expense of his own king. The most serious charge against him was that, 'exceeding the instruction and power committed to him', he had promised to surrender Le Mans and Maine to Henry's 'great enemies', René d'Anjou and his brother Charles, 'without the assent, advice or knowledge of your other ambassadors'.[3]

Was it possible that Suffolk could have given such a momentous promise just to secure the hand in marriage of a woman who was in reality the fourth child and younger daughter of a French duke, even one who claimed to be king of Sicily? Given the geographical proximity of Anjou and Maine, and the disputed claims to their ownership, it is likely that the future of these provinces was a subject of discussion. Charles VII would not countenance the more obvious idea that Margaret might bring Maine to Henry VI as her dowry. As far as he was concerned, the English were the suppliants and they should be making the concessions; he had no intention of creating another Gascony.

The French would later claim that Suffolk had indeed given a verbal undertaking that Maine would be ceded back to Charles d'Anjou but, as nothing was put in writing, there is nothing to prove that such a promise was definitely made, or that it was unconditional. The very fact that it was not documented implies that it was not an issue upon which either the truce or the marriage depended. This suggests that, if such a promise was made at Tours, it was probably offered as an inducement for future Angevin assistance in converting the truce into a concord that would genuinely end the war. In any event Suffolk could not have acted without Henry's knowledge and approval and there is little doubt that Henry himself would willingly have parted with Maine to secure a permanent peace. The problem was that the Truce of Tours was not a final settlement and it did not warrant relinquishing such an important part of Henry's heritage. Henry himself naively assumed that Charles was as anxious for peace as himself and urged 'our very dear uncle of France' to send ambassadors to England as soon as possible to conclude a final peace.[4]

After the apparent triumph of his first commission it was inevitable that Suffolk would be entrusted with the second, more pleasant task of fetching Henry's bride back to England. This time he went in style. The tiny embassy that he had taken to Tours was replaced with a magnificent entourage, which significantly included the warrior Talbot and several members of his family, as well as a contingent of well-born ladies-in-waiting: the duchess of Bedford, the marchioness of Suffolk (Alice Chaucer, granddaughter of the poet), the countesses of Shrewsbury (Talbot's wife) and Salisbury, lady Scales (wife of the lieutenant-general of western Normandy) and lady Grey. In total five barons and baronesses, seventeen knights, sixty-five esquires and 174 valets were selected to escort Margaret of Anjou to England.[5]

Henry was forced to beg and borrow to put on this appropri-ately prestigious display: loans were raised throughout the kingdom and the abbot of Bury Saint Edmunds was even brow-beaten into lending horses, the need for palfreys, which were suitable for women to ride, especially being stressed. Though it was expected to cost just under £3000 (£1.58m), the eventual outlay was £5573 17s. 5d. (£2.93m). When one learns that this ranged from the cost of replacing the arms of Louis de Luxembourg with Margaret's own on silverware she had bought to that of bringing a lion and its two keepers from Titchfield, where it had been presented to her, to the royal menagerie at the Tower, one understands how the expenses built up; even the budget for the fleet to convey the company was overspent by £17 (£8925), though the culprit had to wait ten years for his payment.[6]

Suffolk and the bridal party set out from London on 5 November 1444. They had possibly expected to return to Tours, or to go to Angers, where Margaret was in residence, as arrangements were put in hand at Rouen three weeks later for all the royal officials and notable individuals of the duchy to prepare to accompany York for her formal reception. Instead, however, the party had to travel to Nancy, the capital of René d'Anjou's duchy of Lorraine, where the royal court had been in residence since the autumn. Charles had lent his moral and military sup-port to the duke for a campaign against Burgundian-backed Metz, thirty-five miles north of Nancy, which claimed allegiance to the Empire, rather than to Lorraine. A lengthy siege was in progress, usefully providing employment well away from the centre of France for soldiers made idle by the truce.

Suffolk must have expected to find Margaret at Nancy but he was to be disappointed, for she was still over 350 miles away at Angers and would not arrive until early February. For two full months after its own arrival, therefore, the English embassy was obliged to kick its heels at Charles VII's court. This might have been a genuine misunderstanding or, as the rumour-mill in England soon suggested, a deliberate ploy by Charles to extract more concessions from Suffolk before permitting the bride to leave France. The revocation of Maine was again said to have been on the agenda.[7]

What was definitely discussed, at the request of Richard, duke of York, was the possibility of marrying Edward, his son and heir, to one of Charles's three daughters. Suffolk advocated this scheme as his insurance policy in case Henry's marriage failed to produce an heir: after the elderly Gloucester, York had the best claim to the throne, and it was therefore in Suffolk's interests to cultivate York's favour. Charles too must have known that York was a potential king of England, yet he willingly went along with the proposal, only substituting his youngest daughter, the infant Madeleine, for the older Jeanne, whom York would have preferred.

York's ambition must have blinded him to Charles's motives, for if the latter had refused to allow any of his daughters to marry Henry VI, why would he approve a marriage with his possible successor? By leading York to believe that such a thing was achievable, Charles brought the lieutenant-general and - governor of Normandy into his Francophile fold, ensuring that he too would be willing to endorse the cession of Maine. If such was his aim he was successful: York never explicitly condemned the handover. In the meantime the marriage negotiations dragged on for almost two years, during which time the lieutenant-general did his best to ingratiate himself with the former 'adversary of France': 'I pray the blessed Son of God that he will have you in his safe-keeping and give you a good life and a long one.'[8]

At the beginning of March 1445 Margaret of Anjou finally set out with her English escort for her new home. It was clearly not a prospect she relished. She burst into tears when she parted from her uncle and by the time she arrived in Rouen, a couple of days before her fifteenth birthday, she was apparently too ill to participate in the formal entry that had been prepared to welcome her. One of her English ladies-in-waiting had to take her place in the processions, wearing the robes Margaret had worn for her betrothal at Tours. Her physician, Master Francesco, was kept busy plying her with 'ointments, confections, powders and drugs' but she was seasick on the voyage from Harfleur and by the time she arrived at Portsmouth on 9 April she had broken out in 'the pox'.[9]

In the circumstances it is not surprising that Henry may have paid a surreptitious visit to view his bride before he married her. The Milanese ambassador reported that he disguised himself as an esquire so that he could personally deliver her a letter from himself, enabling him to scrutinise her while she read it. Not realising who he was, Margaret was dismayed to discover afterwards that she had kept the king of England on his knees before her. Whether or not the twenty-three-year-old Henry liked what he saw – Margaret was variously described as 'a good-looking and well-developed girl, who was then "mature and ripe for marriage"' and 'a most handsome woman, though somewhat dark' – the wedding ceremony was performed on 22 April at Titchfield Abbey in Hampshire. Cardinal Beaufort, who might have been expected to carry out such an important duty, did not officiate, though Margaret was placed in his care afterwards; the couple were married by Henry's confessor and councillor, William Aiscough, bishop of Salisbury.[10]

The low-key wedding may have been arranged to accommodate the bride's ill-health and obvious nerves but she could not avoid the extravagant pageantry that was to come. On 28 May she was greeted at Blackheath by the customary assembly of nobles and civic dignitaries, led by the duke of Gloucester with a retinue of five hundred, all 'in one livery', and escorted into London. Her formal entry was an opportunity for propagandist displays and speeches celebrating 'peace and plenty', while the Londoners went wild with joy, aided, no doubt, by the copious

supplies of wine which ran through the water conduits and foun-
tains on such occasions. Two days later, on 30 May, Margaret
was crowned in Westminster Abbey.[11] For better, for worse,
Henry had a new wife and England a new queen. The general
expectation was that a lasting peace with France would follow.

It was Suffolk, of all people, who first sounded a note of cau-
tion. Two days after the coronation, on 2 June, he addressed the
lords in parliament, informing them of his great labours to procure the marriage and reminding them that the truce would
lapse on 1 April 1446 and that Charles had promised to send an
embassy to England 'well instructed and disposed to good conclusion of peace'. Nevertheless, he added,

> it still seemed to him to be entirely necessary, expedient and
> beneficial for the security of this realm and the king's obedi-
> ence overseas, in order to have a more agreeable manner of
> peace in the said treaty and to avoid all manner of ambiguities
> and inconveniences which might arise and occur by breach of
> their promises should they depart without effective conclu-
> sion, which God forbid, that ordinance and provision might
> be made with all good speed in order to be ready at all times
> to defend that land, and for the war and the mighty defence of
> the same . . . and also to stock up the castles, towns and all
> manner of fortresses of the king's obedience in Normandy
> and France.

When he was on his embassy to Tours, he told the lords, he had
advised York 'to stock up the places in Normandy to prevent all
manner of harm and problems which might occur or arise in
those parts in default of such an ordinance and provision'. Were
the French to know that such preparations had been made, he
'truly believed' that it 'would be of great benefit to the better
conclusion of peace'.[12]

Perhaps rumours were already beginning to circulate that he
had promised to cede Maine, for he ended his recommendation
on rearmament with an elliptically phrased assertion that, during
all his time overseas, he had never discussed details of what a

peace treaty might contain, nor of what kind it might be, but had always referred all such queries back to Henry VI. The day after he made his speech in the lords he repeated it in the commons, stating that, 'whatever might happen' in the future, he had answered to the king. He requested that this should be recorded on the parliamentary roll, which was duly done, and he was effusively thanked by the speaker on behalf of parliament for his 'good, true, faithful and notable service to his highness and to his land'.[13]

Suffolk had done all that he could to protect himself against the inevitable backlash that would come from the likes of Gloucester and the Beauforts when they learned that Maine might be returned to the French. He had made it clear that any decision to do so had been, and was still, the king's to make: he had only acted as Henry's agent and bore no personal responsibility in the matter. The timing of his statement in parliament was significant, for it was delivered as preparations were being made to receive Charles VII's ambassadors for the conferences that were to end the war permanently. The ceding of Maine would inevitably be on the agenda.

Suffolk's advice on using the truce as an opportunity to secure Normandy's defences against a possible resumption of war was not acted upon for the simple reason that there was no money available to do so. The savings to the English exchequer on military expenditure occasioned by the truce had been outweighed by the extraordinary costs of the embassy to fetch Margaret of Anjou, her reception in London and the coronation.

The truce had not brought a massive reduction in spending in Normandy either. The estates-general still had to levy taxes to pay the wages of soldiers in garrisons, even if there were no longer field armies to be supported. According to the terms of the Truce of Tours, all forms of protection money levied by frontier garrison captains had been prohibited, including collecting *appâtis* and charging for safe-conducts. This raised the intractable problem posed by Perrinet Gressart in a letter to François de Surienne written in 1425, when local truces were about to be imposed round La-Charité-sur-Loire: 'Tell my lord the Marshal that if he includes

The month of February from the manuscript of *Les Très Riches Heures* of the duke of Berry, painted between 1438 and 1442, depicts a French country household in winter. Note the enclosure to keep out wild animals and the tall oven-house, built of stone and separate from the domestic quarters so as to minimise the risk of fire. In the yard are the sheep in their pen, the pigeons from the dovecot and the four bee-skeps against the far wall. Small farms and peasant households in the open countryside were especially vulnerable to the depredations of soldiers and brigands. (AKG)

Once thought to depict Cardinal Albergati, this portrait by Jan van Eyck, painted in 1430–5, is now identified as one of Cardinal Henry Beaufort. (Kuntshistorisches Museum, Wien)

Humphrey, duke of Gloucester, protector of England during the minority of Henry VI and his wife, Eleanor Cobham, who was convicted of sorcery and forcibly divorced from him in 1441. A miniature from the register of Saint Albans Abbey, of which Gloucester was a patron. (AKG)

The magnificent gilt-bronze effigy of Richard, earl of Warwick, on his tomb in the Beauchamp Chapel, Saint Mary's Church, Warwick. The earl, who died in Rouen in 1439 while serving as Henry VI's lieutenant-general and governor of France and Normandy, is depicted in full plate armour of a Milanese design, clean-shaven and with the pudding-bowl haircut fashionable at the time. The bars around the effigy belong to the curving hearse of carriage design, which, unusually, was included with the tomb, perhaps to illustrate Warwick's corpse's long journey home from Normandy. (Topfoto)

The marriage of Henry VI and Margaret of Anjou, at Titchfield Abbey on 22 April 1445. A fifteenth-century French miniature from the manuscript of the 'Vigiles de Charles VII' by Martial d'Auvergne. (Bibliothèque Nationale de France)

Hay-making in June in a field outside Paris from a miniature in *Les Très Riches Heures* painted in the 1440s. The labourers are all bare-foot; the men cut the grass with their scythes while the women rake it up and pile it into stooks. In the background across the Seine is the walled Île-de-la-Cité, dominated by the Palais Royal, the centre of administration, and, to its right, the soaring finials of the Sainte-Chapelle. Cultivating the fields outside Paris was essential but highly risky when enemy garrisons frequently raided right up to the city gates. (AKG)

French peasants harrowing the fields and sowing winter wheat in October on the right bank of the Seine; a scarecrow, dressed as a *franc-archer* in kettle hat and armed with a bow, stands guard in the field behind them. Citizens of Paris stroll outside the city walls, and the great keep of the Louvre, with its towers and slender chimneys, towers over the city walls on the left bank. Painted for *Les Très Riches Heures* in the 1440s by the same artist as the miniature for June. (AKG)

Henry VI invests John Talbot either as marshal of France (9 May 1436) or, more probably, given the age at which the king is portrayed, as earl of Shrewsbury (20 May 1442). From a miniature in the Talbot Book of Hours presented by Talbot to Margaret of Anjou in 1445. (The Stapleton Collection/Bridgeman Art Library)

François de Surienne and his scaling-master, Thomassin du Quesne, scale the walls of Fougères and seize the town from the duke of Brittany in March 1449. Charles VII claimed that the incident was in breach of the Truce of Tours and therefore declared war on the English, leading to their final expulsion from France. From a fifteenth-century manuscript of the 'Vigiles de Charles VII' by Martial d'Auvergne. (Bibliothèque Nationale de France)

The dauphin Louis leads the assault on the English bastille which Talbot had built to lay siege to Dieppe. The bridges across the ditch surrounding the bastille were wheeled into place or lowered by crane enabling the attackers to scale the walls; the wheels on the furthest bridge can still be seen. The bastille was carried by assault on 14 August 1443 and Talbot's bastard son was among those taken prisoner. From a fifteenth-century manuscript of Jean Chartier's *Chronique du Charles VII*.

(Mary Evans Picture Library)

Raoul Roussel, archbishop of Rouen, acting on behalf of the citizens of Rouen, begs Edmund Beaufort, Henry VI's lieutenant-general in France, to accept Charles VII's terms for surrendering the city in October 1449. From a fifteenth-century manuscript of Jean Chartier's *Chronique du Règne de Charles VII*.

(Bibliothèque Nationale de France)

Cherbourg castle, captured by Thomas, duke of Clarence, in 1418 and surrendered to the French by Thomas Gower on 12 August 1450. Regarded by contemporaries as impregnable it was the last English stronghold to yield in Charles VII's reconquest of Normandy. A sixteenth-century lithograph by Théodore du Moncel.

Mont-Saint-Michel. The fortified abbey on its own island surrounded by treacherous sands which was the only stronghold in Normandy never to surrender to the English. (Giraudon)

A page from the Talbot Book of Hours, compiled and illustrated in Rouen for John lord Talbot. This is a highly personal collection of favourite devotional pieces in both English and French, including the Charlemagne prayer, with its repeated invocation of the sign and name of the Cross of Christ, which was believed to ward off sudden death in battle. This page depicts Talbot and his wife, Margaret Beauchamp, kneeling before the Virgin and Child. Their patron saints stand behind them: Saint Margaret behind Margaret but, significantly, behind Talbot is Saint George of England, rather than Talbot's own name-saint, Saint John. Note beneath this portrait the emblem of the Order of the Garter, of which Talbot was a member, and Saint George the patron saint. (The Fitzwilliam Museum Cambridge/Bridgeman Art Library)

this town within these truces, he must find for me and my companions some means of living: otherwise it must not be included in the truce, for without wages we cannot sustain ourselves unless we make war.' The innovative means introduced by the Truce of Tours was to replace *appâtis* with a direct local tax levied by the civil authorities of each obedience. The totals due from both sides were then to be added together and divided equally: if one party received more than the other it was to hand over the difference.[14]

This complex arrangement was administered jointly by the conservators of the truce appointed by each side and inevitably it led to disputes. The assessments revealed an imbalance of 18,000*l.t.* (£1.05m) a year in favour of the English, so Suffolk, while he was at Nancy, agreed that this sum should be paid into Charles VII's exchequer: a further 2156*l.t.* (£125,767) would be paid directly to the Armagnac garrison at Bellême. As York complained in April 1445, this was still unfair: he disputed the Armagnac claims to jurisdiction at Beaumont-le-Roger, Pontorson, Saint-James-de-Beuvron, Sainte-Suzanne and Granville. He also found that the enemy garrison at Louviers was encouraging the inhabitants of neighbouring Pont-de-l'Arche to resist paying taxes legally levied by the estates-general, driving the collector to resign his commission in frustration.[15]

The biggest problem for both sides was what to do with the soldiers rendered unemployed by the truce. Within days of the start of the Truce of Tours the citizen of Paris was already complaining that Robert Floques and La Hire's bastard brother had established themselves in the villages round Paris with 'a great gang of robbers and cut-throats . . . limbs of Antichrist every one, for they were all thieves and murderers, incendiaries, ravishers of all women', and they were killing, robbing and ransoming with impunity. 'When people complained to the rulers of Paris, they were told: "They've got to live. The King will be seeing to it very soon."'[16]

Charles's solution was to send these soldiers of fortune off under the dauphin's command into Alsace and Lorraine to support the Habsburgs against the Swiss and put pressure on

Burgundy. (It was as part of this campaign that Charles himself moved to Nancy and besieged Metz in the autumn and winter of 1444.) Exactly the same problems with unemployed soldiers were being experienced in Normandy. The novel answer devised there in the summer of 1444 was to allow Matthew Gough to recruit from their numbers one hundred men-at-arms and three hundred archers and lead them to Alsace to enter Charles VII's service and join his campaign.[17] Bizarrely, therefore, they found themselves fighting side by side with men who, just weeks earlier, had been their mortal enemies.

This proved to be only a temporary solution for the Norman companies: while Charles's armies spent the winter living off the land in Alsace, Gough and his men trooped back to Normandy. By December 1444 the *bailli* of Caen was sending messages to the duke of York at Rouen informing him that 'certain Englishmen and other soldiers have just come into the Auge region and this *bailliage* from the company of Matthew Gough and Raynforth' and that they were committing numerous oppressions on the king's subjects. The inhabitants of Lisieux bribed Gough with food and money to keep his men away from their town and by the following February they had moved into the Cotentin, where they were 'plundering and robbing the poor people and committing crimes, pillages, batteries, murders and other numerous excesses and offences'.[18]

So many complaints were pouring into Rouen that York decided drastic measures would have to be taken. He therefore went to Argentan in person to deal with the problem, taking with him a large number of councillors, justiciars and soldiers, many of whom would remain there throughout the spring. He carried out musters of those retinues which seemed genuinely to consist of placeless soldiers and assigned them to various garrisons; the remaining English, Welsh and Irish 'who do not seem to suit soldiering' were given their fare home and repatriated immediately in ships that Thomas Gower, captain of Cherbourg, was ordered to hire at York's expense especially for that purpose. York also gave numerous 'secret gifts to divers persons whom he employed to make the payments to the men who were not in any garrison' and, since the funds were not available from the Norman exchequer and the necessity was urgent, York personally pledged his jewels and plate to raise the money.[19]

On 12 May 1445 York ordered the *bailli* of Caen 'very expressly on our behalf' to have proclamations made in the customary places and at the sound of the trumpet that any remaining soldiers living off the land should leave immediately. If they belonged to a garrison in Normandy or Maine they should return there; those 'of this nation and tongue' who had a trade or employment should go back to it, on pain of being considered rebels and disobedient; all other soldiers should immediately take themselves off

> to the furthermost marches between Normandy and Maine, living there under their chiefs and leaders in an orderly fashion, taking nothing except reasonably adequate victuals for men and horses, and, to avoid a crowd of people, they should only stay in one place for a single night and in moderately sized companies ... and they must be on their guard and abstain at all times from doing anything contrary or prejudicial to the present truces and abstinences of war; and if it happens that, after the said proclamation, anyone should be found acting contrary to our present order, you must arrest and imprison them, or have them arrested and imprisoned in reality and in fact, wherever they may be found, except in sanctuary, and you should inflict such punishment, and so harsh, that it will be an example to others, without fear or favour and using armed force if necessary.[20]

In July York presided over a meeting of the estates-general at Argentan, setting out the huge costs involved in this entire exercise and seeking reimbursement for his personal expenditure; a tax of 30,000*l.t.* (£1.75m) was imposed on the duchy as a result. This was one of York's last formal acts as lieutenant-general and governor, for his five-year term of office was now coming to an end. In September he returned to England in the expectation that his appointment would be renewed and in order to attend

the third session of parliament, which was reconvening in the
wake of the latest peace negotiations.[21]

The great French embassy empowered to seek peace had
arrived in England in July 1445, almost exactly thirty years since
its predecessor had sought and failed to prevent Henry V launching the Agincourt campaign, which was then in the final stages
of preparation. Surprisingly, at least one man served on both
embassies. Louis de Bourbon, count of Vendôme, had returned
to France in 1415 and taken up arms to resist the English invasion. Captured at the battle of Agincourt, he had spent eight
years as a prisoner in England, where he had fathered the
Bastard of Vendôme by an Englishwoman before being released
in 1423. Now he returned to London as an honoured guest,
escorted by Garter king-of-arms from Dover, and accompanied
by Jacques Juvénal des Ursins, the new archbishop of Reims,
together with several other members of the royal council and
representatives of the dukes of Brittany and Alençon, René
d'Anjou and the king of Castile.[22]

Suffolk naturally played a leading role in the negotiations and
did his utmost to flatter both Charles VII and his ambassadors,
repeatedly and openly proclaiming that he was 'the servant of
the king of France and that, excepting the person of the king of
England, his master, he would serve him with his life and his fortune against all men'. Henry VI, he assured them, felt just the
same, as his uncle was the person he loved most in the world
after his wife. Suffolk also commented 'loudly', so that others
could hear, that when he was in France he had heard it
rumoured that the duke of Gloucester would impede the peace
process. This Suffolk now denied, adding in the duke's presence
that Gloucester would not do so and could not, since he did not
have the power.[23]

Suffolk's cosy relationship with the French ambassadors had
Henry VI's approval. The king also had several personal inter-
views with them in which he too was at pains to declare the
warmth of his love for the uncle he had never met. He went into
transports of joy when they conveyed messages of affection from
Charles VII, and publicly rebuked his chancellor for not using

words of greater friendship in his reply. There was also an implicit rebuke for Gloucester, who was at the king's side, in Henry's comment to the chancellor: 'I am very much rejoiced that some, who are present, should hear these words: they are not a comfort to them.'[24]

Despite all these mutual protestations of affection and goodwill, the peace negotiations foundered, as they had always done, on the question of sovereignty. The offer that Suffolk had made at Tours was repeated: the English would abandon their claim to the crown if their right to hold Normandy and Gascony without doing homage to Charles was accepted. Now, as then, this was rejected. Rather than allow the peace talks to fail completely, a face-saving solution was agreed. The archbishop of Reims suggested that a peace settlement was more likely if a summit meeting was held between the two kings in person rather than trying to negotiate through intermediaries. This request had to be referred back to Henry, who professed himself willing to go to France for further discussions in a face-to-face meeting with his uncle, though he warned that this would take time and much preparation to organise. As an earnest of goodwill on both sides, the Truce of Tours, which was due to expire on 1 April, was extended to 11 November 1446.[25]

After the grand French embassy had returned to report to Charles VII, one of its members, Guillaume Cousinot, Charles's councillor and chamberlain, was sent back to England at the head of a smaller working delegation charged with making the preliminary arrangements for the meeting of kings. Suffolk and Adam Moleyns, the keeper of the privy seal, were appointed to treat with them and by 19 December they had decided that the meeting should take place in November 1446, necessitating a further extension of the truce until 1 April 1447.[26] Cousinot and his colleague, Jean Havart, had also been entrusted with a far weightier matter: they had been instructed to demand that Henry should hand over Maine to his father-in-law, René d'Anjou, in return for a lifelong alliance and a twenty-year truce. In this they were nominally acting on René's behalf and at his request – or so it was said – but the fact remained that they were

Charles VII's envoys and there is no doubt that it was Charles himself who was pushing this agenda. And he was doing so entirely for his own ends because the Angevins had just lost their ascendancy at court in one of the periodic palace coups. Charles had told them 'by word of mouth, that they should not return until they were sent for': René d'Anjou disappeared from the list of royal councillors in September; his brother, Charles, in December.[27]

The cession of Maine had never been part of the formal marriage contract but Charles now insisted that Henry should fulfil what he claimed was his nephew's personal promise which had been given on his word as a prince. If that promise had indeed been given, it had been to achieve peace. Charles now demanded its fulfilment merely to extend the truce, though he cleverly played to Henry's susceptibilities, urging him to make the concession 'because we hope that on this account the matter of the principal peace will proceed better, and will come to a more speedy and satisfactory conclusion'. Charles had already enlisted the aid of his niece, Henry's queen. On 17 December Margaret of Anjou replied to letters from her uncle, saying that there could be no greater pleasure in the world for her than to see a treaty of peace between him and her husband, to which end 'we are employing ourselves effectively to the best of our ability so that really you and all others ought to be content'. As to the delivery of Maine, she understood that her husband had written to him at length about this but she would nevertheless do what he wished 'to the best that we can do, just as we have always done'.[28]

Five days after this letter, and three days after the truce was prolonged, Henry VI signed with his own hand a formal engagement addressed to Charles VII promising to hand over Le Mans and all other places, towns, castles and fortresses in Maine to René and Charles d'Anjou by 30 April 1446. He did this, he said, to show the sincerity of his own wish for peace, to please his queen, who had requested him to do it many times, and principally to please and benefit Charles VII. It did not augur well for the future that this crucially important undertaking was not a public document, witnessed, sealed and approved by the royal council, but a private letter conceived, written and sent in secret.[29]

It was an act of supreme folly which played straight into Charles VII's hands. How could Henry possibly expect to keep his written undertaking secret, especially as he had also promised to put it into effect in four months' time? When or how did he imagine he would inform his subjects in either England or France, particularly those whose lands and lordships he had just signed away without any whisper of compensation? By agreeing to surrender Maine he had implicitly renounced his sovereignty over it and effectively declared that future diplomatic or military pressure might persuade him to make similar concessions elsewhere in France. He had made himself – and his French possessions – a hostage to the possibility that this grand gesture would persuade Charles VII to make a final peace. It was a serious and fatal error of judgement.

CHAPTER TWENTY-TWO

Concessions for Peace

If Henry VI had naive illusions about the likely reception of his secret revocation of Maine, the frosty response to the public announcement of just the summit meeting between himself and Charles VII should have given him pause for thought. The longest parliament of his reign ended its fourth and final session at Westminster on 9 April 1446. The chancellor, John Stafford, archbishop of Canterbury, had opened it on 25 February 1445 with a sermon expounding the text 'righteousness and peace kiss each other' in anticipation of the arrival of Margaret of Anjou and the hope she brought of the Truce of Tours being converted into a permanent peace.

Now, on the final day, Stafford 'made a certain declaration in his own name and that of the . . . lords spiritual and temporal, which he desired . . . to be enrolled and enacted in the rolls of the said parliament'.[1] Though couched in courteous and diplomatic language, it was nothing less than a collective washing of hands:

> It has pleased our Lord to incline your highness, to his pleasure and for the well-being of both your realms and of all your subjects of the same, towards appointing a day of convention

for the matter of peace and for the good conclusion of the same to be had between your most royal person and your uncle of France; and therefore you should be within your said realm of France during the month of October next coming, by God's might. To which said motions and promptings, as he knows, it has pleased only our Lord to stir and move you; none of the lords or your other subjects of this your realm have in any way stirred or moved you to do so.[2]

In other words, as Suffolk had done earlier in the same parliament, the king's advisers disclaimed any responsibility for the king's actions in holding the summit meeting or in its outcome. Henry needed no reminder that he alone had the power to determine foreign policy but he was being told in no uncertain terms that he alone would also be held responsible for what transpired. The lords and commons had always done their duty, Stafford declared, and would labour as far as possible to assist him in accomplishing his 'blessed intent', but they wished the king 'in all humility to hold them discharged and excused from anything which goes beyond this'.

The next item on the parliament roll reveals exactly why the king's advisers were so concerned. The Treaty of Troyes, which was the foundation of the English kingdom of France, contained a clause that no 'treaty of peace or accord with the present king's uncle, then called Charles the Dauphin', could be entered into, or concluded, without the assent of the three estates of both realms. This clause was now revoked, freeing Henry legally to conclude peace on any terms he chose, without having to consult his lords and commons in the English parliament. It would, of course, have been difficult to refuse the king's request for this revocation but it would not have been impossible and parliament was as anxious as the country at large for a permanent end to the war with France. The enrolment of Stafford's protestation, however, was an indication of the depth of public disquiet at the prospect of a peace which few knew, but many suspected, would be founded on concession.[3]

It was perhaps an indication of Henry's lack of interest in his

French possessions that he did not seek a similar revocation from the estates-general in his realm overseas. It was true that this body only represented Normandy, whereas the Treaty of Troyes had been approved and registered by the national assembly, to which Henry no longer had access, having lost so much of his kingdom. The estates-general of the duchy were in session throughout January 1446 but no formal revocation was sought or given. Henry did inform the representatives of his great desire for peace and his wish to come to Normandy soon to confer in person with Charles VII, but this was merely a precursor to the usual request for money. The English parliament eventually and in instalments granted two whole subsidies to be collected over two years. The estates-general approved the levying of 130,000*l.t.* (£7.58) followed in July by another 60,000*l.t.* (£3.5m) and the imposition of a tax of twelve *deniers* in the *livre* (5p in the £1). These sums were explicitly designated for the payment of the wages of the soldiers in garrison and to deal with those soldiers living off the land.[4]

This was still a problem twelve months after York's personal intervention at Argentan. The estates-general described their allocation of funds in January 1446 as being 'to put under rule and regulation the soldiers living without order imposed on them'. In February Fulk Eyton, captain of Caudebec, was dispatched from Rouen to Argentan and Caen, 'to put and keep in order and good government a great number of men-at-arms and archers who, on the pretext that they do not have wages or pay from us, are living off our good and loyal subjects in our duchy of Normandy, without regulation, committing great and detestable evils and causing our subjects innumerable losses'. Whether Eyton performed this task as head of an armed force, or purely in his role as a commissioner, accompanied by Sir Robert Roos, is not clear but the council in Rouen awarded him a 100*l.t.* (£5833) bonus on top of his salary for the expenses incurred in his journeys to and from Argentan and Caen.[5]

Containing and preventing military indiscipline was almost more important now than it had ever been in the past: it was no longer just that it caused the king's subjects to suffer, but that it endangered the maintenance of the Truce of Tours. As was the usual practice, conservators of truces had been appointed by both sides to list alleged breaches of the truce and then jointly decide culpability and agree compensation. These were critical appointments, since the effort the conservators made to see fair play in repairing infractions was usually more important than the infringements themselves. For instance, when a temporary truce was made to cover the Vendôme region for the preliminary meetings before the negotiations opened at Tours in 1444, it was a clear indication of the English administration's determination to ensure that the truce was observed that they appointed as conservators Richard Wydeville, captain of Alençon and Fresnay, François de Surienne, captain of Verneuil, Osbern Mundeford, *bailli-général* of Maine, and Talbot himself. Similarly a wish to see the Truce of Tours maintained ensured that once claim and counter-claim had been heard reparation for breaches of its terms was made swiftly. In the summer of 1446, for example, the conservators from both sides meeting at Évreux and Louviers decided that 850*l.t.* (£49,583) should be paid out by the English.[6]

The situation in Normandy was not helped by the fact that it had been left leaderless. Talbot had not returned to the duchy after escorting Margaret of Anjou to England and in March 1445 had been appointed the king's lieutenant in Ireland, a post he had previously held from 1414 to 1419. His dynamic personality was undoubtedly better suited to warfare, but his military knowledge and his ability to inspire his troops would also have been useful in the limbo following the Truce of Tours. No one could better have fulfilled Suffolk's admonition that Normandy should be prepared for a resumption of war if the peace negotiations failed.[7]

But Normandy had lost not just its marshal but also its lieutenant-general and governor. The duke of York's tenure of office, which had expired at the end of September 1445, had been extended by three months, but this too had lapsed by the end of the year. The government of Normandy was therefore temporarily carried out by a committee of the council in Rouen. York himself remained in England, hoping and expecting to return, but his reappointment was apparently delayed by an audit conducted at the exchequer into his accounts for the office. He had claimed that he was owed almost £40,000 (£21m) but at the end of July he was persuaded to accept a settlement that saw him completely forgo £12,666 13s. 4d. (£6.65m) in order to receive guarantees for the remaining £26,000 (£13.65m) due to him. Even then, though he received a substantial part of this sum fairly quickly, the outstanding debt was not paid off in full for another sixteen years.[8]

The empty coffers of the English state were also causing problems for the king, who was himself trying to raise funds to enable him to travel to France for his summit with Charles VII in October 1446. He had already decided that his queen should accompany him and that the historic meeting should take place near Le Mans, but such an occasion demanded lavish pageantry and display on a scale neither he nor his country could afford. His pleas for loans met with a disappointing response but Henry was determined to press ahead with his arrangements.[9]

On 20 July 1446 Adam Moleyns and John, lord Dudley, were sent to France to finalise the details of the meeting. Their mission was somewhat hampered by the fact that, according to their king's written undertaking, Maine should have been surrendered to René and Charles d'Anjou on 30 April. Nothing whatsoever had been done to put this into effect and the English embassy now discovered that Charles VII would not countenance a meeting, nor even an extension of the truce, until Maine had been handed over. Inch by inch he was inexorably turning the screw on his nephew. [10]

Henry and his chief minister, Suffolk, had not anticipated this development: they had counted on the summit meeting to achieve a permanent peace or, at worst, a long truce, to justify the cession of Maine. Now they faced the unenviable task of being forced to reveal that the undertaking had been given with nothing to show for it except a short-term truce which would expire on 11 November 1446. Faced with this calamity, they decided that the cession would have to be forced through in the teeth of inevitable opposition.

The two people who could be guaranteed to lead that opposition were the ones who had most to lose: Edmund Beaufort, who had succeeded his brother as earl of Somerset in 1444 and was the governor of, and greatest landowner in, Maine, and Humphrey, duke of Gloucester, a consistent opponent of any territorial concessions to the French. Suffolk – for it is difficult to believe that the king himself could have displayed such guile – set about disarming them both.

Beaufort had enjoyed effectively vice-regal powers in Maine since the county was granted to him on 19 July 1442. He controlled all military and civilian offices, had his own treasury and centre of government in Le Mans independent of those in Normandy and exercised to the full his right to grant lands to his supporters. There were only two limitations on his extraordinary powers: the grant was made to him for life only and it was revocable – if peace were agreed with Charles VII, Maine could be restored to French ownership. Suffolk relied on this clause as the stick with which to beat Beaufort into surrendering Maine but he needed to offer a carrot as well. The one that he chose was the office of lieutenant-general and governor of Normandy, which was technically vacant, though it had been all but promised to York. The most cost-effective way of preventing York's reappointment was to discredit him, so when Adam Moleyns returned in October 1446 from his fruitless mission to France, he accused the duke of financial improprieties in his administration, in particular, diverting the funds intended for the defence of Normandy to the benefit of his own councillors.[11]

This charge was given added substance by the fact that one of York's foremost captains, Sir Thomas Kyriell, had been found guilty by Talbot, in his capacity as marshal of Normandy, of withholding wages from his garrison at Gisors. Kyriell had appealed the decision and in November 1446 Thomas Bekyngton, bishop of Bath and Wells, the former keeper of the privy seal, and Ralph, lord Cromwell, the former treasurer of England, were appointed to investigate the case. Mired in accusations of corruption, embezzlement and maladministration,

York could legitimately be set aside and the office he had waited for over a year to have renewed could be given to someone else.[12]

On 24 December 1446 Edmund Beaufort was appointed lieutenant-general and governor of Normandy, thereby effortlessly securing the post with the powers that his uncle, Cardinal Beaufort, had fruitlessly schemed so hard to secure for his elder brother. He was to hold the office for three years, commencing on 1 March 1447 (a month before the truce next expired), and he would contract to serve in Normandy at the head of an army of three hundred men-at-arms and nine hundred archers. The price he would be expected to pay for his promotion was his acquiescence and assistance in the handover of Maine.[13]

Beaufort might be bought, but his uncle, Gloucester, could not. The old duke was now in his fifty-seventh year and since 1441 had been sidelined from his natural place at court and in the council chamber by the disgrace of his wife. He could not be completely ignored, however, as he was still the childless king's heir to the two crowns; he also had the best claim in the realm to act in Henry's stead while the latter was absent in France for his proposed meeting with Charles VII. His opposition to the cession of Maine was inevitably going to be profound and vociferous and he would make a powerful figurehead round whom the dispossessed in Maine could rally.

On 14 December 1446 the writs had been issued for a new parliament to meet at Cambridge on 10 February 1447. Fearing that Gloucester would use the occasion as a platform to attack the current trend of peace policies (whether he yet knew of the promise concerning Maine is unclear), Suffolk decided to pre-empt his objections and silence him by having him arrested and impeached for treason. The legal grounds for such a charge are unclear, not least because no formal process was recorded and the Yorkist chroniclers who relate the whole sorry affair had their own reasons for demonising those responsible. The two charges that they allege were that Gloucester was plotting either a rebellion against his nephew in Wales or to stage a coup during parliament, killing the king, seizing the throne and releasing his own wife from her perpetual imprisonment. Though neither accusation seems credible, Henry must have been gullible enough to believe that his uncle was planning his destruction because he sanctioned the actions that followed.

On 20 January 1447 the venue for the forthcoming parliament was suddenly changed 'for certain causes that have been declared to us' to Bury Saint Edmunds, a quiet abbey town in the heart of Suffolk's territorial influence. Gloucester still enjoyed a popular following in both London and the University of Cambridge: the move to Bury meant that there was less chance of a riot when his fate became known. Large numbers of armed men were drafted into the region to prevent the duke's retinue rising to his defence and the duke was ordered to bring only a small company with him. Ten days later the justices of the King's Bench, Exchequer and Common Pleas were ordered to adjourn their hearings from 12 February to 24 April because their presence was required at parliament. There was no precedent for such a step, which suggests that its purpose was to ensure that the most important judges in the land were available to give legal backing to the impeachment proceedings.[14]

According to a memo written the following year by Richard Fox, the abbot of Saint Albans, who attended the parliament, Gloucester arrived at Bury on 18 February, eight days after the chancellor delivered his opening speech on the theme 'But to the councillors of peace is joy'. Stafford had expounded at length on the necessity of rejecting the counsel of the wicked and following that of the Holy Spirit. He announced that the parliament had been summoned to make provision for both 'the safe and secure preservation of the most illustrious and most excellent person of the lord king' on his journey to France to meet Charles VII and 'the safe and secure keeping of the peace' in his realm during his absence.[15]

Gloucester was greeted on his arrival by two knights of the royal household, John Stourton and Thomas Stanley, who urged him to go straight to his lodgings rather than to the king. Later in the day a posse of peers arrived to arrest him: they included Humphrey Stafford, duke of Buckingham, acting in his official capacity as constable of England, Edmund Beaufort, earl of Somerset, and Richard Neville, earl of Salisbury. All were leading members of the faction surrounding Cardinal Beaufort: though there is no suggestion that the cardinal himself was behind the final downfall of his long-term opponent, there is no doubt that his supporters readily lent their assistance.

Although Gloucester demanded to see the king, his petitions were refused and over the next few days more than forty members of his entourage, including his bastard son, Arthur, were arrested and taken away. The speed and efficiency with which the coup was carried out attest to its careful planning but no one had foreseen the effect it would have on Gloucester. He appears to have suffered a major stroke. For three days he lay in bed, unresponsive and possibly unconscious, and that was where, on 23 February 1447, he died.[16]

The circumstances of his death inevitably raised suspicions that he had been murdered, which is why members of both houses of parliament were invited to view his body in the abbey church next day, before it was taken for burial in the tomb he had already built close to the shrine in the abbey of Saint Albans. This public display failed to quell the rumours which would return to haunt Suffolk and his associates who had engineered Gloucester's fall. Suffolk did himself no favours in this regard by presiding in person over the indictment of Gloucester's bastard son and seven other leading members of the duke's retinue on charges of treasonably marching in force to Bury to overthrow the king. Perhaps he felt some tinge of shame, however, for when Henry VI belatedly decided to pardon them as they were on the scaffold, Suffolk himself rushed to the scene of execution at Tyburn to ensure that they were cut down and released.[17]

They were unbelievably fortunate, not only in having their lives spared and property restored but also in being able to resume their careers. There was no such mercy for Eleanor Cobham, Gloucester's forcibly divorced widow. In a final piece of petty vindictiveness, on the last day of parliament a statute was enacted which effectively declared her legally dead, preventing her making any claim on her husband's estate. This meant that all his properties, titles and offices now reverted to the king – who had already promised many of them to the vultures who had circled after Eleanor's conviction. Suffolk, for instance, had been granted the right to succeed Gloucester as earl of Pembroke as long ago as 1443. On the very day that the duke died grants from his estate were made to Queen Margaret, Henry's new foundations at Eton and Cambridge and members of the royal household. At best this was unseemly haste. More sinister was the granting of Gloucester's property to Sir Robert Roos and two royal officials on 13 and 18 February – ten and five days before he died – in anticipation of his conviction and forfeiture for treason. Even if it had got to that stage, it seems unlikely that Gloucester would ever have received a fair trial. Too many people had too much to lose by his exoneration.[18]

Cardinal Beaufort did not long survive the nephew with whom he had quarrelled so bitterly. After Somerset's expedition in 1443, from which so much had been hoped and so little achieved, the cardinal had retired from public life and lived quietly in his episcopal residences in the country. He died, aged about seventy-two, at his magnificent palace of Wolvesey in Winchester, on 11 April 1447. Though more of a prince than a cleric, he had achieved two distinctions in his ecclesiastical career: he had held his episcopal office for almost fifty years, longer than any other English bishop, and he was, controversially, the first cardinal to keep his bishopric and reside in England. The enormous wealth of the see of Winchester had enabled him to fund the conquest and reconquest of the English kingdom of France: on at least two occasions, in 1421 and 1437, his loans amounted to more than £25,000 (£13.13m) and he had provided only slightly less for Somerset's expedition in 1443. Without his money, and his willingness to lend it, English dominion in France might have ended where it began, in the reign of Henry V.[19]

Despite his commitment to the war, Beaufort was also a pragmatist who had been prepared to make territorial concessions to secure a lasting peace. Nevertheless, it is unlikely that he would have approved of the inept handling of the current peace negotiations. Even Suffolk himself appears to have feared a backlash, for once again he sought and gained the king's personal and public sanction for his acts, this time at a meeting of the council: Henry's approval was given added weight by the issuing of proclamations threatening appropriate punishment for anyone who slandered Suffolk.[20]

This suggests that criticism of the conduct of foreign policy was becoming more overt, despite the silencing of Edmund Beaufort and Gloucester. It was readily apparent that the price of peace – even if it was only a temporary truce – was increasing. To obtain an extension of the truce beyond 11 November 1446, Henry had been forced both to express again his determination to hand over Maine and to make a further disastrous concession. On 18 December Suffolk and Moleyns agreed with Charles VII's agents, Guillaume Cousinot and Jean Havart, who were then in London, that ecclesiastical revenues from land in either obedience were to be restored to clergy who resided outside that obedience. On paper this seemed a fair arrangement, but in reality the concession was almost entirely one-sided in favour of the French – which is why a similar proposal in 1439 had been rejected.[21]

On 22 February 1447 a further extension of the truce, to 1 January 1448, was obtained by English ambassadors at Tours in return for an undertaking that Henry would cross the Channel for his summit meeting with Charles VII by 1 November. Also by that date, Henry promised to surrender Maine. This time, however, his promise was backed up by a confirmation of his secret undertaking made in December 1445, which he publicly sealed on 27 July, and by letters patent, issued the following day, appointing Matthew Gough and Fulk Eyton as his commissioners to take into the king's hands all English-held places in Maine and deliver them to Charles VII's commissioners on behalf of René and Charles d'Anjou. They were authorised to seize chattels, to compel cooperation and, if necessary, to use force: intriguingly, they were also ordered to obey not only these written commands but also instructions that Garter king-of-arms would deliver verbally to them. Edmund Beaufort (who had not yet set foot in the duchy since his appointment) and his officials were all ordered to assist Gough and Eyton in their task.[22]

As a reward for the public confirmation of the undertaking to deliver Maine, the Bastard of Orléans, who headed the July embassy to London, extended the truce and deadline for Henry's crossing to France by a further six months to 1 April 1448. The appointment of the commissioners for the handover earned modifications to the terms of the restitution of ecclesiastical revenues and, more importantly, for the first time a genuine concession that 'reasonable provision' should be made for Englishmen who lost their lands in Maine.[23]

How to deal with the dispossessed of either side had always been a stumbling block in any negotiated settlement but it was one that had grown increasingly insurmountable as the years passed, the conquest became entrenched and a whole new generation of land and office holders had emerged who had legitimately and peaceably acquired their possessions from the first wave of invaders. Their rights were arguably as valid as those of the original owners but one or other of them would have to lose out if any territorial concession was made. The cession of Maine brought this problem to the fore.

On 23 September 1447 Matthew Gough and Fulk Eyton presented themselves before Osbern Mundeford, the *bailli-général* of Maine and captain of Le Mans on behalf of Edmund Beaufort. They showed Mundeford their letters from Henry VI ordering the surrender of Maine, and required him to hand over the places in his charge. Mundeford politely but firmly refused, claiming quite correctly that the letters were addressed 'primarily' to Beaufort and contained no official discharge from his office for Mundeford himself.[24]

This was, of course, a useful delaying tactic, but it was also true that a captain was legally obliged by his contract of service to surrender his office only to the person who had appointed him. In 1434, for example, Oliver Adreton, the English lieutenant of Bernay, had similarly refused to surrender his office without letters of discharge from lord Willoughby, who had appointed him; what is more, John Salvein, the *bailli* of Rouen, whose command he refused to obey, had to go to Lisieux to obtain the official discharge before Adreton would relent. Given what was riding on the surrender of Maine, Mundeford was wise to insist on having his formal release from office before he committed the rash act of handing over the capital of the county to the enemy.

Mundeford reproved Gough and Eyton for failing to secure his letters of discharge from Beaufort before they approached him but offered to send for them himself, with all diligence and at his own cost, adding that he needed them 'in order to avoid blame and reproach in times to come'. Till then he would continue to hold the town and castle of Le Mans with all his power.[25]

Since Beaufort was still in England there would be a considerable delay in obtaining his releases and it would be impossible to meet the deadline of 1 November 1447 for implementing the handover. This was, no doubt, what Beaufort himself intended, since he was still holding out for full compensation for his losses in Maine before taking up his post as lieutenant-general in Normandy. Henry was furious at the delay, since it reflected on his honour as a prince, and he suspected that Beaufort was complicit in the prevarication of his officials. On 28 October he wrote a peremptory letter to Beaufort ordering 'as you dread our displeasure' that he, Mundeford, Richard Frogenhalle and all the other officers should deliver their places to his commissioners without further excuses or delays. Anticipating that Beaufort himself might use the same excuse, Henry took the precaution of adding that this letter would be the earl's sufficient warrant, quittance and discharge for the surrender.[26]

Belatedly Henry and Suffolk had realised that if they wanted the cooperation of the men on the ground in Maine they would have to tackle the question of compensation. On 13 November a major meeting of the English council decided that Beaufort should receive an annual pension of 10,000*l.t.* (£583,333), to be drawn from the revenues of Normandy, but no provision was made to recompense those whose livelihoods depended on their small estates and offices. For them compensation would be sought from the French.[27]

On 31 October 1447 a two-day conference had opened in the chapter-house at Le Mans between Charles VII's agents, Cousinot and Havart, and Henry VI's officers, Sir Nicolas Molyneux, master of the king's *chambre-des-comptes* at Rouen, Osbern Mundeford, the *bailli-général* of Maine who had refused to surrender his charge, and Thomas Direhille, *vicomte* of Alençon. It was a measure of the importance of the whole question of compensation that some five hundred interested parties attended, ranging from members of the nobility and the church to citizens and merchants.[28]

The first day of the conference was given over to tedious but necessary formalities. Cousinot related the four-year history of the promise to deliver Maine and produced the documentation, including Henry VI's secret undertaking made in December 1445 and his and Havart's delegated powers from Charles VII to make 'reasonable provision' for the dispossessed. The English queried the authenticity of their letters of appointment on the grounds that there were so many erasures and emendations and that they did not recognise the signature of the notary who had produced the copy.

The whole process took so long that it was not until the following day, 1 November – the day Henry VI had promised to deliver Maine, as Cousinot pointed out – that the conference reassembled after attending high mass in the castle. Molyneux, who acted as the English spokesman throughout the proceedings, then set out his own documentation, stating that Henry VI's letters promising delivery of Maine were conditional on lifelong alliances between his king and René and Charles d'Anjou, a twenty-year truce with Anjou and Maine and 'reasonable provision . . . which is properly understood to mean due compensation'. Cousinot could not produce any letters of alliance or truce, or a licence from Charles VII permitting these to go ahead, claiming he had left them behind at Sablé for fear of attack on the road. Without that security and the 'reasonable provision' agreed beforehand, Molyneux argued that the handover should not take place.

Cousinot insisted that the question of the truce and alliance was irrelevant, since neither was mentioned in Henry VI's letters ordering the handover to take place on 1 November 'all excuses and hindrances notwithstanding'. As for compensation, he agreed that the letter did mention 'reasonable provision' but he pointed out that no date had been set for its being made and he disputed that it was the equivalent of compensation. Any 'reasonable provision' made before the handover took place would turn it into 'a sort of sale', which Charles VII had never intended.

This was as specious an argument as Molyneux's earlier challenge to Cousinot's powers as a commissioner. Molyneux's response was to reiterate his case but beg 'to be excused if he could not speak and articulate in French words as [well as] he could do in his mother tongue'. This was not a denial of his ability to speak and understand French: Molyneux had spent the previous twenty-five years in France and had been Bedford's receiver-general in Anjou and Maine before rising to his present position. His legal and financial skills had also long been employed for his own benefit, beginning with the legally binding agreement he made (in French) at Harfleur on 12 July 1421 with his English brother-in-arms, John Winter, for the division of their spoil and investment of the proceeds, and continuing with a successful career in property speculation in Rouen.[29] None of these things could have been achieved without a good understanding of French and an ability to speak it proficiently.

What Molyneux was actually doing was falling back on the age-old ploy used by English ambassadors whenever they did not wish to concede a point: they declared that they did not understand French, the international language of diplomacy, and wished everything to be conducted and recorded in Latin.[30] Cousinot understood the game, responding that Molyneux 'excused himself for not speaking eloquently in the French language, it not being his mother tongue, however, he possessed intelligence and prudence and knew how to communicate in French and in Latin as well as [Cousinot] himself could do'. Once more he demanded that Maine be handed over without excuses and when many of those present, including the Bastard of Salisbury and lord Fastolf's proctor, added their appeals for compensation to Molyneux's, he stated that it was not for him to interpret Henry VI's letters or cause his promises to be kept. He was unable to do anything more, he added, because his powers as Charles VII's commissioner ran out that very day. All the English could do was feebly announce that they would seek further instructions from Henry VI, leaving Cousinot and Havart with no option but to depart from Le Mans empty-handed.[31]

Like so many earlier Anglo-French negotiations, the conference had foundered on the fundamental problem that neither side trusted the other to do what they promised to do: the French believed the English were determined to avoid delivering Maine, just as the English were convinced that the French would not offer compensation once they had achieved their goal of acquiring the county. The only difference now was that the English at the conference were at loggerheads not only with the French but also with their own government. Henry VI had promised to cede Maine and he was determined to see it through.

CHAPTER TWENTY-THREE

The Surrender of Maine

On 23 October 1447 Henry VI wrote to Matthew Gough and Fulk Eyton, praising their diligence as commissioners, sending them the letters of discharge for Osbern Mundeford and Richard Frogenhalle, and urging them to bring their good work to a swift conclusion so that his intention, wish and desire in ceding Maine could be accomplished and his honour upheld.[1]

Gough and Eyton have been considered a strange choice for such a role. Neither had any diplomatic experience – but then diplomacy was not what was expected of them. They were not members of the council of Rouen, so they had no political influence or authority. Both were self-made men, professional soldiers who had made their careers in France and distinguished themselves in action, not least in Gough's retaking of Le Mans in 1428 and Eyton's cunning recapture of Lillebonne in 1436. Perhaps more important than any of these things was the fact that they appear to have had the trust of both the establishment and the common soldier. When the council at Rouen needed someone to lead the unemployed field armies out of Normandy into the dauphin's service in Alsace in 1444 it chose Gough; when it needed someone to impose order on the soldiers living off the land in 1446 it chose Eyton. It was their experience in dealing with these potentially dangerous bands of trained and armed soldiers, many of whom were disillusioned and disaffected by their enforced idleness and sudden loss of income, which fitted them for the role of commissioners for the delivery of Maine. The authorities obviously expected trouble from the dispossessed.

What they did not expect was that Gough and Eyton would join the resistance. Gough already had long-standing connections with Maine and was himself a property-owner in the county. Neither he nor Eyton appears to have attended the Le Mans conference, at least not in an official capacity, thereby avoiding the unpleasantness of being forced to back the French commissioners against the English landholders. Nevertheless, when Charles decided to send an embassy to press his claims, they were the ones with whom the negotiations had to be held, since no one of higher authority was available in the area.

Gough and Eyton were perhaps fortunate that the French embassy was led by the Bastard of Orléans, an intimidating figure for mere esquires but nevertheless a soldier himself and one who had originally conceded that compensation should be paid to the dispossessed. On 30 December they agreed terms which acknowledged the difficulties facing the English commissioners. Gough's request for a delay was granted, providing he gave his bond that Maine would be handed over on 15 January 1448. The truce was extended to cover that period and as soon as Le Mans itself was surrendered and security given for the surrender of Mayenne-la-Juhez and other places, the recently agreed one-year general truce until 1 January 1449 would apply, even if Gough was unable to force the recalcitrant Mundeford to yield Sillé-le-Guillaume, Fresnay-le-Vicomte and Beaumont-le-Vicomte. These three fortresses stood in a triangle to the north of Le Mans in the marches with Normandy and Mundeford may have been trying to redraw the border along the river Sarthe to include them in the duchy rather than the county.

The agreement allowed any English who wished to leave to go before 15 January, taking their portable property with them:

those who wished to stay could do so. Gough and Eyton also secured a commitment that they would receive Charles VII's letters permitting René and Charles d'Anjou to make the truce and alliance and Charles's personal promise to make the Angevin brothers consent to the articles of their agreement with the Bastard.[2] Given how little room they had for manoeuvre and that they were not diplomats, Gough and Eyton had probably secured the best deal possible in the circumstances.

The fifteenth of January 1448 came and went but Maine was still in English hands. A further period of grace until 2 February was granted 'at the request of the people of Le Mans' but by this time Charles VII had lost patience and decided to back up his demands with the threat of force. Learning that he was 'assembling from day to day a great army of people with the intention of waging war', Thomas Hoo, the chancellor of Normandy, wrote a desperate letter to Pierre de Brézé, the Bastard of Orléans's colleague on the recent delegation to Le Mans: 'for truthfully, whatever words have been said to you, or you have been given to understand, by Fulk Eyton, captain of Caudebec, or others, have no doubt that the promises, which have been made and settled touching the deliverance of the said town of Le Mans, shall be kept and fulfilled point by point, whatever delay there has been or may be'. Hoo begged Brézé

> that for your part you would not put anything into motion by which war or any other disaster may follow, which God forbid: such a thing would not be easily smoothed over, but be the total destruction and desolation of the poor people. The more especially also that if the soldiers were once assembled in the field, either upon the one side or the other, it would be very hard to make them withdraw and depart, and it would be only money wasted and a great expense.[3]

The role of the English commissioners was increasingly compromised as no surrender took place in February. Charles VII complained directly to Henry VI, explicitly naming Gough, Eyton and Mundeford, accusing them of resorting to 'subterfuges, pretences and dissimulations' and telling his nephew that he should declare them disobedient and repudiate them. Henry, in the meantime, had dispatched Adam Moleyns and Robert Roos to France. They landed at Honfleur on 15 February and three days later Hoo wrote again to Pierre de Brézé in a panic on learning that Charles's army had now taken to the field and was rumoured to be on its way to lay siege to Le Mans. Moleyns and Roos had 'ample powers to discuss and settle the affair of Le Mans', he assured Brézé, as once more he begged him to exert his influence to secure the withdrawal of the army.[4]

By the time Moleyns and Roos had made their way into Charles's presence in early March, he was at Lavardin, some nine miles north-west of Le Mans, where he had established himself in the castle so that he could watch the progress of the siege in comfort. The Bastard of Orléans had been given command of the army and, with the aid of Jean Bureau and his famous guns, he began the first formal siege of a town in northern France since the Truce of Tours. The English now had no choice. If there was one thing worse than having to leave their lands and properties to go into exile, it was the prospect of having Le Mans taken by assault and losing everything, including their own freedom and probably their lives as well.

Moleyns and Roos lost no time in confirming the agreement made by Gough and Eyton on 30 December, exempting only Fresnay-le-Vicomte, the fortress closest to the Norman border, which would remain in English hands, and Mayenne-la-Juhez, which, four days later on 15 March, they agreed to surrender 'really and in fact' on 27 March. As a salve to their pride the Treaty of Lavardin also addressed the question of compensation: the vague expression of 'reasonable provision' was turned into a payment of 24,000*l.t.* (£1.4m), a figure which was calculated as being ten times the annual value of the ceded territories. This was not to be paid in cash, but was to be deducted from the *appâtis* levied in Normandy due to Charles VII.[5]

Besieged by the French and betrayed by their own king, the defenders of Le Mans had now no option but to surrender. On 15 March 1448 Matthew Gough and Fulk Eyton reluctantly completed their commission and formally handed the town over to Charles VII. At the gates of Le Mans, however, they staged a final protest, declaring that they had surrendered only to secure the promised peace and that their action was no reflection on the validity of Henry VI's claim to sovereignty: if the French failed to fulfil their side of the bargain, then the English could legitimately resume possession of Le Mans. Their protestation was formally recorded and registered, and endorsed by Mundeford and the English captains who witnessed it.[6]

If Henry VI and his ambassadors had taken such an uncompromising view of the surrender of Maine, the future might have been very different. Instead of seeing it as a binding condition for peace, however, they had seen it as an expression of goodwill which might induce Charles to make peace. The naivety of Henry's secret undertaking was now exposed in all its folly as it secured nothing more than a two-year extension of the Truce of Tours until 1 April 1450, which Charles magnanimously granted on the day that Le Mans was surrendered to him.[7]

It would be the last concession he would ever make, for he had no intention of making a permanent peace. As he told the men of Reims just six months after regaining possession of Maine, he had already decided that he would recover Normandy as well.[8] In preparation for that end, throughout the period of the truce he had been employed in a series of military reforms which would transform his army. With the aid of his constable, Arthur de Richemont, who was the prime mover in the process, he had finally forced through some of the changes he had tried to make in 1439.

The *écorcheurs* were gone, having disbanded, joined the royal army or relocated to more profitable pastures such as Italy. The problem of soldiers left unemployed because of the truce had initially been dealt with by sending them off with the dauphin to Alsace. The following year, 1445, Charles and Richemont went a step further, creating from their ranks what became the first standing army in France. Fifteen captains chosen by the king were each put in charge of a company of one hundred 'lances', each 'lance' being a unit which actually consisted of four or five fighting men rather than a single man-at-arms. The companies were subjected to muster and review by royal marshals and were distributed in groups of lances around the regions. Originally it had been intended that they should be stationed within the walled towns and billeted on the inhabitants, but there was such local hostility that most of the *bonnes villes* obtained exemption by paying a tax instead. (This was in addition to the annual levy established in 1439 to pay the wages of the royal army.) The system proved so successful that it was extended throughout Languedoc the following year, creating a further five hundred lances at the constable's command.[9]

In April 1448, immediately after the surrender of Le Mans, another reform was instituted, creating a body known as the *francs-archers*. In return for exemption from certain taxes (hence the fact that they were called 'free') every community of between fifty and eighty households was now required to provide at its own expense one combatant, usually a crossbowman, to render military service in the royal army. The idea was to create a nationwide body of trained and well-equipped soldiers who could be quickly and easily mobilised when required. An inci- dental effect of their introduction was to give even rural villages and parishes a vested interest in Charles VII's military adven- tures: in future every corner of the country would have its representative in what was now emerging as a truly national army.[10]

No such measures had been taken in England or in Normandy, despite Suffolk's warnings to parliament in June 1445 that all the strongholds of the duchy should be rearmed, restocked and kept in a state of readiness for the resumption of war. Both the polit- ical will and the finances were lacking to put this into effect. There was nothing to be had from England, where Henry's mar- riage and the coronation of Queen Margaret had emptied what was left in the treasury. In the duchy the natural temptation to see the truce as an opportunity to pay less tax for defences which were not needed at the time was reflected in the decision of the estates-general, meeting at Rouen in the spring of 1447, to refuse a request for 100,000*l.t.* (£5.83m). Eventually, and only by a grudging majority vote, the representatives made a grant of just 30,000*l.t.* (£1.75m), obliging the government to impose an extra levy of 10,000*l.t.* (£583,333) by royal prerogative, which did not require their consent.[11]

The speed with which Charles VII had raised an army of six thousand men and moved against Le Mans shocked the English into action. Preparations were at long last put in place for Edmund Beaufort to cross from England to take up his appointment as lieutenant-general and governor of Normandy. On 31 January 1448, 'in case that war follows', Henry ordered the urgent recruitment of a thousand archers to accompany Beaufort to France. On 6 March, as arrangements were being made for the impressing of ships and mariners to convey him across the Channel, Henry authorised that Beaufort should receive the full £20,000 (£10.5m) annual payment due to him in time of war, instead of the half-payment he had received during the truce, because, the king explained, 'it is come to our knowledge that a great power and a mighty siege is laid before our town of Le Mans, and sharp war daily made to our subjects being therein, the which is no sign of peace, but a likelihood to the war'. An extra two hundred men-at-arms and two thousand archers were also added to the earl's company; significantly too Beaufort would be joined by his brother-in-law, John Talbot, who was recalled from his lieutenancy of Ireland for that purpose. At the end of the month, in anticipation of his new role in Normandy, Beaufort was raised to the rank of duke of Somerset and on 8 May 1448, a full fifteen months after his formal appointment, he finally made his official entry into Rouen.[12]

There had been no lieutenant-general resident in Normandy since York's departure in September 1445 and those two and a half years had seen a steady deterioration in the duchy's defences and administration. Only 2100 men were now stationed in garrisons, down from around 3500 before the truce began, a reduction in numbers dictated by the inability to secure higher grants of taxation from the estates-general to pay their wages. Not only did the soldiers have to contend with irregular and sometimes partial payments but also the terms of the truce denied them all the usual legitimate gains of war such as ransoms and booty.[13]

As a result many took the remedy into their own hands, supplementing their official pay as best they could. A detailed receipt for the wages for the last quarter of 1447 paid to the English captain of Coutances, in the southern Cotentin, offers some interesting insights into the state of the garrison there. His lieutenant, Robert Nytes esquire, had seven men-at-arms serving on foot and twenty-two archers under his command. In addition to substantial deductions for unexplained absences, defaulting on service and lacking equipment (one archer had no helmet on the day of muster), large amounts were also withheld for soldiers who did not reside in garrison as they were supposed to do: 30*l.* 6*s.* 8*d.t.* (£1769) was deducted for the wages of two archers who were said to run taverns, a profitable sideline when military wages were uncertain, though one of them was also described as a 'looter of the countryside'. The same amount was also deducted as half the wages of four other archers, Colin Frere, 'who lives in the countryside', Richard Clerc and Henry Havart, 'looters of the countryside and quarrelsome', and John Conway, 'also quarrelsome and living off the countryside'.[14]

That more than a quarter of the archers were not in residence and almost a fifth were pillagers is a striking indictment of the lack of discipline within the garrison. And, of course, they were not the only ones exploiting the neighbourhood. A couple of months later, in February 1448, the *vicomte* of Coutances paid the 6*l.t.* (£350) bounty to Lancelot Howell for bringing to justice a fellow Welshman described as a 'thief, looter, living off the countryside and keeping a great number of dogs at the expense and charge of the poor people'. Why he had the dogs is not explained, but it is possible that it was a hunting pack, enabling him to supplement his wages, or lack of them, with regular supplies of fresh meat.[15]

The problem of unemployed soldiers living off the land was even worse in the lawless frontier areas in the marches of Normandy and Brittany. In the summer of 1447 a large and efficiently led band was operating in the area. Unusually it was led by a member of the English aristocracy. Roger, lord Camoys, had been captured at Le Mans in October 1438 and spent nine years 'in hard prison' because he could not pay his ransom. Despite his title, he was a younger son, and the truce imposed during his captivity deprived him of the opportunity to restore his finances through the profits of war. On his release, therefore, he gathered round him 'a great assembly of soldiers' who were similarly 'unwaged' and, like others before him, made the fortified abbey of Savigny his base and lived off the land, indiscriminately pillaging and ransoming both in enemy territory and his own: the English lieutenant of Harcourt castle even went so far as to reinforce his garrison so that he could better defend the place against Camoys.

In August 1447 the company was in the Exmes region, where the *vicomte* ordered Camoys 'to leave immediately' and threatened to hang any soldiers who joined him. Camoys then moved on to Alençon, where his men were again ordered to abandon him, on pain of death, and by September he was at Saint-James-de-Beuvron, where he began to repair the dismantled fortifications to establish a new base. After several months of living off the land his activities were ended by Thomas Hoo, the chancellor of Normandy, who spent 100*l.t.* (£5833) hiring unemployed soldiers from Fresnay-le-Vicomte to 'suppress his damnable enterprises'. Whether there was an armed confrontation or indeed what happened to Camoys is unclear, though he would later serve with distinction as the last English seneschal of Gascony, suggesting that his rank as a banneret had saved him from serious punishment for his earlier misdemeanours. Many of his men found their way to Le Mans, where they were said to have assisted in the town's defence during the siege, though the reviewer of Gough and Eyton's troops at the end of November 1447 was explicitly ordered to ensure that no men-at-arms or archers associated with Camoys had been employed by the English commissioners.[16]

When Beaufort arrived in the duchy in May 1448 he determined to address some of these problems, holding a simultaneous duchy-wide muster to find out the state of the garrisons and

launching a major drive against corruption among royal officials. His inspectors had the power to scrutinise accounts and
receipts and to fine or imprison offenders. As a result of their
inquiries Beaufort decided to abolish the post of local receivers of
taxes (the customary perquisite of their employment was cream-
ing off a proportion of the money collected) and fined or sacked
officials found guilty of fraud or corruption.[17]

Beaufort's desire to put his house in order did nothing to halt
the rapid decline in relations between the duchy and its neighbours. Though he would later be blamed for this, in reality there
was probably little he could have done: Charles VII was determined to find fault so that he could renew the war when he was
ready to do so. On 22 August 1448 he sent his nephew a long
list of complaints about the behaviour of 'those who are on this
side of the sea', insinuating that things had deteriorated since the
advent of the new lieutenant-general. In particular he accused
Mundeford and some of the other refugees from Maine of seizing and rebuilding the fortress of Saint-James-de-Beuvron,
'which borders on the frontier of Brittany, Mont-Saint-Michel,
Granville and other disputed places', in contravention of the
terms of the truce.[18]

Though it was debatable whether or not Saint-James-de-
Beuvron belonged to the English, refortifying an abandoned
stronghold was unquestionably a breach of the truce. Charles VII
made much of this issue but what he really objected to was not so
much the offence as Beaufort's handling of it. Hoo had acted
decisively to stop Camoys rebuilding the place. Beaufort simply
referred the matter to Moleyns and Roos, 'who had greater
knowledge of the truce than he had', and sent Mundeford himself
to seek them out in Brittany, where they were on another diplomatic mission. Mundeford, not surprisingly, displayed little
enthusiasm for his task and gave up when he did not find them
where he had expected to do so.

Charles also complained that Beaufort had compounded his
fault by his arrogant behaviour: he had allegedly threatened to
withdraw the safe-conducts and arrest Charles's envoys, Raoul
de Gaucourt and Guillaume Cousinot, while they were in Rouen

seeking redress. He had also 'with too much arrogance or ignorance' disrespectfully addressed letters to Charles himself as 'the most high and powerful prince, the uncle in France of the king, my sovereign lord'. This was, as Charles pointed out, a far cry from the former lieutenant-general's flowery 'very high, very excellent, and very powerful prince and very formidable lord' – but then York had been a suppliant seeking a marriage alliance, not a king's lieutenant dealing with alleged breaches of a truce.[19]

That Charles's complaints were largely manufactured for negotiating purposes is evident not only in his avowed intention to regain Normandy, declared only a few weeks later, but also in his response to accusations that his own men had 'seized many places, both in the Caux region and in Maine, and that they have committed numerous murders and robberies' on Henry's subjects. Charles explained this away with the answer that 'with regard to the places seized, none can be found except in disputed territory or where there is disagreement', an argument that also applied to Saint-James-de-Beuvron. His excuse for issuing pardons to malefactors, such as brigands hiding in woods, was equally disingenuous: they had not been given 'because he regarded or held them to be his subjects or obedient to him, but to remove them from their evil and damnable way of life'.[20]

It is abundantly clear that there were violations of the truce on both sides. Saint-James-de-Beuvron, as a border fortress, features regularly in accusations by the English against the men of Mont-Saint-Michel. In February 1447 they were 'by subtle means' imprisoning and imposing fines on Norman subjects; a few months later an inquiry was held into their having seized Richard Holland at Saint-James-de-Beuvron and put him to death. In September they carried off cattle being driven from Brittany to the English garrison of Avranches and in the same month Charles VII pardoned a man who had served at least twenty years in the garrison at Mont-Saint-Michel, during which time he had both waged war against the English and, sometimes working alone, sometimes with his fellow soldiers, acquired large quantities of booty by robbing, pillaging, ransoming and battering those on his own side, including clergymen.[21]

Not all acts of violence and breaches of the truce were committed by individuals or groups acting on their own volition. The agreement allowing clergymen to resume possession of their revenues from lands 'in the other obedience' caused endless trouble in practice and resulted in a series of tit-for-tat confiscations by the state. The abbey of Mont-Saint-Michel was soon in dispute with the English authorities over its rights to collect its customary revenues in Normandy. In September 1448 Beaufort ordered the *bailli* of the Cotentin to seize all 'fruits, profits, revenues and emoluments' from clergymen 'of our uncle's party' as a response to Charles's having prevented the collection of, and appropriated, similar monies in his territories belonging to Norman churchmen. This was evidently a particular problem in the wider Cotentin region because the following March Charles ordered to be taken into his hands all those lands, property, rents and revenues within his jurisdiction belonging to the bishops and cathedral chapters of Coutances and Avranches and the abbots of Savigny, Montmorel and La Luzerne.[22]

This sort of action was not just aggravating for those involved: it was indicative of an escalating tension and hostility which neither side addressed. Henry VI responded to his uncle's catalogue of complaints by referring them back to Beaufort, saying it was impossible to deal with such matters at a distance, but also secretly instructing his lieutenant-general to spin out the negotiations for as long as he could without actually causing a rupture with France. Meetings between the ambassadors of both sides in November failed to achieve any advance towards a permanent peace settlement, only an agreement to meet again for further discussions before 15 May 1449.[23] By that time, however, England and France were already unofficially at war.

Beaufort had seen this coming and had sent Thomas Hoo, the chancellor of Normandy, and Reginald Boulers, abbot of Gloucester, a member of his council at Rouen, to make an appeal on his behalf to the parliament which opened on 12 February 1449 at Westminster. There is no indication whether the speech was composed by Beaufort and his advisers or by the abbot, who made the presentation before both houses, but it was cogently and powerfully argued, presenting three main points.

> The first is to show the great and well equipped army of the enemy, provided with all manner of military gear. The enemy daily fortify, repair, and reinforce all their garrisons on the frontiers of the king's obedience, moving about and riding within the said obedience, armed in large numbers, contrary to the tenor of the truces, committing innumerable murders and taking the king's subjects prisoners, just as if it was full war, along with other great and lamentable injuries, such as countless public robberies, oppressions and plunders.

Beaufort had summoned them many times to answer for their violations of the truce and required them to cease, but he had had neither remedy nor reasonable answer: 'wherefore it may be supposed, by their perverse deeds and contrary disposition, that their intention is not to proceed effectively to any good conclusion of peace'. Further evidence of this was that Charles had ordered all noblemen to arm, equip and hold themselves in readiness to answer a summons to war within fifteen days, on pain of forfeiture, and had recruited in excess of sixty thousand *francs-archers* whom he 'expressly ordered that they do nothing other than exercise with their said bows and armour'.

> The second part is to show that if war should occur, which God forbid, the country of Normandy is in no way sufficient in itself to offer resistance against the great might of the enemies, for many great reasons. First, there is no place in the king's obedience there which is provided for either in terms of repairs, equipment, or any kind of artillery. Almost all places have fallen into such ruin that, even where they are full of men and materials, they are in so ruinous a condition that they cannot be defended and held. To make adequate provision for such repairs and equipment would incur inestimable expense.

The last meeting of the estates-general in Normandy had declared the impossibility of levying future grants because of the general poverty of the duchy, the abbot told parliament: the only alternatives left to the lieutenant-general were that the number of soldiers would have to be reduced, money would have to come from England or the land would have to be abandoned to the enemy.

For his final point the abbot drew attention to the fast-approaching deadline for the end of the truce: 'it will last for only fourteen months more, and therefore it is thought that it is now the right and necessary time to begin your provision for the safeguard of that noble land'. He ended with an emotional appeal from Beaufort himself

> to have that noble land in your good and special remembrance, calling to mind the great, inestimable, and well nigh infinite cost and expenditure both of goods and blood that this land has borne and suffered for the sake of that land; the shameful loss of it, which God forever forbid, would not only be to the irreparable damage of the common benefit, but also an everlasting slur, and permanent denigration of the fame and renown of this noble realm.[24]

Beaufort's appeal fell on deaf ears. Parliament had heard all this many times before and had become inured to such dire prophecies. It sounded unnecessarily alarmist: after all, the truce was still holding and there was no reason to assume it would not be extended again. There was also an increasing divergence of interest between those Englishmen who held lands in France and those who did not. The men who sat in both houses of parliament no longer had the same level of investment in, or commitment to, England's territories in northern France.

Throughout Henry V's reign and indeed until Bedford's death many members of parliament were veterans of the war in France. Many knights of the shire and an even higher proportion of peers had taken part in military campaigns and could claim to have fought at Agincourt or Verneuil. Some had benefited from the conquest by acquiring lands which, after the ending of the Anglo-Burgundian alliance and the recent cession of Maine, had been lost again: the promised compensation never materialised, the French rebate on *appâtis* being swallowed up by the Norman defence budget. Others, who had spent years in France and acquired valuable lands and properties there, had returned to England to invest their profits and pick up the threads of their political and social life.

Sir John Fastolf is a prime and well-documented example of a man from the ranks of the minor gentry who rose to high office and made his fortune through the war in France. From his profits of war he had invested £13,885 (£7.29m) in purchasing property and £9495 (£4.98m) in improving it – but it was all French money spent in England. In 1445 the annual income from his English lands was £1061 (£557,025), compared with £401 (£210,525) from his French lands, a sum that would substantially reduce after the surrender of Maine, where much of his property lay. Despite having fought almost continuously in France since 1412, he never returned there after his retirement to England in 1439. Though he remained passionately committed to the preservation of English possessions in France, and spent much of his old age raging against the ineptitude of English policy there, he had become an absentee landlord and captain.[25] Fastolf's enrichment as a result of his military career was exceptional but his experience was not. There were few old soldiers among the gentry who did not wish to return home for their final years.

But a growing proportion of the knights of the shires had never seen active service in France, let alone acquired lands or offices there. As the opportunity for enrichment declined, so did the attractions of volunteering for campaign duties, resulting in an increasing difficulty in recruiting men-at-arms for the expeditionary forces. It was not that they had no interest in maintaining English lands overseas, just that they had other priorities at home and a pardonable belief that those who had benefited from the conquest should be the first to defend it. The attitude was not new but, for the first time in twenty-five years, the circumstances were. Beaufort and his colleagues in Normandy had seen the dangers of a resurgent French militarism: their compatriots in England did not. The consequences would be fatal for what remained of the English kingdom of France.

CHAPTER TWENTY-FOUR

The Truce Breaks Down

In France the violations of the truce became daily more blatant. On 28 February 1449 Beaufort wrote to Charles VII complaining that since the previous August Robert de Floques and his garrison at Louviers had committed a number of outrages, attacking shipping on the Seine, seizing wine worth 800 *l.t.* (£46,667) and raiding the village of Quévreville, near Pont-de-l'Arche, where they had beaten the inhabitants, calling them false traitors and English dogs, and badly damaged their property. The men of Mont-Saint-Michel and Granville were no better, 'daily committing infinite crimes, murders, robberies, seizing labourers whom they seek out at night ten or twelve leagues away from their bases, putting them to ransom, as they still do, just as if it were war-time and open war at that'.[1]

Worse still, because it was a deliberately planned attack rather than opportunism or the result of a lack of discipline, was a raid led by the men of Dieppe on 25 February, Shrove Tuesday, the last day of feasting before the abstinence of Lent. Between 160 and 180 men, 'armed and armoured as if in time of war', had ridden into the parish of Torcy-le-Grand, ten miles south-west of Dieppe, where an important meeting of royal officials was being held. They had taken a large number of them prisoner, among them the lieutenant-general and the procurator of the *bailli* of Caux, the lieutenant of the *vicomte* of Arques and, most spectacularly of all, Simon Morhier, the royal councillor who had been provost of Paris until the expulsion of the English in 1436, who was there on private business of his own. Two men were killed in the incident and the rest, including some who were wounded, were taken and imprisoned in the dungeon at Dieppe 'as if it were time of war'.[2]

Though Beaufort acknowledged that there had been some provocation in that Norman officials had arrested men from Dieppe, a matter that was being investigated by his conservators of the truce, such action was inexcusable. Since Charles also had cause for complaint in that the English were refortifying Saint-James-de-Beuvron and Mortain, envoys were sent by both sides to attempt to resolve the issues.[3]

Before any conclusions could be reached, however, there was another major breach of the truce, this time by the English. On 24 March 1449 François de Surienne seized the town and castle of Fougères in the marches of Brittany, close to the Norman border. On the face of it this was simply the independent action of a foreign mercenary captain. Fougères was a wealthy trading town which Surienne thoroughly plundered, earning himself booty alleged to be worth 2,000,000 *l.t.* (£116.67m), before installing himself and his men in the castle and preying on the wider district, levying *appâtis*, taking prisoners and 'generally carrying out all the customary exploits of waging war'. When an indignant duke of Brittany sent his herald to Normandy and England, demanding reparation and to know on whose authority this had been done, both Beaufort and Suffolk denied all knowledge and disavowed the action.[4]

This was completely untrue. The capture of Fougères had been carefully planned in London at least fifteen months earlier. According to Surienne's account of the whole affair, written in March 1450, the idea had actually been mooted as long ago as the summer of 1446. In June of that year, under pressure from Prégent de Coëtivy, one of a group of highly influential Bretons

at the royal court, Charles VII had ordered the duke of Brittany
to arrest his Anglophile brother, Gilles, on charges of conspiring
with the English. There was some basis for this allegation as
Gilles held an English pension and had been an important advocate of English alliance at a time when the duke himself was
more inclined towards the French: Gilles may even have hoped
that English arms would restore him to the lands he claimed
from his brother. The English administration in Normandy had
certainly provided him with a bodyguard in the weeks before his
arrest and warned him of plots against him. When he was
imprisoned official protests were made and consideration given
to his rescue: Surienne claimed that 'Matthew Gough and others
were urgent to have Thomassin du Quesne, my scaling-master,
and others of my people to find a way of liberating my lord
Gilles of Brittany.' Suffolk, however, had suggested an alternative
plan to Surienne's marshal at Verneuil who just happened to be
in England at the time: that his master, who was renowned for
similar exploits, should capture Fougères so that it could be
traded for Gilles's freedom. He offered assurances that Surienne
would not suffer any consequences as a result.[5]

Suffolk's choice of Fougères was probably dictated not just by
its wealth and its location close to the Norman border but also
by the fact that it had formerly belonged to Jean, duke of
Alençon. In order to raise funds for his ransom after his capture
at Verneuil in 1424, Alençon had reluctantly mortgaged it to the
duke of Brittany for 80,000 *écus* (£5.83m) and had never forgiven Charles VII for refusing to assist him in getting it back.
Since his involvement in the Praguerie revolt Alençon had been
cold-shouldered by his king and had made several overtures to
the English. In the summer of 1440, for instance, he had sought
military aid from the seneschal of Gascony for his rebellion.
The following summer he had sent his personal pursuivant to
Argentan to warn the captain that the castle-keep had been sold
and betrayed by the English and to give him a list of the traitors'
names so that he could arrest them. It was in Suffolk's interest to
please Alençon and it was in Alençon's interest to take Fougères
from Brittany. Though there is no hard evidence for his

complicity, at least one of Alençon's agents is known to have been in touch with Surienne.[6]

Perhaps testing the water, Surienne said that he could not carry out the scheme without a base in the marches of lower Normandy. Suffolk obliged by persuading lord Fastolf to surrender his castle of Condé-sur-Noireau, some fifty miles north-west of Fougères. As an added inducement Suffolk offered Surienne the most prestigious gift in the king's hands: an invitation to become a knight of the Order of the Garter in place of John Holland, earl of Huntingdon and duke of Exeter, who died in August 1447. For an Aragonese soldier of fortune this was an honour which could not be turned down. His installation on 8 December 1447 provided a convenient cover for him to travel to England to discuss the Fougères scheme in person with Suffolk and with Beaufort, whose appointment as lieutenant-general was about to be confirmed. Reassured of their support, Surienne returned to Normandy and over the course of the following year sent his spies into Fougères to ascertain the state of its defences, and gathered support and intelligence for his enterprise by visiting the garrisons of lower Normandy under the guise of a joint commission with Talbot from Beaufort to muster and review the troops.[7]

In the light of these actions the deployment of Mundeford and the troops withdrawn from Maine to Saint-James-de-Beuvron takes on a more sinister interpretation. The dismantled fortress lay just fourteen miles north-west of Fougères. Perhaps as a result of Charles VII's many complaints about the rebuilding at Saint-James-de-Beuvron and neighbouring Mortain, Beaufort took fright at the last minute and on 26 February 1449 sent his herald to Surienne forbidding him to launch an attack without Henry VI's express command. He was informed in no uncertain terms that Surienne's plans were too far advanced for him to withdraw. Some six hundred troops had been gathered at Condé-sur-Noireau; Thomassin du Quesne had brought his scaling ladders there, and the long pincers and other instruments Surienne needed to break open the gate-fastenings at Fougères, which Beaufort had personally ordered a suspicious workman in Rouen to make, were ready.

Surienne gave the signal to depart on 23 March 1449, setting off in the direction of Avranches to deceive the French spies he knew would be watching, before heading under cover of night for his genuine destination. The next day, at around two in the morning, part of his company scaled the town walls while the rest took the castle by surprise. The operation was, militarily at least, a complete triumph. A relieved Beaufort sent his congratulations, together with bows, arrows, gunpowder and culverins to restock the castle, and ordered Surienne to keep his troops in a state of readiness and await further orders from Talbot.[8]

The capture of Fougères became notorious as the cause of the resumption of war between England and France. In itself, however, it was not sufficient reason for restarting hostilities, not least because the quarrel should have been between England and Brittany. But the incident played straight into the hands of Charles VII. Just as he had done with the cession of Maine, he took up the dispute on behalf of the duke, and turned it into a matter touching on his personal honour as king.

When challenged by a Breton envoy, Surienne had made it clear that he had not been acting independently: 'I have the power to take but not to give back,' he said, then, drawing attention to his Garter insignia which he wore prominently displayed, 'do not ask me any more. Do you not see well enough that I am of the order of the Garter? And that should be sufficient for you!'[9]

At first the matter was treated just like any violation of a truce. The duke of Brittany demanded Fougères's return and reparation and when this was not forthcoming, appealed to Charles VII, who took up his cause with enthusiasm. Charles wrote to Beaufort formally demanding satisfaction for the seizure of Fougères but he also gave his tacit approval for retaliatory action. His choice for its execution fell on Robert de Floques, the maverick captain of Évreux, who, on 21 April, carried out a sabre-rattling raid to the gates of Mantes, thirty miles away, threatening to take it by assault. When the English conservators of the truce objected Charles's representatives airily disclaimed all knowledge and said that Floques had acted without royal orders but in response to the general outrage at the English capture of Fougères.[10]

Early in May, however, with no breakthrough in the deadlock over Fougères, Floques carried out a more spectacular coup with the aid of Jean de Brézé, the Breton captain of Louviers. Guillaume Hoel, a merchant who daily travelled the seven-mile road between Louviers and Pont-de-l'Arche, informed them that the latter town was poorly guarded and suggested a plan to take it. On a designated day the two captains sent a number of their men, one after another to avoid detection, to an inn in the suburbs where Hoel was due to make a call. That night Floques and Brézé hid several hundred soldiers in ambush around the town.

Just before daybreak, having taken the innkeeper prisoner and loaded up a wagon with wine, two of them, disguised as carpenters, accompanied Hoel to the drawbridge of the town. Hoel hailed the porter, saying he was in great haste, and offered him money to let him in. The porter lowered the drawbridge but, as he bent down to pick up a coin Hoel had artfully dropped, the merchant killed him with his dagger. The two 'carpenters' were already on the second bridge and had killed a second Englishman who had been summoned to assist the porter.

With the entrance to Pont-de-l'Arche now open and unguarded, Floques and Brézé sprang the ambush, pouring their men into the town. Significantly, instead of using their usual French battle cry of 'Saint-Denis!', they shouted 'Saint-Yves! Brittany!', making it clear that this was revenge for the taking of Fougères. It was arguably also a way of avoiding a French breach of the truce, since it was not an act of war committed in the name of France. They took the town with ease, since most of its inhabitants were still asleep, and acquired between a hundred and 120 prisoners, including lord Fauconberg, who had unluckily chosen to spend the night there. Hesitating to surrender to a humble archer, he was so seriously wounded that he almost died and was carried off to Louviers, remaining a prisoner in French hands for three years. A few days later Floques and Brézé reprised their success, taking the neighbouring strongholds of Conches, where 'the town [was captured] by surprise and

treason, the castle by composition [agreement to surrender]',
and Gerberoy, 'seized by subtle means very early in the morning'
in the absence of its captain; all thirty Englishmen found in the
latter place were put to death.[11]

Pont-de-l'Arche was a town of enormous strategic importance, being widely considered the gateway to lower Normandy.
Its loss, and the capture of such an experienced captain as
Fauconberg, were major blows to the English administration in
Normandy: Beaufort was said by one observer to have looked as
though he had been hit by a thunderbolt when he received the
news. Though he vowed to recover Pont-de-l'Arche immediately, he got no further than a show of force, sending Talbot
with 'a great number of soldiers' to Pont-Audemer, some thirty
miles west of the lost town. Even Talbot dared not risk a military
confrontation, however, as this would have ended any hope of
patching up the truce.[12]

Talbot had already sent William Gloucester, master of the king's
ordnance, to England before the fall of Pont-de-l'Arche. Beaufort's
plea to parliament in February having gained no response,
Gloucester was charged with reinforcing the message that
Normandy was in desperate need of money, men and munitions.
The English garrisons were becoming mutinous because they were
unpaid. Jean Lampet, the captain of Avranches, had been obliged
to resort to drastic measures: with his men threatening to leave
unless paid and unable to get messengers through to Rouen
because of the dangers of the road, he forcibly took 2170*l.t.*
(£126,583) from the tax-receiver for the *vicomté* – though he did
give him a receipt for the full amount. Richard Harington, the
bailli of Caen, also used the threat of violence against his clerk of
the general receipts to get 600*l.t.* (£35,000) to pay the reinforcements he had brought in for the town's defence.[13]

That men of their calibre should be forced to such means to
obtain their legitimate wages was an indication of the dire state
of the Norman finances. Beaufort had summoned a meeting of
the estates-general in May to secure the garrison wages: originally due to meet at Caen, it was transferred to Rouen as Beaufort
was reluctant to leave the city in the escalating crisis. The news

of the capture of Pont-de-l'Arche came while it was in session, prompting the assembly to grant a general aid, and on 2 June Osbern Mundeford, now the Norman treasurer, issued the orders for its collection.[14]

The same news also prompted Suffolk to agree to send Beaufort and Talbot reinforcements of one hundred men-at-arms and twelve hundred archers: they were ordered to muster in unusually short time on 11 June at Portsmouth and Suffolk intimated to the council in Rouen that he would accompany them himself. Without funds, however, he was in difficulty. According to an assessment presented to parliament earlier in the year, the king was already £372,000 (£195.3m) in debt, 'which is a great and grievous sum'. As Henry was as profligate with his gifts as he was with his distribution of titles, his annual income of £5000 (£2.63m) fell far short of what he spent: his household alone cost him £24,000 (£12.6m) a year.[15] In the circumstances it was not surprising that he had nothing to spare for Normandy or that parliament was unwilling to grant him more taxes. It was not until 16 July, after heated argument, that the House of Commons reluctantly increased the half-subsidy it had granted earlier to a whole tenth and fifteenth. It was to be collected over two years and, strikingly, none of the money was earmarked for the defence of Normandy.[16]

Throughout May and June the conservators of the truce had been continuing their negotiations over Fougères, their meetings being augmented by various embassies in which Guillaume Cousinot, who had been so heavily involved in the surrender of Maine, again played a leading role. Beaufort had steadfastly refused to offer restitution and compensation, probably because he was determined to carry out the original plan to exchange Fougères for Gilles of Brittany. In this he almost succeeded. Arthur de Richemont persuaded Charles VII that Gilles's continuing imprisonment might cause trouble in Brittany and that his liberation would facilitate the restoration of Fougères. Charles therefore sent Prégent de Coëtivy back to the duke, who at first agreed to release his brother but then, at the very last minute, on 30 May 1449, suddenly countermanded his order.[17]

His decision is probably to be explained by another act of English aggression, committed just a week earlier by Robert Wynnington, a Devonshire esquire, who had contracted to serve the king on the sea 'for the cleansing of the same and rebuking of the robbers and pirates thereof, which daily do all the nuisance they can'. Instead of attacking the French and Breton pirates who preyed on English merchant shipping in the Channel and whose activities had been a constant cause of complaint for decades, on 23 April Wynnington captured the entire fleet of ships – over one hundred of them – carrying Breton salt from the Bay of Bourgneuf and brought them to the Isle of Wight. This was a major diplomatic incident, both because the Breton salt trade was extremely valuable and much of Europe depended on it for the preservation of meat and fish, and the ships were sailing under the friendly flags of the Hanseatic League, the Dutch and the Flemish.[18]

It was an action that was typical of the lack of coordination between the governments of England and Normandy and it exacerbated an already tense and delicate situation. Together with English intransigence over reparations for the seizure of Fougères, it drove the duke of Brittany into the arms of Charles VII: less than a month later they concluded an offensive and defensive alliance and the duke began to make his preparations for war.[19]

Our accounts of the final breakdown of the negotiations all come from the French side and are understandably partisan. They include the résumé compiled in July 1449 to justify Charles's declaration that the truce was irreparably broken and an account written in the 1460s when Louis XI was trying to subsume Brittany within the French state.[20]

According to them, and the French chroniclers to whom the 1449 résumé was circulated, Beaufort perversely and obstinately refused all demands for the restoration of Fougères, thereby putting himself in breach of the truce; he likewise refused the reasonable final offer put to him on 4 July, that if he returned Fougères and all its former contents or their value by 25 July, then within fifteen days Charles would do the same for Pont-de-l'Arche, Conches and Gerberoy and release lord Fauconberg. This all sounds very like the propaganda issued by Henry V in 1415 when he was trying to justify his decision to go to war to enforce his 'just rights and inheritances' against an 'unreasonable' and 'obdurate' opponent.

The 1449 résumé reveals the fact that Beaufort made counter-offers, though not what they were, and that he fell back on the standard delaying tactic of referring back to the king for further instruction. More importantly it shows that he sought to have the matter of the sovereignty over Brittany treated as an 'open question' and therefore set aside from any agreement that might be reached. This was a sensible option since the sovereignty belonged to the king of France and both Charles VII and Henry VI claimed that title: over the years since the Treaty of Troyes the dukes of Brittany had done homage to both kings, most recently to Charles VII on 16 March 1446.[21]

Suffolk's failure to include Brittany in the list of English allies when signing the Truce of Tours in 1444 had been remedied by the Treaty of Lavardin in 1448 – though not, as in the ridiculous account compiled in the 1460s, because the English deviously arranged for the treaty to be signed at midnight, without the aid of candles, at the bottom of a ditch at Le Mans, thus deceiving the French envoys in the darkness. In the 1449 negotiations Beaufort evidently tried to use the argument that Brittany was subject to Henry VI to claim that the seizure of Fougères was an action against his own subject and therefore not a violation of the truce with France. Charles responded by angrily insisting that he had always and indisputably enjoyed sovereignty over Brittany: to turn it into an 'open question' impugned his right to do so, 'which is a matter of the highest importance, and one which touches the king nearer than almost any other that can arise in this realm'. It was, he alleged in his résumé of events, proof that Beaufort had no real wish to proceed to a settlement at all. It gave him his excuse to turn a truce violation into a cause for war.[22]

Beaufort seems to have had no idea that anything other than the usual tortuous diplomatic negotiations were taking place: after all, if the French complained that the seizure of Fougères was in violation of the truce, so also was the taking of Pont-de-l'Arche, Conches and Gerberoy. He also seems to have been unaware, despite a spy system that had always been efficient in the past, that Charles was merely using the conferences as a cover for his final preparations for the invasion of Normandy. Several great armies were now gathering on the frontiers of the duchy to launch a three-pronged attack: from Brittany into lower Normandy, led by the duke and his uncle Arthur de Richemont; through the centre, under the command of the Bastard of Orléans, assisted by the duke of Alençon from his base in Anjou; and from Picardy into upper Normandy, led by the counts of Eu and Saint-Pol.

The fact that Louis, count of Saint-Pol, had assumed a commanding role in the French army was significant. The house of Luxembourg had been a mainstay of Bedford's last years as regent of France and after his death its members had refused to take up arms against the English. Jehan de Luxembourg died in January 1441 never having taken the oath to the Treaty of Arras, and in September of that year Jehan's nephew, Louis, count of Saint-Pol, who had served in Charles VII's army during the siege of Pontoise, was permitted to return home early to avoid having to participate in the final assault. Now, however, his ties with the English administration long since severed, he volunteered to raise troops for the invasion.[23]

That he did so with the approval of his feudal overlord, Philippe of Burgundy, was also noteworthy. The duke had maintained peace with both England and France since 1439 but Wynnington's capture of the Bay fleet in May 1449 had alienated him as much as it had the duke of Brittany because Dutch and Flemish vessels had been taken. Burgundy responded by arresting English merchants in his territories, confiscating their goods and sending four warships to patrol the coast of Normandy and Brittany. He refused to be drawn into Charles VII's invasion plans, but he did permit him to recruit volunteers in Burgundian dominions.[24]

Even before the formal declaration of war another major English bastion fell to a combination of treachery and force. A miller from Verneuil, who had been beaten for falling asleep on night-watch, took his revenge by travelling the twenty-four miles to Évreux to offer his services to Robert de Floques and Pierre de Brézé. On 20 July, when he was next on duty, he persuaded his fellow night-watchmen to leave early because it was Sunday and they needed to get to mass. He then showed the waiting French where his mill adjoined the town walls and helped them place their scaling ladders there. They were able to enter unseen and take the town by surprise; some of the garrison fled to the castle but the next morning the miller diverted the waters from the moat, enabling the French to take it by assault.

The remaining English, together with around thirty of the leading townsmen, retreated into the last stronghold, the Grey Tower, which was strongly fortified and surrounded by a moat but lacked a suitable stock of provisions. That same day the Bastard of Orléans, newly appointed as the king's lieutenant for war, arrived at Verneuil at the head of his army and surrounded the tower. The besieged had already sent an urgent appeal for assistance to Talbot and Mundeford, who set out from Rouen at the head of a relief column, expecting only to encounter the French who had taken Verneuil. It was therefore a shock when, as they neared Harcourt, they saw the Bastard and his massive army gathering to intercept them. Talbot quickly drew up his wagons into a circle, placed his men inside the makeshift fortification and refused to be drawn into battle. When night fell he retreated under cover of darkness into the castle at Harcourt. Hopelessly outnumbered and outgunned, Talbot had no option but to return to Rouen, leaving the defenders of the Grey Tower to their fate.[25]

There was a poetic justice in the fact that the town and castle of Verneuil were captured while the Truce of Tours was still in force. The captain of the place was none other than François de Surienne, who was now at Fougères, and both his lieutenant, his nephew Jean de Surienne, and his scaling-master, Thomassin du Quesne, were among the defenders of the Grey Tower.

The seizure of Verneuil – and indeed the Bastard of Orléans's bringing an army into the duchy – were yet more infringements

of the truce which Beaufort could cite in the long catalogue of
violations by both sides. There was, however, little point. On 31
July 1449 his envoys were summoned into Charles VII's presence
at his castle of Roches-Tranchelion: they were obliged to listen to
a recitation of the faults committed by the English administration in Normandy since Beaufort's arrival and then officially
informed that as a result Charles found himself 'completely and
honourably freed and discharged' from his obligation to keep
the truce. It was a declaration of war.[26]

With impressive speed and efficiency the invasion of Normandy
now began in earnest. The counts of Eu and Saint-Pol invaded
from the east, crossing the Seine at Pont-de-l'Arche: on 8 August
they captured the small castle of Nogent-Pré, the garrison capitu-
lating after a brief assault. They were allowed to march out,
leaving their arms behind them, and the castle itself was destroyed
by fire. On 12 August they joined forces with the Bastard,
Gaucourt and Xaintrailles, who had brought two thousand men
from Évreux, to surround Pont-Audemer, a small but important
hub-town thirty-two miles west of Rouen, not far from Honfleur
and Pont-l'Évêque.

The town had evidently been selected both for its position
and the fact that its defences were poor, in part at least consisting of just wooden palisades. Without pausing to lay siege, the
French attacked, hurling fire into the town and forcing their
horses through the moats in water up to their saddles. They
swiftly carried the town by assault but then faced unexpected
resistance. What they did not know was that a few days earlier
Fulk Eyton and Osbern Mundeford had brought reinforcements
into Pont-Audemer. After fierce hand-to-hand fighting in the
streets the English were eventually overwhelmed by numbers
and retreated into a stone house at the end of the town. The
Bastard then led an assault on this last stronghold and, faced
with the prospect of all his men being massacred, Eyton formally surrendered, handing over his sword to the Bastard on the
stairs of the house. Twenty-two Burgundian esquires were
knighted as a result of this exploit.[27]

From Pont-Audemer the triumphant armies turned west,

heading for Lisieux but taking in Pont-l'Évêque, which surrendered at their approach when its garrison fled. Lisieux proved
equally faint-hearted. Its bishop was the chronicler Thomas
Basin, who had led a peripatetic childhood when his parents
fled before Henry V's invading armies. They had returned to
their native Caudebec in 1419, only to be driven out again some
twenty years later by the 'horrifying tyranny' of Fulk Eyton, 'an
abominable Englishman and ferocious brigand' whose men were
not his inferior in wickedness, according to Basin. While his
parents had taken up residence in Rouen, Basin himself had not
returned to Normandy until 1441, spending the intervening
years training as a canon lawyer in Paris, Louvain and Italy.
Having decided that the English conquest was going to be permanent, he came back to take up a post at the new university at
Caen, rising to become the rector, and finally earning his eleva-
tion to a bishopric in 1447.[28]

Basin had no stomach for a fight. When the French hosts
approached he held a town council meeting and undertook to
negotiate a surrender. His years of legal training evidently paid
off, for he succeeded in obtaining permission for the English
garrison to withdraw with all its belongings and for himself,
the cathedral chapter and inhabitants to remain in possession of
all their lands, properties and goods. The price he paid was that
Lisieux became subject to Charles VII, together with seven
dependent castles and fortresses in the neighbourhood, including
Orbec, the head of the *vicomté*. At a single stroke, and without
striking a blow, the Bastard had subjugated the whole district. It
was certainly a clean and efficient way to conquer.[29]

Basin's cooperation was richly rewarded. Twelve days after
surrendering Lisieux he did homage to Charles VII at Verneuil
and was appointed a member of the great council with an
annual pension of 1000*l.t.* (£58,333). Charles was equally generous to the townsmen of Verneuil who had opposed him. On
23 August the Grey Tower had surrendered. Even without
Talbot's supplies its defenders had managed to hold out for
another five weeks, but when they finally capitulated, through
lack of food, only thirty men were found inside. Most of these

were Normans who had supported the English regime, for whom the humiliating term 'French renegades' was now coined. Jean de Surienne, displaying the family resourcefulness and perhaps employing the skills of his scaling-master, had taken advantage of a negligent night-watch to escape, together with most of the other defenders and anything of value left in the tower. Despite his annoyance at this turn of events, Charles magnanimously pardoned all the 'renegades' who had taken refuge in the tower, a gesture designed to win over his future subjects. The pardon, incidentally, mentions by name three men, two officials, the *vicomte* and *grênetier* of Verneuil, and Robin du Val, who were 'the cause and means of the capture', suggesting that there were wider ramifications to the betrayal than simply a disgruntled miller.[30]

Charles's presence at Verneuil was no accident. The scene of Bedford's victory in 1424, the greatest French defeat in battle since Agincourt, had become the first place he would choose to enter in triumph as king of a France that would soon include the duchy of Normandy.

CHAPTER TWENTY-FIVE

Reconquest

Once the reconquest began it seems to have acquired a momentum of its own. On 26 August the combined armies of the Bastard of Orléans and the counts of Eu and Saint-Pol appeared before Mantes. Summoned to yield, several hundred of the inhabitants crammed into the town hall to hear an address urging them to do so by their mayor, who had refused to take the oath of allegiance on his inauguration in November 1444 on the grounds that the truce was in force. They unanimously agreed 'that a way should be found, without having to suffer the destruction of the town by cannon or otherwise, to obtain a good composition, the most advantageous and honourable that could be had'.[1]

Since Thomas Hoo's lieutenant showed signs of wishing to resist, some of the townsmen seized one of the fortified gates and insisted they would open it if he did, forcing him to agree to the surrender. According to the terms of capitulation, the garrison and all those of any nationality who wished to leave were given safe-conducts allowing them to do so, taking their goods but no weapons or armour with them. Those who remained and swore allegiance to Charles were to be confirmed in their property, positions, liberties and privileges 'as they were before the descent of the late king Henry of England'.[2]

The surrender of Lisieux and Mantes set the pattern for the coming campaign. Most walled towns, when forced to choose between capitulation on generous terms which maintained the status quo, and being assaulted and probably losing everything, sensibly chose the former. Often, if the garrison chose to resist, the inhabitants either rose up and forced them to submit or made their own overtures to their besiegers and let them into the town. The French chroniclers naturally saw this as an overwhelming wave of popular support for Charles VII: a crushed and conquered people joyously welcoming their liberator. The prosaic truth was that it owed more to self-interest than patriotism.

This was perhaps more obviously illustrated by the number of captains who accepted money to hand over their strongholds. The most startling example of this was Longny, which was surrendered at the end of August 1449. The captain of Longny was François de Surienne: his wife and family were resident in the castle and in his absence he had entrusted the lieutenancy to his son-in-law, Richard aux Épaules, the last surviving member of an ancient Norman family. It is possible that Épaules was angered by the way the English administration had disowned and abandoned his father-in-law at Fougères: he would later claim – to a French inquiry – that he had tried to dissuade Surienne from undertaking the mission, believing he was dishonouring himself and his family.

The facts remain that he accepted 12,000 *écus* (£875,000) from Pierre de Brézé to let the French into the keep; he stood by while they overcame the resistance and took prisoner some of the castle's defenders, probably the Spanish and other foreign soldiers of fortune whom Surienne regularly employed in his service; he again stood by as his mother-in-law, who was justifiably 'very unhappy' with him, was told to leave, taking her goods with her; then he accepted the captaincy of Longny on behalf of Charles VII and took the oath of allegiance to his new master. He later received 450*l.t.* (£26,250) 'to distribute among twelve French-speaking companions of war, who were in the said place with him and under [him] . . . and of his alliance, both for having been the cause, with him, of the reduction of the said place, as for having reduced and put themselves in the king's obedience . . . and performed the oath'.

Rather than a principled change of allegiance because he felt his family had been dishonoured and betrayed by the English, these facts suggest the self-serving action of a man who saw the opportunity at one stroke to gain the captaincy for himself, throw off the shackles of his Aragonese father-in-law and enrich himself. There is a certain malicious enjoyment to be had in learning that he did not enjoy his ill-gotten gains for long. In 1451 he began an action against the heirs of the original owners of the castle, seeking 10,000*l.t.* (£583,333) in compensation for repairs he had done to it, only to have *parlement* eventually judge that Longny was rightfully theirs and should be returned to them.[3]

Richard aux Épaules was at least a native Norman. Two other turncoats did not have that excuse, though both changed allegiance for the same reason: they had married wealthy Frenchwomen and had more to lose by remaining loyal. John Edwards, the Welsh captain of La-Roche-Guyon on behalf of Simon Morhier, was persuaded by his wife and a bribe of 4500*l.t.* (£262,500) to take the oath to Charles VII and continue in his post. He was followed a month later, in October 1449, by Richard Merbury, an Englishman who had been a member of Bedford's household and, since at least 1425, captain of Gisors. His wife's parents acted as intermediaries and negotiated that, in return for surrendering Gisors and taking the oath, his two sons, John and Hamon, who had been captured at Pont-Audemer, were released without having to pay ransoms. Merbury did not retain his captaincy: it was given to Raoul de Gaucourt as a reward for his lifelong service to the French crown and in consideration of his great age. Merbury's compensation for delivering such an important English stronghold was to be confirmed in possession of his wife's territories and created captain of Saint-Germain-en-Laye. His English lieutenant, one

'Reynfoks' (possibly the 'Raynforth' who had accompanied Matthew Gough to Alsace in the summer of 1444 and was later living off the land in the Caen region), received 687*l.t.* (£40,075) from Pierre de Brézé for his part in delivering Gisors to Charles VII.[4]

By the beginning of September 1449 Vernon, Dangu castle and Gournay had also surrendered. The English garrison at Vernon had maintained a show of defiance, mocking the herald sent to demand the keys of the town by giving him all the old keys they could find. When the *francs-archers*, in their first distinguished action, captured an artillery emplacement on an island in the river, leading to the bridge also being taken, the inhabitants decided to surrender 'whether the English wished it or not'. The garrison, under protest, accepted their decision, requiring sealed letters confirming that they had not consented or wished to capitulate but had been forced to do so, and obtaining a delay in the handover in the hope of relief from Rouen. As this was not forthcoming, town and castle were surrendered together.[5]

The first stronghold to put up any real resistance was Harcourt, where the garrison was commanded by Richard Frogenhalle, one of the captains who had resisted the handover of Maine. The siege lasted fifteen days and was distinguished both by casualties killed by artillery on each side and by the Bastard of Orléans displaying at the gate a painting of Frogenhalle hanging upside down by his feet. This was the standard method of publicly denouncing and humiliating someone who had breached the chivalric code of conduct. Frogenhalle's alleged crime was to have broken his oath not to take up arms again against the French. Tanneguy du Châtel had exacted a similar vengeance against Suffolk, Robert Willoughby and Thomas Blount in 1438, denouncing them for perjury and hanging 'very unpleasant pictures' of them at the gates of Paris: 'each one showed a knight, one of the great English lords, hanging by his feet on a gallows, his spurs on, completely armed except for his head, at each side a devil binding him with chains and at the bottom of the picture, two foul, ugly crows, made to look as if they were picking out his eyes'.[6]

September saw the pace of the reconquest quicken as François, duke of Brittany, and Arthur de Richemont invaded lower Normandy from the west with an army six thousand strong. Leaving the duke's brother, Pierre, to guard the Breton marches, and avoiding the great English frontier fortresses, they pushed their way up the Cotentin peninsula, capturing first Coutances, then Saint-Lô and finally Carentan and Valognes. Not one of them offered any resistance, though the smallest garrison in Normandy, Pont-Douve, just outside Carentan, where Dickon Chatterton was captain, refused to surrender and was taken by assault.[7]

Elsewhere in the duchy the men of Dieppe ventured out and took Fécamp by surprise, their success being crowned by the capture of ninety-seven English soldiers on board a ship which sailed into the harbour immediately afterwards, unaware that the place had just changed hands. Touques, Essay, Exmes and Alençon all fell without a fight; at Argentan the townsmen displayed a French standard to indicate where the French could gain entry; the garrison retreated to the castle but a cannon blew a hole large enough to admit a cart through the walls, forcing the defenders into the keep, where they too made their submission.[8]

And all the while, despite the desperate pleas for assistance or relief, Beaufort and the English administration sat tight in Rouen and did nothing. Even Talbot, once famed for his energy and boldness, was conspicuous by his failure to venture out into the duchy but, unlike the French, he had no field army at his disposal. No soldiers could be spared from the hard-pressed garrisons and the thirteen hundred men promised from England for June 1449 had not materialised: only fifty-five men-at-arms and 408 archers mustered for service under Sir William Peyto at Winchelsea on 31 July.[9]

Without the resources of men and money which Charles VII had in abundance, Talbot could do nothing except ensure that Rouen itself did not fall into French hands. Yet he too was about to share the experience of so many of the captains and garrisons he had been unable to prevent being captured. At the beginning of October the combined armies of the Bastard of Orléans, the counts of Eu and Saint-Pol, René d'Anjou and the indefatigable seventy-eight-year-old Raoul de Gaucourt converged on Rouen and Charles came in person to observe the progress of the siege. Two attempts to summon the city to yield were thwarted by the garrison, who sallied out and prevented the heralds approaching the townsmen.

The Rouennais still had bitter memories of the long and terrible siege of 1418–19. They had also had a foretaste of what was to come as no supplies had been able to get into the town for six weeks before Charles VII's army appeared before their gates. A group of them therefore seized control of a stretch of wall between two towers and signalled their willingness to admit the French. On 16 October the Bastard led a scaling party to the section of wall, placed his ladders against it and, having knighted a dozen of his companions, including Guillaume Cousinot, urged them over the ramparts. They had reckoned without Talbot, who, at last galvanised into action, personally led a counter-attack in which some fifty or sixty Frenchmen, including Rouennais, were killed or captured, the wall was regained and the invaders repulsed. The next day, however, the townsmen went in such numbers to Beaufort to demand that their archbishop should be allowed to negotiate a surrender on their behalf that he reluctantly gave his consent. This was as far as he was prepared to go, for when the terms offered were brought to him Beaufort gave them such a hostile response that the citizens rebelled, forcing him and the rest of the English to retreat into the safety of Rouen castle, where they barricaded themselves inside. The Rouennais therefore opened the gates, handed over the keys to the Bastard and forced the garrison guarding the bridge to surrender.[10]

With the town now in French hands, Beaufort, Talbot and the chancellor, Thomas Hoo, found themselves trapped in the castle with some twelve hundred soldiers, many of them refugees from surrendered garrisons. With food already in short supply and no prospect of relief, they had no realistic option but to negotiate their way out. Charles, who seems to have disliked Beaufort personally as well as for what he represented, was determined to extract the highest price possible. He surrounded the castle with his men and a huge array of guns, as if in preparation for a siege, and demanded that Beaufort surrender not only Rouen but all the strongholds left in English hands in the entire Caux region, namely Caudebec, Tancarville, Lillebonne, Harfleur, Montivilliers and Arques. In addition he was to pay a ransom of 50,000 *saluts* (£4.01m) within twelve months and provide eight hostages for the fulfilment of the terms, including his brother-in-law, Talbot, and his stepson, Thomas Roos, as well as Richard Frogenhalle and Richard Gower, son of Thomas Gower, captain of Cherbourg, the last remaining English fortress in the Cotentin. On these conditions Beaufort, his wife, children and anyone else who chose to go with him would have safe-conducts to leave for England, taking with them all their belongings apart from heavy artillery, prisoners and bonds.[11]

On 29 October 1449 Beaufort set his seal to the surrender of Rouen, purchasing his life at the cost of his honour. The news of the treaty was greeted with shock, outrage and shame in England, particularly because it involved the loss of other key strongholds which were not even under attack at the time. The siege had lasted less than three weeks from start to finish and although the castle had been invested no bombardment of it had begun: Beaufort's capitulation without any show of resistance could properly be regarded as treasonable. This was perhaps brought home to him before he left France, for having boarded ship at Harfleur he did not return to England but instead diverted to Caen.[12]

A week after the surrender of Rouen another iconic place in the history of these troubled times was given up. On 5 November François de Surienne delivered Fougères to the duke of Brittany, alleging that he had held out for five weeks against heavy bombardment in the face of desertion by his men, who had returned to defend their own garrisons, which were now under threat, and abandonment by the English government, which had promised but failed to send him reinforcements under Robert de Vere. Four hundred men had indeed crossed to France with Vere in September, but had got no further than Caen, where the *bailli* and inhabitants had begged them to stay to protect their town. Surienne had received 10,000 *écus* (£729,167) to evacuate Fougères, but he had lost Verneuil, Longny and all his lands in both Normandy and the Nivernais. His bitterness at the way his actions had been disowned by Suffolk and Beaufort would lead him to resign his prized membership of the Order of the Garter, enter the service of the duke of Burgundy and ultimately become a naturalised subject of France.[13]

It was only now, when it was already too late, that the English government took steps to assist Normandy. On 21 and 22 November one thousand longbows, two thousand sheaves of arrows, 2880 bowstrings, 1800 pounds of gunpowder and a host of other armaments were sent to Caen and Cherbourg with two gunners and a 'cunning' or skilled 'carpenter for the ordnance'. On 4 December Sir Thomas Kyriell contracted to serve in France with 425 men-at-arms and 2080 archers, but Suffolk could not find the money to pay their wages or their transport costs. The treasurer had to pawn the crown jewels to raise loans for the expedition because 'we be not as yet purveyed of money' and the king was obliged to plead with the major West Country landowners to be kind enough to lend their naval assistance to lower Normandy. Even in death Cardinal Beaufort was still the crown's banker-in-chief: his executors made loans totalling £8333 6s. 8d. (£4.38m) and Suffolk himself lent £2773 (£1.46m).[14]

Parliament had been hastily summoned on 6 November as news of the fall of Rouen broke: foreseeing the stormy sessions that lay ahead, Sir John Popham, a veteran of Agincourt and the French wars, who had been chosen by the House of Commons as its Speaker, declined to serve, pleading age and infirmity. The most politicised parliament of the century now sought vengeance on those it held responsible for the unfolding disaster: those who had brokered the Truce of Tours. Adam Moleyns, bishop of Chichester, was obliged to resign the privy seal. On 9 January 1450, as he was attempting to deliver their back-pay to Kyriell's unpaid and rioting troops who were waiting to embark at

Portsmouth, he was attacked, denounced as 'the traitor who sold Normandy' and murdered by Cuthbert Colville, a long-serving army captain.[15]

Rumours 'in the mouth of every commoner' that the dying Moleyns had accused Suffolk of treachery forced the duke to make an emotional statement to parliament. He movingly recounted the long service of his family in the king's wars: the deaths of his father at Harfleur, his eldest brother at Agincourt, two others at Jargeau and a fourth in France as a hostage for the payment of his own ransom; his personal thirty-four years in arms, seventeen of them spent 'without coming home or seeing this land'. Would he have betrayed all these things 'for a Frenchman's promise'?

It was meant to be a rhetorical question, but parliament believed he had. On 28 January he was committed to the Tower and ten days later he was formally impeached as a traitor who for years had been a 'follower and abettor' of Charles VII. The release of the duke of Orléans, the handover of Maine, the failure to include Brittany among English allies and, it was implied, Henry's marriage to Margaret of Anjou, disparagingly referred to as 'the French queen', were all now seen as evidence of his diabolical machinations to sell the two kingdoms to the French. Many of the charges were ridiculous, reflecting parliament's desire to find a scapegoat, rather than genuine causes of concern. Suffolk protested that he was not solely responsible: 'so great things could not be done nor brought about by himself alone, unless that other persons had done their part and were privy thereto as well as he'. On 17 March, in an assembly of the lords, Henry 'by his own advice' cleared Suffolk of the capital charge and sentenced him to five years' banishment, beginning on 1 May, for the lesser crimes of corruption and peculation. As he was crossing the Channel on 2 May his ship was intercepted by a royal vessel, he was taken prisoner and, after a mock trial by the crew, beheaded in the name of 'the community of the realm'.[16]

In the meantime the situation in Normandy became increasingly desperate. On 20 November Matthew Gough and his lieutenant, an archer turned man-at-arms turned chronicler,

Christopher Hanson, surrendered the isolated fortress of Bellême after no relief force came to their assistance. Even the supposedly impregnable Château Gaillard, which had previously required many months to starve into submission, capitulated on 23 November after a siege of just five weeks, proof, surely, of the lack of provisions and munitions in the Norman garrisons about which Beaufort had complained. On 8 December the Bastard of Orléans took six thousand soldiers, four thousand *francs-archers* and sixteen great cannon to lay siege to Harfleur. Alone of all the English strongholds required to submit as part of the capitulation of Rouen, Harfleur had refused to surrender. Abetted by the English government, which sent in supplies of barley, wheat and malt, Harfleur managed to hold out until Christmas Day, but then was forced to agree to submit on 1 January 1450. So many English were in the town, among them sixteen hundred soldiers in garrison and a further four hundred ejected from captured strongholds, that an extension of two more days was granted to allow them all to be evacuated by sea.[17]

From Harfleur the Bastard made his way to Honfleur, on the other side of the Seine estuary, which withstood a combination of heavy bombardment and mining for four weeks before it too agreed to yield if no relief was brought before 18 February. The French evidently thought that there might be an attempted rescue as they took the precaution of fortifying their position, but Beaufort remained at Caen and Kyriell's army was still waiting to embark in England, so the surrender went unchallenged and the defeated garrison also took ship for home.[18]

It was not until the middle of March, more than three months after he had contracted to serve, that Kyriell finally arrived in France. Had he landed at Caen, he could have joined forces with Beaufort and begun a campaign to extend the English frontier beyond Caen and Bayeux. Instead, and inexplicably, he landed at Cherbourg, the only other port still in English hands but an isolated outpost on the northernmost tip of the Cotentin. He had with him 2500 men and a great artillery train, which suggests that this was not just a field army but one equipped for recovering captured strongholds. Alarmed, the French authorities at

Coutances sent urgent messages to the duke of Brittany and the admiral, marshal and constable of France, begging them to come 'with all strength and diligence' to repel the enemy.[19]

Kyriell's first action was to lay siege to Valognes, eleven miles from Cherbourg: it surrendered after three weeks but only after the arrival of reinforcements of 1800 men brought from Caen, Bayeux and Vire by Robert de Vere, Matthew Gough and Henry Norbury. This was the first and last success of the campaign. Kyriell now resumed his sixty-mile journey to Caen, avoiding Carentan by taking the direct route across the bay using the fords of Saint-Clément, which were only accessible at low tide. Jean de Bourbon, count of Clermont, was alerted to his crossing by the watchman on the church tower at Carentan and mobilised his forces to follow them while sending to Arthur de Richemont at Saint-Lô for assistance in intercepting them.

On 15 April 1450, with some three thousand men under his command, Clermont caught up with the English near Formigny, a village ten miles west of Bayeux. Warned of their approach, Kyriell had time to choose a defensive position with his back to a small river and to dig ditches and plant stakes to protect his front line against cavalry attack. With his superior numbers and strong position, he was easily able to repel a flanking attack by Clermont's forces and his archers even sallied out to seize two of their small field guns. Pierre de Brézé succeeded in rallying the fleeing men and launched a full-scale attack which could also have been defeated had not Arthur de Richemont arrived at this critical moment with two thousand men of his own. Caught in a pincer movement between the two forces, Kyriell attempted to turn his left flank to meet the new threat but in the confusion his forces disintegrated and were overwhelmed. Gough and Vere managed to fight their way through to the old bridge across the river with the remnants of the left wing and were able to escape to Bayeux. Kyriell, Norbury and many men-at-arms were taken prisoner but the rest of the English army, the unransomable rank and file, were slaughtered where they stood. Three thousand seven hundred and seventy-four Englishmen were buried on the field in fourteen grave pits; the French, by comparison, lost only a handful of men. It was the French revenge for Agincourt.[20]

The battle of Formigny ended what little hope there had been that the reconquest of Normandy could be stopped, least of all reversed. The victorious French swept on to Vire, a choice no doubt dictated in part because its captain, Henry Norbury, was now a prisoner in their hands; Vire offered a perfunctory resistance, then surrendered in return for Norbury's release without ransom and the garrison's freedom to depart for Caen with their belongings intact. The director of the artillery at this siege, incidentally, as at other unnamed places, was John Howell, a Welshman not in the English garrison but in Richemont's service.[21]

Clermont and Richemont now went their separate ways, the former to join the Bastard in laying siege to Bayeux, the latter to assist his nephew at the siege of Avranches. The defence of Bayeux was in the hands of Matthew Gough but even he could not endure the battering of Bureau's guns, which, in the space of sixteen days, reduced the town walls to rubble. Two unauthorised attempts to take Bayeux by storm were repulsed in a single day, resulting in many deaths on both sides from arrows and gunshot, but in the end Gough was forced to capitulate before a full-scale assault took place. The English were allowed to depart for Cherbourg on 16 May, taking their wives and children with them but leaving behind all their property. Since there were over four hundred women, and a great many children, now all destitute, the French charitably provided them with carts to transport them to Cherbourg. Wounded soldiers were allowed a month's grace before having to leave, but the rest of the men, including Gough, had to march out on foot, each carrying a stick in his fist as a sign that they were unarmed and carried nothing with them, this also being the universally recognised symbol of being under safe-conduct.[22]

Four days before the evacuation of Bayeux, Avranches had also surrendered after a spirited defence lasting three weeks which was said to have been inspired by the wife of the captain, John Lampet. She donned male clothing and went from house to house, urging the inhabitants to join in beating off the besiegers with missiles, before reverting to feminine dress to enchant François of Brittany into granting the best terms once resistance was no longer an option. Since the duke died not long afterwards it was assumed she had either poisoned or bewitched him – though her charms did nothing more than secure freedom for the English to depart empty-handed.[23]

At the beginning of June the French armies reunited to lay siege to Caen. Twenty thousand troops surrounded the place and Bureau drafted in hundreds of miners, labourers and carpenters from all over the region to assist in digging mines which ran right into the ditches round the town and brought down a tower and stretch of wall near the abbey of Saint-Étienne. At this point, as both sides were well aware, Caen could be taken by assault. Henry V's sack of the town in 1417 was still such a raw memory that neither side had the resolution to go through with one again. On 24 June 1450 Beaufort signed his second capitulation in eight months. The four thousand Englishmen in Caen, including Beaufort's family, the *bailli* Richard Harington, Robert de Vere and Fulk Eyton, were again to be allowed to leave with all their movable goods, including hand weapons, but this time they must take ship for England and nowhere else. And the price had risen from 50,000 *saluts* (£4.01m) to 300,000 *écus* (£21.88m).[24]

Beaufort understood all too well the enormity of what he was doing, which is why he apparently made a desperate attempt to secure a different outcome. He offered 4000 *écus* and £50 (£291,667 and £26,250) to Robin Campbell, the lieutenant of Robert Cunningham, captain of Charles VII's Scots bodyguard, to organise the kidnapping of either the Bastard of Orléans or one of three other named royal intimates and lead fifteen hundred Englishmen out of Caen. A third of these men were to be mounted and would descend on Charles's lodgings 'in order to seize him, and take him to Cherbourg, and put him to flight'; the rest would destroy the French artillery by torching the powder kegs and spiking the guns. The plot, if it was genuine, obviously failed, though when it was discovered some years later Campbell

and another Scots guard were beheaded and quartered as traitors and their captain was dismissed and banished from court.[25]

The surrender of Caen spelled the end of the line for the few
remaining English garrisons. On 6 July, after a brief struggle,
Falaise yielded to Xaintrailles and Bureau in return for the
unconditional liberation of its captain, John Talbot, who had
been kept a prisoner after the surrender of Rouen because the
terms of the capitulation had been breached by Harfleur's refusal
to submit. In a proud but forlorn gesture of defiance Falaise's
defenders secured the right to defer their submission until 21
July in case a relieving army came to its assistance. The last
great stronghold on the southern frontier, Domfront, followed
suit on 2 August.[26]

All that now remained in English hands was Cherbourg, a
fortress capable of holding a garrison of a thousand men, which
had never fallen to assault since the building of the town walls in
the mid-fourteenth century. Standing on a narrow spit of solid
rock, its triple concentric man-made defences were supplemented by a fourth, the sea, which twice daily turned the place
into a virtual island. If ever a stronghold had the potential to be
an English Mont-Saint-Michel it was Cherbourg. It had even
survived as an isolated outpost before, spending sixteen years in
English hands between 1378 and 1394. In 1418 it had taken
Gloucester five months to reduce it, a feat he had achieved only
with the assistance of a traitor in the garrison. Now it took just
a few weeks.

The constable of France, Arthur de Richemont, personally
conducted the siege and Jean Bureau again deployed his heavy
artillery which had proved so effective in persuading other
strongholds to surrender. Displaying the innovative skills which
made him feared and admired in equal measure, Bureau even
planted three bombards and a cannon on the sands, covering
them with waxed hides pinned down by stones to protect them
when the tide came in. By this means he kept up a regular bombardment from every side, though up to ten of his guns were said
to have exploded on firing, a common problem with medieval
artillery. The most notable casualty was the admiral of France,

Prégent de Coëtivy, who was killed by cannon-fire from the garrison, but many others died from disease, which spread rapidly in the unhealthy conditions of the siege.[27]

Unlike so many other strongholds, Cherbourg had the benefit of supplies ferried across the Channel from England: two gunners were dispatched to its aid in June 1450, together with vast quantities of saltpetre, sulphur, bows, arrows and bowstrings, as well as wheat, malt and hops, Cherbourg then being 'in great jeopardy and peril' because it was 'not so furnished with military hardware and victuals as necessity demands'. On 14 August two of the king's sergeants-at-arms were paid for their expenses in seizing ships in western and northern ports 'to be sent forth to the sea, for the rescue of our town and castle of Cherbourg'.[28]

It was too little and too late. Cherbourg had already surrendered on 12 August 1450. The very fact that it held out for so long, compared with the ignominious speed with which most fortresses fell, made its captain, Thomas Gower, a popular hero. He was praised as a 'wise and valiant' esquire 'who had spent most of his life continuously in the service of the king and in warfare for the conservation of the public good in the realms of France and England'. What most people did not know, however, was that underpinning the usual public treaty of capitulation was a private deal which reveals that Gower had, in fact, been bribed to surrender. His son, Richard, who was, like Talbot, a hostage for the handover of Rouen, was to be released unconditionally; 2000 *écus* (£145,833) was to be paid to the members of the garrison; further sums were to be paid towards the ransoms of certain English prisoners, including 2000 *écus* for Dickon Chatterton, the captain of Pont-Douve; all expenses of returning the English and their possessions were to be paid; finally, and most incriminating of all, money was also spent 'on gifts that it was necessary to make in secret to certain knights and gentlemen of the English party'.[29]

So the last bastion of the English kingdom of France did not fall after a heroic but futile defence: it was simply sold to the French. 'Cherbourg is gone' James Gresham wrote to John Paston a few days later, 'and we have not now a foot of land in

Normandy.' The humiliation and anger felt in England were matched only by the jubilation in France. Just as Henry V had made the anniversary of Agincourt a day to be celebrated with special masses in England, so Charles VII decreed that the anniversary of the fall of Cherbourg should henceforth be a national festival of thanksgiving. The reconquest of the English kingdom of France was complete.[30]

EPILOGUE

It was a nice irony that the stronghold which was sold to the English in 1418 should be sold back to the French in 1450, for there was nothing inevitable about Cherbourg's fall. It had held out before, and it could have done so again. After all, Calais would spend another century in English hands. The difference was that Calais was crucial to the English economy and its survival was ensured by the financial support and political muscle of the powerful mercantile lobby in England. Nowhere in the English kingdom of France, not even Rouen, had ever matched Calais's financial importance to the crown and the realm. Individuals had won – and lost – great estates and fortunes in France but the cost to the public purse of defending these private interests far outweighed any benefits they brought to the wider English economy.

The reconquest of Normandy had taken just one year and six days, 'which is a great miracle and a very great marvel', wrote one French chronicler.

Also it clearly seems that Our Lord gave it his blessing: for never before was so great a country conquered in so small a space of time, nor with less loss to the people and soldiers, nor with less killing of people and soldiers, nor with less destruction and damage to the countryside; which is greatly to the honour and praise of the king, princes and other lords . . . and of all others who accompanied them in recovering the said duchy.'[1]

The reconquest was achieved in exactly the same way as the original conquest. Charles VII had belatedly adopted his greatest adversary's methods: his troops were trained and disciplined, he had invested heavily in the latest artillery, he had a deep war chest to finance his campaigns and he had taken to the field in person. Like Henry V, he used a mixture of threat of violence and promise of pardon to secure the submission of the towns and fortresses, and he was not above using bribery to secure a swift and painless surrender.

That he was able to achieve so much in such a short time was also due to the disintegration of the English administration: despite warnings from Suffolk, Beaufort and many others, both England and Normandy had been lulled into a false sense of security by the truce. When war came they were unprepared, disorganised and did not have either the will or the means to resist. And, just like the French in 1417, they had no one to whom they could turn for incisive and charismatic leadership. Henry VI, the least martial of kings, had neither the desire nor the ability to lead the defence of the duchy in person. Years of factional infighting among his advisers had seen the role of lieutenant-general politicised and emasculated: not one of the appointees had enjoyed the talents or powers of Bedford and as a consequence had been unable to rally the two nations to unite against a common foe. Henry V had met with greater opposition in his original conquest because there had always been hope of assistance; the Norman towns and garrisons in the last days of the English kingdom of France knew that no one would come to their rescue. They therefore chose to submit voluntarily rather than be forced to do so.

Henry V had invaded France as an independent power acting unilaterally and exploiting the French civil wars for his own benefit. The fatal flaw in his creation of an English kingdom of France was the Treaty of Troyes, which drew him into those wars, turning him into a Burgundian partisan and committing him to an unsustainable war to conquer the rest of France. When Burgundy withdrew from the alliance the English cause was left high and dry. The fact that Normandy remained in

English hands for another fifteen years owed as much to French failure as to English success. Had Charles heeded some of his advisers, the duchy might have been reconquered in the wake of Jehanne d'Arc's victories and his own coronation: it certainly came perilously close to being lost in 1436 after the death of Bedford and the Treaty of Arras.

Had Henry V been content with just the conquest of Normandy, the outcome might also have been different. His land settlement there could have made the duchy capable of defending itself from its own resources as well as providing the security necessary for agriculture and trade to prosper. An English king as duke of Normandy would certainly have been more acceptable to the French than an English king of France: Gascony had, after all, provided just such a model for almost three hundred years. Though Gascony belonged to the English crown by right of inheritance rather than conquest, there was a common heritage between the Normans and the English which Henry had identified and started to build upon.

The land settlement and the establishment of permanent garrisons, each with its own quota of Englishmen, encouraged intermarriage at every level of society, creating a new bond between conquered and conquerors. When the end came there must have been hundreds, if not thousands, of people who had to make the bewildering decision whether to stay in France or return to England. Many who had employment and families in France chose to stay, among them Bedford's embroiderer, Thomas Bridon, whose daughter had married a Frenchman and whose grandson took up his trade and represented him in the Rouen embroiderers' guild. Both the constable, Richemont, and the new seneschal of Normandy, Pierre de Brézé, were happy to employ skilled English and Welsh soldiers in their armies. And in an early example of a traditional English occupation, the duke of Alençon even had an English valet in the 1450s.[2]

On the other hand, many Frenchmen who had worked for the English chose to go into voluntary exile with their employers: men such as Gervase le Vulre, a royal secretary, who was still employed by the crown thirty years after leaving France; or the

unnamed manuscript illuminator who followed Fastolf from
Paris to Normandy to England so that he could continue to
enjoy his patronage; or even John de Labowley and Hermon the
page, who were each bequeathed 20s. (£525) in Fulk Eyton's
will in 1454 'for they both came with me out of Normandy'.[3]

There was nevertheless a steady stream of English refugees
pouring into London 'in right poor array, piteous to see': not just
dispossessed landowners, expelled soldiers and Englishmen
returning home, but men with French wives and children who
had never set foot in England before. Thomas Gower, for
instance, brought his Alençon-born wife, whom he had had the
foresight to have naturalised as an English subject in 1433, as
well as the son whose freedom had been purchased by the surrender of Cherbourg. The fortunate exiles came with all their
worldly goods piled into carts, but many arrived destitute with
nothing but the clothes upon their backs, having lost their homes
and livelihood.[4]

For them, as for many Englishmen, the personal cost was
unbearably high: for every Cornewaille or Fastolf who had
reaped great wealth, there was a John More, who was left a
pauper after being captured seven times, or a John Kyriell, who
was still a French prisoner twenty years after the loss of
Normandy because neither he nor his brother could afford his
ransom.[5] Though few paid so heavy a price as Suffolk, who lost
his father, four brothers and ultimately his own life to the cause,
decades of constant warfare saw thousands of fathers, brothers
and sons from both sides meet violent and untimely ends.

The England to which the refugees returned was more like the
France they had left than the peaceful, prosperous and ordered
realm Henry V had ruled. Jack Cade's rebellion had erupted in
May 1450, prompted in part by anger at Suffolk and the 'traitors' by whom 'the realm of France was lost . . . and our true
lords, knights and esquires, and many a good yeoman . . . lost
and sold ere they went'. The murders of Suffolk and Moleyns
were swiftly followed by those of their closest associates: lord
Saye and Sele, the former treasurer, was beheaded in the street at
the behest of the mob, and William Aiscough, bishop of

Salisbury, who had married Henry VI to the 'she-wolf of France', was dragged from the altar while celebrating mass and stoned to death. Matthew Gough, who had survived so many daring exploits in France, was killed trying to capture London Bridge from the rebels.[6]

The terrible irony was that the first and last holder of the two crowns of France and England had not inherited his English father's abilities but his French grandfather's madness. He was unable to prevent the bitter quarrel between Beaufort and York, occasioned by the loss of Normandy, spiralling into faction and out of control. When the English Achilles, the sixty-six-year-old Talbot, was killed on the field of Castillon in 1453, and Gascony also fell to Charles VII, the news tipped Henry over the edge. Physically helpless and mentally uncomprehending, he became a pawn in the struggle between the houses of Lancaster and York, and England was set on the path to civil war. The last two lieutenants-general of Normandy were killed fighting each other instead of the French, and Henry VI, the last Lancastrian monarch, was murdered in the Tower in 1471 on his successor's orders, just as the last Plantagenet king, Richard II, had been assassinated at the command of Henry's own grandfather in 1400.[7] For Henry VI the greatest tragedy was that his desire for peace in France fuelled violent conflict and civil war in England and ultimately led to his losing the crowns of both kingdoms.

NOTES

For abbreviations used in the Notes see p. 438.

CHAPTER ONE: INVASION

1 *Foedera*, ix, 436; *PR*, ix, 196–7, where the prohibited wood is strangely mistranscribed as 'aspe' and translated as aspen.
2 Ibid., 182.
3 For a full account of the Agincourt campaign see Juliet Barker, *Agincourt: The King, the Campaign, the Battle* (Little, Brown, 2005).
4 Ibid., 4, 7–14.
5 W&W, ii, 279; Bernard Guenée, *La Folie de Charles VI Roi Bien Aimé* (Paris, 2004).
6 Gérard Bacquet, *Azincourt* (Bellegarde, 1977), 103.
7 Anne Curry (ed.), *The Battle of Agincourt: Sources and Interpretations* (Woodbridge, 2000), 63. See also ibid., 74–5.
8 Barker, 217; Anne Curry, 'Harfleur et les Anglais, 1415–1422' in Pierre Bouet and Véronique Gazeau (eds.), *La Normandie et l'Angleterre au Moyen Âge: Colloque de Cerisy-la-Salle* (Caen, 2001), 256–7.
9 Christopher Allmand, *Henry V* (New Haven and London, 1997), 102–3.
10 Anne Curry, 'After Agincourt, What Next? Henry V and the Campaign of 1416' in Linda Clark (ed.), *Conflicts, Consequences and the Crown in the Late Middle Ages* (Woodbridge, 2007), 31–2; *Gesta Henrici Quinti* ed. and trans. Frank Taylor and John S. Roskell (Oxford, 1975), 134–49, 144 n. 3.
11 W&W, 18–19. For the text of the treaty see *PR*, ix, 182–8.
12 *PR*, ix, 178.
13 Ibid., ix, 175; *Gesta Henrici Quinti*, 176–84. See also W&W, 41–8.

14 Ibid., 46, 50–3; Curry, 'After Agincourt', 41.
15 Newhall, 54–5.
16 Curry, 'Harfleur et les Anglais', 256.
17 Newhall, 46.
18 Ibid., 58. This was clearly a lesson learned from the Agincourt campaign: it had taken three days to disembark the army at Sainte-Adresse: Barker, 165.
19 *Foedera*, ix, 482.
20 *Brut*, 383.
21 Walsingham, 424; M.-L. Bellaguet (ed.), *Chronique du Religieux de St-Denys* (Paris, 1844), vi, 104.
22 Walsingham, 424–5; *Brut*, 383–4.
23 Deuteronomy, ch. 22, vv. 13–14. See Barker, 181.
24 *Brut*, 384; Newhall, 60.
25 Monstrelet, iii, 208ff; *Bourgeois*, 104–7; Newhall, 62–8.

CHAPTER TWO: CONQUEST

 1 R. A. Newhall, 'Henry V's Policy of Conciliation in Normandy, 1417–1422' in C. H. Taylor and J. L. La Monte (eds.), *Anniversary Essays in Medieval History by Students of Charles Homer Haskins* (Boston and New York, 1929), 207–8.
 2 Ibid., 208.
 3 Allmand, 84; W&W, 62–3; Anne Curry, 'Isolated or Integrated? The English Soldier in Lancastrian Normandy' in S. Rees Jones, R. Marks and A. J. Minnis (eds.), *Courts and Regions in Medieval Europe* (Woodbridge, 2000), 191.
 4 Anne Curry, 'The Impact of War and Occupation on Urban Life in Normandy, 1417–1450', *French History*, vol. i, no. 2 (Oct. 1987), 165; Walsingham, 426–7; W&W, 64–5.
 5 W&W, 26–9, 67–8.
 6 Ibid., 65–6; Newhall, 71–4.
 7 W&W, 66–7. Henry IV had married, as his second wife, Joan, widow of Jean V, duke of Brittany. Her children by her first marriage included the present duke, Jean VI, his younger brother, Arthur de Richemont (Henry's prisoner since Agincourt), and Marie, mother of Jean II, duke of Alençon.
 8 Ibid., 68–9. Anjou and Maine, though distinct from the duchy of Normandy, were adjacent to it. Part of the ancient patrimony of the Plantagenets, they were also claimed by Henry as part of his 'just rights and inheritances'.
 9 Walsingham, 427; Newhall, 78–80; W&W, 69–72.
10 See above, 15; Newhall, 'Henry V's Policy of Conciliation', 210 n.

27, though he assumes it was aimed at French men-at-arms rather than Norman refugees.

11 J. A. C. Buchon (ed.), *Les Chroniques de Sire Jean Froissart* (Paris, 1913), ii, 41; Newhall, 92–5.

12 André Plaisse and Sylvie Plaisse, *La Vie Municipale à Évreux Pendant la Guerre de Cent Ans* (Évreux, 1978), 115–16; Curry, 'Impact of War', 160.

13 Robert Massey, 'Lancastrian Rouen: Military Service and Property Holding, 1419–49' in David Bates and Anne Curry (eds.), *England and Normandy in the Middle Ages* (London and Rio Grande, 1994), 270; W&W, 124.

14 Monstrelet, iii, 259–74; *Bourgeois*, 111–19. Jean de Touraine had died in 1417.

15 Newhall, 103.

16 Monstrelet, iii, 281–3; Newhall, 105; Le Cacheux, xiv–xvi.

17 Monstrelet, iii, 283–5; *Brut*, 387–9; W&W, 59 n. 1, 128–9. The bridge had already been used in the sieges of Caen, Louviers and Pont-de-l'Arche.

18 Walsingham, 432; Monstrelet, iii, 299; *Brut*, 390–1, 400–3, 410, 414; John Page, 'The Siege of Rouen' in J. Gairdner (ed.), *The Historical Collections of a Citizen of London in the Fifteenth Century*, Camden Society, New Series, xvii (1876), 18, 30.

19 Monstrelet, iii, 294–303, 305–10; Newhall, 115–22; *Brut*, 420–2.

20 W&W, 148–9: Monstrelet, iii, 284–5; W&W, 131–2.

21 *Brut*, 418; Le Cacheux, xix–xxiv. The fine was never paid in full, Bedford writing part of it off eleven years later in return for an immediate cash payment.

22 Monstrelet, iii, 308, 242–3; Keen, 46; Juliet Barker, 'The Foe Within: Treason in Lancastrian Normandy' in Peter Coss and Christopher Tyerman (eds.), *Soldiers, Nobles and Gentlemen* (Oxford, 2009), 306.

23 Monstrelet, iii, 308–9; W&W, 176–7; Newhall, 124–32.

24 Anne Curry, *The Hundred Years War* (Palgrave, 1993), 100; *POPC*, ii, 246; Henry Ellis (ed.), *Original Letters Illustrative of English History*, series ii (London, 1827), ii, 76–7.

25 Ibid., 77.

26 Maurice Keen, 'Diplomacy' in G. L. Harriss (ed.), *Henry V: The Practice of Kingship* (Oxford, 1985), 189–92.

27 Monstrelet, iii, 321–2.

28 Ibid., 322–34; Walsingham, 432–3; *Bourgeois*, 139–40.

29 Ibid., 139–41; Monstrelet, iii, 338–45.

30 W&W, 187; Richard Vaughan, *John the Fearless* (Woodbridge, 2002), 274–86.

31 W&W, 187; Ramsay, i, 276.
32 Keen, 'Diplomacy', 192; Allmand, *Henry* V, 137–41.
33 Monstrelet, iii, 390–402; Walsingham, 435–6; Keen, 'Diplomacy', 193–6; Allmand, *Henry V*, 136–46; Allmand, 19–20.
34 Monstrelet, iii, 388–90; W&W, 204; *PR*, ix, 246–8.
35 *Bourgeois*, 150; Allmand, *Henry V*, 147.
36 Monstrelet, iii, 400, 393–4; W&W, 197.
37 *Bourgeois*, 151.

CHAPTER THREE: HEIR OF FRANCE

1 W&W, 208; Monstrelet, iii, 208.
2 Ibid., 409–11.
3 The best European example of a mine and counter-mine is in the castle at St Andrews in Fife, Scotland. They were dug through sheer rock, hence their excellent state of preservation, and date from the siege of 1546–7. I am grateful to my son, Edward Barker, for drawing my attention to them.
4 Keen, 48–50. For brotherhood-in-arms see Barker, 160–1 and K.B. McFarlane, 'A Business Partnership in War and Administration, 1421–1445', *English Historical Review*, 78 (1963), 290–310.
5 Monstrelet, iii, 412–13; Gerald Harriss, *Shaping the Nation: England 1360–1461* (Oxford, 2005), 328; Frederick Devon (ed.), *Issues of the Exchequer* (London, 1837), 363.
6 Alain Chartier, quoted in Michael Brown, 'French Alliance or English Peace? Scotland and the Last Phase of the Hundred Years War, 1415–53' in Clark (ed.), *Conflicts, Consequences and the Crown in the Late Middle Ages*, 81.
7 Vale, 73; Bernard Chevalier, 'Les Écossais dans les Armées de Charles VII jusqu'à la Bataille de Verneuil', in *Jeanne d'Arc*, 87; Brown, 'French Alliance or English Peace?', 85–8.
8 Walsingham, 434–5; W&W, 216.
9 Monstrelet, iv, 12–13.
10 Monstrelet, iv, 15–17; *Bourgeois*, 153–4. The *Benedictus qui venit* ('Blessed is he who comes in the name of the Lord') was particularly appropriate, recognising Henry's divinely sanctioned status.
11 Monstrelet, iv, 17–20, 36–7; W&W, 226–7, 230–1, 234.
12 Beaurepaire, 10–14.
13 *PR*, ix, 246–8. All these issues were dealt with in the parliament of May 1421, which Henry attended in person: ibid., 262–4, 278–9, 305–6.
14 *Brut*, 425–7; Walsingham, 439; W&W, 267–70.
15 Monstrelet, iv, 25.

16 Harriss, 103, 204–5.
17 Chevalier, 'Les Écossais dans les Armées de Charles VII', 88; Monstrelet, iv, 37–9; Walsingham, 441–2; W&W, 312; Michael Stansfield, 'John Holland, Duke of Exeter and Earl of Huntingdon (d. 1447) and the Costs of the Hundred Years War' in Michael Hicks (ed.), *Profit, Piety and the Professions in Later Medieval England* (Gloucester and Wolfeboro Falls, 1990), 102–18.
18 Vale, 33; W&W, 311, 310 n. 11.
19 Bellaguet (ed.), *Chronique du Religieux de St-Denys*, vi, 380.
20 *POPC*, ii, 312–15.
21 *PR*, ix, 262–3, 312–13.
22 *Foedera*, x, 131.
23 Thompson, 90–1, 93.
24 Chevalier, 'Les Écossais dans les Armées de Charles VII', 88; Newhall, 279, 281–2, 277.
25 Ibid., 282; W&W, 326–30; Walsingham, 442; *Bourgeois*, 162; Léon Puiseux, *L'Émigration Normande et la Colonisation Anglaise en Normandie au XVe Siècle* (Caen and Paris, 1866), 95.
26 Monstrelet, iv, 70–1; W&W, 337–41; *Bourgeois*, 173–5.
27 Monstrelet, iv, 81–3, 91–6; *Bourgeois*, 168–72; Louis Carolus-Barré, 'Compiègne et la Guerre 1414–1430', *FAMA*, 385, 390–1; Philippe Wolff, *Commerces et Marchands de Toulouse (vers 1350–vers 1450)* (Paris, 1954), 56.
28 W&W, 348, 339 n. 9; Barker, 159.
29 Walsingham, 444.
30 Henrietta Leyser, *Medieval Women: A Social History of Women in England 450–1500* (London, 1995), 134–6; Nicholas Orme, *Medieval Children* (New Haven and London, 2001), 113.
31 *Bourgeois*, 176–7; Monstrelet, iv, 98–100, 107; W&W, 414–15.
32 Patrick and Felicity Strong, 'The Last Will and Codicils of Henry V', *English Historical Review*, 96 (1980), 97, 99–100.
33 Walsingham, 446–7; Griffiths, 16–17.
34 Walsingham, 445; *Bourgeois*, 177; *Brut*, 429–30.
35 Walsingham, 447; *Brut*, 430; Chastellain, i, 334, quoted in W&W, 424.

CHAPTER FOUR: THE ENGLISH KINGDOM OF FRANCE

1 *PR*, x, 13; Ecclesiastes: ch. 10 v. 16, quoted, for instance, in Walsingham, 446.
2 *PR*, x, 6–9, 26–7.
3 André Leguai, 'La "France Bourguignonne" dans le Conflit Entre la "France Française" et la "France Anglaise" (1420–1435)',

FAMA, 44–5, 47; Vale, 25–6.

4 Monstrelet, iv, 119–20; Leguai, 'La "France Bourguignonne"', 47.

5 Ibid. and C. A. J. Armstrong, 'La Double Monarchie et la Maison du Bourgogne (1420–1435): Le Déclin d'une Alliance', *Annales de Bourgogne*, 37 (1965), 81–3, both argue that Bedford effectively staged a coup against Burgundy, an argument which is demolished by Griffiths, 17–19.

6 *Bourgeois*, 183; Griffiths, 18; André Bossuat, 'Le Parlement de Paris Pendant l'Occupation Anglaise', *Revue Historique*, 229 (1963), 21–3.

7 Griffiths, 26 n. 27; Armstrong, 'La Double Monarchie', 83. Anne had three sisters: the marriage contract stated that she would inherit the county of Artois if Burgundy died without issue.

8 B. J. H. Rowe, 'The *Grand Conseil* Under the Duke of Bedford, 1422–35', *Oxford Essays in Medieval History Presented to Herbert Edward Salter* (Oxford, 1934), 209; Guy Thompson, '"Monseigneur Saint Denis", his Abbey, and his Town, under the English Occupation, 1420–1436' in Christopher Allmand (ed.), *Power, Culture and Religion in France c.1350–c.1550* (Woodbridge, 1989), 26; Thompson, 138–42; Le Cacheux, xcvi–xcvii; Reynolds, 'English Patrons and French Artists', 312.

9 Philippe Contamine, 'The Norman "Nation" and the French "Nation" in the Fourteenth and Fifteenth Centuries' in David Bates and Anne Curry (eds.), *England and Normandy in the Middle Ages* (London and Rio Grande, 1994), 215–34.

10 Newhall, 'Henry V's Policy of Conciliation in Normandy', 222–3.

11 Newhall, 154. The seven *bailliages* were the Cotentin, Caen, Alençon, Évreux, Rouen, Gisors and Caux.

12 Ibid.

13 Beaurepaire, 137–9; Anne Curry, 'L'Administration Financière de la Normandie Anglaise: Continuité ou Changement?', in Philippe Contamine and Olivier Mattéoni (eds.), *La France des Principautés: Les Chambres des Comptes aux XIVe et XVe Siècles* (Paris, 1996), 90–2. The exchequer established at Harfleur in January 1416 had accounted in pounds sterling and in Latin, like the English exchequer; it was absorbed into the Caen *chambre-des-comptes*: ibid., 93.

14 See above, 15. Legal documents referred to this date as 'the descent of the king on Normandy' or 'the day of Touques'.

15 Newhall, 'Henry V's Policy of Conciliation', 208–9; Puiseux, *L'Émigration Normande*, 17–18, 38–40.

16 Ibid., 91–3. The families of the chroniclers Percival de Cagny and Blondel also fled Normandy at the English invasion: Puiseux, *L'Émigration Normande*, 35.

17 Newhall, 'Henry V's Policy of Conciliation', 212–21.

18 Dupont, André, 'Pour ou Contre le Roi d'Angleterre', *Bulletin de la Société des Antiquaires de Normandie*, liv (1957–8), 164–6; *POPC*, ii, 351.

19 Allmand, *Henry V*, 203 n. 61.

20 Robert Massey, 'The Land Settlement in Lancastrian Normandy' in Tony Pollard (ed.), *Property and Politics: Essays in Later Medieval English History* (Gloucester and New York, 1984), 81; Allmand, 90–1.

21 Ibid., 53, 91.

22 *Actes*, i, 89 n. 2; Allmand, *Henry V*, 204.

23 Allmand, 55 n. 14.

24 Newhall, 162–5, 165 n. 96.

25 Newhall, 'Henry V's Policy of Conciliation', 207 n. 11.

26 To avoid confusion with the town of Séez in south-eastern France, I have used the modern name of Sées, though the medieval bishopric was properly termed Séez.

27 *Actes*, ii, 5 n. 1; Newhall, 163 n. 91; S. H. Cuttler, *The Law of Treason and Treason Trials in Later Medieval France* (Cambridge, 1981), 83.

28 C. T. Allmand, 'The English and the Church in Lancastrian Normandy' in Bates and Curry (eds.), *England and Normandy in the Middle Ages*, 294; P. S. Lewis, *Later Medieval France: The Polity* (London, 1968), 170–2.

29 Allmand, 'The English and the Church', 295.

30 W&W, 101, 263; Newhall, 163 n. 91.

31 Newhall, 'Henry V and the Policy of Conciliation', 220; Allmand, *Henry V*, 196–7; Le Cacheux, cxv–cxvi, 27–32.

32 Ibid., cxvii–cxviii.

33 *Actes*, ii, 5–13, 22–4.

34 Barker, 211; Dupont, 'Pour ou Contre le Roi d'Angleterre', 165.

35 *CMSM*, i, 87–91, 93–5.

36 Ibid., i, 88 n. 1, 96–7, 96 n. 3, 108–9, 109 n. 1; Ellis (ed.), *Original Letters*, 72–3, wrongly dated to 1419.

CHAPTER FIVE: RESISTANCE

1 *CMSM*, i, 118 n. 1; W&W, 413; Newhall, 290–1. A Bernay weaver captured in this raid, who was unable to pay a ransom, was eventually released only on condition that he fought for the French: *Actes*, i, 31–2.

2 Ramsay, i, 328 n. 3, 329, 294–5.

3 *Bourgeois*, 176, 184; Monstrelet, iv, 104–5, 134; Newhall, 296.

4 Ibid., 291; *CMSM*, i, 119–20; *Bourgeois*, 185; Monstrelet, iv, 137–42.

5 Beaurepaire, 17; Newhall, 293–5.

6 Newhall, 294, 296, 297–9; Monstrelet, iv, 154–6; Christopher Allmand, 'L'Artillerie de l'Armée Anglaise et son Organisation à l'Époque de Jeanne d'Arc' in *Jeanne d'Arc*, 78 n. 36; Monstrelet, iv, 166–9. The challenge replaced the usual clause that the place would surrender if not relieved within a certain time-limit: it also allowed for the principals to be represented by others.

7 *CMSM*, i, 24–5, 116–17; *Actes*, ii, 285 n. 1; Beaurepaire, 25.

8 *CMSM*, i, 126–7; Monstrelet, iv, 157–62; Chartier, i, 32; Brian G. H. Ditcham, '"Mutton Guzzlers and Wine Bags": Foreign Soldiers and Native Reactions in Fifteenth-Century France' in Allmand (ed.), *Power, Culture and Religion in France*, 1; Vale, 33.

9 Chartier, i, 33–8; Monstrelet, iv, 172.

10 Beaurepaire, 19–20.

11 See, for example, Jouet; G. Lefèvre-Pontalis, 'La Guerre de Partisans dans la Haute-Normandie (1424–1429)', *Bibliothèque de l'École des Chartes*, 54 (1893), 475–521; 55 (1894), 259–305; 56 (1895), 433–509; 57 (1896), 5–54; 97 (1936), 102–30; Édouard Perroy, *The Hundred Years War*, with an introduction to the English edition by David C. Douglas (London, 1951), 252. Modern French historians take a more balanced view: see, for example, Dominique Goulay, 'La Résistance à l'Occupant Anglais en Haute-Normandie (1435–1444)', *Annales de Normandie*, 36 (Mar. 1986), 37–55; Claude Gauvard, 'Résistants et Collaborateurs Pendant la Guerre de Cent Ans: Le Témoignage des Lettres de Rémission', *FAMA*, 123–38.

12 Beaurepaire, 21.

13 B. J. Rowe, 'John Duke of Bedford and the Norman "Brigands"', *English Historical Review*, 47 (1932), 591–2; Jouet, 23–7.

14 *CMSM*, i, 133; ii, 66–7, 67 n. 1; Jouet, 114, 172, 105, 168.

15 Jouet, 43–7, 176.

16 Rowe, 'John Duke of Bedford and the Norman "Brigands"', 584–6; *Actes*, i, 55–8.

17 *Actes*, i, 120–2; Rowe, 'John Duke of Bedford and the Norman "Brigands"', 595.

18 *Actes*, i, 302–6, 336–40; ii, 345. Quesnoy was himself pardoned for supplying the gang with shoes and victuals.

19 Ibid., i, 325–8.

20 Ibid., i, 315–20, 342–4.

21 Ibid., i, 336–7.

22 Ibid., ii, 338.

23 Ibid., i, 327; 318–19, 339, 344.
24 Ibid., i, 337. See also i, 317.
25 Rowe, 'John Duke of Bedford and the Norman "Brigands"', 595.
26 *Actes*, i, 49–52, 168–71, 250–9, 262–4, 379–81; ii, 332, 333. Murders by brigands are mentioned in ibid., i, 133–6, 195–6; ii, 341. Ibid., i, 21–2 is a rare example of an unprovoked killing of a lone English traveller by the villager in whose house he was lodging.
27 Ibid., ii, 341.
28 Ibid., i, 196–200, 6–8, 13–15, 44–7.
29 See above, 64 and below, 183–4; Jouet, 116.
30 *Bourgeois*, 208.
31 Keen, 137–8; Kenneth Fowler, 'Truces' in Kenneth Fowler (ed.), *The Hundred Years War* (London, 1971), 204.
32 *Actes*, i, 62–5.
33 Ibid., i, 82–7; *Bourgeois*, 245. Curiously Lointren was sentenced to death by hanging, though he should have been beheaded for being in breach of his oath of allegiance. The Armagnacs at Nogent-le-Rotrou had also wanted to execute him for changing sides but were dissuaded by the captain of Senonches, who intervened on his behalf.
34 B. J. Rowe, 'Discipline in the Norman Garrisons under Bedford, 1422–1435', *English Historical Review*, 46 (1931), 202–6.
35 Newhall, 307–8.

CHAPTER SIX: A SECOND AGINCOURT

1 Newhall, 311–12; Stevenson, ii, 15–24; Le Cacheux, ci; Chevalier, 'Les Écossais dans les Armées de Charles VII', 88–9. The Scots 'with axes' were Highlanders.
2 Newhall, 314. See above, 62–3.
3 B. J. H. Rowe, 'A Contemporary Account of the Hundred Years' War from 1415 to 1429', *English Historical Review*, 41 (1926), 512; Carolus-Barré, 'Compiègne et la Guerre 1414–1430', 385–6; C. A. J. Armstrong, 'Sir John Fastolf and the Law of Arms' in Allmand (ed.), *War, Literature and Politics in the Late Middle Ages*, 47–9.
4 Carolus-Barré, 'Compiègne et la Guerre 1414–1430', 386; Newhall, 312–13; Monstrelet, iv, 186.
5 *Bourgeois*, 192, 194; *Actes*, i, 76–9.
6 Matthew Strickland and Robert Hardy, *The Great Warbow* (Stroud, 2005), 347; Newhall, 317, 319.
7 Griffiths, 185; Stevenson, ii, 24–8; *CMSM*, i, 137–8.

8 *Bourgeois*, 196–7.
9 The wages of archers in the English army who could not shoot ten aimed arrows a minute were withheld: Barker, 87.
10 *Bourgeois*, 197–200; Monstrelet, iv, 192–6; Chartier, 41–3; Newhall, 319–20.
11 Ramsay, i, 344–5; Chevalier, 'Les Écossais dans les Armées de Charles VII', 92. Some sixteen thousand Scots had entered the dauphin's service since 1418: ibid., 88.
12 *Bourgeois*, 200–1.
13 Newhall, 320–1; Monstrelet, iv, 199–206.
14 Ibid., i, 138–9, 115 n. 1, 149–50; ii, 44 n. 1.
15 *CMSM*, i, 26–7, 146–9, 160–1, 163–5, 170–1.
16 Ibid., i, 27 n. 3, 199–200, 201, 204–5, 259–60.
17 *Actes*, i, 145–7.
18 Ibid., 74–6, 397–9; ii, 331, 333, 335, 338, 346.
19 Ibid., i, 103–4.
20 Ibid., i, 104–6, 113–15, 124–7.
21 Ibid., ii, 47–53; Le Cacheux, civ–cvii. See also *Actes*, ii, 44–5, 358.
22 Vaughan, 31–8; Monstrelet, iv, 206ff.
23 Vaughan, 38–9. For trials by battle, including Henry V's challenge to the dauphin in 1415, see Barker, 207–11.
24 Bossuat, 52; Vaughan, 20.
25 Ibid., 9; Armstrong, 'La Double Monarchie', 84–5.
26 Barker, 369–70; Beaurepaire, 15.
27 Ramsay, i, 354; Bossuat, 52–3; Little, 189.
28 Ramsay, i, 364.
29 *PR*, x, 205; Griffiths, 73–7.
30 *CMSM*, i, 225–8.
31 *Bourgeois*, 221–2, 226; *English Suits*, 176 n. 24; Thompson, 71, 99, 103.
32 Ramsay, i, 365.
33 *PR*, x, 276–8, 280; Ramsay, ii, 365–7. See Allmand, *Henry V*, 260–1 and Harriss, 94 ff. for Henry denying his uncle the cardinalship.
34 *PR*, x, 319; *POPC*, iii, 231, 237.
35 *PR*, x, 280; Griffiths, 187; Ramsay, i, 371–2; Pollard, 12.
36 Little, 187–8; *CMSM*, i, 242 n. 3, 262.
37 *Bourgeois*, 216, 219; Ramsay, i, 374–5; Chartier, i, 54–5; Bossuat, 86–7.
38 Chartier, i, 55–6; Rowe, 'A Contemporary Account', 512.
39 *Actes*, ii, 359; *English Suits*, 220–30, where the fall of La-Ferté-Bernard is wrongly ascribed to February 1427. The court decided in Stafford's favour on 13 February 1434.

40 *Bourgeois*, 223–4; Pollard, 13; Keen, 33; *English Suits*, 205–8.
41 *Actes*, ii, 359, 361; Pollard, 13–14.

CHAPTER SEVEN: THE PUCELLE

1 Vaughan, 48–9. The Treaty of Delft was signed on 3 July 1428.
2 *PR*, x, 322–3, 347–9.
3 Stevenson, i, 403–21; Anne Curry, 'English Armies in the Fifteenth Century' in Anne Curry and Michael Hughes (eds.), *Arms, Armies and Fortifications in the Hundred Years War* (Woodbridge, 1994), 43.
4 *PR*, x, 322.
5 Stevenson, ii, 76–8; Beaurepaire, 30; *POPC*, iv, 223. As late as 8 September 1428 it was still expected that Angers would be Salisbury's objective; on that date the estates-general meeting at Rouen granted money for the recovery of Angers: Beaurepaire, 33–4.
6 Keen, 160–1; Thomas Montagu, *ODNB*, 3.
7 Ramsay, i, 381–2.
8 Bernard Chevalier, *Les Bonnes Villes de France du XIVe au XVIe Siècle* (Paris, 1982), 50–1.
9 Barker, 178ff., 370–2.
10 Jacques Debal, 'La Topographie de l'Enceinte d'Orléans au Temps de Jeanne d'Arc' in *Jeanne d'Arc*, 30–9; Kelly Devries, *Joan of Arc: A Military Leader* (Stroud, 2003), 55; Ramsay, i, 383–4.
11 Devries, *Joan of Arc*, 56–7; Monstrelet, iv, 299–300; *Brut*, 434–5; Chartier, i, 63–4.
12 Monstrelet, iv, 300.
13 Devries, *Joan of Arc*, 58; Debal, 'La Topographie de l'Enceinte d'Orléans', 26–7, 38; Monstrelet, iv, 298–301; Taylor, 278.
14 Debal, 'La Topographie de l'Enceinte d'Orléans', 30–9.
15 Monstrelet, iv, 301.
16 *Bourgeois*, 227–30; Monstrelet, iv, 310–14; Strickland and Hardy, *The Great Warbow*, 349–50, where it is wrongly ascribed to 1428.
17 Chevalier, 'Les Écossais dans les Armées de Charles VII', 93–4; Brown, 'French Alliance or English Peace?', 91–3.
18 Taylor, 179–81.
19 Pernoud, 20–1.
20 Taylor, 142. According to her uncle, her first visit was in May 1428, but his account is full of contradictions and the siege of Orléans did not begin until 12 October 1428.
21 Taylor, 271, 273, 275.
22 Ibid., 303.
23 André Vauchez, 'Jeanne d'Arc et le Prophétisme Féminin des XIVe et XVe Siècles', in *Jeanne d'Arc*, 159–64.

24 Ibid., 162–3.
25 Taylor, 142–3; Vale, 49–50; Léo Germain, 'Recherches sur les Actes de Robert de Baudricourt depuis 1432 jusqu'à 1454', *Bulletin Mensuel de la Société d'Archéologie Lorraine et du Musée Historique Lorrain*, 2 (1902), 221–30.
26 Taylor, 272, 276. Colet de Vienne was later paid a messenger's wages for bringing news of the relief of Orléans to Tours: Jan van Herwaarden, 'The Appearance of Joan of Arc' in Jan van Herwaarden (ed.), *Joan of Arc: Reality and Myth* (Hilversum, 1994), 38.
27 Taylor, 271–2, 274, 275–6; Thomas Aquinas, *Summa Theologica*, quoted in Robert Wirth (ed.), *Primary Sources and Context Concerning Joan of Arc's Male Clothing* (Historical Academy for Joan of Arc Studies, 2006), 11; Vaughan, 39–40.
28 Taylor, 142–3, 277–8.
29 Ibid., 144, 317–18; Pierre Duparc (ed.), *Procès en Nullité de la Condamnation de Jeanne d'Arc* (Paris, 1977), i, 326.
30 Vale, 54, 43; Herwaarden, 'The Appearance of Joan of Arc', 41; Taylor, 11–12.
31 Ibid., 46–9, 311, 340, 347.
32 Ibid., 157 n. 45; Vale, 55. Martin V had ruled that the devotion was acceptable if accompanied by the sign of the cross.
33 Taylor, 73–4; Little, 99–105, 108–12; Vale, 55–6.
34 Chartier, i, 65; Monstrelet, iv, 317–19; Claude Desama, 'Jeanne d'Arc et la diplomatie de Charles VII: L'Ambassade Française auprès de Philippe le Bon en 1429', *Annales de Bourgogne*, 40 (1968), 290–9; Little, 93–4.
35 Ibid., 106.

CHAPTER EIGHT: THE SIEGE OF ORLÉANS

1 Taylor, 312–13.
2 Jean-Pierre Reverseau, 'L'Armement Défensif à l'Époque de Jeanne d'Arc. L'Armure de l'Héroïne' in *Jeanne d'Arc*, 68; Pernoud, 59; Taylor, 157, 312.
3 Taylor, 144, 155; Chartier, i, 69–71. Ibid., i, 122–3 claims magical qualities for Martel's sword: when it broke it could not be repaired and Jehanne's success in arms ended.
4 Taylor, 18–19, 77–8, 285; Déborah Fraiolo, 'L'Image de Jeanne d'Arc: Que Doit-elle au Milieu Littéraire et Religieux de son Temps?' in *Jeanne d'Arc*, 194. Jehanne knew of the Merlin prophecy at the time of her trial but did not believe it: Taylor, 151.
5 See above, 105.

6   Taylor, 74–5. When a copy of this letter was read to Jehanne at her trial, she said that it should have read 'Surrender to the King', not to the Pucelle, and denied using the phrases 'commander of war' or 'body for body': ibid., 143–4, 160–1.

7   Ibid., 160–1, 74.

8   Ibid., 298, 314, 309, 338.

9   www.jeannedarc.com.fr/centre/vignolles.html; J.-E.-J. Quicherat, *Procès de Condamnation et de Réhabilitation de Jeanne d'Arc dite la Pucelle* (Paris, 1843), iii, 32; Taylor, 303.

10 Ibid., 278–9; Devries, *Joan of* Arc, 69–70.

11 Taylor, 279–80; Chartier, i, 69. Blois was the nearest river crossing in Armagnac hands.

12 Taylor, 340, 356–7.

13 Ibid., 295; Quicherat, *Procès de Condamnation*, iv, 154–5.

14 *POPC*, iii, 322. The letter must have been sent before Burgundy withdrew his men and probably before the dauphin approved Jehanne's involvement.

15 Beaurepaire, 30–6; *CMSM*, i, 264–70, 272–83; Stevenson, ii, 79–84, 89–92. The clergy had granted a generous two-tenths solely for recovering Mont-Saint-Michel.

16 Taylor, 239 n. 22.

17 Ibid., 280, 313, 341.

18 Taylor, 295–6, 313–14, 342–3; Quicherat, *Procès de Condamnation*, iv, 157.

19 Taylor, 84, 314. In a postscript Jehanne demanded the return of her herald in exchange for some of her English prisoners from Saint-Loup.

20 Ibid., 318–19, 343–4. Gaucourt did not include this story in his evidence at the nullification trial but another witness, the president of the *chambre-des-comptes*, said Gaucourt had told him it.

21 Taylor, 158, 280, 296, 315–16.

22 Ibid., 315–17; Matthew Strickland, 'Chivalry at Agincourt' in Anne Curry (ed.), *Agincourt 1415: Henry V, Sir Thomas Erpingham and the Triumph of the English Archers* (Stroud, 2000), 120, pl. 56; Eamon Duffy, *Marking the Hours: English People and their Prayers 1240–1570* (New Haven and London, 2006), 77.

23 Taylor, 280–1, 315–16. For Glasdale see *English Suits*, 294–5; Newhall, *Muster and Review*, 109.

24 Monstrelet, iv, 321–2; Taylor, 87.

25 Taylor, 86, 281; Devries, *Joan of Arc*, 88.

26 Ibid., 96–101; Taylor, 158, 306–8; Stevenson, ii, 95–100.

27 Chartier, i, 82–3; *Third Report of the Royal Commission on Historical Manuscripts* (London, 1872), Appendix, 279–80.

28 Devries, *Joan of Arc*, 102–3; A. D. Carr, 'Welshmen and the Hundred Years War', *The Welsh History Review*, 4 (1968–9), 39, 36; Rowe, 'A Contemporary Account', 512.
29 Taylor, 308; Chartier, i, 83–4.
30 Monstrelet, iv, 329–33; Chartier, i, 85–7; Jehan de Waurin, *Anchiennes Cronicques d'Engleterre*, ed. Mlle Dupont (Paris, 1858), i, 293–5; Hugh Collins, 'Sir John Fastolf, John Lord Talbot and the Dispute over Patay: Ambition and Chivalry in the Fifteenth Century' in Diana Dunn (ed.), *War and Society in Medieval and Early Modern Britain* (Liverpool, 2000), 114–40.
31 Ibid., 124–5, 128–36; *English Suits*, 264.
32 *ODNB*, Thomas Scales, 1; ibid., Thomas Rempston, 2; Collins, 'Sir John Fastolf, John Lord Talbot and the Dispute over Patay', 126–7; Michael K. Jones, 'Ransom Brokerage in the Fifteenth Century' in Philippe Contamine, Charles Giry-Deloison and Maurice Keen (eds.), *Guerre et Société en France, en Angleterre et en Bourgogne XIVe –XVe Siècle* (Villeneuve d'Ascq, 1991), 223–4; J. L. Bolton, 'How Sir Thomas Rempston Paid his Ransom: Or, the Mistakes of an Italian Bank' in Clark (ed.), *Conflicts, Consequences and the Crown in the Late Middle Ages*, 101–18.
33 *Actes*, ii, 150 n. 1; *English Suits*, 289; Little, 106–7, 174.
34 Collins, 'Sir John Fastolf, John Lord Talbot and the Dispute over Patay', 123. See below, 297.
35 Taylor, 45–6. For the making of the legend see Timothy Wilson-Smith, *Joan of Arc: Maid, Myth and History* (Stroud, 2006).

CHAPTER NINE: A NEW KING OF FRANCE

1 *POPC*, iii, 330–8.
2 Ibid., 339; Harriss, 184–8; *PR*, x, 370; Ramsay, i, 401–2, 409.
3 Little, 114–15; Taylor, 283, 94–5.
4 Ibid., 31–2, 169–70; *Bourgeois*, 230–3, 238–9; Monstrelet, iv, 335.
5 Taylor, 165 n. 56; Chartier, i, 97–8; Georges Peyronnet, 'Un Problème de Légitimité: Charles VII et le Toucher des Écrouelles', in *Jeanne d'Arc*, 197–8.
6 Chartier, i, 96–8; Taylor, 203; Pernoud, 124–6.
7 Taylor, 95.
8 *Bourgeois*, 237–8. Griffiths, 220 describes the reading as a pageant, which would have been even more striking in its effect.
9 Stevenson, ii, 101–11.
10 *CMSM*, i, 283–4, 288 n. 1; Beaurepaire, 37–9; Richard A. Newhall, *Muster and Review: A Problem of English Military Administration* (Cambridge, Mass., 1940), 111–12.

11 *Bourgeois*, 236; Thompson, 108, 91.

12 *POPC*, iii, 322.

13 *PR*, x, 369–70; Stevenson, ii, 120–1.

14 Thompson, 105; *Bourgeois*, 238; Ramsay, i, 401–4.

15 Taylor, 119–22; Monstrelet, iv, 340–4. The friar was Brother Richard: see above, 126.

16 Chartier, i, 103–5; Monstrelet, iv, 344–7; Pernoud, 132–3. Senlis surrendered to the Armagnacs on 22 August: *Bourgeois*, 239; Thompson, 106.

17 Monstrelet, iv, 348–9; Pernoud, 133, 139; Ramsay, i, 402–3; Vaughan, 21–2.

18 Ramsay, i, 404; Germain Lefèvre-Pontalis, 'La Panique Anglaise en Mai 1429', *Moyen Âge* (1891), 9–11.

19 Jouet, 95–6, 100; *CMSM*, i, 291.

20 Ibid., i, 289.

21 Ibid., ii, 22–4; *Actes*, ii, 146–9.

22 Jouet, 130; Siméon Luce, 'Un Complot contre les Anglais à Cherbourg à l'Époque de Jeanne d'Arc', *Mémoires de l'Académie de Caen* (1887–8), 96–116; *Actes*, ii, 176–8; Monstrelet, iv, 350–1; Puiseux, *L'Émigration Normande*, 55.

23 Le Cacheux, cvi–cviii; *Actes*, ii, 368–9; Chartier, i, 114–15; Newhall, *Muster and Review*, 125, 126 n. 282; Allmand, 189; Monstrelet, iv, 372.

24 *Bourgeois*, 242; Thompson, '"Monseigneur Saint Denis"', 28–9; Pernoud, 136–7.

25 Stevenson, ii, 118–19.

26 Pernoud, 134–8; *Bourgeois*, 240–2; Taylor, 124–5.

27 Pernoud, 141; Ramsay, i, 406.

28 Bossuat, esp. 24–5, 49–50, 66–7.

29 Ibid., 112–23, 118, 212–13; Taylor, 130–1; Pernoud, 143–5.

30 Ibid., 145–6; Taylor, 132–3.

CHAPTER TEN: CAPTURE

1 Ramsay, i, 413–14; Griffiths, 189; Vaughan, 22; *Bourgeois*, 242–3.

2 Rowe, 'The *Grand Conseil*', 218; Stevenson, ii, 85–7; *CMSM*, i, 291; Le Cacheux, 162–3; Jouet, 86.

3 Anne Curry, 'The Nationality of Men-at-Arms Serving in English Armies in Normandy and the Pays de Conquête, 1415–1450: A Preliminary Study', *Reading Medieval Studies*, 18 (1992), 139–40.

4 Plaisse, *La Vie Municipale à Évreux*, 121; Newhall, *Muster and Review*, 88, 90.

5 Rowe, 'Discipline in the Norman Garrisons', 207–8; *Actes*, i, 294–6.
6 Ibid., i, 295 n. 1; ii, 158, 206–8.
7 Ibid., ii, 158.
8 Ibid., ii, 157–60.
9 Keen, 167; Bossuat, 134 n. 3, 138.
10 Pollard, 17.
11 Griffiths, 37, 39.
12 *PR*, x, 368–9; Griffiths, 190.
13 *PR*, x, 437; Anne Curry, 'The "Coronation Expedition" and Henry VI's Court in France, 1430 to 1432' in Jenny Stratford (ed.), *The Lancastrian Court* (Donnington, 2003), 30–5; Dorothy Styles and C. T. Allmand, 'The Coronation of Henry VI', *History Today*, 32 (May 1982), 30.
14 *PR*, x, 437; Vaughan, 8, 54–7; Monstrelet, iv, 373–5.
15 *PR*, x, 373; Vaughan, 22–4.
16 Carolus-Barré, 'Compiègne et la Guerre 1414–1430', 386; Devries, *Joan of Arc*, 164; Pernoud, 147.
17 Taylor, 175–6; Pernoud, 149–53; Monstrelet, iv, 388.
18 Pernoud, 150–1; Devries, *Joan of Arc*, 169–74.
19 Taylor, 192–3, 191–2, 320, 329; Pernoud, 153–6.
20 Ibid., 157–8.
21 Bernard Guillemain, 'Une Carrière: Pierre Cauchon' in *Jeanne d'Arc*, 217–25.
22 Pernoud, 156–7, 159, 161.
23 Beaurepaire, 39, 40; Stevenson, ii, 128–39.
24 Ibid., 140–1; Curry, 'The "Coronation Expedition"', 36–8, 40–1.
25 *PR*, x, 436; Rowe, 'The *Grand Conseil* under the Duke of Bedford, 1422–35', 224–5; Harriss, 202.
26 Ramsay, i, 419; Beaurepaire, 40–1; *Bourgeois*, 251.
27 Ibid., 248–52.
28 Vaughan, 60–6; Monstrelet, iv, 406–8; Chartier, i, 131–2.
29 Monstrelet, iv, 409–20.
30 Ibid., 421–5; Ramsay, i, 420 n. 1; Vaughan, 63.
31 Ibid., 24–5; Stevenson, ii, 156–81.
32 Curry, 'The "Coronation Expedition"', 32, 42; *PR*, x, 447.
33 Ibid., 437.
34 Harriss, 103, 187, 204–5; *PR*, x, 443; Griffiths, 191. Edmund Beaufort's youthful affair with Katherine may have resulted in the birth of Edmund 'Tudor', father of Henry VII: *ODNB*, Edmund Beaufort, 1–2.

CHAPTER ELEVEN: TRIAL AND EXECUTION

1 *Bourgeois*, 254–67; Stevenson, ii, 424–6; Ramsay, i, 431 n. 5.
2 *Bourgeois*, 257–8; Curry, 'The "Coronation Expedition"', 45.
3 Pernoud, 160–1; Beaurepaire, 40. The difficulty of categorising the Pucelle is reflected in the ambivalent phrase describing her as '*personne de guerre*'.
4 Taylor, 31, 132–3 and see above, 138–9.
5 M. G. A. Vale, 'Jeanne d'Arc et ses Adversaires: Jeanne, Victime d'Une Guerre Civile?' in *Jeanne d'Arc*, 207–9; Norman P. Tanner (ed.), *Heresy Trials in the Diocese of Norwich, 1428–31*, Camden Fourth Series, 20 (1977), 8. William Alnwick, the bishop of Norwich, who carried out these prosecutions, was one of the few English people to attend Jehanne's trial.
6 Vale, 'Jeanne d'Arc et ses Adversaires', 208–9, quoting Matthew ch. 24 v. 24.
7 Taylor, 136.
8 Vale, 47–8.
9 Taylor, xix, 22–3; Vale, 48; Vale, 'Jeanne d'Arc et ses Adversaires', 210–14.
10 Ibid., 23–5, 25 n. 79; Pernoud, 206–7.
11 Taylor, 321–31, esp. 322–3, 330–1.
12 Adorating: from the Latin, as in praying to rather than simply adoring or worshipping.
13 Taylor, 218.
14 Ibid., 220–2. It was claimed at the nullification trial (Pernoud, 218–20) that Jehanne was forced or tricked into wearing male clothing again so that she could be executed but, as the marginal note makes clear, this was not the capital offence and it was not in the interest of the English to procure her relapse into heresy: Vale, 'Jeanne d'Arc et ses Adversaires', 214–15.
15 Pernoud, 233 asserts that Thérage was an Englishman: he was in fact Norman and had been executing traitors since at least 1421: Le Cacheux, 34–5.
16 Pernoud, 229–33; Taylor, 228.
17 *Bourgeois*, 260–4; Pernoud, 233–4.
18 *Bourgeois*, 337–8; Vauchez, 'Jeanne d'Arc et le Prophétisme Féminin', 166–7; Pernoud, 241–9.
19 Taylor, 225–8; Pernoud, 236–7, 239.
20 Taylor, 227; *Bourgeois*, 264–5.
21 Ibid., 230–3, 234–5, 238. See above, 126.
22 Taylor, 235 n. 17; *Bourgeois*, 253–4.
23 Taylor, 25 n. 77, 35, 172–3, 177.

24 Vauchez, 'Jeanne d'Arc et le Prophétisme Féminin', 165; Little, 121–3.
25 Taylor, 173; Pernoud, 159.
26 Ibid., 237; Vale, 58–9.
27 Quicherat, *Procès de Condamnation*, v, 168; *Bourgeois*, 266; Chartier, i, 133. The 'holy fool' was a popular concept in the medieval period.
28 Monstrelet, iv, 433–4; *Bourgeois*, 266; Chartier, i, 132–3.
29 *Bourgeois*, 264; Chartier, i, 133–4; Ramsay, i, 433–4.
30 *Actes*, ii, 154–7; Le Cacheux, 210–11.
31 Beaurepaire, 42–3; Newhall, *Muster and Review*, 118.
32 Ibid., 142–3.
33 *Bourgeois*, 265–6; Harriss, 205. A Dutchman from the Évreux garrison was pardoned on 4 April 1433 for crimes including holding hostage two priests and a woman in Louviers after the siege and stealing hens and fish from them: *Actes*, ii, 248–50.
34 *Bourgeois*, 268–9; Monstrelet, v, 1–3.
35 The Nine Worthies included three Old Testament heroes, Joshua, Judas Maccabeus and David; three classical heroes, Hector, Julius Caesar and Alexander; and three romance heroes, Arthur, Charlemagne and Godfrey de Bouillon.
36 Ramsay, i, 432 n. 4; *Bourgeois*, 268–71; Monstrelet, v, 1–4; Thompson, 199–205.
37 *Bourgeois*, 271.

CHAPTER TWELVE: A YEAR OF DISASTERS

1 Griffiths, 192; Monstrelet, v, 5; *Bourgeois*, 271–3.
2 Ibid., 268.
3 Stevenson, ii, 196–202; Griffiths, 193.
4 Curry, 'The "Coronation Expedition"', 50; Thompson, 200.
5 Maurice Keen, *England in the Later Middle Ages* (London, 2003), 311.
6 Rowe, 'The *Grand Conseil*', 225.
7 Ibid., 226–7; Harriss, 208–9.
8 Ibid., 212–22; *PR*, xi, 1–4.
9 Monstrelet, v, 12–15; Le Cacheux, c, cxi–cxii, cxxvi, 224–5, 230–3, 253–5; *Actes*, ii, 186 n. 1; Stevenson, ii, 202–4. Ricarville had previously led raids from Beauvais c.1430–1: *Actes*, ii, 171. See also below, 313.
10 Monstrelet, v, 21–5; Chartier, i, 141–3; *Bourgeois*, 276–7.
11 *Actes*, ii, 233–7.
12 Vale, 122; Thompson, 226–7; *Bourgeois*, 281.

13 Ibid., 278; Jouet, 186–7.
14 *Bourgeois*, 274–81.
15 Beaurepaire,43; Stevenson, ii, 208–9.
16 *Actes*, ii, 234; Chartier, i, 150–3 wrongly dates this raid to 1432.
17 Cagny, 185–7; Chartier, i, 134–41, where Saint-Cénéry is mistakenly transcribed as Saint-Célerin and Vivoin as Vinaing: Beaumont-le-Vicomte is now Beaumont-sur-Sarthe. Monstrelet, v, 100–2 wrongly dates this episode to 1434.
18 *CMSM*, i, 34 n. 2; ii, 13–14; Monstrelet, v, 31–5; Chartier, i, 143–7; *Bourgeois*, 278–81.
19 Ibid., 282; Harriss, *Shaping the Nation*, 328–9.
20 Griffiths, 192; Harriss, 225–6; *Bourgeois*, 282–3.
21 *CMSM*, i, 289–90, 293, 314–16, esp. 315.
22 Ibid., ii, 14–15, 30–2; *Actes*, ii, 382, 383.
23 *Bourgeois*, 283.
24 Griffiths, 193–4; Harris, 221.
25 See above, 49.
26 Monstrelet, v, 56; *ODNB*, John, duke of Bedford, 11; Vaughan, 132–3 suggests this figure may be an exaggeration and posits 'perhaps fifteen'.
27 Monstrelet, 55–6; *ODNB*, John, duke of Bedford, 9; Armstrong, 'La Double Monarchie', 107–9.
28 Monstrelet, v, 57–8; Harris, 229; Vaughan, 27.

CHAPTER THIRTEEN: RECOVERY

1 Harriss, 227; Griffiths, 195–6.
2 *PR*, xi, 67; Harriss, 227–8.
3 *PR*, xi, 67.
4 Ibid., 77–8.
5 Harriss, 231; Griffiths, 196.
6 Harriss, 232–3; *PR*, xi, 102. I cannot reconcile Cromwell's statement in parliament with the annual deficit of £21,447 or £22,000 calculated by Harriss, 232 and *PR*, xi, 70 respectively.
7 *PR*, xi, 67; Stevenson, ii, 250–6.
8 *Bourgeois*, 285, 289, 328.
9 Little, 195–6; Stevenson, ii, 229; Vale, 71; Chartier, i, 170–2; Monstrelet, v, 73–4.
10 Stevenson, ii, 220, 241, 248.
11 Keen, 'The End of the Hundred Years War', 308–9.
12 Ibid., 221, 239–40, 231–8; *CMSM*, i, 223 n. 1; Harriss, 183.
13 Stevenson, ii, 250, 257–8.
14 Ramsay, i, 448 n. 4; Stevenson, ii, 540–6, 551–2.

15 Bossuat, 184, 197–8, 200; Stevenson, ii, 427–9.
16 Vaughan, 66–7; Pollard, 18–19; Harriss, 228 n. 40; Monstrelet, v, 62–70.
17 *Actes*, ii, 383; Chartier, i, 160, 164–5; Beaurepaire, 44–5, 48, 45 n. 93. Arundel's campaign is wrongly dated to 1432 by Chartier and to 1434 by Ramsay, i, 462–3.
18 Chartier, i, 165–8.
19 Monstrelet, v, 79–81.
20 *Bourgeois*, 286–8.
21 *CMSM*, ii, 27.
22 Le Cacheux, 270–3.
23 *CMSM*, ii, 34.
24 *Bourgeois*, 288–9.
25 *PR*, xi, 83–4.
26 Ibid., 84–8.
27 See above, 28.
28 *PR*, xi, 71–2.
29 Beaurepaire, 44–5, 48.
30 Pollard, 19; *CPR 1429–36*, 353; Monstrelet, v, 91.
31 Ibid., 91; *Bourgeois*, 290.
32 Harriss, 236–7; *POPC*, iv, 410–16.
33 Harriss, 222–6.

CHAPTER FOURTEEN: DISORDER AND DEFEAT

1 Monstrelet, v, 91–2; Pollard, 19–20.
2 Monstrelet, v, 93–4; *CMSM*, ii, 64; Beaurepaire, 47.
3 *CMSM*, ii, 28–9. Curry, 'The Nationality of Men-at-Arms', 156 suggests Pleuron was the product of an Anglo-French marriage; this is not impossible but it would have made him less than sixteen years old.
4 *CMSM*, ii, 39–40, 43.
5 Rowe, 'Discipline in the Norman Garrisons', 195 n. 3; *CMSM*, i, 144–6; Lefèvre-Pontalis, 'La Panique Anglaise en Mai 1429', 9, 12, 20; *CCR 1429–35*, 47–8; Stevenson, ii, 147.
6 Rowe, 'Discipline in the Norman Garrisons', 196; Jouet, 35; *CMSM*, ii, 17.
7 Ramsay, i, 460 n. 2; Chartier, i, 175–7.
8 *CMSM*, ii, 41, 42; Rowe, 'John Duke of Bedford and the Norman "Brigands"', 598–9; Chartier, i, 177.
9 Monstrelet, v, 104–5; *Bourgeois*, 290, 292. Jouet, 35 and those following him are wrong in merging the Venables and Waterhouse affairs into a single incident and in suggesting it was a massacre of

peasants. Monstrelet wrongly locates Saint-Pierre-sur-Dives to 'near Tancarville' in upper Normandy.

10 *CMSM*, ii, 48–9, 47.
11 Ibid., 49, 67–8.
12 Curry, 'Isolated or Integrated?', 201; Newhall, *Muster and Review*, 118.
13 Curry, 'L'Effet de la Libération de la Ville d'Orléans', 104–5; Newhall, *Muster and Review*, 119–20; *CMSM*, ii, 46.
14 Monstrelet, v, 183; Beaurepaire, 46–8.
15 *Bourgeois*, 292–3; Vaughan, 67.
16 Beaurepaire, 133; *CMSM*, ii, 19. See above, 187–8.
17 Jouet, 62; *CMSM*, ii, 50–1, 53–4; Monstrelet, v, 113.
18 Chartier, i, 172–3; Cagny, 188–92; Monstrelet, v, 113–14; *CMSM*, ii, 51–2, 54–66.
19 Monstrelet, v, 118–23.
20 Very Rev. Canon Tierney, 'Discovery of the Remains of John, 7th Earl of Arundel, (*obit.* 1435)', *Sussex Archaeological Collections*, 12 (1860), 236.
21 *CPR 1429–1436*, 491; *CCR 1435–1441*, 138–9; *ODNB*, John Fitzalan, seventh earl of Arundel, 3; Tierney, 'Discovery of the Remains', 237–9.
22 Chartier, i, 179–80; Monstrelet, v, 125.
23 *Bourgeois*, 295.
24 Bossuat, 214; Vaughan, 63, 67.
25 Monstrelet, v, 106–10; Ramsay, i, 464–5; Harriss, 241–2.
26 Ibid., 108.
27 *Bourgeois*, 294–5.

CHAPTER FIFTEEN: THE TREATY OF ARRAS

1 Griffiths, 207–8.
2 Beaurepaire, 48; Harriss, 246; Pollard, 20.
3 *PR*, xi, 158; Ramsay, i, 467 n. 4.
4 Harriss, 247; Griffiths, 199; Ramsay, i, 467–9; Monstrelet, v, 132; *PR*, xi, 115. For a list of all the delegates see Chartier, i, 185–92.
5 Any renunciation of the Treaty of Troyes would not affect the status of Calais and Gascony, which would remain English by right of conquest and inheritance respectively.
6 Stevenson, i, 51–64.
7 Harriss, 250–1. See above, 221.
8 Harriss, 250; Ramsay, i, 473; Joycelyne Gledhill Dickinson, *The Congress of Arras 1435* (Oxford, 1955), 174–6.
9 Monstrelet, v, 151–82; Chartier, i, 194–204; Cagny, 195–209.

10 Vaughan, 99–101.

11 *Bourgeois*, 297; *ODNB*, John, duke of Bedford, 11. Richard I's heart was buried in Rouen, his body at Fontévrault.

12 Catherine Reynolds, '"Les Angloys, de leur droicte nature, veullent touzjours guerreer": Evidence for Painting in Paris and Normandy, c.1420–1450' in Allmand (ed.), *Power, Culture and Religion in France c.1350–c.1550*, 51–5; Jean-Philippe Genet, 'L'Influence Française sur la Littérature Politique Anglaise au Temps de la France Anglaise' in *FAMA*, 87–9; Thompson, '"Monseigneur Saint Denis"', 26; Thompson, 139–42; Le Cacheux, lvi, xcvi–xcvii.

13 *Actes*, ii, 127–9; *Bourgeois*, 307; Le Cacheux, lvi; *ODNB*, John, duke of Bedford, 12.

14 *Bourgeois*, 296–9; Monstrelet, v, 184–7; Chartier, i, 181; Thompson, '"Monseigneur Saint Denis"', 31–3.

15 Chartier, ii, 181–2; Cagny, 212; Monstrelet, v, 199–201.

16 Chartier, i, 215–16; Monstrelet, v, 201; Keen, 191; Cagny, 212–13.

17 Monstrelet, v, 201–2; Cagny, 213; Curry, 'Impact of War', 158–9, 163; Pollard, 21–2.

18 Newhall, *Muster and Review*, 131–2.

19 *CMSM*, ii, 69–70.

20 Beaurepaire, 50–2.

21 Harriss, 256–9; *PR*, xi, 163.

22 Beaurepaire, 55–7; Stevenson, i, 508–9, where the mandate is wrongly dated to 1450.

23 Beaurepaire, 57; Griffiths, 201; Harriss, 251, 258 n.16, where Norbury's departure is wrongly dated to December 1435.

24 Pollard, 22–3.

25 Monstrelet, v, 204–5, 281–2, 297–8; Pollard, 23.

26 *CMSM*, ii, 72–7, 94–5; Jouet, 131–41; Allmand, 41.

CHAPTER SIXTEEN: THE FALL OF PARIS

1 Thompson, 231. The abbess had form as a traitor: she and nuns from the same convent had been arrested in September 1432 in connection with a similar but unsuccessful plot: ibid., 226, 227–8.

2 Le Cacheux, 308; Chartier, i, 217–18.

3 Thompson, 234. See above, 135–6.

4 Thompson, 229, 232.

5 *Bourgeois*, 299–301; Thompson, 231.

6 *Bourgeois*, 300–1; Barker, 249.

7 *Bourgeois*, 301–2; Chartier, i, 221–2, 226–7; Monstrelet, v, 217–18; Thompson, '"Monseigneur Saint-Denis"', 33.

8 *Bourgeois*, 303–5; Monstrelet, v, 218–20; Chartier, i, 223–6; Cagny, 215–17.

9 *Bourgeois*, 305–6.

10 Thompson, 237; *Bourgeois*, 306–8; Monstrelet, v, 221; Chartier, i, 226.

11 *Bourgeois*, 309–12.

12 Little, 190–1; Thompson, 238.

13 André Bossuat, 'L'Idée de Nation et la Jurisprudence du Parlement de Paris au XVe Siècle', *Revue Historique*, 204 (1950), 54–7. The ultimate fate of both parties is not known.

14 Ibid., 57–9.

15 Monstrelet, v, 231; Curry, 'Isolated or Integrated?', 110; Pollard, 37–8.

16 *CMSM*, ii, 78–9, 82–3, 87–92.

17 *PR*, xi, 162; Harriss, 262; Griffiths, 455; *ODNB*, Richard of York, 3 distinguishes York's one-year military indentures from his commission as lieutenant, which does not specificy a time-limit; in practice, as York's later difficulties reveal, the two were clearly intended to be concurrent.

18 Harriss, 261; Stevenson, ii, lxxii–lxxiii; Griffiths, 208.

19 *ODNB*, Richard Neville, 2. See above, 235, 239.

20 Monstrelet, v, 271–2; Cagny, 276–7.

21 Beaurepaire, 69; Barker, 'The Foe Within', 312–13.

22 Ramsay, i, 476; Vaughan, 75–6.

23 Harriss, 258, 260–1; Vaughan, 76.

24 Monique Sommé, 'L'Armée Bourguignonne au Siège de Calais de 1436' in Contamine, Giry-Deloison and Keen (eds.), *Guerre et Société en France, en Angleterre et en Bourgogne XIVe–XVe Siècle*, 202–6.

25 Vaughan, 79; Sommé, 'L'Armée Bourguignonne au Siège de Calais de 1436', 207–9.

26 Monstrelet, v, 238–60; Vaughan, 79–82; Keen, 120 n. 4.

27 Monstrelet, v, 263–4; Vaughan, 82–3; *PR*, xi, 194; Griffiths, 204–5.

CHAPTER SEVENTEEN: DEFENDING NORMANDY

1 *Bourgeois*, 313–14; Pollard, 44–5; Beaurepaire, 60.

2 *Bourgeois*, 313–14; Chartier, i, 233–5; Cagny, 229–30; Pollard, 48.

3 *Bourgeois*, 316–17.

4 Andrew Baume, 'Les Opérations Militaires Anglaises pour Expulser les Compagnies Françaises du Pays de Caux et du Vexin Normand 1436–1437', *FAMA*, 398.

5 *PR*, xi, 237; *CMSM*, ii, 93–4; Beaurepaire, 60; Griffiths, 455; Newhall, *Muster and Review*, 137–42.

6 Ibid., 143–6, 146 n. 326.

7 Baume, 'Les Opérations Militaires Anglaises', 398; Newhall, *Muster and Review*, 143; Pollard, 49, 72–3; Allmand, 'L'Artillerie de l'Armée Anglaise', 78.

8 Harriss, 278–9; *PR*, xi, 237–8; Griffiths, 455–6; Stevenson, lxvi–lxxi.

9 Vaughan, 84; Pollard, 49; Monstrelet, v, 308–16.

10 Bossuat, 264–6, 231–3, 258; Cagny, 237–43; Newhall, *Muster and Review*, 147.

11 Cagny, 230–3; *Bourgeois*, 315–16. An oubliette was a windowless, doorless cell accessed only by a trapdoor in the ceiling.

12 Bossuat, 262–4, 267–9; Cagny, 247–8; Beaurepaire, 66.

13 Pollard, 49–50.

14 *Bourgeois*, 322, 326–7; Monstrelet, v, 338–40; Cagny, 245–8.

15 Christopher Allmand, 'The War and the Non-Combatant' in Fowler (ed.), *The Hundred Years War*, 172; Christopher Allmand, *The Hundred Years War: England and France at War c.1300–c.1450* (Cambridge, 1988); Puiseux, *L'Émigration Normande*, 85.

16 Vale, 74; Cagny, 233–4, 237.

17 Monstrelet, v, 355–6; *CMSM*, ii, 108–10, 112; Harriss, 281.

18 Monstrelet, v, 346–7; Griffiths, 456.

19 Harriss, 281–3; Stevenson, ii, 449–50.

20 Harriss, 282.

21 For this and what follows see Griffiths, 248–51.

22 Newhall, *Muster and Review*, 150 n. 234; Stevenson, ii, 443; Griffiths, 446–7.

23 Monstrelet, v, 352–3; Harriss, 296; Griffiths, 446–7.

24 Allmand, *The Hundred Years War*, 35; Harriss, 296–304; Griffiths, 447–50; C.T. Allmand (ed.), 'Documents Relating to the Anglo-French Negotiations of 1439', *Camden Miscellany*, vol. xxiv, Fourth Series, 9 (Royal Historical Society, 1972), 79–149.

25 Ibid., 135–46; Stevenson, ii, 446.

26 *PR*, xi, 238; Harriss, 304–5; Griffiths, 450, 472.

CHAPTER EIGHTEEN: GAINS AND LOSSES

1 Cagny, 254–5; *Bourgeois*, 327–8; Bossuat, 270–1. Talbot was reimbursed 1462*l*. 10*s*.*t*. (£85,313) for his expenses in taking Saint-Germain: Beaurepaire, 91.

2 Cagny, 254–5; Monstrelet, v, 387–90; Chartier, i, 249–50; Pollard,

52; Keen, 125; Collins, 'Sir John Fastolf, John Lord Talbot and the Dispute over Patay', 127–8.

3 *Bourgeois*, 332–3.

4 Ibid., 329; Chartier, i, 250–1; *CMSM*, ii, 121–2, 125–6.

5 Chartier, i, 252–3.

6 C. T. Allmand, 'Changing Views of the Soldier in Late Medieval France' in Contamine, Giry-Deloison and Keen (eds.), *Guerre et Société en France, en Angleterre et en Bourgogne XIVe–XVe Siècle*, 179–80; Chartier, ii, 12–13; Lewis, *Later Medieval France*, 102.

7 Vale, 75–82; Chartier, i, 253–9; Monstrelet, v, 410–17, 458.

8 *PR*, xi, 245–6; Harriss, 308–11; Stevenson, ii, 440–51.

9 Griffiths, 452; Stevenson, ii, 451–60.

10 *PR*, xi, 246; Griffiths, 452–3; Monstrelet. v, 433–44, 452–4.

11 Harriss, 279–80; Michael Jones, 'John Beaufort, duke of Somerset, and the French expedition of 1443' in Ralph A. Griffiths, *Patronage, the Crown and the Provinces in Later Medieval England* (Gloucester, 1981), 80–1.

12 Griffiths, 457–8; *ODNB*, John Beaufort, 1; *PR*, xi, 238; Jones, 'John Beaufort', 83.

13 Ibid., 84–5; Harriss, 312–13.

14 Ibid., 312–13; Griffiths, 459; Stevenson, ii, 585–91. See also above, 248, 282.

15 Jones, 'John Beaufort', 83; Pollard, 51; Stevenson, ii, 317–19.

16 Monstrelet, v, 405–9; Michael K. Jones, 'Ransom Brokerage in the Fifteenth Century' in Contamine, Giry-Deloison and Keen (eds.), *Guerre et Société en France, en Angleterre et en Bourgogne XIVe –XVe Siècle*, 222.

17 Beaurepaire, 68, 72–3; Stevenson, ii, 308–16; i, 442; Bossuat, 272.

18 Monstrelet, v, 419–20; A. D. Carr, 'Welshmen and the Hundred Years War', 37. See Barker, 178ff. This was Gaucourt's second experience of being taken prisoner in 1440; he had also been captured by the Praguerie rebels earlier in the year: Vale, 80.

19 Monstrelet, v, 418–24.

20 Jones, 'John Beaufort, 85; Beaurepaire, 73–4; Curry, 'The Impact of War', 160–1; Chartier, ii, 7–8.

21 Pollard, 54.

22 Chartier, ii, 15–17.

23 Ibid., 20–2; Stevenson, ii, 463–4; Monstrelet, vi, 10; *Bourgeois*, 341.

CHAPTER NINETEEN: MISSED OPPORTUNITIES

1 Stevenson, ii, 603–7.

2 Griffiths, 459–60; Jones, 'John Beaufort', 100 n. 57; *PR*, xi, 199.

3 Griffiths, 459–61.
4 Monstrelet, vi, 12–21; Chartier, ii, 22–5.
5 Ibid., 25–7; Monstrelet, vi, 21–4; Ditcham, '"Mutton Guzzlers and Wine Bags"', 4.
6 Allmand, 'L'Artillerie de l'Armée Anglaise', 81.
7 Chartier, ii, 17–18, 32; Plaisse, *La Vie Municipale à Évreux*, 130–1, 135, 141, 144.
8 Griffiths, 470.
9 Bossuat, 276–7; Chartier, ii, 33–4.
10 Bossuat, 277, 278 n. 1.
11 Griffiths, 461; Harriss, 318.
12 *PR*, xi, 316.
13 Lewis, *Later Medieval France*, 24–6.
14 Hilary Carey, *Courting Disaster: Astrology at the English Court and University in the Later Middle Ages* (London, 1992), 50, 121; Allmand, *Henry V*, 397 n. 52.
15 Monstrelet, v, 425–6; Lewis, *Later Medieval France*, 17–18. See above, 124.
16 *ODNB*, Eleanor Cobham, 1–3; Harriss, 321–3.
17 *PR*, xi, 316; Barker, 115–16.
18 Pollard, 59; Ramsay, ii, 42; Barker, 87–90; Stevenson, i, 431–2.
19 Vale, 85–6; Perroy, *The Hundred Years War*, 310; Ramsay, ii, 46–7.
20 Jones, 'Ransom Brokerage', 223–4, 233 n. 4; J. L. Bolton, 'How Sir Thomas Rempston Paid his Ransom', 101–18; Williams, *Renewal and Reformation*, 169. For Rempston's previous captivity see also above, 123. I am grateful to M. Jack Thorpe of Erquinghem-Lys for the information on the 'lahire' playing-card.
21 Bossuat, 278–80; Pollard, 59; Stevenson, ii, 331–3, 360–1.
22 Chartier, ii, 36–7; Stevenson, i, 483–4; ii, 463–4; Pollard, 59–60; Allmand, 'L'Artillerie de l'Armée Anglaise', 77.
23 *CMSM*, i, 43; ii, 142, 145–7, 155–6, 164–5, 192–5, 148–9; Stevenson, ii, 335–40.
24 *CMSM*, ii, 200–1.
25 Ibid., 192–5.

CHAPTER TWENTY: A LAST MILITARY EFFORT

1 Harriss, 325–6.
2 Ibid., 333–4; Griffiths, 465, 479 n. 141.
3 Harriss, 334–5; Ramsay, ii, 50–1; Jones, 'John Beaufort', 86–9.
4 *ODNB*, John Fastolf, 1–3; Stevenson, ii, 575–85, esp. 580.
5 Jones, 'John Beaufort', 87–91; Harriss, 334–6.
6 Harriss, 329, 338, 340.

7 Michael K. Jones, 'L'Imposition Illégale de Taxes en "Normandie Anglaise": une Enquête Gouvernementale en 1446', *FAMA*, 462; Griffiths, 467–8; *POPC*, v, 258–63; Pollard, 60.

8 Jones, 'John Beaufort', 87–9, 92; Griffiths, 468–9.

9 Jones, 'John Beaufort', 88, 93; Jones, 'L'Imposition Illégale de Taxes', 462–4, 466; Harriss, 341; *CMSM*, ii, 157–60.

10 Jones, 'L'Imposition Illégale de Taxes', 464; *CMSM*, ii, 159–60.

11 Jones, 'John Beaufort', 95.

12 Ibid.; Ramsay, ii, 7, 26, 55.

13 Harriss, 343; Jones, 'John Beaufort', 95–6; Stevenson, i, 439–41.

14 Harriss, 342; Jones, 'John Beaufort', 96; Stevenson, ii, 347; Jones, 'L'Imposition Illégale de Taxes', 465 n. 12.

15 Ibid., 465–8; *CMSM*, ii, 172–3.

16 Chartier, ii, 37–40; Monstrelet, vi, 77–8. For Ricarville's coup see above, 180.

17 Chartier, ii, 40–2; Monstrelet, vi, 78–80; Cuttler, *The Law of Treason*, 35.

18 Jones, 'L'Imposition Illégale de Taxes', 464–5.

19 *CMSM*, ii, 160–5; Harriss, 341.

20 *POPC*, vi, 32; Griffiths, 483–4; Harriss, 343–4; Ramsay, ii, 58–9; *ODNB*, William de la Pole, 8.

21 Griffiths, 484; *ODNB*, Adam Moleyns, 1–4.

22 Griffiths, 485; Ramsay, ii, 59–60.

23 Vale, 91; *ODNB*, Margaret of Anjou, 1–2.

24 Vale, 73, 84; Barker, 14.

25 Monstrelet, vi, 96–107; Griffiths, 485–6.

26 Ibid., 485–6; *Bourgeois*, 352–3.

27 Barker, 374.

CHAPTER TWENTY-ONE: A TRUCE AND A MARRIAGE

1 *Bourgeois*, 353–4; Ramsay, ii, 60–1; *ODNB*, William de la Pole, 7.

2 Harriss, *Shaping the Nation*, 576.

3 *PR*, xii, 95–6, 98.

4 Harriss, 345–7.

5 Griffiths, 486; Stevenson, ii, 356–60; Ramsay, ii, 61.

6 Ibid., i, 450; Griffiths, 535 n. 28.

7 Ibid., 486–7; Chartier, ii, 43–7; *CMSM*, ii, 176–8.

8 *ODNB*, Richard of York, 5; Stevenson, ii, 79–86, 160–3, 168–70, esp. 85–6.

9 Ramsay, ii, 63–4; Griffiths, 487–8; Stevenson, ii, 452.

10 Griffiths, 487–8; *ODNB*, Margaret of Anjou, 5.

11 Griffiths, 488–9; Ramsay, ii, 64.
12 *PR*, xi, 412.
13 Ibid., 410–12.
14 Fowler, 'Truces', 207–8; Keen, 82.
15 Fowler, 'Truces', 208–9; Beaurepaire, 85–6.
16 *Bourgeois*, 354–5.
17 Vale, 95–6; Beaurepaire, 87; Carr, 'Welshmen and the Hundred Years War', 40.
18 *CMSM*, ii, 178–80; Curry, 'The Impact of War', 170.
19 *CMSM*, ii, 182–8; Carr, 'Welshmen and the Hundred Years War', 40.
20 *CMSM*, ii, 182–4.
21 Beaurepaire, 86–8, 189–92; *ODNB*, Richard of York, 4; *PR*, xi, 391; Stevenson, i, 160–3.
22 Barker, 123–7, 373; Griffiths, 490.
23 Stevenson, i, 115–16, 123.
24 Ibid., 110–11.
25 Ibid., 129–30, 144, 147, 149–52; Griffiths, 493.
26 Ibid., 492–3.
27 Vale, 97.
28 Stevenson, i, 164–7; Griffiths, 495.
29 Stevenson, ii, 638–42.

CHAPTER TWENTY-TWO: CONCESSIONS FOR PEACE

 1 *PR*, xi, 395, 471–2.
 2 Ibid., 471.
 3 Ibid., 471–2.
 4 Beaurepaire, 89–91; *PR*, xi, 392.
 5 *CMSM*, ii, 196–7.
 6 Keen, 207, 214–15; Pollard, 61; Bossuat, 281 n. 1; Beaurepaire, 92–3.
 7 *ODNB*, John Talbot, 1, 4.
 8 Harriss, 357; Ramsay, ii, 72 n. 3.
 9 Griffiths, 391, 493.
10 Harriss, 357.
11 Michael K. Jones, 'Somerset, York and the Wars of the Roses', *English Historical Review*, 411 (1989), 292; *ODNB*, Adam Moleyns, 3; ibid., Richard of York, 6; Harriss, 357–8.
12 *ODNB*, Thomas Kyriell, 1; Griffiths, 506–7.
13 *PR*, xii, 2; Griffiths, 507; Harriss, 358.
14 Griffiths, 496–7; *PR*, xii, 2–3, 32.
15 Ibid., 5, 8.

16 Ibid., 5–6; Griffiths, 496–7; *ODNB*, Humphrey, duke of Gloucester, 8–9; Ramsay, ii, 75; *PR*, xii, 32.
17 Ibid.; Griffiths, 498.
18 *PR*, xii, 6–7; Griffiths, 356; Ramsay, ii, 77.
19 *ODNB*, Henry Beaufort, 12; Harriss, 411.
20 Ramsay, ii, 79.
21 Ibid., ii, 72; *Foedera*, xi, 152; Allmand, 280.
22 *PR*, xii, 34, 7; Ramsay, ii, 80–1; Stevenson, ii, 696–702, 655.
23 *PR*, xii, 34; Ramsay, ii, 80–1; Stevenson, ii, 665.
24 Ibid., 704–10.
25 Ibid., 708–10; *Actes*, ii, 269–71.
26 Stevenson, ii, 692–6; Jones, 'Somerset, York and the Wars of the Roses', 293.
27 Ibid.; Stevenson, ii, 685; Allmand, 281 n. 28; *ODNB*, Edmund Beaufort, 3.
28 For this and the following account of the conference see Stevenson, ii, 634–92.
29 *English Suits*, 120 n. 18; McFarlane, 'A Business-Partnership in War and Administration', 309–10; Massey, 'The Land Settlement in Lancastrian Normandy', 275.
30 Dickinson, *The Congress of Arras*, 116–17. For two examples of this in 1413 see Barker, 64.
31 Stevenson, ii, 676–7, 682–90.

CHAPTER TWENTY-THREE: THE SURRENDER OF MAINE

1 Stevenson, ii, 702–3.
2 Ibid., 710–18.
3 Ramsay, ii, 83; Stevenson, i, 198–201.
4 Ibid., ii, 361–8, wrongly dated to 1445; i, 202–6.
5 Stevenson, ii, 717–18; Griffiths, 503, 541 n. 120; Jones, 'Somerset, York and the Wars of the Roses', 298.
6 MS E30/508, National Archives; *Foedera*, v, i, 189; Griffiths, 503.
7 Ibid., i, 207–8.
8 Auguste Vallet de Viriville, *Histoire de Charles VII, Roi de France, et de Son Époque* (Paris, 1865), iii, 144.
9 Vale, 104; Lewis, *Later Medieval France*, 102; Chevalier, *Les Bonnes Villes de France*, 119. See also above, 278.
10 Claude Gauvard, Alain de Libera and Michel Zink (eds.), *Dictionnaire du Moyen Âge* (Paris, 2002), 560; Allmand, *The Hundred Years War*, 148.
11 Beaurepaire, 93–5; see also above, 329.
12 Stevenson, ii, 479–83; Ramsay, ii, 85; Pollard, 63.

13 Curry, 'English Armies in the Fifteenth Century', 51; Harriss, *Shaping the Nation*, 581.

14 *CMSM*, ii, 214–15.

15 Ibid., 215 n. 1.

16 Jones, 'Ransom Brokerage', 226; Bossuat, 320 n. 2; Jouet, 152–4; *CMSM*, ii, 209; Stevenson, ii, 480 n. 1; Beaurepaire, 95; Margaret Wade Labarge, *Gascony: England's First Colony 1204–1453* (London, 1980), 224, 227–8. See above, 210–12, 216–17.

17 Jones, 'Somerset, York and the Wars of the Roses', 299.

18 Stevenson, i, 209–20, esp. 211.

19 Ibid., 209–20, 245–6, 83–6.

20 Ibid., 218–20.

21 *CMSM*, ii, 206, 208–10, 212–13.

22 Ibid., 212–13, 219–20.

23 *POPC*, vi, 64; Ramsay, ii, 86.

24 *PR*, xii, 54–5.

25 *ODNB*, John Fastolf, 1–3.

CHAPTER TWENTY-FOUR: THE TRUCE BREAKS DOWN

1 Stevenson, i, 223–8.

2 Ibid., 228–32.

3 Ibid., 233–8.

4 Chartier, ii, 60–1; Bossuat, 323–4.

5 Stevenson, i, 280–2; Bossuat, 309–12; C. D. Taylor, 'Brittany and the French Crown: the Legacy of the English Attack on Fougères (1449)' in J. R. Maddicott and D. M. Palliser (eds.), *The Medieval State: Essays Presented to James Campbell* (London and Rio Grande, 2000), 245 n. 5, 252–3.

6 Vale, 79, 156–7; Stevenson, ii, 189–94, where Garter's letter is wrongly dated to 1447.

7 Bossuat, 313–19; Stevenson, i, 283–5.

8 Bossuat, 320–3; Stevenson, i, 287–9; Pollard, 64.

9 Bossuat, 326.

10 Anne Curry, 'Towns at War: Relations between the Towns of Normandy and their English Rulers 1417–1450' in John A. F. Thomson (ed.), *Towns and Townspeople in the Fifteenth Century* (Gloucester and Wolfboro, 1988), 151.

11 Blondel, 23–6; Berry, 245–50; Chartier, ii, 69–71, 74 with a carter rather than a merchant as the protagonist; Stevenson, ii, 619; Jean Glénisson and Victor Deodato da Silva, 'La Pratique et le Rituel de la Reddition aux XIVe et XVe Siècles', in *Jeanne d'Arc*, 114.

12 Thomas Bassin, *Histoire des Régnes de Charles VII and Louis XI* (Paris, 1855), i, 204.
13 Bossuat, 334.
14 Beaurepaire, 100–2; Bossuat, 334.
15 Stevenson, ii, 496–9; Bossuat, 333; *PR*, xii, 107.
16 Ibid., 36–7.
17 Taylor, 'Brittany and the French Crown', 254–5.
18 Stevenson, i, 489; Ramsay, ii, 102.
19 Bossuat, 332, 339; Ramsay, ii, 94 n. 4, 95; Taylor, 'Brittany and the French Crown', 255.
20 *Escouchy*, iii, 145–251; Stevenson, ii, 243–64, wrongly dated to April 1449; Taylor, 'Brittany and the French Crown', 243–5, 256–7.
21 Stevenson, i, 263; Taylor, 'Brittany and the French Crown', 250–1.
22 Ibid., 249; Stevenson, i, 263. See above, 324.
23 Monstrelet, v, 454; Chartier, ii, 27.
24 Vaughan, 110; Stevenson, i, 264–73.
25 Bossuat, 339–41; Plaisse, *La Vie Municipale à Évreux*, 142; Chartier, ii, 80–3; Blondel, 50–63; Berry, 257–61.
26 Stevenson, i, 243–64; Bossuat, 332; Blondel, 37–45.
27 Chartier, ii, 84–7; *Escouchy*, ii, 191–2; Blondel, 65–70; Berry, 262–4.
28 Stevenson, ii, 620; Puiseux, *L'Émigration Normande*, 91–5, esp. 94; Mark Spencer, *Thomas Basin: The History of Charles VII and Louis XI* (Nieuwkoop, 1997), 13–21.
29 Stevenson, ii, 620; Chartier, ii, 93–4; Blondel, 70–3.
30 Spencer, *Thomas Basin*, 25; Bossuat, 340–1; Plaisse, *La Vie Municipale à Évreux*, 142; Chartier, ii, 92–3; Blondel, 77; Berry, 265.

CHAPTER TWENTY-FIVE: RECONQUEST

1 Stevenson, i, 223–8.
2 Chartier, ii, 94–101; Blondel, 78–81; Curry, 'Towns at War', 149–53, esp. 150.
3 Chartier, ii, 102–3; *Escouchy*, iii, 374; Bossuat, 286–7, 320, 342, 346–7, 372–3; Vale, 123.
4 Chartier, ii, 116–19, 159; Blondel, 88–9; Berry, 277; Vale, 123–4; Stevenson, ii, 621. See above, 332.
5 Chartier, ii, 103–14; Blondel, 83–4; Berry, 269–71.
6 Chartier, ii, 115–16; Berry, 273–5; *Bourgeois*, 323–4.
7 Chartier, ii, 121–2, 126–7, 130–2.
8 Ibid., ii, 122–6; Blondel, 89–96; Stevenson, ii, 625–6.
9 Pollard, 65; *PR*, xii, 38.
10 Chartier, ii, 137–52.

11 Stevenson, ii, 609–17; Chartier, ii, 152–4; Jones, 'Somerset, York and the Wars of the Roses', 302. Honfleur is sometimes mistaken for Harfleur in some accounts of the terms of surrender, but Honfleur is in Calvados and Harfleur is clearly the place meant.

12 Ramsay, ii, 100. See above, 90, 275.

13 Stevenson, i, 291–5; Chartier, ii, 172–4; Bossuat, 344–5, 348–53, 371.

14 Stevenson, i, 501–8, 510–12; Griffiths, 519; Harriss, 382; *ODNB*, William de la Pole, 10.

15 *PR*, xii, 71, 73–5; *ODNB*, Adam Moleyns, 3.

16 *PR*, xii, 92–106; *ODNB*, William de la Pole, 13.

17 Rowe, 'A Contemporary Account', 504, 507–8; Blondel, 119–20; Berry, 288, 322; Chartier, ii, 174–80; Jones, 'Somerset, York and the Wars of the Roses', 304.

18 Chartier, ii, 188–9.

19 *CMSM*, ii, 225–7.

20 Chartier, ii, 192–9; Blondel, 170–6; Berry, 330–7; Strickland and Hardy, *The Great Warbow*, 358–60.

21 Chartier, ii, 201–2; Berry, 336; *CMSM*, ii, 229.

22 Chartier, ii, 204–11; Berry, 340–3; Keen, 110 n. 2.

23 Blondel, 206–8; Chartier, ii, 202–3.

24 Griffiths, 521; *CMSM*, ii, 236; Chartier, ii, 214–21.

25 Vale, 138; Cuttler, *The Law of Treason*, 30.

26 Chartier, ii, 223–8; Blondel, 227–30.

27 Chartier, ii, 231–2.

28 Stevenson, ii, 634; i, 502, 517–18, 520–1

29 *CMSM*, ii, 237–9; André Plaisse, *La Délivrance de Cherbourg et du Clos du Cotentin à la Fin de la Guerre de Cent Ans* (Cherbourg, 1989), 180–5; Barker, 'The Foe Within', 305–8.

30 Ibid., 305; Griffiths, 522.

EPILOGUE

1 Chartier, ii, 234.

2 Reynolds, 'English Patrons and French Artists', 309; Curry, 'The Nationality of Men-at-Arms', 157; Vale, 157 n. 6.

3 Thompson, 237; Reynolds, 'English Patrons and French Artists', 307; Tierney, 'Discovery of the Remains', 236.

4 Harriss, *Shaping the Nation*, 584; *PR*, xi, 117.

5 Jones, 'Ransom Brokerage', 228, 222.

6 Keen, *England in the Later Middle Ages*, 407; Ramsay, ii, 129–30.

7 Edmund Beaufort was killed at Saint Albans in 1455; Richard, duke of York, at Wakefield in 1460.

BIBLIOGRAPHY

I: Abbreviations used in the Notes

Actes Paul Le Cacheux (ed.), *Actes de la Chancellerie d'Henri VI Concernant La Normandie sous la Domination Anglaise (1422–1435)* (Société de l'Histoire de Normandie, 1907; 1908), 2 vols.

Allmand C. T. Allmand, *Lancastrian Normandy 1415–1450: The History of a Medieval Occupation* (Oxford, 1983).

Barker Juliet Barker, *Agincourt: The King, the Campaign, the Battle* (London, 2005).

Beaurepaire Charles de Beaurepaire, *Les États de Normandie sous la Domination Anglaise* (Évreux, 1859).

Berry Berry Herald, 'Le Recouvrement de Normendie' in Rev. Joseph Stevenson (ed.), *Narratives of the Expulsion of the English from Normandy* (London, 1863), 239–376.

Blondel Robert Blondel, 'De Reductione Normanniae' in Rev. Joseph Stevenson (ed.), *Narratives of the Expulsion of the English from Normandy* (London, 1863), 1–238.

Bossuat André Bossuat, *Perrinet Gressart et François de Surienne* (Paris, 1936).

Bourgeois Janet Shirley (ed.), *A Parisian Journal, 1405–1449: Translated from the Anonymous Journal d'un Bourgeois de Paris* (Oxford, 1968).

Brut F. W. D. Brie (ed.), *The Brut or The Chronicles of England* (London, 1908), vol. ii.

Cagny H. Moranvillé (ed.), *Chroniques de Perceval de Cagny* (Paris, 1902).

CCR *Calendar of the Close Rolls, Preserved in the Public*

	Record Office: Henry V, vols. i–ii, *1413–22*; *Henry VI*, vols. i–v, *1422–54* (London, 1929–32; 1933–47).
Chartier	Vallet de Viriville (ed.), *Chronique de Charles VII, Roi de France, par Jean Chartier* (Paris, 1858), 2 vols.
CMSM	Siméon Luce (ed.), *Chronique du Mont-Saint-Michel (1343–1468)* (Paris, 1879, 1883), 2 vols.
CPR	*Calendar of the Patent Rolls, Preserved in the Public Record Office: Henry V*, vols. i–iii, *1413–22; Henry VI*, vols. i–v, *1422–52* (London, 1910–11; 1901–09).
English Suits	C. T. Allmand and C. A. J. Armstrong, (eds.), *English Suits Before the Parlement of Paris 1420–1436*, Camden Fourth Series, 26 (Royal Historical Society, 1982).
Escouchy	G. du Fresne de Beaucourt (ed.), *Chronique de Mathieu d'Escouchy* (Paris, 1863–4), 3 vols.
FAMA	*La 'France Anglaise' au Moyen Âge: Actes du IIIe Congrès National des Sociétés Savantes (Poitiers, 1986)* (Paris, 1988).
Foedera	Thomas Rymer (ed.), *Foedera, Conventiones, Litterae* (London, 1726–35), 10 vols.
Griffiths	R. A. Griffiths, *The Reign of King Henry VI* (Stroud, 2004).
Harriss	G. L. Harriss, *Cardinal Beaufort: A Study of Lancastrian Ascendancy and Decline* (Oxford, 1988).
Jeanne d'Arc	*Jeanne d'Arc: Une Époque, un Rayonnement: Colloque d'Histoire Médiévale: Orléans – Octobre 1979* (Paris, 1982).
Jouet	Roger Jouet, *La Résistance à l'Occupation Anglaise en Basse-Normandie (1418–1450)*, Cahier des Annales de Normandie, no. 5 (Caen, 1969).
Keen	Maurice Keen, *The Laws of War in the Late Middle Ages* (London and Toronto, 1965).
Le Cacheux	Paul Le Cacheux (ed.), *Rouen au Temps de Jeanne d'Arc et pendant l'Occupation Anglaise (1419–1449)* (Société de l'Histoire de Normandie, 1931).
Little	Roger G. Little, *The Parlement of Poitiers: War, Government and Politics in France 1418–1436* (London, 1984).

Monstrelet   L. Douët-D'Arcq (ed.), *La Chronique d'Enguerran de Monstrelet* (Paris, 1859–62), vols. iii–vi.

Newhall   Richard A. Newhall, *The English Conquest of Normandy 1416–1434: A Study in Fifteenth Century Warfare* (New Haven and London, 1924).

ODNB   *Oxford Dictionary of National Biography*: online version.

Pernoud   Régine Pernoud, *Joan of Arc: by Herself and her Witnesses*, trans. Edward Hyams (New York and London, 1982).

Pollard   A. R. Pollard, *John Talbot and the War in France, 1427–1453* (London and New Jersey, 1983).

POPC   Nicholas Harriss Nicolas [sic] (ed.), *Proceedings and Ordinances of the Privy Council of England* (London, 1834–7), vols. ii–vi.

PR   Chris Given-Wilson (ed.), *The Parliament Rolls of Medieval England 1275–1504* (Woodbridge and London, 2005), vols. ix–xii.

Ramsay   James H. Ramsay, *Lancaster and York: A Century of English History (1399–1485)* (Oxford, 1892), 2 vols.

Stevenson   Rev. Joseph Stevenson (ed.), *Letters and Papers Illustrative of the Wars of the English in France during the Reign of Henry the Sixth of England* (London, 1861, 1864), 2 vols.

Taylor   Craig Taylor (ed. and trans.), *Joan of Arc: La Pucelle: Selected Sources* (Manchester and New York, 2006).

Thompson   Guy L. Thompson, *Paris and its People under English Rule* (Oxford, 1991).

Vale   M. G. A. Vale, *Charles VII* (London, 1974).

Vaughan   Richard Vaughan, *Philip the Good: the Apogee of Burgundy* (Woodbridge, 2002).

Walsingham   David Prest (trans.), *The Chronica Maiora of Thomas Walsingham 1376–1422*, with introduction and notes by James G. Clark (Woodbridge, 2005).

W&W   James Hamilton Wylie and William Templeton Waugh, *The Reign of Henry the Fifth* (Cambridge, 1914–29), vol. iii.

II: Other Frequently Cited Printed Sources

Bibliographical details of books and articles cited only once are given in full in the relevant note.

Allmand, Christopher (ed.), 'Documents Relating to the Anglo-French Negotiations of 1439', *Camden Miscellany*, vol. xxiv, Fourth Series, 9 (Royal Historical Society, 1972), 79–149.

(ed.), *War, Literature and Politics in the Late Middle Ages* (Liverpool, 1976).

'L'Artillerie de l'Armée Anglaise et son Organisation à l'Époque de Jeanne d'Arc', in *Jeanne d'Arc*, 73–83.

The Hundred Years War: England and France at War c.1300–c.1450 (Cambridge, 1988).

(ed.), *Power, Culture and Religion in France c.1350–c.1550* (Woodbridge, 1989).

'The English and the Church in Lancastrian Normandy' in David Bates and Anne Curry (eds.), *England and Normandy in the Middle Ages* (London and Rio Grande, 1994), 287–97.

Henry V (New Haven and London, 1997).

Armstrong, C. A. J., 'La Double Monarchie et la Maison du Bourgogne (1420–1435): Le Déclin d'une Alliance', *Annales de Bourgogne*, 37 (1965), 81–112.

'Sir John Fastolf and the Law of Arms' in Christopher Allmand (ed.), *War, Literature and Politics in the Late Middle Ages* (Liverpool, 1976), 46–56.

Barker, Juliet, 'The Foe Within: Treason in Lancastrian Normandy' in Peter Coss and Christopher Tyerman (eds.), *Soldiers, Nobles and Gentlemen* (Woodbridge, 2009), 305–20.

Bates, David and Curry, Anne (eds.), *England and Normandy in the Middle Ages* (London and Rio Grande, 1994).

Baume, Andrew, 'Les Opérations Militaires Anglaises pour Expulser les Compagnies Françaises du Pays de Caux et du Vexin Normand 1436–1437' in *FAMA*, 393–400.

Bellaguet, M.-L. (ed.), *Chronique du Religieux de Saint-Denys* (Paris, 1844), 6 vols.

Bolton, J. L., 'How Sir Thomas Rempston Paid his Ransom: Or, the Mistakes of an Italian Bank' in Linda Clark (ed.), *Conflicts, Consequences and the Crown in the Late Middle Ages* (Woodbridge, 2007), 101–18.

Bossuat, André, 'L'Idée de Nation et la Jurisprudence du Parlement de Paris au XVe Siècle', *Revue Historique*, 204 (1950), 54–9.

'Le Parlement de Paris Pendant l'Occupation Anglaise', *Revue Historique*, 229 (1963), 19–40.

Brown, Michael, 'French Alliance or English Peace? Scotland and the

Last Phase of the Hundred Years War, 1415–53' in Linda Clark (ed.), *Conflicts, Consequences and the Crown in the Late Middle Ages* (Woodbridge, 2007), 81–99.

Carolus-Barré, Louis, 'Compiègne et la Guerre 1414–1430', in *Fama*, 383–92.

Carr, A. D., 'Welshmen and the Hundred Years War', *The Welsh History Review*, 4 (1968–9), 21–46.

Chevalier, Bernard, 'Les Écossais dans les Armées de Charles VII jusqu'à la Bataille de Verneuil' in *Jeanne d'Arc*, 85–94.

Les Bonnes Villes de France du XIVe au XVIe Siècle (Paris, 1982).

Clark, Linda (ed.), *Conflicts, Consequences and the Crown in the Late Middle Ages* (Woodbridge, 2007).

Collins, Hugh, 'Sir John Fastolf, John Lord Talbot and the Dispute over Patay: Ambition and Chivalry in the Fifteenth Century' in Diana Dunn (ed.), *War and Society in Medieval and Early Modern Britain* (Liverpool, 2000), 114–40.

Contamine, Philippe, 'The Norman "Nation" and the French "Nation" in the Fourteenth and Fifteenth Centuries' in David Bates and Anne Curry (eds.), *England and Normandy in the Middle Ages* (London and Rio Grande, 1994), 215–34.

Contamine, Philippe, Giry-Deloison, Charles, and Keen, Maurice (eds.), *Guerre et Société en France, en Angleterre et en Bourgogne XIVe –XVe Siècle* (Villeneuve d'Ascq, 1991).

Curry, Anne, 'L'Effet de la Libération de la Ville d'Orléans sur l'Armée Anglaise: Les Problèmes de l'Organisation Militaire en Normandie de 1429 à 1435' in *Jeanne d'Arc*, 95–106.

'The Impact of War and Occupation on Urban Life in Normandy, 1417–1450', *French History*, vol. i, no. 2 (Oct. 1987), 157–81.

'The Nationality of Men-at-Arms Serving in English Armies in Normandy and the Pays de Conquête, 1415–1450: A Preliminary Study', *Reading Medieval Studies*, 18 (1992), 135–63.

The Hundred Years War (Palgrave, 1993).

'English Armies in the Fifteenth Century' in Anne Curry and Michael Hughes (eds.), *Arms, Armies and Fortifications in the Hundred Years War* (Woodbridge, 1994), 39–68.

'L'Administration Financière de la Normandie Anglaise: Continuité ou Changement?' in Philippe Contamine and Olivier Mattéoni (eds.), *La France des Principautés: Les Chambres des Comptes aux XIVe et XVe Siècles* (Paris, 1996), 83–103.

'Isolated or Integrated? The English Soldier in Lancastrian Normandy' in S. Rees Jones, R. Marks and A. J. Minnis (eds.), *Courts and Regions in Medieval Europe* (Woodbridge, 2000), 191–210.

'Harfleur et les Anglais, 1415–1422' in Pierre Bouet and Véronique Gazeau (eds.), *La Normandie et l'Angleterre au Moyen Âge: Colloque de Cerisy-la-Salle* (Caen, 2001), 249–63.

'The "Coronation Expedition" and Henry VI's Court in France, 1430 to 1432' in Jenny Stratford (ed.), *The Lancastrian Court* (Donnington, 2003), 29–52.

'After Agincourt, What Next? Henry V and the Campaign of 1416' in Linda Clark (ed.), *Conflicts, Consequences and the Crown in the Late Middle Ages* (Woodbridge, 2007), 23–51.

Cuttler, S. H., *The Law of Treason and Treason Trials in Later Medieval France* (Cambridge, 1981).

Debal, Jacques, 'La Topographie de l'Enceinte d'Orléans au Temps de Jeanne d'Arc', in *Jeanne d'Arc*, 23–41.

Desama, Claude, 'Jeanne d'Arc et la Diplomatie de Charles VII: L'Ambassade Française auprès de Philippe de Bon en 1429', *Annales de Bourgogne*, 40 (1968), 290–9.

Devon, Frederick (ed.), *Issues of the Exchequer* (London, 1837).

Devries, Kelly, *Joan of Arc: A Military Leader* (Stroud, 2003).

Dickinson, Joycelyne Gledhill, *The Congress of Arras 1435* (Oxford, 1955).

Ditcham, Brian G. H., '"Mutton Guzzlers and Wine Bags": Foreign Soldiers and Native Reactions in Fifteenth-Century France' in Christopher Allmand (ed.), *Power, Culture and Religion in France c.1350–c.1550* (Woodbridge, 1989), 1–13.

Duparc, Pierre (ed.), *Procès en Nullité de la Condamnation de Jeanne d'Arc* (Paris, 1977–89), 5 vols.

Dupont, André, 'Pour ou Contre le Roi d'Angleterre', *Bulletin de la Société des Antiquaires de Normandie*, liv (1957–8), 147–71.

Ellis, Henry (ed.), *Original Letters Illustrative of English History*, Series ii (London, 1827), vol. i.

Fowler, Kenneth (ed.), *The Hundred Years War* (London, 1971).

'Truces' in Kenneth Fowler (ed.), *The Hundred Years War* (London, 1971), 184–215.

Goulay, Dominique, 'La Résistance à l'Occupant Anglais en Haute-Normandie (1435–1444)', *Annales de Normandie*, 36 (Mar. 1986), 37–55.

Harriss, Gerald, *Shaping the Nation: England 1360–1461* (Oxford, 2005).

Herwaarden, Jan van, 'The Appearance of Joan of Arc' in Jan van Herwaarden (ed.), *Joan of Arc: Reality and Myth* (Hilversum, 1994).

Jones, Michael, 'John Beaufort, Duke of Somerset and the French Expedition of 1443' in Ralph A. Griffiths (ed.), *Patronage, the*

Crown and the Provinces in Later Medieval England (Gloucester, 1981), 79–102.

Jones, Michael K., 'L'Imposition Illégale de Taxes en "Normandie Anglaise": une Enquête Gouvernementale en 1446' in *FAMA*, 285–307.

'Somerset, York and the Wars of the Roses', *English Historical Review*, 411 (1989), 285–307.

'Ransom Brokerage in the Fifteenth Century' in Philippe Contamine, Charles Giry-Deloison and Maurice Keen (eds.), *Guerre et Société en France, en Angleterre et en Bourgogne XIVe–XVe Siècle* (Villeneuve d'Ascq, 1991), 221–35.

Keen, Maurice, 'Diplomacy' in G. L. Harriss (ed.), *Henry V: The Practice of Kingship* (Oxford, 1985), 189–92.

'The End of the Hundred Years War: Lancastrian France and Lancastrian England' in Michael Jones and Malcolm Vale (eds.), *England and Her Neighbours, 1066–1453: Essays in Honour of Pierre Chaplais* (London, 1989), 297–311.

Lefèvre-Pontalis, Germain, 'La Panique Anglaise en Mai 1429', *Moyen Âge* (1891), 5–20.

Leguai, André, 'La "France Bourguignonne" dans le Conflit entre la "France Française" et la "France Anglaise" (1420–1435)'in *FAMA*, 41–52.

Lewis, P. S., *Later Medieval France: The Polity* (London, 1968).

Massey, Robert, 'The Land Settlement in Lancastrian Normandy' in Tony Pollard (ed.), *Property and Politics: Essays in Later Medieval English History* (Gloucester and New York, 1984), 76–96.

'Lancastrian Rouen: Military Service and Property Holding, 1419–49' in David Bates and Anne Curry (eds.), *England and Normandy in the Middle Ages* (London and Rio Grande, 1994), 267–86.

McFarlane, K. B., 'A Business Partnership in War and Administration, 1421–1445', *English Historical Review*, 78 (April 1963), 290–310.

Newhall, Richard A., 'Henry V's Policy of Conciliation in Normandy, 1417–1422' in C. H. Taylor and J. L. La Monte (eds.), *Anniversary Essays in Medieval History by Students of Charles Homer Haskins* (Boston and New York, 1929), 205–29.

Muster and Review: A Problem of English Military Administration 1420–1440 (Cambridge, Mass., 1940).

Patourel, John Le, 'The Origins of the War' in Kenneth Fowler (ed.), *The Hundred Years War* (London, 1971), 28–50.

Perroy, Édouard, *The Hundred Years War*, with an introduction to the English edition by David C. Douglas (London, 1951).

Plaisse, André and Plaisse, Sylvie, *La Vie Municipale à Évreux Pendant la Guerre de Cent Ans* (Évreux, 1978).

Puiseux, Léon, *L'Émigration Normande et la Colonisation Anglaise en Normandie au XVe Siècle* (Caen and Paris, 1866).

Quicherat, J.-E.-J. (ed.), *Procès de Condamnation et de Réhabilitation de Jeanne d'Arc dite la Pucelle* (Paris, 1841–9), 5 vols.

Reynolds, Catherine '"Les Angloys, de leur droicte nature, veullent touzjours guerreer": Evidence for Painting in Paris and Normandy, c.1420–1450' in Christopher Allmand (ed.), *Power, Culture and Religion in France c.1350–c.1550* (Woodbridge, 1989), 37–55.

Rowe, B. J. H., 'A Contemporary Account of the Hundred Years War from 1415 to 1429', *English Historical Review*, 41 (1926), 504–13.

'Discipline in the Norman Garrisons under Bedford, 1422–1435', *English Historical Review*, 46 (1931), 194–208.

'John Duke of Bedford and the Norman "Brigands"', *English Historical Review*, 47 (1932), 583–600.

'The *Grand Conseil* under the Duke of Bedford, 1422–35', *Oxford Essays in Medieval History Presented to Herbert Edward Salter* (Oxford, 1934), 207–34.

Sommé, Monique, 'L'Armée Bourguignonne au Siège de Calais de 1436' in Philippe Contamine, Charles Giry-Deloison and Maurice Keen (eds.), *Guerre et Société en France, en Angleterre et en Bourgogne XIVe –XVe Siècle* (Villeneuve d'Ascq, 1991), 197–219.

Stansfield, Michael, 'John Holland, Duke of Exeter and Earl of Huntingdon (d. 1447) and the Costs of the Hundred Years War' in Michael Hicks (ed.), *Profit, Piety and the Professions in Later Medieval England* (Gloucester and Wolfeboro Falls, 1990), 102–18.

Strickland, Matthew, and Hardy, Robert, *The Great Warbow: From Hastings to the Mary Rose* (Stroud, 2005).

Taylor, C. D., 'Brittany and the French Crown: the Legacy of the English Attack on Fougères (1449)' in J. R. Maddicott and D. M. Palliser (eds.), *The Medieval State: Essays Presented to James Campbell* (London and Rio Grande, 2000), 243–57.

Thompson, Guy, '"Monseigneur Saint Denis", his Abbey, and his Town, under the English Occupation, 1420–1436' in Christopher Allmand (ed.), *Power, Culture and Religion in France c.1350–c.1550* (Woodbridge, 1989), 15–35.

Tierney, Very Rev. Canon, 'Discovery of the Remains of John, 7th Earl of Arundel (*obit*. 1435)', *Sussex Archaeological Collections*, 12 (1860), 232–9.

Vale, Malcolm, 'Jeanne d'Arc et ses Adversaires: Jeanne, Victime d'Une Guerre Civile?' in *Jeanne d'Arc*, 203–16.

Vauchez, André, 'Jeanne d'Arc et le Prophétisme Féminin des XIVe et XVe Siècles' in *Jeanne d'Arc*, 159–68.

Williams, *Renewal and Reformation: Wales c.1415–1642* (Oxford, 1993).

Wolff, Philippe, *Commerces et Marchands de Toulouse (vers 1350– vers 1430)* (Paris, 1954).

CHRONOLOGY OF KEY EVENTS

1417 1 August   Henry V lands at Touques to begin conquest of Normandy

       9–20 September   Siege and formal surrender of Caen

1418 29 May   Paris seized by Burgundians in a successful coup

       29 July   Henry V lays siege to Rouen

1419 19 January   Surrender of Rouen and Henry V's formal entry into the city

       11 June   Treaty of Pouilly: John the Fearless, duke of Burgundy, and the dauphin reconciled and agree to cooperate against the English

       10 September   Meeting of duke of Burgundy and the dauphin on the bridge at Montereau-sur-Yonne; Burgundy is assassinated by the dauphin's men

1420 21 May   Treaty of Troyes: Henry V recognised as heir and regent of France by Charles VI and the Burgundians

       2 June   Henry V marries Katherine of France at Troyes

1421 February   Henry V and Katherine sail for England; coronation of Katherine at Westminster Abbey

       22 March   Battle of Baugé: English defeated by combined French and Scottish forces; duke of Clarence killed; John, earl of Huntingdon,

		and John Beaufort, earl of Somerset, captured
	June	Henry V returns to France
1422	31 August	Death of Henry V at Bois-de-Vincennes; accession of Henry VI as king of England; duke of Bedford becomes regent of France, duke of Gloucester protector of England
	21 October	Death of Charles VI; Henry VI becomes king of France
1423	17 April	Treaty of Amiens: triple alliance between England, Burgundy and Brittany; duke of Bedford and Arthur de Richemont to marry duke of Burgundy's sisters
	14 June	Bedford marries Anne of Burgundy at Troyes
	31 July	Battle of Cravant: Anglo-Burgundian forces defeat Scottish-Armagnac army
	26 September	Earl of Suffolk defeated at La Brossinière; his brothers William and John taken prisoner
1424	17 August	Battle of Verneuil: duke of Bedford leads English to crushing defeat of Scottish-Armagnac forces; count of Aumâle and earl of Buchan killed; duke of Alençon captured
	16 October	Duke of Gloucester begins military campaign to claim and occupy Hainault in the name of his wife, Jacqueline of Hainault; abandons campaign and returns to England in April 1425
1425	8 March	Arthur de Richemont abandons the English alliance and becomes constable of France for the dauphin
	7 October	Treaty of Saumur: alliance between Brittany and the dauphin
	December	Duke of Bedford goes to England to broker peace between duke of Gloucester and Cardinal Beaufort
1426	15 January	English declare war on Brittany

1427	19 March	Duke of Bedford returns to France with major reinforcements
	5 September	Lord Fastolf's forces surprised and defeated at Ambrières
	8 September	Duke of Brittany makes new English alliance, accepting the Treaty of Troyes
1428	12 October	Earl of Salisbury lays siege to Orléans
	3 November	Salisbury dies of injuries sustained at siege of Orléans
1429	c.28 February	Jehanne d'Arc arrives at Chinon to see the dauphin
	29 April	Jehanne enters Orléans with relief forces
	8 May	English abandon siege of Orléans
	12 June	Jehanne takes Jargeau by assault; earl of Suffolk captured
	18 June	Battle of Patay: Armagnac forces defeat Talbot and Fastolf; Talbot, Scales and Rempston captured
	17 July	Coronation of the dauphin as Charles VII at Reims
	26 August	Jehanne and duke of Alençon take Saint-Denis
	8 September	Jehanne and Alençon fail in assault on Paris; Jehanne wounded
	6 November	Coronation of Henry VI as king of England at Westminster Abbey
	c.24 November	Jehanne lays siege to La-Charité-sur-Loire but is forced to withdraw a month later
	8 December	La Hire captures Louviers for Charles VII
1430	7 January	Duke of Burgundy marries Isabella of Portugal, half-cousin of Henry VI
	23 April	Henry VI and the 'coronation expedition' land at Calais
	23 May	Jehanne d'Arc captured by Burgundians in sortie from Compiègne
1431	9 January	Jehanne d'Arc's trial begins at Rouen
	30 May	Jehanne condemned to death and burned at the stake in Rouen
	25 October	Louviers recaptured by English after five-month siege

	2 December	Henry VI makes formal entry into Paris
	13 December	Treaty of Lille: establishes six-year general truce between Burgundy and Charles VII
	16 December	Henry VI crowned king of France in Notre Dame, Paris
1432	29 January	Henry VI sails from Calais; he never returns to France
	13 November	Death of Anne of Burgundy, the duchess of Bedford
	27 November	English, Burgundian and French envoys meet at Auxerre for peace talks mediated by Cardinal Albergati
1433	February	Mutiny of the Calais garrison
	20 April	Marriage of the duke of Bedford and Jacquetta of Luxembourg
	24 June	Bedford and Jacquetta sail to England
1434	July	Duke of Bedford returns to France with an army of 1400
1435	January	Popular revolt in lower Normandy; Caen besieged by rebels but they are repelled
	6 February	Dukes of Burgundy and Bourbon sign preliminaries of peace and agree to meet again at Arras
	7 May	Earl of Arundel mortally wounded and captured by La Hire at Gerberoy
	12 June	Death of Arundel
	12 August	English, Burgundian and French envoys attend peace conference at Arras
	6 September	English envoys break off negotiations and leave Arras
	14 September	Death of duke of Bedford at Rouen
	21 September	Treaty of Arras: duke of Burgundy and Charles VII reconciled
	28 October	French seize Dieppe; popular uprising in upper Normandy
	25 November	French seize Harfleur, followed by much of the surrounding area

1436 January–March   Popular uprising (Boschier revolt) in lower Normandy

13 April   French seize Paris

May   Richard, duke of York, appointed lieutenant-general of Normandy and leads expeditionary army there; the subsequent campaign, led by Talbot, safeguards Rouen and recovers Caux region

9–28 July   Unsuccessful Burgundian siege of Calais

August   Duke of Gloucester's expedition for relief of Calais diverted into raid through Flanders

1437 12–13 February   Talbot recovers Pontoise by surprise, launching year-long campaign that recovers most of Normandy – except Harfleur and Dieppe – and reopens the Normandy–Paris corridor

16 July   Richard, earl of Warwick, appointed lieutenant-general of Normandy but storms at sea delay his arrival until November

6 December   Minority government ends with Henry VI's sixteenth birthday; beginning of his personal rule

1438 March   Henry VI empowers ambassadors to treat for peace with France

May   John Beaufort, earl of Somerset, released in exchange for count of Eu

May–June   Peace conference at Vannes under presidency of duke of Brittany

1439 14 January   Talbot recaptures Saint-Germain-en-Laye

30 April   Death of earl of Warwick at Rouen

July–September   Peace talks at Calais; no agreement is reached except Anglo-Burgundian commercial treaty

12 September   Meaux – last remaining English stronghold east of Paris – falls to French

1440 February   John Beaufort, earl of Somerset, acting lieutenant-general, leads expeditionary army to France

April–September   Praguerie revolt against Charles VII

	2 July	Duke of York appointed lieutenant-general of Normandy
	October	Harfleur recovered by English after three-month siege
	November	Release of Charles, duke of Orléans, prisoner since Agincourt, with objective of mediating peace between England and France
1441	June	Duke of York arrives in Rouen at head of expeditionary army; relieves Pontoise
	15 September	Évreux captured by French and never recovered by English
	19 September	Pontoise taken by assault and never recovered by English
	6 November	Duke of Gloucester divorced from Eleanor Cobham, who is convicted of sorcery
1442	June	Talbot leads expedition recruited from England to recover Évreux, Conches, Louviers and Dieppe; unable to recruit sufficient men-at-arms so only recovers Conches (September)
	1 November	Talbot builds bastille and lays siege to Dieppe
1443	July	Earl of Somerset leads major expedition to wage 'mortal war' against French beyond the Loire; has extraordinarily independent powers and makes no contact with Norman government throughout
	14 August	English bastille at Dieppe taken in assault by French; Somerset subsequently seizes Breton town of La Guerche
	December	Somerset's expedition abandoned, never having crossed the Loire
1444	11 February	Earl of Suffolk authorised to conclude peace with Charles VII and leads embassy to Tours
	24 May	Henry VI formally betrothed to Margaret of Anjou at Tours
	1 June	Truce of Tours – a general two-year truce

between England and France – begins, and
will be prolonged as further concessions are
made

1445	22 April	Henry VI marries Margaret of Anjou at Titchfield Abbey
	July	French embassy arrives in London to negotiate a final peace
	22 December	Henry VI secretly undertakes to surrender Maine to René and Charles d'Anjou 'on behalf of' Charles VII
1446	26 June	Arrest of Gilles of Brittany by his brother, the duke of Brittany, for conspiring with the English
	24 December	Edmund Beaufort appointed lieutenant-general of Normandy to secure his assistance with surrender of Maine
1447	23 February	Death of duke of Gloucester, five days after his arrest for alleged treason
	11 April	Death of Cardinal Beaufort
	27 July	Henry VI formally seals public agreement to surrender Maine
	31 October	Conference at Le Mans: English captains and residents refuse to surrender Maine to French commissioners without compensation
1448	16 March	English captains surrender Maine under protest, after Charles VII lays siege to Le Mans
	May	Edmund Beaufort arrives in Rouen as lieutenant-general
1449	24 March	François de Surienne captures Fougères in marches of Brittany on behalf of the English
	13 May	Pont-de l'Arche seized in retaliation by French
	23 May	Breton salt fleet, sailing under friendly flags, captured by English privateer
	20 July	Verneuil betrayed to French
	31 July	Charles VII formally declares war on the

		English and launches campaign for the conquest of Normandy
	29 October	Edmund Beaufort surrenders Rouen after brief siege and takes refuge at Caen; most of Normandy now in French hands
1450	1 January	English surrender Harfleur
	February	Earl of Suffolk impeached for treason; banished for five years from 1 May
	March	Sir Thomas Kyriell leads expeditionary army to recover Normandy; lands at Cherbourg and captures Valognes
	15 April	Battle of Formigny: French inflict heavy defeat on English
	2 May	Suffolk assassinated as sails into banishment
	June–July	Jack Cade's rebellion in England
	1 July	Edmund Beaufort surrenders Caen to the French
	12 August	Cherbourg, the last English stronghold in Normandy, surrenders to the French
1451	April	French invasion of English Gascony
	24 June	Surrender of Bordeaux
	20 August	Surrender of Bayonne
1452	17 October	Talbot launches campaign for recovery of Gascony and retakes Bordeaux
1453	17 July	Battle of Castillon: French inflict heavy defeat on English and Talbot is killed. The only English possession now left in France is Calais

ACKNOWLEDGEMENTS

I am grateful, as always, to the universities of Leeds and Oxford for allowing me to use their libraries, and to my agent, Andrew Lownie, for his support and expertise. I would also like to thank Richard Beswick and Stephen Guise of Little, Brown who were responsible for the original idea. The book was written in very difficult personal circumstances and I am especially grateful to my editors, Tim Whiting and Viv Redman, who could not have been more kind, understanding and encouraging. Finally, I am indebted to my family. My father, Richard Bateson, encouraged me by his eagerness to read the next instalment while the book was a work in progress. My saintly husband James and my children Edward and Sophie have always suffered for my art: quite simply, there would be no book and I would have no life without them.

INDEX

Born in Yorkshire, Juliet Barker was educated at Bradford Girls' Grammar School and St Anne's College, Oxford, where she gained a doctorate in medieval history. Widely acclaimed for setting new standards of literary biography with her prize-winning and bestselling books, *The Brontës* (1994) and *Wordsworth: A Life* (2000), she is also an expert on medieval chivalry and tournaments; her most recent book *Agincourt* (2005) was the fourth bestselling history book of 2006. She was awarded an honorary Doctorate of Letters by the University of Bradford in 1999 and elected a Fellow of the Royal Society of Literature in 2001. She is married, with two children, and lives in the South Pennines.

www.julietbarker.co.uk